Howard Hughes

Howard Hughes

Power, Paranoia, and Palace Intrigue

Revised and Expanded

Geoff Schumacher

UNIVERSITY OF NEVADA PRESS *Reno & Las Vegas*

Howard Hughes: Power, Paranoia & Palace Intrigue was first published by Stephens Press, LLC, in 2008. The 2020 University of Nevada Press edition is a revised and expanded version.

University of Nevada Press | Reno, Nevada 89557 USA
www.unpress.nevada.edu

Cover photographs courtesy of *Las Vegas Review-Journal*. Back cover photo: Howard Hughes Public Relations Photo Collection. Special Collections and Archives, University Libraries, University of Nevada, Las Vegas. Spine photo: Author's collection.

LIBRARY OF CONGRESS CATALOGING-IN-PUBLICATION DATA
Names: Schumacher, Geoff, author.
Title: Howard Hughes : power, paranoia, and palace intrigue / Geoff Schumacher.
Description: Revised and expanded. | Reno ; Las Vegas : University of Nevada Press, [2019] | Includes bibliographical references and index. | Summary: "*Howard Hughes* chronicles the life and legacies of one of the most intriguing and accomplished Americans of the twentieth century. Hughes made big-budget movies, built the world's fastest and largest airplanes, and helped transform and grow Las Vegas. He was a respected trailblazer and firebrand, but behind the facade his physical and mental health declined to the point of incapacitation. This book takes you behind the curtain to understand what really happened to Howard Hughes and what he has left behind"—Provided by publisher.
Identifiers: LCCN 2019052075 (print) | LCCN 2019052076 (ebook) | ISBN 9781948908603 (paperback) | ISBN 9781948908610 (ebook)
Subjects: LCSH: Hughes, Howard, 1905-1976. | Hughes, Howard, 1905-1976—Influence. | Hughes, Howard, 1905-1976—Friends and associates. | Millionaires—United States—Biography. | Air pilots—United States—Biography. | Motion picture producers and directors—United States—Biography. | Real estate developers—Nevada—Las Vegas—History—Biography. | Recluses—United States—Biography. | Las Vegas (Nev.)—Politics and government—20th century. | Las Vegas (Nev.)—Social life and customs—20th century. | Las Vegas (Nev.)—History—20th century. | LCGFT: Biographies.
Classification: LCC CT275.H6678 S38 2019 (print) | LCC CT275.H6678 (ebook) | DDC 338.7/67092 [B]—dc23
LC record available at https://lccn.loc.gov/2019052075
LC ebook record available at https://lccn.loc.gov/2019052076

The paper used in this book meets the requirements of American National Standard for Information Sciences—Permanence of Paper for Printed Library Materials, ANSI/NISO Z39.48-1992 (R2002).

Manufactured in the United States of America

For Erin, Sara, and Tammy,
and to all those whose lives were touched by Howard Hughes.

Why have we made a folk hero of a man who is the antithesis of all our official heroes, a haunted millionaire of the West, trailing a legend of desperation and power and white sneakers?

—Joan Didion, *Slouching Towards Bethlehem*

I have heard him described as Dracula, Bluebeard and Satan. I have heard stories about him that I know are completely untrue and read others equally false. And yet I know that I do not know the truth, the whole truth and nothing but the truth about him. I'm not sure that anyone does. He is so complex that there must be times when he is a stranger even to himself.

—Louella Parsons, *Tell It to Louella*

Hughes is the champion artful dodger of them all, with the possible exception of the Loch Ness Monster and the Abominable Snowman.

—Bob Considine, *1968*

In this world you can't just be neutral or you can't just go about your business and live your life in what seems to you to be a normal way. This just doesn't seem possible. You apparently have to do certain things and follow a certain kind of conduct in order to satisfy people.

—Howard Hughes, *1972 telephone interview*

In the end, his lifetime of manipulating others, his capricious misuse of wealth and power, his callousness to friendship, funneled down to no lessons other than the banalities that money can't buy happiness, and that monstrous power can corrupt monstrously.

—James Phelan, *Scandals, Scamps, and Scoundrels*

Contents

PREFACE
The Hughes–Las Vegas Connection

In many ways, Howard Hughes was a detestable character. He wielded his money and power to manipulate the democratic process. He treated women like property. He was an unabashed racist. He didn't seem to have an artistic bone in his body, yet he arrogantly declared himself a movie director. He was an irrational Red baiter who fired numerous alleged Communists working for his movie company. Hughes was intermittently generous to friends and allies, but he was not a great philanthropist. For the most part, Hughes saw his fellow human beings as pieces on a chess board to be moved here and there to suit his needs.

But while I recognize his many flaws, Hughes is endlessly fascinating to me. He was smart—some say a genius—and largely self-educated. He was an important aviation innovator, despite having no formal training in aerodynamics. His flying boat was an incredible achievement, even if it flew only once. He was a maverick. He never ran with the pack, and he didn't back down from a fight. He was a rich man who had little interest in expensive clothes, cars, or houses. He wined and dined beautiful actresses, then drove them home in an unassuming Chevrolet. Hughes spent hundreds of millions of dollars in pursuit of his passions: airplanes, movies, and, later, casinos. In the process, he employed tens of thousands of people, many of whom were fiercely loyal to him even if they had never met him.

Hughes also was a tragic figure. His gradual descent into drug addiction, germ phobia, paranoia, seclusion, and obsessive-compulsive disorder—all steadily worsening while doctors toyed with his drug intake and aides sat on their hands—is one of the saddest stories of the twentieth century.

Indeed, Hughes was "the last private man," as Joan Didion called him in 1967 while he was living in the penthouse of the Desert Inn in Las Vegas, with only a handful of personal aides granted access to his suite. Hughes' insistence on total privacy in the final years of his life is eternally intriguing. People just want to know what was happening up there. Did he really keep his urine in jars? (Yes.) Were his fingernails really six inches long? (No.) Is it true that his top Las Vegas executive, Bob Maheu, never spoke with his boss in person? (Yes.) Is it true that he snuck out of the hotel a few times to visit a prostitute in rural Nevada? (No.) Did he really watch the same movie, *Ice Station Zebra*, over and over? (Yes.) A whole book could be written just confirming and debunking the legends generated by his privacy obsession.

I am also fascinated by Hughes' impact on Las Vegas. Today, more than forty years after his death, his name has an uncanny way of popping up in conversation. Everybody in Las Vegas, it seems, knows somebody who worked for Hughes in some capacity. His former employees are still scattered across the city, and most of them love to talk about the man, even if they never met him.

Soon after I started working on the first edition of this book, my mom put me in touch with her neighbor, eighty-eight-year-old Russ Hudson, who said he played golf with Hughes in the early '50s. Hudson proudly showed me the pair of red cowboy boots he wore while playing with Hughes and that Hughes admired. In his final years, Hudson wore gloves much of the time, an homage of sorts to Hughes' fear of germs.

I also sat down with Bob McCaffery, a former design engineer for Hughes Helicopter Company who regularly delivered public lectures about Hughes. McCaffery campaigned successfully in the 1980s to save Hughes' flying boat from being dismantled and distributed to nine different museums. Then, with the plane facing eviction from Long Beach, California, he campaigned to bring it to Las Vegas. He identified a spot at the south end of the Strip where the giant plane could be put on display. Alas, Las Vegas lost out to a bid from the Evergreen Aviation & Space Museum in McMinnville, Oregon, where the flying boat resides today.

I interviewed Linda Gray, a longtime Las Vegan who was married to the late Dick Gray, Hughes' personal attorney in the late 1960s. Linda told me about Hughes calling her husband in the middle of the night. Hughes would tell him to have his wife leave the room so they could speak privately. Dick would rustle the bedcovers to suggest her departure, but in truth she would remain by his side while her husband discussed whatever was on Hughes' mind at three a.m. After Hughes died and the Mormon Will came to light, memos written by Hughes in Linda's possession were used to compare with the handwriting of the will to determine its legitimacy.

After the first edition of the book was released in 2008, I was contacted by an array of individuals who claimed special knowledge about Hughes. At one public event, I met a man who insisted he was the love child of Hughes and Katharine Hepburn. I also met a man who believes he is the son of Hughes. The man did, in fact, look eerily like the billionaire in his prime. More common, however, were longtime Las Vegans who enjoyed reminiscing about the days when Hughes was living at the Desert Inn.

There is no shortage of books about Hughes. Published works about him fill two wide shelves in my home office, and all of them were useful in the preparation of this book. Seemingly every aspect of his life—as secret as it was—has been examined in print, including Hughes' activities in Las Vegas. Three books focus on his eventful four-year sequestration on the top floor of the Desert Inn, while a few others contain extensive material on Hughes' Las Vegas years. But for all the reams of paper devoted to the Hughes-Las Vegas connection, this remains the only book that explores the long-term impact Hughes had on America's fastest-growing city and the people living there.

It would be folly to try to pack everything about Hughes into one book, but this second edition is longer than the first. I have attempted to provide a more complete picture of Hughes' life, while retaining a primary focus on Las Vegas. But I couldn't cover everything. The guy just had too much going on.

Howard Hughes: Power, Paranoia, and Palace Intrigue is a product of two things. Much information was culled from the innumerable newspaper stories, magazine articles, and books about Hughes written by my journalistic and academic predecessors. From Hollywood tell-alls to in-depth biographies, Hughes has been a popular topic in publishing over the past fifty years (even though in the '60s he aggressively sought to suppress books about him). My personal library includes all the major books and magazine articles about Hughes, plus an array of memoirs that discuss him and some oddball works that may or may not offer credible information. I also benefited from access to archives at the University of Nevada, Las Vegas, the Nevada State Museum, and the *Las Vegas Review-Journal.*

The book also is based on the many interviews I conducted with people who knew Hughes, worked for Hughes, or whose lives were affected by Hughes. Their memories, perspectives, and opinions constitute the freshest and most valuable portion of this project.

I like how this book came together, because it's not just another Howard Hughes biography. I have pursued the threads of his life that interested me. Most of those threads include a generous slice of Las Vegas history—covering when Hughes was there and the messy aftermath. Writing about Hughes has given me an opportunity to delve into segments of the city's past that one might ignore in a more conventional format.

As a result, you don't have to be a member of the Howard Hughes fan club to find valuable and entertaining information between these covers. If you are interested in the history of Las Vegas, this book offers information you will want to know.

Part 1:

Before Las Vegas

1
Young Maverick: *Becoming Hughes*

Howard Robard Hughes was born in 1905, the same year Las Vegas became a town. But a whole lot would happen to both of them before his life intersected with the city.

Howard is most often associated with Texas, where he was born and where he was buried, as well as California, where he spent the most time during his life. It is often overlooked that he is a progeny of a family, on his father's side, with deep roots in the Midwest.

After serving in the U.S. Army during the Black Hawk War, Howard's great-grandfather, Joshua Waters Hughes, settled in southern Illinois. His Army service entitled him to a land grant, which he took advantage of in the form of forty acres in northeast Missouri. He built a log cabin there and lived in it for fifty years.

Howard's grandfather, Felix Turner Hughes, grew up in that log cabin. He worked as a lawyer (without benefit of a college education) and became solicitor general of the Missouri, Iowa & Nebraska Railroad in Lancaster, Missouri. He married Jean Summerlin Hughes and they had several children, including Howard's father. In 1880, Felix moved the family to the Mississippi River town of Keokuk, Iowa, where he opened a law firm and was hired as president and general counsel of the Keokuk & Western Railroad. He was elected mayor of Keokuk in 1895.

Felix Hughes championed the idea of damming the Mississippi River at Keokuk to smooth the rapids and generate hydroelectric power. His vision was realized in 1913 with the completion of the dam and powerhouse, which was, at the time, the largest electricity-generating plant in the world. It provided power to Keokuk and other cities across the Midwest. The Lock and Dam No. 19, added to the National Register of Historic Places in 2004, is still in operation today.

Howard's father, Howard; uncles Rupert and Felix; and aunt, Greta, grew up in Keokuk, in a large red brick house at 312 N. Fifth Street. Howard's father was known as something of a "mechanical genius," according to local historian Francis J. Helenthal. Helenthel says he "invented a fire escape for business buildings and a dentist's drill which was used extensively at the old Keokuk Dental College."

Howard Sr. studied briefly at Harvard, dropping out after one year, and at the University of Iowa College of Law. He left law school early, but passed the bar exam and started working in his father's firm. But as he reported back to Harvard years later, he "found the law a too-exacting mistress for a man of my talent, and I quit her between dark and dawn, and have never since been back. I decided to search for my fortune under the surface of the earth."

Showing an interest in mining, he explored silver in Colorado, zinc in Oklahoma, and lead in Missouri before eventually following the hordes of fortune seekers to Houston, center of the fledgling oil industry.

According to family lore, Howard's father invented the rotary drill bit that would make him rich while sitting at the dining room table in the family house in Keokuk. The real story is more complicated. Hughes picked up the seed of the idea for the rotary bit from a man named Granville Humason, whom he met in a bar in Shreveport, Louisiana. Hughes Sr. bought Humason's model for $150. Then Hughes caught a train to Keokuk, where he sought his father's financial and legal help to secure a patent for the revolutionary drill bit. While there, he sat down at the dining room table and sketched out detailed drawings of the device, as well as technical documents. The patents were granted on August 10, 1909. Howard Jr. was not yet four years old.

When the drill bit made him rich, Howard Sr. built his mother a second house in Keokuk, at 925 Grand Avenue. This was known in the family as the "summer house," because it offered a view of the Mississippi River and the cool breezes that came with it. Family members recalled episodes when Jean and Felix were not getting along, and Jean occupied the Grand Avenue house while Felix was relegated to the "winter house" on Fifth Street.

Although Howard Jr. was born in Texas, he was baptized in St. John's Episcopal Church in Keokuk. As a youth, he occasionally visited his grandparents there.

Howard's mother, Allene Gano, was a Dallas heiress, described by Charles Higham in *Howard Hughes: The Secret Life*, as "darkly pretty" and "high-strung, a hypochondriac." The Hughes-Gano marriage—on May 24, 1904, in Dallas—was important enough to be chronicled in the city's society pages. The young couple settled in Houston, but moved a year later to Humble, a small town northeast of the city, where Howard Jr. was born on Christmas Eve 1905.

In 1907, the family moved to Oil City, Louisiana, outside Shreveport, where Howard Sr. served as postmaster and deputy sheriff while chasing his oil dreams. A year later Howard Sr. pursued the invention that would make him rich. He purchased two patents for drill bits, one for $2,500, the other for $9,000. Working with partner Walter Sharp, he tested, experimented, and eventually invented the Hughes drill bit. Hughes and Sharp started the Sharp-Hughes Tool Company. When Sharp died in 1912, Hughes bought out his interest in the company. This clever piece of hardware became the foundation of the family fortune.

What made the Hughes drill bit so innovative? As the oil business started taking off in Texas just after the turn of the century, miners were having trouble drilling through underground rock. The bits then in use scraped their way through the rock and wore out quickly. The Hughes drill bit had two rotating steel cones that cut through rock much more efficiently. Oil companies wanted the Hughes drill bit because it cut a ton of time out of the drilling process, and they could go deeper into the earth in search of oil than ever before. It wasn't long before the Hughes drill bit became the industry standard.

The family did not enjoy the riches of its drill bit fortune right away, in part because Howard Sr. spent much of his income on gambling and expensive equipment. But by 1913, the Hughes fortune had solidified. The family moved into a pricey apartment and became part of Houston's country club set.

Their child, nicknamed Sonny, started out life as a sickly boy, partly a result of his mother's hypochondria. But several summers at Camp Dan Beard in Pennsylvania bolstered his fitness and taught him to appreciate nature and to learn the ins and outs of woodcraft. He also briefly excelled at the private Fessenden School, near Boston, where he edited the school paper, learned to play golf, and played saxophone in the school band.

Hughes' parents began to spend more time in Southern California. They purchased a home on Coronado Island, near San Diego, and in 1921 Sonny transferred to the Thacher School in Ojai, where he excelled in math and science and rode horses. During summer vacation, Hughes spent time with his uncle, Rupert Hughes, a bestselling novelist and screenwriter who exposed the teenager to the movie business.

Multiple tragedies struck the family about this time. In 1922, Hughes' mother, hemorrhaging from her womb, died in a Houston hospital while receiving anesthesia. She was thirty-eight. A year later, Hughes' Aunt Adelaide, Rupert's wife, hanged herself during a trip to Asia. Finally, in 1924, Howard Sr. died of an embolism at his office in Houston. He was fifty-four.

Hughes had withdrawn from the Thacher School and was attending the California Institute of Technology when the devastating trio of deaths hit his family. But rather than falling apart, the eighteen-year-old decided to take control of his father's company. To accomplish this, he had to pay off his father's considerable debts and fend off an attempt by his uncle to run the show.

Helping to establish his maturity to run his father's affairs, in 1925 Hughes wedded a childhood friend, Ella Rice, a member of the oil family for which Rice University is named. But after the newlyweds moved to Los Angeles later that year, the marriage gradually collapsed. Hughes' obsession with business and golf left his wife out in the cold, and she found little comfort from Hollywood society. Hughes' infidelity with the actress Billie Dove was a contributing factor in Ella's return to Houston in 1928. They divorced the following year.

The filmmaker

Hughes moved to Southern California to break into the movie business. His first venture was *Swell Hogan*, starring Ralph Graves, a friend of Hughes' father. Hughes, a novice producer, trusted Graves, a veteran actor, to direct the film, and this proved to be a mistake. "It was rubbish," wrote Tony Thomas in *Howard Hughes in Hollywood*. "It had no structure, no plot, no tension, and the acting was ludicrous. Hughes ordered the film to be placed in a vault, from which it never emerged."

The *Swell Hogan* disaster changed Hughes' approach. He studied every aspect of moviemaking and become a more careful judge of talent. His next project was called *Everybody's Acting*. Hughes hired proven talent to write and direct the film, and after he secured a distribution deal with Paramount, the movie was financially successful in 1926.

After starting his own movie company, Caddo Productions, Hughes hired Lewis Milestone to direct his next project, a World War I comedy called *Two Arabian Knights*. With a large budget, a good script, and Milestone's expert direction, *Two Arabian Knights* was a hit with moviegoers and critics. The film, released in 1927, earned a Best Director honor for Milestone at the first Academy Awards ceremony in 1929. (Three decades later, Milestone directed *Ocean's Eleven*, a film with legendary connections to Las Vegas.)

With just three movies under his belt and barely twenty-two years old, Hughes had nonetheless earned a measure of respect in Hollywood. Now he was eager to rise to the top of the heap with his next film. Hughes was fascinated by aviation and wanted to merge that interest with filmmaking. When he came across the World War I story of *Hell's Angels,* he saw the perfect opportunity.

Unlike his previous films, Hughes decided to become intimately involved in the production of *Hell's Angels*. With Hughes hovering relentlessly, original

Portrait of Hughes at age twenty-five in 1930. Courtesy of Prints and Photographs Division, Library of Congress.

director Marshall Neilan quit after a few weeks. When the second director, Luther Reed, departed after two months, Hughes decided to direct the picture himself.

This proved to be a costly and time-consuming decision. Hughes labored over every detail, constantly making changes to the script and camera angles. This, along with the long hours Hughes demanded on the set, strained the cast and crew. "He could work for twenty and thirty hours at a stretch, and he seemed to show little regard for the more regular time schedules of other people," according to author Tony Thomas. "He never wore a watch and he appeared to be oblivious of time."

Hughes bought dozens of airplanes to be used in the film's aerial combat sequences. It was dubbed the largest private air force in the world. He also purchased and leased real estate across Southern California to stage the ground scenes.

Instead of using military airplanes and pilots, as had been done in the 1927 epic *Wings*, Hughes hired stunt pilots because he thought they were more capable of performing the dramatic maneuvers he wanted to film. But Hughes' demand for dangerous stunts took its toll on the airplanes and the pilots. Four men—three pilots and a mechanic—died in flying accidents during the filming.

The first of Hughes' many flying accidents occurred during the filming of *Hell's Angels*. Trying an unadvised maneuver in a Thomas Morse Scout, Hughes crashed. Pulled from the wreckage, he was in the hospital for a week.

Shooting began in the fall of 1927, and continued through 1928 and 1929. When Hughes was frustrated by the absence of clouds in the Southern California skies, he picked up the giant production and moved it to the Oakland Airport in Northern California, where there was more reliable cloud cover.

While *Hell's Angels* was in production, Hughes released two other films in 1928: *The Racket*, a gangster flick directed by Milestone, and *The Mating Call*, starring the French actress Renée Adorée. *The Racket* was a critical success, and *The*

Hell's Angels movie poster. Courtesy of The Mob Museum.

Mating Call was a popular success, especially because of its steamy sexual undercurrents. Hughes had become a force in the silent film era.

But he also was something of a victim of the switch to talking pictures. Midway through production on *Hell's Angels*, Hughes decided it needed to become a talkie. He brought in new actors (including a teenage Jean Harlow to replace the heavily accented Swedish actress Greta Nissen) and reshot dramatic scenes.

Hughes orchestrated a grand premiere for *Hell's Angels* on May 27, 1930. Fifty airplanes flew in formation over Grauman's Chinese Theatre in Hollywood. Thousands of people crowded onto closed-off Hollywood Boulevard to watch celebrities arrive by limousine. Hughes attended the event alongside Dove. While the movie's dialogue and plot lines did not impress critics, the aerial battles left them breathless. The critic for *The New York Times* called it "a strange combination of brilliance and banality."

Film historian Thomas, writing in 1985, argued that Hughes deserves a place of honor in movie history if only for the astonishing battle scene between Allied and German fighter pilots. "The dogfight between the fighter pilots, involving thirty planes, not only was the most astonishing aerial warfare filmed to that time, but nothing done since has surpassed it. . . . His pilots and photographers achieved a breathtaking sequence, with the planes ferociously attacking each other like angry hornets, zipping, swooping, looping, and tumbling."

The movie was a huge hit across the country and in England, but it did not earn more than its $4 million price tag. Hughes opted for more modest budgets for subsequent movie projects.

Hughes' affair with Dove prompted him to sign her to a contract and to produce *The Age for Love*, which Hughes hoped would reignite her career. Instead, the 1931 drama was a dismal failure. Hughes arranged for Dove to receive flying lessons and she earned her pilot's license, after which she starred in the World War I film *Cock of the Air*. The film received tepid reviews, and moviegoers were disappointed there weren't more flying scenes.

Dove was under contract to do five movies for Hughes, but when their relationship disintegrated, she wanted to terminate her contract. Dove retired from acting after just one more film.

Pressing on, Hughes produced *Sky Devils*, another World War I flying movie, this one starring a young Spencer Tracy. Despite using aerial footage left over from *Hell's Angels*, the film was another dud.

Three straight failures suggested to Hollywood observers that Hughes had lost his touch, but Hughes still had a couple of celluloid gems in the works. *The Front Page*, a rapid-fire comedic dissection of the newspaper business, written by Ben Hecht and Charles MacArthur, was a wildly successful Broadway play in 1928. Hughes bought the rights to bring it to the silver screen and hired Milestone, who had by now won a second Oscar, to direct. The combination of great script, great director, and veteran actors such as Adolph Menjou and Pat O'Brien turned *The Front Page* into an instant classic. (The movie has been remade twice: a 1940 remake titled *His Girl Friday* starring Cary Grant and Rosalind Russell is perhaps the best of the three, while the 1974 version starring Walter Matthau and Jack Lemmon is arguably the weakest.)

Hughes' other ambitious film project was *Scarface*, a violent gangster flick whose main character was obviously patterned after Chicago mob kingpin Al Capone. Written by Hecht and directed by Howard Hawks, *Scarface* was too violent for the sensibilities of legendary censor Will Hays, who demanded an array of cuts and changes. Hughes initially agreed to some cuts and to film a new ending. In addition, the title was changed to *Scarface: The Shame of a Nation*. But when it still wasn't enough for some state censorship boards, Hughes became defiant, restoring the cuts and reviving his original ending.

Hughes released *Scarface* in 1932 without an official seal of approval, and received wide support for his cause. He showed the film in places that did not have censorship boards. It opened in New Orleans, then in Los Angeles and other cities, receiving rave reviews. Meanwhile, Hughes sued the censorship board in New York and other places that refused to screen the movie. He won those battles, and the film eventually gained wide exposure.

Today, *Scarface* is regarded as one of the great early gangster movies. Among other things, it provided a breakout part for actor George Raft, who in several scenes is repeatedly flipping a nickel. While the coin-flipping worked perfectly for Raft's role in *Scarface*, it became an affectation forever linked to him and to movie gangsters.

The censorship wars over *Scarface* and Hughes' growing interest in aviation contributed to one of his trademark antithetical moves: Just as he reached the pinnacle of Hollywood success at age twenty-six, he quit the film business to concentrate on flying. Hughes would return to filmmaking eight years later, but he could not equal the success of his earlier stint in Hollywood.

The aviator

Since *Hell's Angels* was an aviation picture, Hughes believed he needed to learn to fly to understand his subject and took lessons during the filming. But he didn't dedicate himself to flight until a few years later.

In 1933, Hughes purchased an S-43 Sikorsky Amphibian airplane and hired engineer Glenn Odekirk to help him rebuild it. Hughes was prone to taking risks. Testing the Sikorsky with Odekirk, Hughes ran into a storm, lost an engine, and landed on the Mississippi River. "He and Odie bobbed around for hours in the damaged aircraft, in drenching rain, branches and logs hitting the plane violently," biographer Higham wrote. Hughes finally made contact with the Coast Guard, which sent a cutter that towed him and his plane to New Orleans.

Hughes' next goal was to build a plane that would break the air speed record. Hughes and Odekirk worked around the clock on the Hughes *Racer*, or H-1, which cost $120,000 to build. The authors of *Empire: The Life, Legend, and Madness of Howard Hughes* summarized their achievement: "A series of innovations . . . made the H-1 the most advanced plane of its time. Rivets were placed flush with the fuselage to reduce drag. The wings were shortened to increase speed. The single most revolutionary feature was its unique landing gear which did not remain permanently in place during the flight, but retracted neatly after takeoff into a snug compartment under the wings."

On September 13, 1935, at an air field in Santa Ana, California, Hughes flew the H-1 352 miles per hour, shattering the previous record of 314 mph. After receiving his accolades, the excited Hughes got back into the plane to resume

Hughes with his H-1 *Racer*. Author's collection.

flying. Something went wrong and he was forced to crash-land in a bean field. When emergency crews arrived, they found him sitting on the plane, uninjured.

Hughes' next big feat was to set the transcontinental speed record. With the H-1 in the shop for repairs, he bought a Northrop Gamma and changed out the engine. On January 13, 1936, Hughes took off from Burbank, California, and landed nine hours and twenty-seven minutes later in Newark, New Jersey. On his first try, he had set the record. But Hughes knew his H-1 could do better. On January 19, 1937, Hughes flew the H-1—retrofitted for the longer flight—from Los Angeles to Newark in seven hours, twenty-eight minutes. He had cut an incredible two hours off his year-old record. His feats earned him the Harmon Trophy, awarded annually to the world's outstanding aviator.

Hughes had one more record in his sights: the speed for a round-the-world flight. Choosing a twin-engine Lockheed 14 Super Electra for the attempt, Hughes equipped the plane with the latest communications and navigational innovations. Accompanied by four skilled aviators, Hughes took off on July 10, 1938. He traveled from New York City to Paris in sixteen hours and thirty-eight minutes, cutting in half Charles Lindbergh's transatlantic record. Then Hughes flew to Moscow, Omsk and Yakutsk in the Soviet Union, Fairbanks, Alaska, Minneapolis, and back to New York. The 14,716-mile flight took three days, nineteen hours and seventeen minutes: another record.

AROUND THE WORLD IN LESS THAN FOUR DAYS

After circling the top of the globe over three continents, Howard Hughes landed at his starting point yesterday, halving the previous record for the flight. The black line shows his course

Map showing the path Hughes took on his round-the-world flight. Courtesy of Howard Hughes Public Relations Photo Collection, Special Collections and Archives, University Libraries, University of Nevada, Las Vegas.

More than his previous record-setting flights, Hughes' round-the-world flight made him a major celebrity. New York, Chicago, Washington, D.C., and Houston celebrated Hughes' achievement with ticker-tape parades attended by millions, and he earned another Harmon Trophy, presented to him by President Franklin Roosevelt.

The onset of World War II spurred Hughes to seek contracts to build military aircraft. The D-2 fighter, designed at his new Culver City, California,

Hughes waves to cheering crowds during a July 15, 1938, parade in New York City celebrating his record-breaking round-the-world flight. Courtesy of Howard Hughes Public Relations Photo Collection, Special Collections and Archives, University Libraries, University of Nevada, Las Vegas.

research facility, did not garner a military contract. His larger XF-11, however, was commissioned as a photo-reconnaissance plane. The contract, signed in late 1943, called for Hughes to build one hundred planes. But the war ended before the XF-11 could see action.

Hughes also secured a contract for a "flying boat"—a giant eight-engine transport plane designed to carry seven hundred soldiers into war zones. The idea for the flying boat came from shipbuilder Henry Kaiser, who was dismayed that Nazi submarines were sinking his freighters as fast as they could be built. If the boats had wings, he reasoned, they could evade the Nazi assault. Kaiser, however, could not convince the military to entrust an aviation project to a shipbuilder. Enter Hughes. Intrigued by the challenge of building such a large aircraft, Hughes joined forces with Kaiser in 1942 and they obtained an $18 million contract to build three prototype flying boats. The contract contained a vexing condition: They could not use steel or aluminum, which were in short supply.

Using wood, Kaiser and Hughes set to work on the HK-1, or *Hercules*, which would weigh 300,000 pounds and have a wingspan of 320 feet. It was a

long and difficult process, and the Allies had since gained the advantage in the
war. The government moved to cancel the flying boat contract, but Hughes insisted it was a valuable research project, if nothing else. The federal government
ultimately allowed Hughes to complete the one flying boat under construction.
In 1946, the giant aircraft, finally ready for a test flight, was transported in three
pieces from Culver City to Long Beach Harbor and reassembled.

In the meantime, the XF-11 was finally ready to go airborne. On July 7,
1946, Hughes took off and flew over Los Angeles for about forty-five minutes.
As he was returning to his Culver City plant, a propeller problem sent the
plane into a spiral. Hughes crashed into the roof of a house in the Los Angeles
Country Club, and the plane's fuel tanks exploded. Hughes, critically injured,
somehow pulled himself from the wreckage. A Marine master sergeant named
William L. Durkin rushed up to the flaming plane and rescued Hughes. Just
before Christmas of that year, Hughes wrote a letter to Durkin thanking him for
his assistance and offering him a job after he left the Marines. In the meantime,
Hughes said, his company would send him a "small check"—$200—each month.

After Durkin died in 2006, his daughter insisted he had declined to accept any
money from Hughes. However, company records indicate that Hughes dutifully
sent the monthly checks for years—and that they were cashed. Hughes also gave
Durkin the damaged yoke—the steering control—from the crashed plane, which he
kept until his death. In 2009, Swann Galleries announced plans to auction the yoke,
with an estimated value of $40,000-$60,000. It's not clear if the auction took place.

Immediately after the crash, doctors thought it would be a miracle if
Hughes survived, considering the extent of his injuries. According to *Empire*:
"His chest was crushed. He suffered fractures of seven ribs on the left side, two
on the right, a fracture of the left clavicle, a possible fracture of the nose, a large
laceration of the scalp, extensive second- and third-degree burns on the left
hand, a second-degree burn on the lower part of the left chest, a second-degree
burn on the left buttock, cuts, bruises, and abrasions on his arms and legs, and
many small cuts on his face. His left lung had collapsed and his right was also
injured. His heart had been pushed to one side of his chest cavity. He was in
severe shock." Hughes walked out of the hospital in five weeks, attributing his
rapid recovery in part to drinking fresh-squeezed orange juice. Hughes fixed the
problems with the XF-11 and delivered one to the military in 1947. But with the
war over, the aircraft was not needed. Hughes built only two XF-11s.

After recovering from his accident, Hughes was ready to test the flying
boat. He was motivated by U.S. Senate hearings during which he was accused
of war profiteering and the flying boat was derided as the "Spruce Goose."

Hughes' defiant four days of testimony effectively squelched suggestions of wrongdoing on his part.

On November 2, 1947, Hughes taxied the flying boat into Long Beach Harbor with thousands of spectators and reporters lining the shore. When the plane reached one hundred miles per hour, it lifted into the air. The plane flew one mile and reached a top altitude of seventy feet. Hughes continued to make improvements over the next few years, but eventually his attention turned to other pursuits and the plane never flew again. Today, the flying boat is on display at the Evergreen Aviation & Space Museum in McMinnville, Oregon.

The ladies' man

Hughes was linked with most of Hollywood's female elite throughout the '30s, '40s, and early '50s. Here is an incomplete list of actresses, in alphabetical order, who dated or had more involved relationships with Hughes during this period: Cyd Charisse, Linda Darnell, Bette Davis, Yvonne De Carlo, Olivia de Havilland, Marlene Dietrich, Faith Domergue, Billie Dove, Ava Gardner,

Hughes' flying boat docked near Los Angeles Harbor on July 16, 1947. With Hughes at the controls, the giant plane took flight on November 2, 1947. Courtesy of Howard Hughes Public Relations Photo Collection, Special Collections and Archives, University Libraries, University of Nevada, Las Vegas.

Mitzi Gaynor, Kathryn Grayson, Jane Greer, Susan Hayward, Rita Hayworth, Katharine Hepburn, Dorothy Jordan, Hedy Lamarr, Janet Leigh, Carole Lombard, Ida Lupino, Marian Marsh, Ann Miller, Terry Moore, Jean Peters, Ginger Rogers, Gail Russell, Yvonne Shubert, Jean Simmons, Gene Tierney, and Lana Turner.

Although Hughes clearly focused on actresses, he also dated a few rich socialites, including Barbara Hutton and Gloria Vanderbilt, and Las Vegas showgirls, including Phyllis Applegate and Gloria White.

In a 2016 memoir, *The Rainbow Comes and Goes*, Vanderbilt describes her relationship with Hughes in 1941. Vanderbilt was seventeen at the time, and Hughes was thirty-six. She remembers him fondly: "When I was with Howard, I always felt that he was concentrating on me exclusively, and he was so easy to be with. Silences in our conversation were not empty spaces I wondered how to fill; they were as natural as breathing. It was as if we had known each other forever, yet whenever we got together, we plunged into wild joy as if it were our first meeting."

She says Hughes often would pick her up in a "shabby Oldsmobile" and they would embark on some kind of adventure. "Often he would fly me in his plane to Catalina for dinner in a seaside restaurant. There were nights in his private screening room when he'd proudly show me films he produced and directed. . . . Some nights when he was working he'd ask me to wait for him in the screening room. I'd watch movies until he'd suddenly appear with a picnic dinner we'd prop on our laps and enjoy." Vanderbilt believed they were in love and might get married. But after she returned to New York to complete her senior year of high school, the affair ended.

Two famous names are missing from the list above. Contrary to some accounts, Hughes' relationships with Harlow, star of *Hell's Angels*, and Jane Russell, star of *The Outlaw*, appear to have been strictly business-related.

While Hughes chalked up an astonishing record of romantic connections, two relationships stand out. In both cases, Hughes found someone to whom he was attracted for more than mere good looks.

Katharine Hepburn

In 1936, Hughes became involved with actress Katharine Hepburn. After success on the New York stage, Hepburn went to Hollywood in 1932 and earned an Academy Award for one of her first film roles, 1933's *Morning Glory*. She followed that with a great performance in the beloved *Little Women*. Her acting success caught Hughes' attention, and he introduced himself, in the summer of

Actress Katharine Hepburn and Hughes were a couple in the mid-1930s. Courtesy of The Mob Museum.

1935, in an unusual way: He landed his Sikorsky amphibian airplane on Malibu, California's Trancas Beach where Hepburn was shooting scenes for *Sylvia Scarlett*. At the time, she was sitting down to a picnic lunch with costar Cary Grant and director George Cukor.

Hepburn was perturbed at first. "It landed beautifully but I was angry," she told Charlotte Chandler, author of *The Real Kate: A Personal Biography of Katharine Hepburn*. "It was obvious the pilot was good, but I didn't think it was right to gamble with our lives. I wondered who it was and why anyone would do such a crazy stunt."

Grant soon realized his friend Hughes was the daredevil pilot, because Grant had suggested he drop by the movie set to meet Hepburn. "I wasn't dazzled as I suppose I was meant to be," Hepburn recalled. "It was too obvious a maneuver, done for effect by a show-off. But there was no doubt—Howard had a lot of pizzazz."

Hepburn did not see Hughes again for about a year, but their next meeting echoed the first. Hepburn was playing golf at the Bel-Air Country Club when Hughes landed a small plane on the seventh-hole green. "He got out of the small plane, and he was carrying his golf clubs," Hepburn said. "He joined us. The people at Bel-Air were really angry, but they were appeased when he said he'd pay for everything. . . . He asked me if I could have dinner with him the next week."

Hepburn was going to be in Boston the following week to appear in the play *Jane Eyre*, but that did not deter Hughes. When she arrived in Boston, he was waiting for her, and they saw each other every day.

The budding relationship between two of Hollywood's biggest names was fodder for reporters for months. The publicity helped Hepburn, according to William J. Mann, author of *Kate: The Woman Who Was Hepburn*: "Her relationship with Hughes, just as she was setting off on tour with *Jane Eyre,* was extraordinarily well timed. Soon after she opened in Chicago, the newspapers were filled with stories of Hepburn and Hughes, which certainly didn't hurt the box office; the play was extended for a week in the Windy City."

They may have wanted their fame, but they didn't like being hounded by the celebrity press, which worked overtime to snap pictures of Hughes and Hepburn together. During the traveling theater production of *Jane Eyre*, Hughes followed along in his plane, landing in Chicago, Cleveland, Pittsburgh, and other cities. As Charles Higham reported in *Kate: The Life of Katharine Hepburn*, the actress was "forced to dodge reporters, leaving cars several blocks before they reached her destination and darting behind buildings, using freight or servants' elevators, putting 'Do not disturb' notices on all of her doors."

They shared a love of golf and flying—he taught her how to pilot a plane. "I loved flying with Howard," Hepburn told Chandler. "We flew all over. With Howard, I had less than zero fear. I felt like a bird." More than once, Hughes landed his seaplane on the water in a secluded place and they would swim—sans clothes—with Hepburn diving from the wing into the water.

Hepburn eventually moved into Hughes' Los Angeles home at 211 Muirfield Road. In her autobiography, *Me: Stories of My Life*, Hepburn described their relationship:

> I think that reluctantly he found me a very appropriate companion. And I think that I found him extremely appropriate too. He was sort of the top of the available men—and I of the women. We were a colorful pair.

Hepburn said Hughes asked her to marry him several times, but she always said no. "I wasn't looking for a husband—even Howard," she said. Looking back late in life, Hepburn was a little perplexed by why she had rejected his proposals. "I'm not sure why I didn't marry him. I said no without giving much thought to it. . . . Well, one day, or rather one night, Howard asked me to marry him, and I, having come to take for granted one of the most brilliant, exciting, bravest, kindest, most attractive men in the world, who cared about me, said no without any serious thought. I didn't know it was the last time he would ask me—that he finally got tired of hearing me say no."

The relationship ended in the months after a hurricane flooded the Hepburn family home in Connecticut in September 1938. Hepburn and other family members escaped the house through a window, then watched the structure literally float away. Soon after, Hughes sent an airplane to deliver bottled water to Hepburn and her family. "I thought it would be Howard," Hepburn said, "but it wasn't. He had sent someone else to deliver the bottled water. . . . I understood that Howard and me, as it had been, was over."

Although Hughes and Hepburn gradually grew apart, he had one more kind gesture that reflected his lingering feelings for her. In late 1938, Hepburn started performing in a play called *The Philadelphia Story*. The part of Tracy Lord was made for her, and the play was a Broadway hit. The logical next step would be to turn the story into a movie. Hughes advised Hepburn to buy the movie rights to ensure she would secure the starring role. She didn't have the money at that time, so Hughes bought the movie rights for $30,000 and gave them to Hepburn as a gift.

The Philadelphia Story film, starring Hepburn, Grant, and a young Jimmy Stewart, was released in 1940. The romantic comedy was a box office success and nominated for six Academy Awards, winning two (Stewart for Best Actor and Donald Ogden Stewart for Best Adapted Screenplay). Today, *The Philadelphia Story* is shown often on classic movie networks.

Hepburn died in 2003. She was ninety-six.

Ava Gardner

Hughes met the actress Ava Gardner in 1943, after she had initiated divorce proceedings with actor Mickey Rooney. Hughes invited her to dinner—beginning a relationship that ranged from tender to tempestuous. In interviews with Peter Evans for a memoir that was not published during her lifetime, Gardner said Hughes asked her to marry him multiple times.

"Howard was in my life, on and off, for more than twenty years but I never loved him," she said. "I don't think he ever loved me, although he was a dogged sonofabitch. He wanted me to marry him so much. He was driving me crazy. I thought, Shit, I'll marry the man and be done with it. I mean, it was not a bad move marrying Howard Hughes, the richest man on the planet. I was still waiting for my California divorce from Mickey to come through. That was going to take a year, I reckoned. Howard didn't want to wait that long. He wanted me to go to Nevada to get a divorce." Gardner asked movie producer Louis B. Mayer for advice, and he talked her out of a quickie divorce.

Gardner remembered Hughes as a shy man. "He was partially deaf, of course," she said. "That may have accounted for the longueurs in his conversation, and probably explained his shyness, too. Anyway, he never talked much. He was no raconteur; I called him the Quiet Texan."

She marveled at Hughes' often shabby and ill-fitting attire. One time he arrived to pick her up wearing a "shiny blue serge suit, the trousers held up by a tie, the sort you usually wear around your neck, the coat slung over his shoulder, his shoelaces undone." Another time, attempting to impress her, he showed

Actress Ava Gardner, pictured in 1946, had a tempestuous relationship with Hughes. Courtesy of Howard Hughes Public Relations Photo Collection, Special Collections and Archives, University Libraries, University of Nevada, Las Vegas.

up dressed in an "ice cream-colored affair that he must have worn at some high school or college function about twenty years before. Howard, the shy one, the invisible one, pirouetting like a god-damn male mannequin, oblivious to the belt in the back and pleats that must have gone out with dueling. As usual the sleeves were four inches too short and the trouser legs six inches above the socks."

Calling Hughes "more eccentric . . . than anyone I ever met," Gardner described his eating habits: "His taste in food . . . was bizarre to the point of absurdity. I never saw him eat anything for dinner but a steak, green peas, perhaps a few potatoes, and a small salad, followed by ice cream topped with caramel sauce. Night after night, year after year."

Hughes bought her dozens of pieces of expensive jewelry, intending to give her one before each meal and one before bed for seven days, leading to his proposal. Gardner, however, was not impressed by the gifts. "Most women would have given their souls for some of that stuff," she said. "I admit it would have kept me for the rest of my life. But at that moment, with my temper aroused, I just didn't care."

Gardner and Hughes once got into a physical fight. Hughes had hired private detectives to follow Gardner and bug her house. They discovered that even as Gardner was divorcing Rooney, they continued to meet for conjugal visits. Using a key, Hughes entered Gardner's house while she slept and walked into her bedroom, perhaps expecting to catch her with Rooney. In the ensuing conversation, Hughes slapped Gardner. Enraged, Gardner reached for something to hit him with and found either an onyx ashtray or a bronze bell—Gardner told the story both ways. She smashed the object into his face. As Hughes collapsed to the floor, Gardner reached for a chair to hit him with but her sister rushed into the room and stopped her. "I practically had him laid out on a slab," Gardner told Evans. "We fought all the time but I nearly put a lily in his hand that night." Covered in blood and with two missing teeth, Hughes was carried out of the room by two of his bodyguards.

At the time, Gardner thought she had seen the last of Hughes, but he was undeterred. Not long after the fight, he proposed marriage again. When she started seeing Frank Sinatra, Hughes tried to convince her the crooner wasn't good enough for her. "Howard never took no for an answer," she said. "What can you expect from someone who shrugged off a brass bell tossed at the side of his head? Believe me, there was something scary about Howard's stop-at-nothing determination."

Gardner and Hughes continued to see each other over the next few years, but marriage was out of the question. "The mix was too volatile," Gardner said. "Our chemistry was the stuff that causes hydrogen bombs to explode. Till death do us part would have been a whole lot sooner than later if we had tied the knot."

Gardner died in 1990. She was sixty-seven.

Part 2:

Las Vegas

Early Las Vegas: Hughes' Safe Haven

Howard Hughes was familiar with Las Vegas long before he moved into the Desert Inn in 1966. He had an affinity for the city dating back at least to the early '40s.

It's not easy to track all his Las Vegas visits and activities before the Desert Inn years. There are a couple of good reasons: 1) Hughes usually came to Las Vegas to escape the spotlight, and 2) Las Vegas was eager to accommodate his desire for privacy.

Still, Hughes did not hide while in Las Vegas. In the 1940s and early '50s he gambled, dined, and watched shows amid thousands of other tourists. He hobnobbed with local honchos such as Benjamin "Bugsy" Siegel and Wilbur Clark, and he often was accompanied by a beautiful actress such as Ava Gardner or perhaps a Las Vegas showgirl he admired. In his 1966 biography, John Keats described Hughes' affinity for Sin City: "So far as Hughes was concerned, the twenty-four-hour-a-day town suited him to the ground. The restaurants were always open at any hour of the day or night, and there is probably no better place than a gambling hall for a man who wishes to be unnoticed and undisturbed."

As much as he enjoyed the Las Vegas nightlife, Hughes was not a high-rolling gambler. And he was very demanding of the hotels in which he stayed. Keats interviewed Abe Schiller, a Flamingo Hotel public relations man, who said Hughes once rented an entire hotel wing. "Whereupon, he promptly refused maid service," Keats wrote. "Towels and linens, when called for by a young Mormon, were left outside Hughes' room. The rooms to either side of Hughes' room were kept vacant."

Then Hughes made another demand. According to longtime Las Vegas journalist and publicist Dick Odessky's memoir *Fly on the Wall*, Hughes asked Schiller to help him pin a pink blanket—standard issue on Flamingo beds—over the

Silent film star Billie Dove was Hughes' first true love. Why they broke up was never revealed. Author's collection.

window in his suite. "That's absolutely perfect, Abe," Hughes reportedly said. "Now, I want the exact same blankets placed over every window in my rooms." Schiller and hotel manager Dick Chappel did some quick math and realized they needed seventy-eight more blankets to fulfill Hughes' wish. The blankets were found and placed on the windows. When Hughes left the Flamingo, Odessky wrote, he took the blankets with him, as well as some furniture he liked.

Billie Dove

It's probably impossible to pinpoint the first time Howard Hughes set foot in Nevada, but his first known trip was in 1931, when the twenty-four-year-old accompanied silent film star Billie Dove, whom he hoped to marry, to Nevada so she could establish residency and obtain a divorce from director Irvin Willat.

Dove was one of Hollywood's biggest stars at the time, competing with Clara Bow for box office supremacy. In an interview with William M. Drew, Dove recalled: "In those days, I had my picture on the cover of every motion picture magazine. Clara Bow had the most fan mail of everybody in Hollywood, I was second, and then one summer, I beat her. I have a letter the Burbank postmaster gave me and it says I received in one month inclusive 37,320 letters—that's more than a thousand letters a day."

Dove met Hughes at a party at the Biltmore Hotel in Hollywood. Hughes asked the actress Marion Davies to escort him to Dove's table for the introduction. He did not make a good first impression.

"He was deadpan and look at me stiff-faced like a statue," Dove said. "I don't know whether he spoke even. I tried to make polite conversation and there was nothing, nothing. He was absolutely blah. He didn't smile. He just kept looking at me and I thought, 'Good God! Is this the guy they're talking about who's making a famous picture, *Hell's Angels*, and is the heir to $84 million? Is this the one they're talking about?' I was glad when he left the table."

Despite their uninspired first meeting, Hughes and Dove eventually became a couple. "I got to know him and found out that he was brilliant, that he was charming and had a lovely sense of humor. We laughed together and then we fell in love. That's how it happened. He was very much in love with me, very, very, very much, and I was in love with him."

Hughes and Dove tended to spend their weekends together, often going out on a boat to Catalina Island, off the coast of Southern California, where they kept a couple of horses to ride. One time, Hughes brought Dove aboard a 170-foot-long yacht. "It was big, big, big," Dove recalled. "You could barbecue there, you could dance there, you could get sun, you could fish, you could do anything. There were white cushions that were water-proof all the way around— it was just wonderful." Hughes asked her what she thought of the yacht. "Oh, Howard, it's the most beautiful thing I ever saw." And he said, "Okay, it's yours."

Although they had been separated for several years, Willat at first refused to grant Dove a divorce. Hughes convinced him to do so in exchange for $325,000.

"That story about the money is true," Dove said. "Howard gave him $325,000 to let me divorce him and that's a hell of a lot of money, especially in those days. I begged Howard not to, but there was nothing I could do once he gave the money to Irvin. I felt like I'd been bought and sold. I lost all my respect for Irvin."

Dove planned to go to Las Vegas and establish her six-week residency to get a divorce. But Hughes came up with a plan to spend the six weeks on a farm outside Las Vegas. They dressed very plainly as they boarded a train. "You wouldn't take him for Howard Hughes and you wouldn't take me for an actress, believe me," Dove said.

Hughes had devised a scheme in which he and Dove became "George Johnson" and his sister, "Marion," and they stayed and worked on a farm owned by Floyd and Arlene Struck.

"The building where I was to stay was a funny-looking thing, not half as large as your kitchen probably," Dove said. "I think maybe it was built to store food for the winter and then they abandoned it. . . . The building was nothing but concrete. It had a place for a door but no door, it had a place on two sides for windows but no windows."

After they lived a few days on the farm, Hughes' lawyers informed him the shed would not qualify as a residence under Nevada divorce law. His plan was sunk. The couple returned to California, and Dove went through her divorce in the glare of the Hollywood spotlight.

Despite the foiled plan, Dove recalled the farm experience fondly, reflecting that Hughes seemed happier working as a farmhand than he ever did in the city.

Hughes and Dove broke up about a year later. For the rest of her life, Dove never revealed the reason. "People have been so interested in knowing why we split up and I think it's none of their damn business. . . . It had nothing to do with any man, nothing to do with any woman—nothing at all. It was something personal but nothing important. It was really such a tiny thing that you wouldn't believe it if I told you."

Dove died in 1997. She was ninety-four.

Sky Haven Airport

During the 1930s, Hughes almost certainly touched down in Nevada a few times while testing new airplanes and breaking speed and endurance flying records. But the first solid evidence of his landing in Las Vegas came in 1942.

Florence Murphy and her husband, John, opened Sky Haven Airport north of Las Vegas on December 7, 1941. Hughes became a regular customer soon afterward.

"The first time he came in he called us from Los Angeles and told us he was coming in," Murphy said in a 2003 interview. "He said he might come in after dark and so we should be sure to have some lights on the runway. We didn't have lights, so we got some automobiles parked at the terminal building and got them out beside the runway [with their lights shining on the runway]. He came in and landed."

Over the next few years, Hughes frequently used Sky Haven, Murphy recalled, including one landing in which he ground-looped, damaging a wingtip. "He came into the office and said, 'Now, none of you saw that.'"

One holiday season, Hughes had stationed mechanics at Sky Haven to work on his plane. "They hadn't heard anything from him for a week, so we told the crew to go home for Christmas," Murphy said. "They didn't want to because Mr. Hughes would be very mad if they did. They finally left, and wouldn't you know it, he came in. He found them gone and fired them all. I told him it was my fault and he put them all back to work."

Hughes was a "very nice fellow, very soft-spoken," Murphy said. He invited her and her husband to the El Rancho Vegas hotel for dinner a few times. "He'd invite a whole bunch of us, and he'd have a table ready for twelve or fifteen of us. He'd come in and say, 'You can have anything you want.' He never did sit down to eat with us. He always had some business to take care of."

Murphy later served as vice president of Bonanza Airlines, becoming the nation's first woman airline executive. She died in 2006 at age ninety-four.

When Hughes returned to Las Vegas in the 1960s, he acquired Murphy's airport. In 1987, his heirs sold it to Clark County for $16 million. It is now known as North Las Vegas Airport.

Lake Mead crash

The May 18, 1943, issue of the *Boulder City News* featured a banner headline: "One Man Dies in Plane Tragedy on Lake Mead." The secondary headline elaborated: "Howard Hughes, Noted Pilot, Builder of Planes, Three Others Survive Crash."

The newspaper reported that the aircraft, a Sikorsky S-43 twin-engine amphibian, "suddenly went out of control and crashed into Lake Mead," killing William M. Cline, a Civil Aeronautics Administration inspector from Santa Monica, California. The four survivors were Hughes, who was "slightly injured"; Richard Felt, a flight mechanic from Burbank, California, who was seriously injured; Charles Walter Von Rosenberg, a test pilot, who suffered two broken vertebrae; and Gene Blandford, a flight engineer from Santa Monica, who was not seriously hurt.

According to the newspaper, after the plane crashed about one thirty in the afternoon, the drama played out like this: "Four of the five men aboard were able to get out atop of the plane as it floated, a few miles from the Vegas Wash boat landing, and Hughes and two companions, Charles W. Von Rosenberg and Gene Blandford, had placed Richard Felt, seriously injured with a gash in his forehead, on an inflated life raft."

The survivors saw a boat coming toward them, "a small craft in which were Mr. and Mrs. B.A. Robertson and Mr. and Mrs. Willard Parrish, all of Las Vegas."

The *News* continued: "When the boat reached the slowly settling amphibian, the men helped place Felt, the injured flight mechanic, in the small craft, and Gene Blandford . . . went with him, while Hughes and Von Rosenberg . . .

Hughes' Sikorsky S-43 sits on the shore of Lake Mead after it was pulled out of the water in 1943. Courtesy of Howard Hughes Public Relations Photo Collection, Special Collections and Archives, University Libraries, University of Nevada, Las Vegas.

stayed with the plane." Felt was taken to the boat landing at Hemenway Wash, then by Army ambulance to Camp Williston Hospital in Boulder City.

Meanwhile, another small boat, piloted by Slim Powell of Boulder City, arrived to rescue Hughes and Von Rosenberg. Cline's body was not immediately recovered from the plane.

Two days after the crash, Felt died from his injuries, which included a fractured skull.

"Though the plane eventually sank completely, Rangers Bywater and Campbell, though off duty at the time, took a sight from shore from which they believed they could later locate fairly closely the spot where the plane went down," the *News* reported.

A more organized search for the plane ensued the following day. The May 20, 1943, issue of the *News* explained: "Search for the sunken plane continued yesterday, with help of National Park Service boats and planes. The approximate place where it sank was located, and the water was said to be from 150 to 175 feet deep." Hughes, naturally, assisted in the search. He "flew over the spot Tuesday with Glenn E. Odekirk, locating by memory of the terrain the place where he had landed the plane."

The following week, Hughes started salvaging the aircraft. With the help of Navy divers, the plane was brought to the surface, dragged to the beach, and separated into pieces that were transported by truck and trailer back to California.

Just days after the crash, a coroner's jury heard testimony concerning Cline's death and absolved Hughes of blame.

Hughes was conducting test flights of his experimental Sikorsky amphibian in anticipation of obtaining Civil Aeronautics Administration approval before delivery to the U.S. Army Corps of Engineers. Hughes originally planned to use the Sikorsky for his 1938 round-the-world flight but eventually chose a modified Lockheed 14. Since then, the Sikorsky had sat in a hangar in Glendale, California.

The Army Corps wanted the plane to transport its engineers to far-flung air bases. At first, Hughes didn't want to part with it, but when the Army Corps suggested it might take possession of the plane anyway, Hughes reluctantly consented to sell, and the test flights were scheduled. Civil Aeronautics Administration approval was required to complete the deal.

But Hughes being Hughes, the process took a strange turn. With the test flights looming, Hughes suddenly disappeared with the Sikorsky. He turned up in Southern Nevada. He spent his days at Lake Mead flying the plane, and his nights in Las Vegas soaking in the nightlife along the burgeoning Strip, often alongside actress Ava Gardner.

According to *Empire*, "For hours at a stretch, he taxied the plane while speedboats loaded with cameramen trailed alongside shooting hundreds of feet of film of the Sikorsky's hull as it glided through the water." Hughes filmed the water landings not to gauge the readiness of the Sikorsky but for use in the development of his giant flying boat.

A month after his disappearance, Hughes returned to California and declared the Sikorsky ready for testing. The land-based test flights occurred in California but when it came time for the water flights, Hughes recommended Lake Mead.

With Hughes at the controls, the plane took off from a small airstrip near the lake and soon was ready to test some landings on the water. Hughes had landed the plane at Lake Mead literally thousands of times before. All went well until Hughes set the plane down on the lake's surface. According to *Empire*: "The Sikorsky started settling in, displacing water, and picking up drag. It pitched forward slightly and became a little unstable, but that was normal during the first few seconds. It started to go left, but Hughes straightened it out. Then, without warning, the Sikorsky lunged forward on its nose and veered sharply right. Before Hughes could react, the plane turned in the water and began skipping sideways on the lake."

Now the plane was "hurtling diagonally at eighty miles an hour," according to *Empire*, and the craft started coming apart. As the cockpit filled with water, four of the five occupants scrambled to get out.

As the *Boulder City News* reported, Felt and Blandford were brought ashore by a nearby boat, while Hughes, whose forehead had been gashed, and Von Rosenberg clung to a life raft.

Hughes' longtime aviation partner, Odekirk, had witnessed the crash from the ground. He found Hughes at the Boulder City Airport and tried unsuccessfully to convince him to go to the hospital. When Hughes refused, he took him to the Boulder Dam Hotel, where he treated Hughes' cuts.

During his recovery at the Boulder Dam Hotel, Hughes told the proprietor, Chauncey Spilsbury, that he wanted only one maid he could depend on to take care of his room. Edna Dryden got the assignment. "I waited on him and did his room," Dryden recalled in a history of the hotel written by Dennis McBride. "He must have been there a couple of months. When he got able to go down to the lobby, then I'd do his room. When he was even better, he took walks outside. He was very quiet and never had much of anything to say. He just thanked me for doing his room, and for going and getting him coffee and things. And when he left, he gave me a $100 tip."

Federal investigators later determined that the accident occurred because the plane had been loaded improperly, throwing off its center of gravity. Hughes was officially cleared of wrongdoing, but there's no question he was not on his game the day of the crash. The authors of *Howard Hughes: The Untold Story* contend the federal probe was whitewashed because Hughes was a major contractor for the war effort. And they note that the crash occurred just months before Hughes' first major psychological breakdown.

Hughes paid the medical bills of everyone involved in the crash. After retrieving the plane from the lake bottom, at a cost of $100,000, and hauling it back to California, he rebuilt it (at a cost of $500,000) and flew it again.

Cline's body was never recovered from Lake Mead.

George and Peg Crockett

Peg Nickerson was a teenager when her family moved from Pasadena, California, to Las Vegas in 1937 and built the Hidden Well Ranch south of town. The small ranch attracted a variety of paying guests, including movie stars and authors. Among the celebrities who signed the guest book were Alfred Hitchcock, William Powell, and Irene Dunne. They came for a respite from the Hollywood rat race, or, in the case of bandleader Benny Goodman's wife, to establish six-week residency to get a divorce.

The ranch was a big change for Nickerson, who was used to city living. "It was a total change in culture for me, but I loved it," she said. "I was kind of a tomboy."

A few years later, a man named George Crockett knocked on the door and said he was going to build an airport nearby. George asked Peg, who was still in high school at the time, "You ever been up in a plane?" Peg went flying with George, and she soon told her parents she wanted to be a pilot. "I took a few lessons and really got hooked on it," she said. When Peg ran out of money for lessons, George put her to work at the airport.

Crockett opened Alamo Airways in 1941, Peg earned her pilot's license in 1943, and the two were married in 1948. Alamo was a successful operation. The Crocketts had eighty-five people working for them at one point. They had a restaurant, motel, and rental car agency.

Peg said she first met Howard Hughes in 1945 when he was dating a guest staying at the Hidden Well Ranch, a model named Florence Pritchett. He only came to the ranch one time that she remembered. "He was very tall and quiet," Peg recalled. "He came in and sat down and was talking to my mother, waiting for Florence." Peg remembered her mother's assessment of Hughes: "fascinating but the hardest man to hold a conversation with."

Hughes started flying into the Alamo Airways terminal near Las Vegas Boulevard about the same time, and he kept George busy with tasks big and

Peg Crockett and her husband, George, ran Alamo Airways in Las Vegas and knew Hughes well. Author's collection.

small. "George would do everything for him," Peg said. One time, Peg said, Hughes summoned George to the men's room at the airport. He had broken the zipper on his pants and wondered if Peg would fix it for him. She did.

Hughes could be very demanding of George, his requests varying in tone from "I wonder if you'd do me a favor" to "George, I need you." The Crocketts lived in a house on the airport property, and Hughes started using their telephone. "He started making a habit of showing up at the house to use the phone," Peg said, noting that she would come home to find empty milk glasses he had used.

The Crocketts often saw the various women Hughes brought to town. When Hughes escorted actress Terry Moore to Las Vegas in 1949 to get a divorce, he had George drive her around.

The heavy demands Hughes placed on George Crockett were typical of the way he treated his employees. "He knew what he wanted to do, and didn't realize that other people needed to be considered," said Peg, who nevertheless relished being of assistance to Hughes. "It was interesting. We got an insight into the man."

In 1948, the Crocketts relinquished their lease of government land on which their airport sat and it was taken over by Clark County, which built McCarran Field (later McCarran International Airport). The Crocketts leased back forty acres to continue operating Alamo Airways as a fixed-base operation. In 1960, they completed construction on a large house on a hill south of McCarran that afforded them breathtaking views of Las Vegas and the surrounding mountains.

After Hughes moved into the Desert Inn Hotel in 1966, he bought Alamo Airways from the Crocketts for $1.75 million. A year later, Hughes got Crockett into a mess when he bought Air West Airlines. In 1973, Hughes, Bob Maheu, Chester Davis, and two others were indicted on charges of stock manipulation in the Air West deal. Crockett, who had sold his shares at Hughes' request, was named a co-conspirator but was not indicted. U.S. District Judge Bruce Thompson of Nevada threw out the case twice, but the United States Court of Appeals for the Ninth Circuit disagreed and sent it back to his court in 1976. Crockett, frustrated by the proceedings, went fishing in Mexico instead of appearing for the next hearing. When the Justice Department requested a delay, Thompson, perhaps even more frustrated than Crockett, dismissed the case a third time. The Justice Department did not appeal.

The growth of Las Vegas, which the Crocketts helped nurture, eventually came back to bite them. In 1990, just two weeks after George Crockett's death, the county acquired the house and surrounding property to be used for a freeway connection to the airport. "They just took my husband, and now they're going to take my home," a teary Peg Crockett told reporters.

Husite purchase

In the early '50s, Hughes generated rampant speculation and anticipation in Nevada over his purchase of 25,000 acres west of Las Vegas, presumably with the intention of building some kind of aviation-related industrial facility. Using anonymous sources, a *Las Vegas Review-Journal* article printed November 6, 1953, reported that Hughes had acquired 11,829 acres. The same article reported that earlier on June 9, 1952, Hughes had obtained a patent for the first 13,536-acre parcel. This brought his land holdings west of Las Vegas to 25,365 acres The article described the land buyer as "the Hughsite company," although the acreage later became known as "Husite."

The article concluded: "There has been much speculation as to what type of factory the Hughsite firm would establish on the property, when the land acquisition has been completed, ranging from an atomic jet engine to guided missiles, but there has been no announcement made by firm officials . . . Company spokesmen reported, however, that 'none of the guesses thus far made are even close.'"

In 1955, when Hughes formally recorded the patents on all the Husite land, Las Vegans were still wondering what he planned to do with it. "Reports have persisted for several years that Hughes might develop the huge property for aircraft construction or guided missile work as part of a decentralization of industry move being studied by the federal government," the *Review-Journal* reported on September 15, 1955. "The industrialist, however, has maintained silence on whatever plans, if any, he has for the property."

Development of the vast property did not begin until the 1980s, when Hughes' heirs started building the Summerlin master-planned community.

Grace Hayes Lodge

In 1942, the singer and actress Grace Hayes was invited to perform at the El Rancho Vegas hotel in Las Vegas. Her show was a hit, and she continued to perform in Las Vegas over the next few years. In 1947, she bought a nightclub in Las Vegas, the Red Rooster, for $15,000. It was on the west side of the Las Vegas Strip, where the Mirage Hotel stands today.

Renamed the Grace Hayes Lodge, the club attracted an array of movers and shakers, from mobster Benjamin "Bugsy" Siegel to Hughes. In a 1981 interview with the *Review-Journal*, Hayes estimated Hughes was in the place an average of three times a week.

"I don't know what I served him," Hayes said. "I know I served him a drink. I mixed a drink; he didn't care what it was. He never drank it, and he never paid me for a drink in his life. All he was concerned about was getting me out from behind that bar."

Hayes' most vivid memory of Hughes revolved around a business opportunity. "He came in one night and I fixed him a drink," Hayes said. "And I looked around and he was gone. So I figured he had gone and I dumped out his drink. I went around to the other customers, singing and telling dirty jokes. And when I turned around, he was back again. I said, 'What the hell happened to you?' He said, 'I went to wash my shirt.'"

Hughes had gone into the restroom, where he washed out his shirt and dried it over an oil heater. "He said, 'I've got a deal for you. I want you to be in on this. This is what they're going to call "wash and wear."'"

Hayes assumed he was joking, and Hughes never brought up the subject again. However, according to Hughes' longtime publicist, Walter Kane, Hughes

did play a role in the development of wash-and-wear—or permanent press—
cotton fabric and "made a lot of money off it."

The timeline fits, at least. Wrinkle-free cotton was indeed first developed in the
1940s and became available commercially in the 1950s. However, a chemist named
Ruth Benerito, who worked for the U.S. Department of Agriculture, is widely credited with creating the chemical process that made wrinkle-free cotton fabric possible.

Grace Hayes died in 1989. She was ninety-three.

The Green House

On January 25, 1954, the *Review-Journal* printed a brief story headlined, "Howard
Hughes Likes to Live in Las Vegas." The newspaper report was based on an article
in an unnamed magazine detailing the "secret life of the film and financial tycoon."

Hollywood had grown "too complicated," Hughes told the magazine, while
Las Vegas is "close enough to Los Angeles to make the trip the merest of chores
and active enough to supply excitement when excitement is wanted."

The article said Hughes conducted all facets of his business from Las Vegas, either
by phone or by summoning people to the desert for meetings. He once called a Trans
World Airlines board of directors meeting in Las Vegas, according to the story.

Hughes was not an easy man to find, even though Las Vegas was a fairly
small place at that time. "In a roaring resort city that consists essentially of a
strip two-and-one-half miles long and a few hundred yards wide, Hughes manages to keep himself almost completely inaccessible," the magazine article stated.

In 1953, Hughes leased a five-room house east of the Strip, which was
dubbed the "Green House" because of its color. He spent time in the house
over the next year, but it's unlikely he ever slept there, since he also kept rooms
at the Flamingo Hotel. When Hughes returned to Los Angeles, he ordered aide
Bill Gay to have the house sealed. Hughes presumably planned to return to the
Green House at some point but never did.

The early '50s were a trying time for Hughes, who probably had only himself to blame. Hughes Aircraft Company was in turmoil over his inability to
get along with the men he hired to run it, and he had the Air Force on his back
over completing defense contracts. The same could be said of RKO Pictures,
where Hughes dramatically cut film production and faced lawsuits from angry
shareholders. Meanwhile, Hughes was seeing Communists everywhere as the
Red Scare and McCarthyism took hold. Las Vegas, then, provided Hughes with
a safe haven, an escape from the pressures of running his many enterprises.

When Hughes died in 1976, company employees opened the house looking
for a will. They found the house exactly as it had been left in 1954. According to

This house in Las Vegas, known as the "Green House" to Hughes' staff, served as his residence in 1953-54. Author's collection.

Empire, "The Green House contained an electric Westinghouse refrigerator—still running—two newspapers dated October 13, 1953, and April 4, 1954, keys to Room 186 at the Flamingo Hotel and Room 401 of the Hotel Miramar, twin beds with soiled sheets, some Sahara casino gambling chips, eight telephones in five rooms, a letter from 'Jane to Howard' dated December 5, 1952, a script titled *Son of Sinbad*, two yachting caps, a 1953 appointment diary believed to belong to Jean Peters, a box of Christmas decorations, and a fruitcake."

Paul Winn, one of the employees who scoured the house, said there also was a box with a beautiful silk robe in it, apparently a gift Hughes had received. Also, Winn said, there were "two pairs of white tennis shoes, size ten, slightly worn."

The employees who entered the house brought a metal detector with them, and the machine indicated something metal beneath the floor. Thinking it might be a safe, they obtained a jackhammer and used it to open up the floor. There was no safe, just a pipe or something, Winn recalled. "We made a valiant effort to find a will."

After the company employees departed, some employees of the adjacent KLAS Channel 8 television station, which Hughes also owned, snagged a few more souvenirs from the house, including a toilet seat. The Nevada State Museum in Las Vegas has one of the telephones, equipped with an amplifier because Hughes was hard of hearing.

Mark Smith, Channel 8's general manager at the time, had the house renovated and used it for occasional cocktail parties and conferences. When Bob Stoldal became a news executive at the station, the house was transformed into something of a shrine to Hughes, with movie posters and other memorabilia

Jean Peters married Hughes in 1957 in Tonopah, Nevada. Author's collection.

honoring his residence there. The house still stands, and Channel 8 occasionally opens it up for special guests and events.

Secret wedding

Upon returning to Los Angeles, Hughes went deeper into seclusion, living at the Beverly Hills Hotel, where his mental instability became more pronounced. He had just one known foray back into the Silver State in the years before his hermitic four-year stint at the Desert Inn.

In 1957, Hughes asked the actress Jean Peters to marry him, and she accepted. Ever obsessed with privacy, Hughes decided the wedding would occur in a secret location—Tonopah, Nevada, an old mining town about 200 miles north of Las Vegas.

Hughes asked his tax attorney, James Arditto, to make the arrangements. Arditto, in turn, consulted with Howard Cannon, the Las Vegas city attorney, to help smooth the way for a very private wedding. (A year later, Cannon would be elected to the first of four terms as a U.S. senator.)

On the morning of January 12, 1957, the couple traveled from Los Angeles to Tonopah in a Lockheed Constellation, flown by a TWA pilot and co-pilot. They landed at an abandoned air strip outside of town. Only a handful of Hughes' personal aides were there, and they were told to dress as if they were going on a hunting trip. No women accompanied Peters.

The ceremony was held on the second floor of the L&L Motel, a nondescript roadside lodge that was demolished in 2005. Nye County Justice of the Peace Walter Bowler presided. After the brief ceremony concluded, Hughes and Peters returned to the airplane and flew back to Los Angeles.

The secrecy of the affair extended to the marriage certificate, for which the bride and groom did not provide their real names. Instead, they were listed as G.A. Johnson and Marian Evans. They even used fake ages on the form.

Thus began one of the most unusual marriages in history, with the couple living together for only a short period until their amicable divorce in 1971.

Bob Maheu, Part 1: *Rise of the Alter Ego*

When Howard Hughes lived in Las Vegas between 1966 and 1970, he never made a public appearance. A handful of Las Vegans spoke with him on the telephone, but they couldn't know for sure he was making a local call. They accepted that he was a Las Vegas resident largely on faith in the word of others.

When Las Vegans had business dealings with Hughes or watched television news reports about his activities, the person they saw was Bob Maheu. After Hughes went into deep seclusion in the late '50s, but before he came to Las Vegas, he hired Maheu to represent his interests in the public eye. He called Maheu at three a.m. to give him the news. Maheu recalled what he said: "'Congrats, Bob. I've just chosen you to be my alter ego.' He said he's never again going to make a public appearance. When I spoke, the world would know it was Hughes speaking."

Although flattered by the offer, Maheu worried about the pitfalls of such a high-profile post. For one thing, the arrangement would be awkward when seeking licenses and approvals from regulatory bodies. "If I go before a regulatory body and I am asked who's going to be in charge of this project, I have to say I'm going to be in charge," Maheu told Hughes. "Because if I don't, there's no way to accomplish what you're trying to accomplish." Hughes wasn't fazed.

Maheu said he knew from the outset that he could end up embroiled in a power struggle within Hughes' vast empire. He told Hughes: "I'm going to become too powerful in your organization." Maheu worried that once he started making decisions, other executives would come to feel he had more power than he should have. Hughes responded that if Maheu had a problem with the board of directors, he would back Maheu.

As it turned out, Maheu was able to navigate the regulatory process in Nevada, but his fears about an internal struggle proved accurate. Before the arrangement fell apart in 1970, however, Maheu had an amazing run as Hughes' alter ego and the leading force in several aspects of his business. And he accomplished all this while never meeting Hughes in person.

Maheu said he actually glimpsed Hughes twice. The first time was in a hotel in the Bahamas. "I was sitting in the lobby reading a newspaper, and he came by and took the elevator," Maheu said. The second time was when Hughes secretly came to Las Vegas via train on Thanksgiving 1966. "We stopped the train five miles outside Las Vegas at night," Maheu said. "They were just taking him off the train on a stretcher, and I saw the engineer from the front start coming in that direction and I went to intercept the engineer."

Maheu wanted to meet Hughes in person and actually tried to see him at a critical moment in 1968. Maheu awoke in the middle of the night in a cold sweat. "I had the realization at that moment that I had to make three $150 million decisions on his behalf with full authority to make those decisions," Maheu said. "At the time that was big stuff. I made up my mind that I was going to talk to this man in person, and I was not going to take no for an answer. I finally got him on the phone, and four-plus hours later this man started actually crying on the phone. 'Bob,' he said, 'your Jesuit logic has finally caught up with me. You've got me so mentally fatigued and I can't go on at this pace anymore, and I have to tell you the truth.' He says, 'If you saw the condition under which I have allowed myself to deteriorate . . .' Now, I knew he was not good. The guys would tell me piecemeal. Hughes said, 'If you ever see it, you'll never be able to represent me again with as much effectiveness as you have in the past. Please promise me that you will let this one die.' And I have to tell you, I started crying. I really did. I thought, my God, how can any person allow this to happen?"

Born in Waterville, Maine, Maheu grew up wanting to be a lawyer. He earned his bachelor's degree at the College of the Holy Cross and attended Georgetown Law School. But then his plans took a dramatic turn. "I am about four weeks in law school when I am taking an exam with the FBI as a translator. I speak French. And the job paid two hundred bucks a year more than the job I had. I had to work through college. So I took the exam and as a consequence they asked me if I'd like to be an FBI agent. I thought they were pulling my leg at first. They explained to me that they had found themselves with a shortage of agents who could speak foreign languages and they were giving them some kind of entitlements with the exam. . . . I figured the hell with law school, this was exciting."

He entered the FBI Academy in December 1940. Because of the urgent need for agents, the training period was reduced from three months to two. Maheu

A portrait of Bob Maheu during the time he worked for Hughes in the 1950s and 1960s. Courtesy of *Las Vegas Review-Journal* Archive.

recalled that he was a horrible trainee. He contracted pneumonia and broke his thumb during the training. "I've always described myself as the least educated and least trained agent in the FBI."

Maheu nonetheless had some success during his seven years with the agency. During the war, he worked undercover for two years. His first undercover assignment was to monitor two Nazi spies operating in the United States. One became a double agent, and Maheu gave him misleading information to send to the Germans about U.S. military plans for the D-Day invasion of Normandy. "The Germans bought our story," Maheu wrote in his memoir, *Next to Hughes*. "It's impossible to say how many German troops were diverted south because of the Bureau's broadcasts. But it's known that the German high command expected the invasion to take place there, and it is certain that one critical aspect of D-Day's success was the fact that it took the Nazis by surprise."

After the war, Maheu moved to the New York office, serving under E. J. Connelley, assistant director in charge of major cases. But when Maheu's pregnant wife, Yvette, came down with tuberculosis, FBI Director J. Edgar Hoover transferred the young agent back to his hometown, where his wife could recuperate. "I was so happy about that," Maheu said. "But six weeks later, I'm beginning to realize that there's nothing for the FBI to do in Waterville. Once in a while there'd be a guy who'd steal an automobile. It became very, very depressing and finally I submitted my resignation."

As his wife recovered, Maheu went into business, first in the distribution of goods between the United States and Canada. Then he got involved with a business enterprise that had the potential to make him very rich. "In Canada some fellow had developed a process for canning pure cream without any additives at all and retaining the taste," Maheu said. "I managed to get the [distribution] rights for the world, except Canada."

"Dairy Dream" was an immediate hit. A manufacturing plant was set up in Wisconsin, and before long the product was available in seventeen states. "The world was my oyster," Maheu said. "This was a hot item." He and his wife moved to New York and bought a large house in New Rochelle.

Then disaster struck. "I reached the office one morning, and the phone was ringing. It was a chemist at the plant. He said, 'Bob, I hope you are sitting down.' And I said yes. He said, 'I have some bad news. The lacquer on the inside of the can had oxidation.' I said, 'What does it mean?' He said, 'It means we gotta get this stuff off the shelves right now.'"

Dairy Dream had become a nightmare. Maheu spent five days in the office getting the cream back from across the country. He obtained a settlement from the can company, but it was hardly enough to cover his debts.

"I am flat-ass broke, and I owe money all over the place," Maheu said. "Now I sit down and write Hoover a letter. I told him about the situation, and [said] if you hear of anything that comes up in the government, please keep me in mind." On Hoover's recommendation, Maheu landed a job in the Small Defense Plants Administration, a new agency, where he set up the security and compliance division. The SDPA became the Small Business Administration, and Maheu served as a special assistant to the administrator.

But the salary wasn't enough to pay Maheu's mounting bills. Attending an ex-FBI agents' monthly dinner in Washington, D.C., he got involved in a craps game and went home about $4,000 richer. Maheu promptly resigned from the government job and decided to use his gambling winnings to open his own business, Robert A. Maheu and Associates, in 1954. He would conduct investigations and solve problems for clients.

Maheu said he learned early in life that he was a good listener, and that this was the key to solving problems. "I learned when I was in high school, when I was in college, that I had the ability to listen to people's problems, help them identify the problem, and realized that you have no prayer of solving a problem unless you *identify* the problem. As long as you leave it in the realm of the unknown, you can't solve it, nobody can solve it. No person in the world is smart enough to solve the unknown. And as devastating as the problem may be, if you identify it properly, you may have a shot at solving it."

In addition to this talent, Maheu had a lot of friends from his FBI days and contacts within the CIA (from his World War II espionage experience) who could refer clients to him and help with some of his projects. Within a week of opening the doors of his consulting firm, Maheu had a job working for a group of stockholders for the New York Central Railroad who wanted a change in management. He came up with a plan, and it was successful.

Maheu's next job was much bigger. Greek shipping magnate Stavros Niarchos hired him to help stop his biggest competitor, Aristotle Onassis, from reaping the rewards of an exclusive contract to handle oil shipments out of Saudi Arabia. A representative for Niarchos met him in Washington, D.C. "He said, 'We want to hire you, if you think this is something you can do, to make sure that there is no oil shipped under that contract and hopefully to scuttle the contract. Is that something you think you can do?' I said I think so. They gave me a retainer check, we made arrangements to meet the following day, and he left. I called my secretary in and I asked, 'Peg, do we have an atlas here?' and she said, 'Of course, why?' I said, 'Where in the hell is Saudi Arabia?'"

Maheu met Niarchos the next day and was given the assignment "with the understanding that [cost] was of no consequence." Maheu learned that the contract, known as the Jiddah Agreement, would give Onassis control of forty-five percent of the world's oil shipping. Onassis was widely regarded as an "international gangster," using bribery and intimidation to profit and gain power. (Later, Onassis' image would soften when he married Jacqueline Kennedy.)

To succeed, Maheu determined he would need the assistance of the U.S. government. Through his contacts, Maheu secured a meeting with Vice President Richard Nixon, who expressed strong support. Nixon then presented the case to the National Security Council, after which the State Department publicly denounced the contract. Other nations did as well.

The next part of the plan was to discredit Onassis in the eyes of the Saudi government. With the CIA's help, Maheu traveled to Saudi Arabia to meet with the king and tell him about Onassis' bribes to secure the contract. Maheu did not meet the king in person, but he made his case to the finance minister and the king's assistant with a degree of confidence that the king was listening in from another room.

The next day, the king's assistant instructed Maheu to leak the story of the Onassis bribes in the press. An Athens newspaper printed the story. "Once the bribe was made known, King Saud got out of the contract with Onassis without losing face," Maheu wrote in *Next to Hughes*. "Onassis's dreams of an oil monopoly were dashed forever."

Howard Hughes heard about Maheu's role in the oil contract and started using him for some small jobs. Maheu didn't know who his client was at first. "I get a phone call from one of the partners in the biggest law firm in Washington, D.C., saying they have a client who wants to find out something pertaining to an individual [Stuart Cramer] who claimed that he was a big shot in the CIA in an undercover capacity, and did I have any way of checking that. I did not tell them I was on retainer to the CIA, but I called my guys and gave them his name. The guy was lying, so that impressed Hughes, I found out later."

At the time, Cramer was married to actress Jean Peters, who was being pursued by Hughes. Peters and Hughes later married in Tonopah, Nevada. Cramer later married Terry Moore, an actress who claims she married Hughes in a secret ceremony on a boat anchored in international waters.

A few months later, the same law firm, Hogan & Hartson, wanted Maheu to surveil Ava Gardner at Lake Tahoe. Gardner was staying in Nevada to get a divorce from Frank Sinatra. Maheu hired a private eye in Reno. When Sinatra showed up and took Gardner out on a boat ride, the private eye followed in a boat of his own. Sinatra caught him and called the police. "It was very embarrassing," Maheu said. "I figured that's the end of the client. It was in the papers and everything."

However, Hughes respected Maheu's work and his connections enough to cut him some slack on the private eye screw-up. A few months later, in early 1955, Maheu's presence was requested in Los Angeles to take on another job. "It turned out that some joker was trying to get some money out of Hughes," Maheu said.

Maheu wrote a memo in which he laid out how the blackmail situation should be handled. Maheu explained that he did not want to be involved if Hughes was prepared to pay the man off. "I can guarantee you in advance that it will never work," Maheu said. "If you acquiesce, you are giving someone a blank check for the future."

The blackmailer was a minister who learned that one of his parishioners allegedly had an affair with Hughes. He threatened to go to the press if he wasn't paid. Maheu did a little checking and discovered the minister had been charged with child molestation (though never convicted). Confronted by what Maheu knew about him and the threat of public exposure, the man dropped his demand and was never heard from again.

Maheu's next task for Hughes also involved an extortion attempt. Another blackmailer wanted money to keep quiet about a starlet Hughes was keeping in an apartment. But this time, Maheu didn't have anything to hold over the guy's head. Maheu rented an apartment and called the would-be blackmailer to meet him there. Maheu and the man had a drink and talked, then Maheu handed him the few thousand dollars he wanted for his silence. But when the guy got up to leave, Maheu stopped him and told him he wanted to play him some music first. He pulled out a wire recorder and played back the man's verbal admission that he was a blackmailer. Maheu told the man he was going to take the recording to the police and the man could be convicted and put in prison. "He gave me back the money and left," Maheu recalled.

When Hughes heard about the successful mission, he called Maheu himself. Maheu recalled how the conversation started: "'Hey, Bob! This is Howard. What a deal! Tell me exactly what happened!' He insisted I call him Howard. He said, 'You and I are going to do a lot of things together.'"

In 1955 and '56, Hughes kept Maheu busy with assignments of various kinds, including local and national politics. Hughes wanted Maheu to move to Los Angeles, but Maheu resisted. After all, he had several other very good clients he was working for in Washington, D.C.—and they paid better than Hughes.

Still, Hughes and Maheu got along well. "He and I had a great relationship," Maheu said. "I may have been the only guy who would tell him to go to hell, who'd hang up on him. We had a lot of fights, but he'd always say, 'Bob, you and I should not do this to each other.' It was a great relationship."

Noah Dietrich was Hughes' chief executive for thirty-two years and a key reason for the success and growth of his companies. But Dietrich's tenure ended abruptly in 1957 when he and Hughes feuded over Dietrich's demand to finally enjoy a larger piece of the profits. In that same year, Hughes moved to the Bahamas, where he started buying real estate. Maheu handled many of the details.

But the Bahamas and Hughes were not meant to be. Locals were threatening a general strike, which could close down all transportation on and off the island. In addition, Hughes was unhappy with the telephone system. He was constantly on the phone, and the connection between the islands and the mainland was poor, interrupting his conversations.

Hughes returned to Los Angeles in the fall of 1957, and Maheu's assignments increased. Finally, in 1959, Maheu agreed to spend his summers in L.A.—if Hughes provided a house, maid service, and two Cadillacs. "He said no problem, consider it done," Maheu said. In 1961, Maheu moved to L.A. for good.

Maheu's high-flying lifestyle in Los Angeles irked Hughes' other top aides, such as Bill Gay. Maheu had a big house in Pacific Palisades and a yacht. In hindsight, he admitted he probably overdid it. "High-class hotels, four-star restaurants, and Hollywood parties. There were dinners at Perino's, Chasen's, LaRue's, and the Coconut Grove. I was on a first-name basis with the town's heavy hitters—politicians, film executives, and Hollywood legends. Like good champagne, it can go right to your head. It went to mine."

In the early '60s, Hughes focused much of his time on legal wars over TWA, the airline he had owned for years but gave up control of in a power struggle with his managers. Concerned about being subpoenaed to appear in court, Hughes moved to a house in Bel Air and staked guards outside to keep process servers at bay. Then Maheu came up with a diversion: He hired a look-alike actor to make appearances in restaurants and nightclubs across the country. Process servers tracked the impersonator's whereabouts like hawks, but didn't catch up with Hughes.

Hughes eventually faced a $145 million judgment in the TWA case (which he didn't end up having to pay). But a few years later he sold his TWA stock, receiving what at the time was the largest single check in U.S. history: $546 million.

After selling the stock, Hughes was looking for ways to avoid the big tax bill that would accompany the windfall. At first, Maheu recalled, Hughes wanted to move to Tucson, Arizona, where he had invested heavily in real estate and airport hangars. But then, mysteriously, Hughes decided he wanted to go to Boston—and the world-famous pilot wanted to take the train.

"He told me he did not feel well enough to fly himself and did not trust anyone else to fly, which did not come to me as a great surprise," Maheu said. "I could not change his mind, and it was a problem."

The project presented Maheu with multiple challenges. "To accomplish this, I needed the presidents of three railroads to cooperate with me. Luckily, one was an ex-FBI agent friend of mine." Complicating matters, Hughes wanted his train trip to occur right in the middle of a strike by airline machinists, so the trains were particularly busy that July 1966. "We were finally able to get a date, and upon that date, the train was already full, so they made up an extra section and put it in front of the train," Maheu said. "He was to embark the train at Pasadena. The train stopped in Pasadena and he doesn't show. In the meantime, the big trains behind it can't move. We're tying up traffic all over the place. We finally convinced him to board the train."

The "mystery train" generated news coverage across the country, but nobody actually saw Hughes. Soon he was safely ensconced on the fifth floor of the Ritz-Carlton Hotel in Boston.

Boston proved to be a very temporary destination for Hughes. For one thing, local reporters had figured out Hughes was on the train and in the Ritz-Carlton. They were on the story like vultures, trying every which way to get a look at Hughes.

Soon, Hughes was talking about moving back to the Bahamas, or perhaps to Montreal. "In the beginning, he had no intention of coming back to the West," Maheu recalled. "Then, at three a.m. or thereabouts, my phone rang. 'Bob, put on your seat belt.' I had learned that whenever he started a conversation with those words, my life was about to have a sudden change. He said we're going to Nevada. At first he wanted Lake Tahoe, the Cal-Neva Lodge. I'm just about ready to call him to tell him that everything is okay at Lake Tahoe, and he calls me and says, 'I've changed my mind, it's Las Vegas.'"

Outside Looking In: *What Las Vegas Saw*

When Howard Hughes secretly arrived in Las Vegas on Thanksgiving Day 1966, *Las Vegas Review-Journal* associate editor Colin McKinlay knew something unusual had happened involving the Union Pacific Railroad, but he couldn't nail down the details.

He finally got his story into the December 1 edition: "Billionaire Hides in Las Vegas." The article offered fairly specific details about Hughes' special train arrangements to arrive secretly in Las Vegas, including that he had been unloaded from the train on a stretcher at the Carey Avenue crossing in North Las Vegas.

McKinlay said there were "conflicting stories circulating about his health." Some people, McKinlay reported, said Hughes looked to be in "poor shape," while attorney Cliff Jones, a longtime Nevada politician and casino operator, said Hughes' health was "fine." Jones admitted, however, that he hadn't actually seen Hughes.

The story also reported conflicting reasons for Hughes' coming to town. While friends told McKinlay that Hughes came to relax and "do some business here," others (correctly) said he intended to make Las Vegas his home. The uncertainty of his motivations undoubtedly contributed to the relatively small headline on the story.

The following day, McKinlay produced another story, with a slightly larger headline: "Hughes Stays Hidden." The article offered just a few new details. "He is occupying a plush suite which has a large living room, bedrooms, a bar, and kitchen. It is lavishly furnished," wrote McKinlay, who had no way of knowing that Hughes himself stayed in one small room on the penthouse floor of the Desert Inn, and his aides occupied the rest. McKinlay had some insight on another part of the penthouse operation. "He is being constantly attended to by a physician, and has a special dietician in his room preparing meals every two hours." The reference to a dietician is clearly exaggerated. McKinlay closed the story in comic fashion: "Calls for the billionaire industrialist through the hotel switchboard are answered, 'We don't show him registered.'"

Hank Greenspun, publisher of the rival *Las Vegas Sun*, had played a role in Hughes' move to Las Vegas. As a result, his paper did not report or comment on the billionaire's arrival until after the *Review-Journal*'s early stories revealed his presence. On December 2, 1966, Greenspun broke his silence with a front-page column urging the press and public not to invade Hughes' privacy.

"Continuous snooping and harassment forced him out of our community years ago and he built giant industries elsewhere," Greenspun wrote. "The same thing could happen again (if the community doesn't respect his wishes for privacy)."

Greenspun saw Hughes as a major catalyst for Las Vegas growth. "Nevada has an opportunity to gain as a permanent resident this man who stands foremost among all giants of industry, finance and humanity," he wrote. "He alone is bigger than any other single Nevada industry or combination of all."

It wasn't long before Greenspun was proved prescient. Hughes went on a spending spree the likes of which Las Vegas had never seen. The press struggled to keep up with all his activities.

The March 10, 1967, *Review-Journal* had a banner headline: "Hughes Will Buy LV's Desert Inn." Four days later, another banner story by United Press International reporter Myram Borders confirmed Hughes had purchased the hotel where he had been living since November. The article provided few details on the sale, but it did include what turned out to be two inaccurate statements. First, Borders wrote, "Despite rumors that the one-time playboy was seriously ill, a spokesman said persons close to Hughes 'assure me that he has never been in better health.'" Also, the story closed by reporting that Hughes' wife, former actress Jean Peters, had joined him at the resort. In fact, Hughes had not been truly healthy, mentally or physically, for years. And Peters never did visit her husband at the Desert Inn.

On March 15, the paper reported that negotiations to buy the Desert Inn had begun in mid-December, after hotel officials asked Hughes to vacate the penthouse suites so that high-rolling customers could use them during the New Year's celebrations. According to the article, Hughes "refused to vacate for the expected influx of high rollers and told a DI official, 'I'll buy the place then.'"

Hughes bought the Desert Inn for $13.25 million from a group headed by longtime Las Vegas casino operator and organized crime figure Moe Dalitz. The Nevada Gaming Commission gave Hughes a license to operate the casino and waived the requirement for him to appear in person. "Hughes' life and

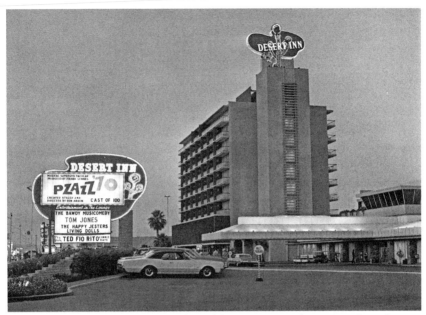

Hughes lived for four years on the ninth floor of the Desert Inn on the Las Vegas Strip. Courtesy of LVCVA News Bureau.

background is well known to this board and he is considered highly qualified," said Gaming Control Board Chairman Alan Abner.

The Clark County Gaming Licensing Board, chaired by Sheriff Ralph Lamb, also waived the requirement that Hughes show up in person. Asked why, Lamb said, "Because I feel this is a good thing for the county." He added, "It is a great honor to have a man like Hughes as resident of Nevada. He can—and already has—done a great deal for the state. Just his presence in this area will benefit the entire state." Clark County District Attorney George Franklin offered similar sentiments. "This is the best way to improve the image of gambling in Nevada by licensing an industrialist of his stature. It will be an asset and a blessing."

It didn't hurt Hughes' relations with state and local officials that he recently had announced his intention to contribute $6 million to the state university system to build a medical school. In a letter to Governor Paul Laxalt, Hughes said he would not require that the medical school be located in Las Vegas.

In June, Hughes bought the 518-acre Krupp Ranch in Red Rock Canyon west of Las Vegas for $1 million. In July, Hughes bought the Sands Hotel for $14.6 million. The Gaming Control Board gave its approval to the purchase by month's end. That same month, Hughes bought George Crockett's Alamo Airways, adjacent to McCarran Airport, for $1.5 million.

In August, the *Houston Chronicle*, in a copyrighted story, reported that Hughes was "exploring the possibility of establishing a huge industrial complex in the Las Vegas area." *Chronicle* reporter Charlie Evans said that in the first seven months of the year, Hughes had invested $70 million in Las Vegas. The *Chronicle* quoted a Hughes "associate" as saying that he had planned to purchase the Desert Inn before arriving in Las Vegas. "It had come to his attention that hotel-casino operations were good, sound investments," the anonymous source said. "And it was decided he would move into the hotel he intended to buy."

Maheu, Hughes' top executive at that time, denied this chronology, insisting the billionaire did not intend to buy the Desert Inn until he was threatened with eviction. "When Hughes came here initially, he had no intention of ever buying a hotel," Maheu said in a 2007 interview. "He's still in Boston now when he's telling me this. He wants to buy a TV station, he wants to buy the airport, he wants to buy a newspaper, and he wants to buy land. He wanted to buy all the land he could get his hands on."

In September, Hughes acquired the Frontier Hotel for $14 million, as well as the North Las Vegas Airport for $2.3 million. Hughes bought the airport from Ralph Engelstad, who later opened the Imperial Palace hotel-casino on the Strip. Also in September, Hughes filed papers with the Federal Communications Commission to purchase KLAS Channel 8, the Las Vegas CBS affiliate, from Greenspun for $3.6 million.

In late September, Laxalt gave a television interview in which he extolled the virtues of Hughes' investments in Nevada. He said Hughes "has put the Good Housekeeping stamp of approval" on the state and helped improve its image. Laxalt said he was "working daily to induce Hughes to come into Northern Nevada."

One enterprising news story printed September 27 revealed that powerful local banker E. Parry Thomas had been helping Hughes expand his Las Vegas empire. "Thomas has been buying parcel after parcel of Strip property, worth millions of dollars, which dovetail into acquisitions by the Hughes Tool Company," the report explained. The article noted that on Hughes' behalf, Thomas bought twenty acres immediately south of the Frontier Hotel, 41.5 acres near Caesars Palace, more than one hundred lots adjacent to the Desert Inn Country Club, three parcels behind the North Las Vegas Airport, and two lots in the Ridgeview Tract Estates, a subdivision off East Oakey Boulevard.

In his memoir, Thomas explained the effect Hughes' investments had on Las Vegas. "The impact of Howard Hughes moving here when he did was just enormous. I think more than anyone else who was here at the time, I realized the depths of the financial depression this city was in just before Hughes came

Las Vegas journalist Don Digilio covered many Hughes-related front-page stories. Courtesy of *Las Vegas Review-Journal* Archive.

here. We were having real troubles in Las Vegas, corporate influence hadn't yet set in, and we were scrambling at the bank to keep things on an even keel."

While September 1967 was a busy month for Hughes, nothing could top sensational reports about crooner Frank Sinatra's Hughes-related meltdown. First, the local press reported on Sinatra's angry departure from the Hughes-owned Sands Hotel, where he had performed for more than a decade. "I built this hotel from a sand pile, and before I'm through, that is what it will be again," said Sinatra, who promptly signed a contract with Caesars Palace. Speculation in town suggested Sinatra was upset that Hughes had purchased the Sands. Hughes and Sinatra held a mutual resentment based on their shared interest in Ava Gardner—Sinatra left his wife for her, and they married and subsequently divorced. The raging Sinatra parted ways with his old stomping grounds in dramatic fashion.

"The announcement of Sinatra moving to Caesars came after a wild weekend at the Sands that eventually led to his casino credit being stopped," *Review-Journal* managing editor Don Digilio reported. "He drove a baggage cart through a plate-glass window, injured a security guard, fought with casino bosses, pulled all the hotel telephone jacks at the switchboard, threw his furniture from his room, and caused a near-riot in the Garden Room."

Digilio's follow-up story provided a more detailed account of the event that culminated Sinatra's rampage. "Singer Tony Bennett left his heart in San Francisco and Frank Sinatra left his teeth—at least two of them—in Las Vegas," Digilio wrote. Enraged that his credit had been cut off, Sinatra confronted Carl Cohen, longtime Sands Vice President, who was sitting at a table in the Garden Room restaurant. Sinatra shoved the table onto Cohen, and the 275-pound casino executive responded with a punch that bloodied Sinatra's nose and knocked out two capped teeth.

Sands employees praised their boss's action. "As far as I'm concerned, Carl Cohen is a national hero," a bellman told Digilio. "Why should [Sinatra] be allowed to act like a wild animal?" A floorman added: "I came into the Garden Room right after the fight and Sinatra was still screaming about being punched. I don't have any thing to say about it, but if I did, I would have got rid of Sinatra long ago."

Longtime Hollywood reporter Vernon Scott analyzed the situation a few days later. "Until billionaire Hughes moved to town . . . millionaire Sinatra was more or less king of the gambling town. But now the principal dominant figure in the city of glamour and gambling is Hughes, not Sinatra. When Frank played the hotel, it was practically his for sixteen years. But once Hughes bought the Sands, Sinatra became second banana in a hurry, not an easy comedown for a man of Sinatra's pride."

Also in September, Hughes revealed his idea to build a new airport outside Las Vegas to handle supersonic jets. Hughes believed these giant aircraft would be the wave of the future in aviation, and he envisioned Las Vegas as the "southern West Coast terminus" for their flights. Maheu delivered a long written statement to the media, marking Hughes' first public comments in fifteen years. In the rambling statement, in which Hughes equivocated on many points, he reasoned that McCarran Field would not be able to handle "supersonic transport," or SST, aircraft. He envisioned an SST airport outside Las Vegas serving the entire American Southwest.

"From this terminus, passengers may be flown by regular jet aircraft to any normally located present-day airport," Hughes wrote. Or, Hughes suggested, they could hop onto helicopters and fly to terminals "closer to the passenger's ultimate destination—on top of buildings downtown, on top of hotels and residential areas."

In response to concerns that all these connections could add time and hassle for Las Vegas travel, Hughes suggested building a high-speed train on track laid "down the present freeway right of way" and with "air-conditioned cars just as plush as the present airliners which could transport all of the passengers arriving or accumulated at the airport to a point at or near Las Vegas, suitable for transfer to taxi." Hughes suggested the trains could leave every ten minutes and make the trip into Las Vegas in just six and a half minutes.

In a separate article, the *Review-Journal* interviewed three Clark County commissioners who expressed enthusiasm for Hughes' proposed SST airport. "We have the potential of being the world's largest air center and this announcement dovetails with our efforts to make a dream become a reality," Commissioner Bill Briare said. Commissioners met the following week with officials from the Federal Aviation Administration and the Air Transport Association to discuss Hughes' proposal. The federal officials were less impressed with Hughes' plan.

On September 14, the *Review-Journal* featured a long story based on a second Hughes public statement in which he "fired back at aviation experts." Officials from the FAA and ATA urged Clark County officials to forget about building a new airport and to concentrate on expanding McCarran. The aviation officials said the city was fortunate that McCarran was built on "the best site in the valley."

Hughes responded that the McCarran site was selected in the early '40s by George Crockett, founder of Alamo Airways (and Hughes' good friend), and indeed was a good location. "There is only one trouble," Hughes wrote. "Somebody built a city on the same site."

Hughes turned out to be the prescient figure in this part of the debate. "If you feel that Las Vegas will remain unchanged without any further growth . . . then, in that event, McCarran should be able to offer the same service it has in the past. However, I do not believe Las Vegas will remain dormant without further growth. There is no reason in the world why this city should not, within a reasonable number of years, be as large as, say, Houston, Texas, is today. If this sort of growth should take place, the present location of McCarran Field would be approximately comparable to having the airport for Los Angeles located on Wilshire Boulevard at the Miracle Mile."

(Although McCarran is theoretically landlocked, it has managed to expand to accommodate the growth of Las Vegas and its tourist trade. It opened another terminal in 2012 to handle the growing number of flights and passengers. For years, aviation officials have wanted to build a second airport for cargo in the Ivanpah Valley, thirty miles south of Las Vegas. But as of 2019, construction had not started.)

While Hughes correctly predicted that Las Vegas would grow, he was wrong about the prospects for supersonic aircraft. At that time, he suggested that airports serving these huge planes should be built all over the world. It didn't happen. Cost and noise concerns doomed what had once been touted as the future of air travel.

But in 1967, Hughes' advocacy of supersonic aircraft was very exciting to the Clark County Commission. Hughes proposed to build the supersonic airport himself outside Las Vegas. He wanted to turn it over to the county and the county would give him McCarran in return. In December 1967, the commission approved a resolution to pay for a feasibility study.

By the fall of 1967, Hughes had spent an estimated $100 million in Southern Nevada. He completed his first year in the penthouse by purchasing the Castaways and Frontier hotels. But according to a curious banner headline in the November 17 *Review-Journal*, Hughes was far from finished investing in the state. "Hughes Promises Small Industry for Nevada," the headline declared. The story was made up almost entirely of quotations from Hughes derived from a written statement and offered no context. It appears that Hughes issued the statement after Maheu made some kind of public comment that riled the locals. But the reporter did not explain what Maheu said and neither did Hughes. "He was only carrying out my instructions," Hughes stated. "So, if criticism is due, I am afraid I am the one who should receive it."

Hughes was also vague about his plans. "I will promise some kind of a small industrial effort in some part of Nevada with no agreed or committed time schedule," Hughes said, then became almost comically ambiguous. "I promise one thing, it won't be as favorable a schedule as you expect, or as favorable a schedule as you would like it to be, or as favorable a schedule as I would like it to be."

That press release appears to have come in response to rampant speculation that Hughes was planning to bring industry to the valley. A few months before, Maheu urged local land speculators not to buy up properties adjacent to Hughes properties on the premise that Hughes was going to do something soon with his land. "We have no desire to cause investment on the strength of rumors for which we are not responsible," Maheu said.

In its December 3, 1967, edition, the *Review-Journal* offered readers a full-page pictorial status report on Hughes' "Desert Empire." At the top, an aerial photo of the North Las Vegas Airport spread across the page. Below were photos of the Castaways, Frontier, Sands, and Desert Inn hotels, and KLAS Channel 8. In the brief text accompanying the photos, the *Review-Journal* reported that the "mysterious industrialist" had invested an estimated $100 million in the state, becoming Nevada's biggest taxpayer. The text also noted his purchase of the Krupp Ranch near Blue Diamond, Alamo Airways, and "vast amounts of undeveloped property," including the 25,000-acre Husite property.

1968: Investments, setbacks

The January 1, 1968, edition of the *Review-Journal* featured a predictable headline: "Howard Hughes Tops Nevada '67 News." Hughes was the talk not only of Las Vegas but of the entire state. The article reviewed Hughes' investments from the past year. "Although not a single reliable source admits to ever having seen him, Hughes is reported to have spent the past twelve months in his penthouse atop the Desert Inn," the newspaper said. "His comings and goings, if any, are closely kept secrets. But out of this seclusion have come orders for acquisitions that have been a continuing story in the Las Vegas economy."

The year 1968 proved to be again exhilarating for Las Vegas, with Hughes providing much of the news. Just a few days into the new year, Governor Laxalt revealed that he had spoken with Hughes on the telephone. Laxalt said he told Maheu during a meeting in Reno that he felt it was time he talked with Hughes. Laxalt declined to provide details, but he said the "low-key" conversation settled his mind about Hughes. "It took the situation out of the phantom stage," Laxalt said, noting that Hughes apologized for not having contacted him earlier. "Hughes told me he was satisfied with Nevada and that he would like to work closely with the administration in the future."

Hughes made the front pages again in late January when he announced he would build the world's largest resort in Las Vegas. Hughes issued a handwritten statement in which he described the $150 million, 4,000-room addition to the Sands as "a complete city within itself." The resort would include an entire floor of stores open twenty-four hours, "the largest bowling alley and billiard and pool facility in any hotel in the world," an ice skating rink, rooms for chess, bridge, skeeball, and table tennis, and a movie theater. Hughes said the resort would be "aimed at providing the most complete vacation and pleasure complex anywhere in the world." His superlatives continued as he described "a resort, so carefully planned and magnificently designed, that any guest will simply have to make a supreme effort if he wants to be bored, whether he is a sophisticated VIP or jet set type, or one of the children of a family spending their vacation with us." Only years later did the public learn that Hughes invented this Sands expansion plan as a ploy to deter Kirk Kerkorian from building the International Hotel.

On a writing spree, Hughes in February wrote a personal letter to Laxalt formally pledging his financial support for a medical school in Nevada. "When the medical school has been constructed and opened for academic session, and to ensure its successful operation, I hereby commit to furnish . . . from $200,000 to $300,000 per year for twenty years to make up any deficit in annual operating funds," Hughes wrote. "These sums will be available from time to time as required by the trustees."

Also in February, a special session of the Nevada Legislature approved a bill authorizing Clark County to enter into an agreement with Hughes to construct the supersonic airport. Under the agreement, the "jetport" would be turned over to Clark County in exchange for the county-owned McCarran Airport.

March proved another blockbuster month as *Review-Journal* managing editor Digilio reported on Hughes' bid to buy the Stardust. The prospect of Hughes adding the Stardust and Silver Slipper to his casino portfolio raised concerns among some political leaders and gaming regulators about a monopoly.

With his four Las Vegas casinos, Hughes still trailed Del Webb and William Harrah in the size of his Nevada casino empire, although he owned more Las Vegas properties than either magnate. But if he added two more properties, he would eclipse their dominance.

While state officials were wringing their hands over Hughes' growing economic power, enterprising Las Vegans, from entrepreneurs to politicians, looked for ways to cash in. Reporter Borders described the atmosphere: "There is an aura of excitement which fringes on anticipation, anxiety and even greed. . . . Classified advertisements, designed to lure both big and small investors, scream in bold type about 'land for sale near Hughes property.' Politicians gather at out-of-the-way taverns in hopes of figuring out which candidate will get the biggest chunk of Hughes money for upcoming campaigns."

In April and May, Hughes:

- Paid $225,000 for 480 acres of the historic Comstock Lode near Virginia City in Northern Nevada. This was just one of many mining claim purchases he would make across the state, including another big piece of the Comstock the following year.
- Exerted pressure to delay a large hydrogen bomb test at the Nevada Test Site, sixty-five miles northwest of Las Vegas. His efforts, including appealing directly to Vice President Hubert Humphrey, proved unsuccessful.
- Donated $250,000, half to bail out the financially strapped Elko Community College in Northeastern Nevada, and half to study the feasibility of creating a statewide community college system.

On the last day of April, the Nevada Gaming Commission voted 3-2 to approve Hughes' purchase of the Stardust and Silver Slipper. The split vote reflected continuing concerns about his growing power. "I see a great possibility of the stifling of competition," said Commissioner George Dickerson, who voted against Hughes. Fellow board member George Von Tobel also voted no. "I do not wish to see Las Vegas become a company town," Von Tobel said.

In June, Hughes encountered two major setbacks. First, he moved to buy the ABC television network, but ran into a buzzsaw of opposition and a demand from the FCC to make a public appearance. He eventually dropped the bid. Then the U.S. Justice Department's Anti-Trust Division launched an investigation into whether Hughes was building a Nevada monopoly. Pressured by federal authorities, Hughes dropped plans to purchase the Stardust. (His purchase of the smaller Silver Slipper proceeded.) In September, Hughes suffered another blow when a judge ordered him to pay a $137 million judgment in the long-running TWA legal battle.

Despite the Justice Department scrutiny, Hughes wasn't done building his casino empire. In October, he bid $17.3 million for the Landmark. Since the Landmark had faced numerous financial problems and sat unfinished for years, Hughes' purchase was seen in a different light than his Stardust bid.

As the year wound down, Hughes continued to campaign against nuclear testing, commissioning studies and preparing exhaustive reports on the dangers. In December, Hughes appealed directly to President Lyndon Johnson—again without success.

He also spent $11 million for two large pieces of real estate on the north end of the Strip: the former El Rancho Vegas property at the southwest corner of the Strip and Sahara Avenue, and a twenty-seven-acre piece across the street just south of the Sahara Hotel. (The latter property later became the Wet 'n Wild water park.)

All in all, 1968 was a momentous year for Hughes—and for Las Vegas. Reporter Borders interviewed entertainer and real estate agent Norman Kaye, who summed up Hughes' impact: "Hughes has revolutionized this town. We have left the 'Green Felt Jungle' era behind and are now in the 'Greenback Forest.'"

1969: Mining claims, nuclear tests

The year began with an in-depth feature about Hughes in the *Los Angeles Times* Sunday magazine. While the article provided a serviceable survey of Hughes' business activities in Las Vegas, it conjectured wildly about the activities of Hughes himself. Citing what they considered a reliable source, the authors said Hughes "works around the clock and drives himself for about four days at a time with little sleep. Then, exhausted, he heads for the former Krupp Ranch for several days. Mrs. Hughes, the former Jean Peters, like a good many women, isn't exactly enthralled by Las Vegas, this source insists. But she likes the ranch and has entertained there."

The *Times'* "reliable source," of course, wasn't reliable in the slightest. But for a large, reputable newspaper to so completely misrepresent Hughes' habits in 1969 speaks volumes about the secrecy machine that encircled him.

Another magazine article about Hughes reflected the public's fascination with the bashful billionaire. *Esquire*'s March 1969 issue featured a series of photographs on the cover allegedly showing Hughes poolside wearing a bathrobe. The headline read, "We See You!" Some readers were duped by the snapshots, but *Esquire*'s editors said they never pretended the staged photos were authentic.

Beyond the bogus cover, however, the *Esquire* article, by Ovid Demaris, effectively captured the energetic vibe of Las Vegas in the spring of 1969. Demaris, already familiar with Las Vegas through his work as co-author of *The Green Felt Jungle*, interviewed an array of people in Las Vegas, all of whom had an opinion about their mystery investor. "Mr. Hughes' involvement here has absolutely done us wonders," Governor Laxalt told him. "I just returned from a trip to the East where I spoke to some industrialists in midtown Manhattan and, later, insurance executives in Hartford, and their questions no longer are concerned with the Mafia, the skimming, the underworld. This has gone, it's by the board. Now they are interested in Mr. Hughes and other corporate types here and how they are getting along. I can see the change in the national press."

Demaris also interviewed Maheu at his Mount Charleston chalet. The chief executive for Nevada Operations exulted in his good fortune at working for Hughes: "I often tell my wife that it's not fair earning such a lucrative salary while having so much fun. In addition to being my sole boss today, I consider him a very dear friend." (Maheu's relationship with Hughes would change dramatically less than two years later.)

January was dominated by two big victories for Hughes: The Air West board of directors approved his purchase of the regional airline, and the U.S. Justice Department announced it had no objection to his acquisition of the Landmark. The deal's economic benefits assuaged concerns that the hotel-casino purchase would give Hughes a gaming monopoly in Las Vegas. Hughes was rescuing an unfinished, financially troubled project. He agreed to pay all Landmark creditors every penny they were owed, and he would employ 1,000 people.

In February, Hughes' mining claim buying spree reached critical mass. The *Los Angeles Times* reported that Hughes had purchased 503 claims covering 10,000 acres in eight Nevada counties. Most of Hughes' claims were in the Tonopah and Manhattan mining districts of Nye County. Hughes' consultants on the claim purchases, John Meier and E.L. Cleveland, told reporters that plans were in the works to reopen some of the old mines using new mining processes.

Hughes' campaign against nuclear testing raged into 1969, with his consultants meeting regularly with Atomic Energy Commission officials and urging a halt to the underground explosions. In April, the *New Yorker* magazine saluted Hughes' efforts. "He has hired his own team of experts—his personal atomic energy commission—to look into the dangers of the explosions, and his team has concluded that the experimentation is a lot more hazardous than the U.S. Atomic Energy Commission says it is."

1970: Deals and departure

Hughes' final year in Las Vegas began with the news that he and his wife were getting divorced. "This is not a decision reached in haste, and it is done only with the greatest of regret," Jean Peters said in a press release.

In February, a rare bit of naysaying crept into the local newspapers as Beldon Katleman, an old-time Las Vegas casino operator, accused Hughes of having a "stranglehold on the Strip." "I don't believe Hughes should have control of Las Vegas," Katleman said.

Katleman had owned the old El Rancho Vegas when it had burned down in 1960 and was not rebuilt. In 1968, Katleman had agreed to sell the property to Hughes for $7.5 million but, with the transaction sitting in escrow, he decided he wanted to cancel the deal—he claimed he had subsequently received better offers. Hughes objected, insisting the sale go through. The title company went to court seeking a resolution. "All I want is clear title to the property and I will pay them interest on the money which has been in escrow," Katleman said.

If Hughes were allowed to obtain the Strip property, Katleman contended, he would be in violation of antitrust laws by raising "barriers to the entry of new competition in the hotel-casino market." "Hughes is a fine man and I am not critical of him," Katleman said. "But the El Rancho property is the last bastion of independence on the Strip and I don't want it to become stagnant."

Hughes finally obtained the former El Rancho Vegas site later in the year after reaching a settlement with Katleman in which Hughes agreed to pay $11 million for the acreage.

(Katleman's comment about the property's stagnation would prove prophetic: As of 2019, no owner of the property at the southwest corner of Las Vegas Boulevard and Sahara Avenue had built a resort on the former El Rancho Vegas site. The current owner, MGM Resorts International, has set up the property as a festival grounds.)

In April, Hughes' takeover of Air West Airlines was finally completed, with a final price tag of $94 million. The following month, rumors of Hughes buying the legendary Harolds Club casino in Reno were confirmed. His first venture into Northern Nevada gaming—and his seventh casino—cost Hughes $11.5 million, and he even acquired a Lake Tahoe estate and a Reno gun club in the deal.

Asked if Hughes was growing too big in the gambling industry, Laxalt said he wasn't concerned. "The advent to Northern Nevada by Mr. Hughes had been eagerly awaited for some time," the governor said. "Personally I feel the acquisition of Harolds Club is a healthy development for western Nevada."

And then, in early December, all hell broke loose. The *Las Vegas Sun* broke the news with the banner headline, "Howard Hughes Vanishes!" A Hughes company spokesman, responding to the chatter, distributed a bit of misinformation: Hughes had left Las Vegas "on a business trip" and was "retaining his living quarters at the Desert Inn." A few days later, the *New York Times* reported that Hughes was at a hotel in the Bahamas.

But Las Vegans soon learned the reasons underlying Hughes' abrupt departure: a power struggle within his executive ranks. The *Review-Journal's* Digilio had the gist of the story December 5, reporting that attorney Chester Davis and longtime Hughes executive Bill Gay had "made a power move on the present regime headed by Robert Maheu." Davis and Gay said they had a proxy signed by Hughes giving them authority to fire Maheu and assume control of the Nevada operations. Davis and Gay took over the suites of the Sands Hotel and started giving orders, while Maheu defiantly remained in his offices at the Frontier Hotel and questioned whether Hughes had been kidnapped.

Details of the ensuing battle are outlined in other chapters of this book, but for Las Vegans following the press reports, it was an anxious and confusing time, especially for the eight thousand people in town employed by Hughes. Laxalt was among those looking for answers. "As far as I am personally concerned," Laxalt told reporters, "this matter is of such grave importance to this state's people that it probably can only be solved by Mr. Hughes' personal appearance indicating a change in his desire and the reasons justifying the change."

Of course, that wasn't going to happen. But Hughes did call Laxalt and District Attorney Franklin soon afterward, and they had a thirty-minute conversation, during which Hughes confirmed that he had put Davis and Gay in charge and terminated Maheu. Hughes also promised the politicians that he would return to Las Vegas and, according to Laxalt, "live the rest of his life here."

Amid the power struggle in Hughes' executive ranks, Nevada's attorney general-elect, Robert List, offered the understatement of the century: "We have to admit it could all have been handled a little better."

5

The Penthouse: *In the Hermit's Kingdom*

When he decided to move to Las Vegas, Howard Hughes told Bob Maheu he wanted the top floor of one of the hotels on the Strip. The Dunes was his first choice. But when he learned there was a restaurant and dance club above the top floor, he rejected the Dunes.

"So we ended up at the DI," said Maheu, who came to Las Vegas a month early to make the preparations. "They made me promise that we would be guests for only ten days." At the time this seemed all right, Maheu said, because Hughes was talking about buying a house and trying to get his wife, Jean Peters, to move there with him.

Hughes bought three different residences: the 518-acre Krupp Ranch (now Spring Mountain Ranch State Park), twenty-five miles southwest of town; the Major Riddle estate, a large house near Rancho Drive and Charleston Boulevard; and a house on Maria Elena Drive near East Oakey Boulevard. According to Richard Hack's *Hughes: The Private Diaries, Memos and Letters*, Hughes had photo albums made up for Peters. "I had no interest in moving to Las Vegas," Peters said in a sealed court deposition obtained by Hack. "It is not my kind of town, although he did try to make it sound very attractive and I agreed to go, but I didn't want to."

Peters said she preferred the Riddle house, because she worried that at the Krupp Ranch she'd be stuck out in the middle of nowhere. But Peters conditioned a move to Las Vegas on Hughes and her living together in a house, not a hotel, and Hughes was getting comfortable at the Desert Inn.

Hughes had arrived in Las Vegas about four a.m. on Thanksgiving Day 1966. His train from Boston stopped in North Las Vegas, where he was placed on a stretcher and carried to a van by his aides. Within minutes, they were at the Desert Inn, through the service entrance and up to the ninth floor, the arrival of the world's richest man somehow undetected in twenty-four-hour Las Vegas.

Maheu had prepared the ninth floor for Hughes and his aides. A key was required for the elevator to reach the ninth floor. A guard desk was stationed in front of the elevator, in case any intruders got their hands on a key. The guard kept meticulous logs of who came and went. Behind the guard was a partition with a locking door. Most of the eighth floor had been rented as well. His aides kept the room directly beneath Hughes' empty and locked to prevent somebody from bugging the penthouse, according to James Phelan's *Howard Hughes: The Hidden Years*.

Hughes' room was among the smallest on the ninth floor, fifteen by seventeen feet. The windows were blacked out. He sometimes sat naked in a lounge chair, with stacks of newspapers and magazines piled around him. Aides came in when they heard the noise Hughes made by flicking a brown paper bag. They would deliver food or pick up a memo, but interaction was minimal.

From his lair, Hughes proceeded to buy Las Vegas. With Maheu as the front man, Hughes purchased casinos, land, a television station, an airport, a golf course, mining claims, and politicians. He tried unsuccessfully to buy a few other things, such as the *Las Vegas Review-Journal* newspaper and the ABC television network. He campaigned to stop nuclear testing, and he wanted to ban rock concerts in Las Vegas. When he wasn't watching late-night movies or writing memos on yellow legal pads, Hughes plotted strategy in phone calls with Maheu and a few of his lawyers.

Six aides attended to Hughes for most of his four years in Las Vegas: John Holmes, Howard Eckersley, George Francom, Levar Myler, Mell Stewart, and Gordon Margulis. The first four had been Hughes aides before he moved to Las Vegas. Margulis, a room service waiter at the Desert Inn, came on board after Hughes arrived. Stewart was Hughes' barber. (Two others, Chuck Waldron and Jim Rickard, served on the ninth floor later.) Along with a couple of doctors, they were the only people who had personal interaction with Hughes at the hotel. He did not see Maheu in person, nor did he see his wife, Jean Peters. "He wasn't interested in seeing anybody," Margulis said in a 2005 interview.

Fueled by his debilitating drug addiction, Hughes' obsessive-compulsive habits and germ phobia came to the fore at the Desert Inn. According to Stewart, Hughes would rub himself down with alcohol, drenching paper towels laid out on the ground around him. He went through as many as four pints of alcohol a day. Despite his germ fears, Hughes refused to allow the aides to dust in his room.

Hughes' use of pain-killing drugs started after his near-fatal 1946 plane crash. He initially became addicted to morphine but then switched to the milder codeine.

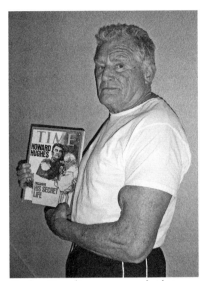

Gordon Margulis was a personal aide to Hughes from the late 1960s and early '70s. Author's collection.

By the late 1960s, he was heavily dependent on codeine and Valium (to help him sleep). Holmes orchestrated an elaborate system of illegal prescriptions and secret couriers to provide Hughes with his fix.

Hughes always was a picky eater, but his dining habits at the Desert Inn were comical. Margulis said Hughes would discover a new food item and have it every day for a long period. For example, he saw a commercial for Campbell's chicken soup and ate that for a while. Then he saw a commercial for Swanson TV turkey dinners and wanted them. However, Hughes said he didn't like the dark meat mixed with the white and he didn't care for the peach cobbler that came with the meal. Hughes wanted his aides to call the Swanson people and convince them to change the meal. Instead, Margulis asked the Desert Inn chef to help him put in all white meat and a new dessert before it was presented to Hughes. When he saw a commercial for Arby's roast beef sandwiches, Hughes sent Margulis to get one. But he told Margulis that he wanted the restaurant to purchase a stainless steel slicer for the meat. Sometimes Hughes would nod off when he was supposed to be eating. "I'd kick the bed to wake him up, and he'd start eating again," Margulis said.

The most famous food story: Every day, Hughes ate Baskin-Robbins banana nut ice cream. The aides bought large amounts and kept it at the hotel. When the supply ran low, Margulis went to a Baskin-Robbins outlet and learned the company had discontinued the flavor. Panicked, the aides came up with the idea of calling Baskin-Robbins' main office and asking if it would take a special order for the discontinued flavor. Baskin-Robbins said it would make the ice cream on the condition that at least 350 gallons were ordered. Margulis agreed, the banana nut ice cream was made in Los Angeles, and two Hughes aides transported it to Las Vegas in a refrigerated truck. It was stored in the Desert Inn's restaurant freezer. Problem solved. But that very night, Hughes announced that it was time for a change and he wanted French vanilla. It took the hotel a year to rid itself of the 350 gallons of banana nut ice cream.

In a 2007 interview, Burton Cohen, who managed the Desert Inn while Hughes was on the ninth floor, remembered getting a call at home at three o'clock in the morning. "The voice says to me, 'Do you want to fire the son of a bitch or should I?' I said, 'I don't know what you're talking about.'" Apparently Hughes had been served milk poured in a glass with a piece of saran wrap on top of it instead of his usual half-pint in a sealed container. "He kept talking and talking, close to two hours. I said I'm not going to fire him. 'You're a stubborn bastard, aren't you?' 'Yes I am.'" Cohen said he did not know for sure whether it was Hughes on the other end of the line. Margulis, who handled all of Hughes' food at the Desert Inn, said he doubted it was Hughes.

Not eating a proper diet, feeding his drug addiction, and cooped up in a small, dirty room, Hughes continued to deteriorate, and his attention to basic hygiene disappeared. Margulis said at one point he was very thin and disheveled, with long fingernails and a beard down to his waist. In 1970, he received a blood transfusion to counter pneumonia and anemia.

Poor health, coupled with a deteriorating opinion of Nevada—he failed to stop the nuclear tests, among other things—led Hughes to start talking about another move, perhaps back to the Bahamas. Attorney Chester Davis and executive Bill Gay recognized that it was a perfect time to launch their Machiavellian plan to oust Maheu and wrest control of the company.

Did he ever leave the ninth floor?

It's not just Melvin Dummar. People from all walks of life have told tales of having seen Howard Hughes while he lived in Las Vegas from 1966-1970. In 1968, *Newsweek* magazine reported: "There have been reports of Hughes sightings in various sectors of Las Vegas' glittery galaxy. Some say he is given to wee-hour walks on the Desert Inn golf course, savoring the unpolluted desert air. Others claim to have spotted him in the casinos. 'I've seen three men in here who I think might have been him—tall, undernourished looking, kind of,' says the red-haired change girl at the Desert Inn. . . . One woman, who claims she still sees Hughes, bears out the rumors. 'He goes out frequently,' she says, 'walking around the hotel lobby and casino, sitting at a table in the restaurant sometimes.'"

However, the best evidence suggests people who claimed to have seen Hughes during this period were lying, hallucinating, or mistaking someone else for him. Margulis, one of a small handful of people who did see Hughes during this period, said he was too sick to go anywhere. "It's absolutely ridiculous," he said. "I was there. I saw the condition the man was in at that time." If Hughes wanted to stand up, Margulis would help him up and then he would have to hold on to the back of a chair. "If you had seen the man, you would have known it was impossible."

Among the aides and doctors who spent time with Hughes while he was at the Desert Inn and those who had regular phone contact with him, none ever publicly said he left the ninth floor. In addition, others close to Hughes dismissed the notion. Maheu said Hughes often was too sick to leave and he was too busy with various projects. Maheu related a recent incident in which he went to lunch with a man who wanted to make a presentation to one of Maheu's clients. "For two hours the guy convinced me he was as honest as fallen snow. But then he said, 'Oh, did I ever tell you that I went to the penthouse to see Howard?' It was a complete, unadulterated lie."

Jack Real, Hughes' best friend in his final years, said one reason Hughes never left the Desert Inn was he did not want to be exposed to dust contaminated by radiation from the nuclear tests conducted sixty miles away.

Skipping town

Hughes' aides spirited him out of the Desert Inn on Thanksgiving Eve 1970. Whether he left of his own volition remains a subject of debate, although the accumulation of evidence over four decades all but confirms he was very sick, heavily drugged, and brainwashed into moving to the Bahamas.

The plan to move Hughes was several days in the making, the secret kept within a small circle of executives and aides. On the night before Thanksgiving, Hughes' aides brought him out of his suite on a stretcher. Author Phelan described the scene:

His gray hair, a foot and a half long, was incongruously topped by a snap-brim brown Stetson, the kind that had been his trademark back in the 1930s when he was breaking world records as a pilot. . . . His eyes were sunken, with dark circles under them, and his weight was down around 115 pounds. He was clad in a pair of blue pajamas, and . . . his legs and lower arms were almost bone thin. He was lying face up on the stretcher with a pillow covered by a plastic bag under his head.

Hughes, awake and aware, was carried down a fire escape, with Margulis in charge of the delicate operation. "They descended carefully, a step at a time, for nine floors, like a solemn religious procession bearing aloft a sacred relic or icon," Phelan wrote.

When they reached the ground, the stretcher was placed in a van, the aides piled in, and they headed to Nellis Air Force Base. When they reached the base northeast of Las Vegas, they put the stretcher aboard a waiting Lockheed Jet Star and climbed aboard. The two pilots were ordered not to look at their secret cargo during the flight.

The plan went off without a hitch. Las Vegas had no clue what happened for several days, as aides who remained behind acted as if Hughes still lived in the penthouse. Margulis retrieved Hughes' meals from the Desert Inn kitchen as if nothing had changed. Meanwhile, others cleaned up the ninth floor, which included disposing of Hughes' drug supply and Mason jars full of urine.

Hughes departed Las Vegas as quietly as he had arrived, but his shadow would loom over the city for years to come.

6

The Landmark: *The Hard Luck Hotel*

The rise of the Las Vegas resort industry is a story of many successes and only a handful of failures. Perhaps the best known of the latter was the Landmark Hotel.

The Landmark's space-age design echoed that of Seattle's Space Needle, which opened in 1961. It also suggested the shape of the mushroom clouds generated by nuclear explosions at the Nevada Test Site. Frank Caroll, a contractor from Kansas City, acquired land on Paradise Road east of the Strip in 1959 and obtained a $3 million loan from a Whirlpool subsidiary. Construction began in 1961. The Landmark originally was to be fourteen stories, but when the Mint Hotel in downtown Las Vegas went higher and the Sahara Hotel initiated a twenty-four-story addition, Caroll changed his plans to maintain the Landmark's distinction as Nevada's tallest building. It would be thirty-one stories.

Caroll ran into financial problems, however, and construction halted in 1963, with the project eighty percent completed. For several years, the Landmark sat vacant, prompting smirking locals to dub the place "Frank's Folly" and "The Leaning Tower of Las Vegas," because it appeared to lean. The building actually was straight but nearby power poles that were not straight created the illusion. Despite its unfinished state, the hotel's distinctive look was featured in several scenes of *Viva Las Vegas*, the 1964 movie starring Elvis Presley and Ann-Margret.

After Caroll obtained a $5.5 million Teamsters Pension Fund loan in 1966, work on the tower resumed, and it was finally ready in late 1967. An estimated $12 million in debt, Caroll desperately needed to open the hotel-casino to start generating revenue. But Nevada gaming authorities rejected his license application in March 1968, citing his financial instability. (Caroll's ties to organized crime also concerned gaming regulators.) Unable to open, Caroll had to sell the Landmark or face foreclosure.

Frank Caroll of Kansas City was the original builder of the Landmark Hotel in Las Vegas. Courtesy of *Las Vegas Review-Journal* Archive.

Finding a buyer proved to be a challenge. While a distinctive element of the Las Vegas skyline, the 500-room Landmark would be a logistical and financial nightmare to operate, requiring hundreds more employees than a conventional hotel-casino. The owners of Caesars Palace turned Caroll down first, then Del Webb took a pass. The unusual resort's drawbacks were obvious to experienced hotel managers but they did not deter Howard Hughes, who bought the white elephant for $17.3 million.

Hughes' Nevada chief executive, Bob Maheu, advised against buying the Landmark. In a 2007 interview, Maheu recalled that he asked Moe Dalitz, the former Desert Inn owner, for his opinion on how much money the Landmark would lose. "Moe wrote what might have been the only memo he'd written in his life," Maheu said. "He predicted the first year of operation we'd lose between $5.5 million and $5.7 million."

But Hughes saw the Landmark from a different perspective. Down the street, Kirk Kerkorian was building the International (later the Las Vegas Hilton and Westgate), which, with 1,500 rooms, would be the biggest resort in town at that time. Hughes did not want Kerkorian to take away his title as the king of Las Vegas. "Hughes never intended to be in the hotel business, much less the gaming business," Maheu explained. "But once he got in, he wanted to be the biggest."

Hughes initially tried to stop Kerkorian from building the International by announcing plans for a giant "Super Sands" resort. The news shook Kerkorian initially, because it could in fact make it more difficult for him to secure construction money. The prospect of the two projects adding thousands of hotel rooms in Las Vegas could cause risk-averse bankers to pull back. But *Las Vegas Sun* publisher Hank Greenspun urged Kerkorian to call Hughes' bluff. "In the end, Kirk bet on that assessment, shoving more of his chips onto the table," according to Kerkorian biographer William Rempel.

As for the Sands, "nothing happened—no architects hired, no plans submitted for approval, no dates set for groundbreaking or completion," Rempel wrote. "After a few months, it was clear that the 'unique and novel' Hughes plan was dormant or abandoned."

Hughes opened the Landmark Hotel in 1969. Courtesy of *Las Vegas Review-Journal* Archive.

When the Sands scare didn't work, Hughes tried another approach: He would persuade Kerkorian to suspend his International project out of concern about ramped-up nuclear testing north of Las Vegas. Hughes claimed architectural experts were advising him not to build high-rises as a result, and that his Desert Inn had sustained damage as a result of a recent underground nuclear explosion. Kerkorian wasn't deterred.

Yet another idea Hughes floated to Maheu was to sell the Stardust to Kerkorian and, in turn, buy the International site and close it down. But when the U.S. Justice Department prevented Hughes from acquiring the Stardust, that scheme was scuttled. In any case, Kerkorian wasn't interested in selling to Hughes.

In January 1969, the Justice Department announced that it did not object to Hughes buying the Landmark. Although Justice officials had blocked Hughes from acquiring the Stardust, citing antitrust concerns, the Landmark presented special circumstances. Hughes' promise to pay three dozen long-suffering creditors one hundred percent of what they were owed played a significant role in the softened federal stance. U.S. Senator Howard Cannon of Nevada worked to convince them that Hughes would help small businesses and put hundreds of people to work. "It appears to me the case involves a question of business distress rather than any threat of restraint of trade," Cannon said. "This is a clear opportunity to assist the economy of Nevada and the employment opportunities of its citizens."

With the Justice Department hurdle cleared, Maheu began making plans to open the Landmark. Hughes, however, was in a mood to micromanage the task. Perhaps remembering the extravagant events he orchestrated for the premieres of his movies *Hell's Angels* and *The Outlaw*, Hughes thought he was the man for the job of putting on a big party—even though he would not be attending.

Hughes told Maheu he wanted to choose the opening date, as well as approve every person invited to the opening-night party. He even wanted to choose the entertainment and the menu. The problem was that Hughes couldn't make a decision on any of it. "If I had been prone to ulcers, I would have had blood coming out of my ears," Maheu said. "I had many sleepless nights."

Maheu had proposed an opening date of July 1, 1969, intending to capitalize on the busy Independence Day weekend. But as of mid-June, Hughes still hadn't committed to a date. Kerkorian's International Hotel was scheduled to open about the same time, which increased the billionaire's anxiety over how to proceed. Should he open before Kerkorian and steal his thunder, or should he open afterward and leave the last impression?

In a memo to Maheu, Hughes wrote: "Re: the date of the opening, why don't we leave that open. If the show and all other elements shape up very rapidly, fine, but I urge that a July 1st date not be committed any further in any publicity or word of mouth. I just don't want it to be embarrassing if the opening should be a little later." This left Maheu in a bind, because it would be difficult to plan a big event when he could not provide anyone involved with a firm date.

Maheu outlined the guest list fiasco. "We dickered over every name on the proposed invitation list. Back and forth it went, with Hughes first crossing off names, then adding them back." Just a week before the hotel was slated to open, not a single invitation had been sent out.

Apparently with plenty of time on his hands, Hughes went through proposed guest lists name by name, questioning almost everybody for one reason or another. For example, if he noticed that one local auto dealer had been invited, he wondered why the others had not been invited as well. He wanted to turn the routine task of party invitations into a science.

Hughes and Maheu also battled over the entertainment. Kerkorian had raised the stakes by announcing that Barbra Streisand would be the featured performer at the International's opening. Hughes wanted to counter with Dean Martin. Martin had previously performed at the Sands, but he was now under contract at the Riviera, where he was a part owner. This did not deter Hughes, however, and he brainstormed ideas to entice Martin. For example, Hughes suggested offering to finance a movie for Martin. "Bob, there is not an actor alive who does not have some pet idea he would like to make into a movie," Hughes wrote in a memo published in *Citizen Hughes*.

Other ideas surfaced as well. Somebody told Hughes that trumpeter Herb Alpert & the Tijuana Brass could be hired for $25,000 per week, two shows per night. Maheu knew this was an absurdly low figure. "I sent him a note saying you'll be lucky if Herb allows you to display one of his brass pieces in the lobby of the hotel for that amount," Maheu said. "He called me and told me to go to hell and hung up on me."

With the opening just days away, Maheu's frustration boiled over:

> Howard: I really don't know what you are trying to do to me, but if your desire is to place me in a state of complete depression, you are succeeding. . . . Now, Howard, this may come to you as a shock, but we are soon entering the realm of not being believable. All I know is that we have an opening taking place in a few days. Everyone seems prepared for it, except you. There have been many hours of sweat and blood poured into this project, and all we need is evidence of confidence from you. . . . Howard, all I can tell you in conclusion is that I have no desire to be identified with a fiasco. But if you are hell-bent on being the author of one, I am afraid there is nothing else I can do to prevent you from accomplishing just that.

In response, Hughes stood his ground: "Just as convinced as you appear to be that I am wrong and that you are getting the bad end of the deal, just as convinced as you appear to be that you are mistreated, and that you have to take some kind of revenge, just as firmly convinced of this as you seem to be, you may rest assured I feel equally strongly that you are 100 percent wrong."

The memo war continued, with a distraught Maheu suggesting that if Hughes didn't make some key decisions soon, Maheu would have to leave town, "because I just simply cannot continue facing all these people any further." This statement pushed the limits of what Hughes would tolerate. "If, under these circumstances, you think my failure to give you a specific date has placed you in a position of embarrassment under which you don't want to be in Las Vegas, I think maybe the time has come when, for my health's sake, a somewhat less efficient and less successful man, but one who would not find it so difficult to put up with my admittedly less-than-perfect operation, should perhaps be the resident managing executive here in Las Vegas."

On June 29, Hughes finally supplied Maheu with an approved guest list—containing a paltry forty-four names. Fearing embarrassment for all concerned, Maheu took a "calculated risk" and sent out four hundred additional invitations without Hughes' approval. Finally, just two hours before guests were scheduled to arrive, Hughes approved the food order for the party. One of Maheu's favorite memories is of Hughes' memo delivered just minutes before the party started. Expressing best wishes to Maheu and his staff, Hughes asked, "Is there anything further I can do to be helpful?"

In the three weeks before the Landmark opening, forty-seven memos had passed between Hughes and Maheu and they spoke by phone an average of four times per day, according to *Hughes: The Private Diaries, Memos and Letters*. "The relationship had gone from unconventional to barely tolerable," author Richard Hack wrote.

But from the public's standpoint, the Landmark's July 1 opening was a success. Hughes had funded $3.5 million in finishing touches. Views from the top-floor lounge were breathtaking. Dean Martin and Danny Thomas both performed, while NASA astronauts were flown in to cut the ceremonial ribbon. "It was great," Maheu said. "Nobody knew."

But as Dalitz and others predicted, the Landmark was a chronic money-loser. Maheu's initial concerns that the design was too unorthodox proved correct. The air conditioning did not work well on the higher floors, and keeping the glass-walled elevators running was a major hassle. "Frank's Folly" had become "Howard's Headache."

After Hughes died in 1976, his heirs, led by cousin Will Lummis, decided to get out of the gambling business. The first thing they did was put the Landmark up for sale. But the search for a buyer was delayed the following summer by a disastrous event. In July 1977, a gas leak at the Landmark left one man dead and 138 people hospitalized. About four a.m., a broken water pipe short-circuited an electrical power panel. The resulting power outage knocked out ventilation blowers in the basement power plant, and exhaust from an auxiliary generator was pumped into the hotel via the air-conditioning system. More than nine hundred guests and employees were evacuated to escape the deadly carbon monoxide.

In 1978, the heirs sold the Landmark to Mark III Corporation, a partnership of Lou Tickel of Salina, Kansas; Zula Wolfram of Toledo, Ohio; and Las Vegas casino executive Gary Yelverton. The $12.5 million price was significantly less than Hughes had paid for the property almost ten years before. Wolfram later bought out Tickel's and Yelverton's interests. However, Wolfram's tenure with the Landmark ended after her husband, Edward, pleaded guilty to defrauding a Toledo brokerage firm out of $36 million. Edward Wolfram was accused of using $15 million of that amount to buy and operate the Landmark under his wife's name. To pay back the brokerage firm, the Wolframs were forced to sell the Landmark. (Edward Wolfram also was sentenced to twenty-five years in prison.)

Bill "Wildcat" Morris bought the hotel for $18.4 million in 1983. A longtime Las Vegan and successful casino operator, Morris brought passion to the task of making the Landmark work. He told reporters that the Landmark had never been given a fair chance. "First, there has never been hands-on management on a day-in, day-out basis," he told the *Las Vegas Review-Journal*. "Second, the operators have all tried to make the property do something it was not meant to do. They tried to compete with superstar productions, and a lot of money was lost in that competition. The property is ideally situated to serve the convention authority, and our operational thrust will be in that direction." To take advantage of the growing convention traffic, Morris vowed to build three fifteen-story towers totaling 1,500 rooms and a domed family entertainment center on acreage west of the Landmark tower.

Morris spent $4 million to spruce up the property but couldn't turn a profit with it. He lost an estimated $9 million in his first two years of operation and fell deeply into debt. The hotel went into Chapter 11 bankruptcy reorganization in 1985 and Chapter 7 liquidation in 1990. It closed for good on August 6, 1990.

History suggests that no matter who was in charge, the Landmark would have lost money. But Bill Friedman, who turned a healthy profit at the Castaways and Silver Slipper casinos for Summa Corporation between 1976 and 1989, disagreed. In a 2007 interview, Friedman said that after he transformed the Castaways and Silver Slipper, his bosses offered him the chance to do the same with the Landmark. He turned them down because he already had two properties under his direction, but Friedman believed he could have worked his magic with the Landmark as well. "I could have turned it into a monster property," he said, noting that he would have followed the principles outlined in his best-selling book, *Casino Management*.

A big problem with the Landmark, Friedman said, was the way in which prospective customers approached the casino. After parking their cars, they were forced to traverse a two-block-long shopping plaza before reaching the gambling floor. Friedman would have reconstructed the property so that customers could get into the casino faster and easier. "Gamblers are very impulsive people," he said. "They expect action the moment they arrive."

The Las Vegas Convention and Visitors Authority acquired the Landmark for $15.1 million in 1993. It imploded the tower on November 7, 1995, a dramatic thirteen-second event that director Tim Burton filmed and included in his movie *Mars Attacks!* For years afterward, the property was used as a parking lot for the Las Vegas Convention Center. Today the property is part of a $935 million convention center expansion.

The year after the Landmark turned to rubble, a tower featuring a similar design debuted in Las Vegas. The Stratosphere Tower, built by Bob Stupak on the site of his Vegas World hotel-casino, reached a height of 1,149 feet—the maximum allowed by the Federal Aviation Administration. Stupak learned some

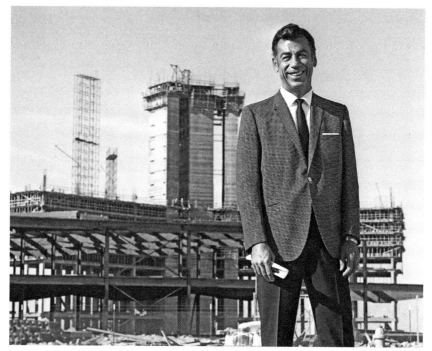

Hughes saw Kirk Kerkorian as a competitor for top dog in the Las Vegas casino industry. Courtesy of LVCVA News Bureau.

valuable lessons from the Landmark. First, the Stratosphere would be substantially taller than any other building in town. (The 350-foot-high Landmark lost its status as the state's tallest building as soon as the International was completed in 1969.) Second, Stupak did not try to stuff the narrow structure with hotel rooms. Instead, the tower was an attraction in itself, with tickets required to ascend to the observation deck, revolving restaurant, thrill rides, and other amenities at the top. Meanwhile, the hotel and casino were contained in more conventional structures around the tower. Third, Stupak equipped the Stratosphere with fast, high-quality elevators capable of carrying large numbers of people efficiently up and down the tower.

If the Landmark was a predictable failure, the Stratosphere was an unlikely success story—eventually. When Stupak was building the tower, his doubters were legion. Stupak had a reputation as a notorious character in the casino industry, not a person whom Wall Street investors were likely to entrust with hundreds of millions of dollars. But he wisely surrounded himself with experienced business executives, engineers, and architects, among them Maheu, who served on his board of directors. Running short of funds to finish the tower, Stupak persuaded respected Minneapolis casino operator Lyle Berman to become his partner. The $550 million tower and resort opened on April 30, 1996. It performed poorly at first, conjuring memories of the doomed Landmark. But after a series of expansions, renovations, and marketing tweaks, the Stratosphere eventually became a dependably money-making resort.

As for Kerkorian, the International was just the beginning of what would become the largest casino empire in Las Vegas history—dwarfing anything Hughes envisioned. In Kerkorian's view, bigger was always better. After he sold the International, he built the 2,100-room, movie-themed MGM Grand in 1973. He sold it in 1986 and the name changed to Bally's. Amid the megaresort boom of the early '90s, Kerkorian built the biggest resort of them all, a new MGM Grand with more than 5,000 rooms. He opened New York-New York in 1997. In 2000, Kerkorian bought Steve Wynn's Mirage Resorts for $6.7 billion, acquiring the Mirage, Bellagio, and Treasure Island resorts in the process. Then, in 2004, he spent $7.9 billion to acquire Mandalay Resort Group, adding the Mandalay Bay, Luxor, Excalibur, and Circus Circus to his menagerie. Kerkorian was now in control of most of the largest and best resorts on the Strip. But he wasn't done. In 2006, Kerkorian's MGM Mirage launched CityCenter, a $7.4 billion "casino community" on seventy-six acres between the Bellagio and Monte Carlo (now the Park MGM). With three hotels, two high-rise condos, and a massive shopping complex, CityCenter was, in 2007, the largest privately funded building project in the United States.

Meanwhile, Kerkorian, who in the late '60s was touted as the anti-Hughes because he lived a down-to-earth life with his family, became, in later years, something of a reclusive figure, living a quiet life in Beverly Hills, California, and rarely granting interviews or appearing in public. But Kerkorian did not adopt any of Hughes' eccentricities.

Although Hughes had used some nasty tactics to try to cripple Kerkorian's International project, Kerkorian did not hold a grudge against his fellow billionaire or his right-hand man, Maheu. Kerkorian and Maheu played tennis together for years afterward.

Kerkorian died in 2015 at age ninety-eight.

The Palace Coup: *The Manipulation of Hughes*

Howard Hughes lived one of the most interesting and varied lives of the twentieth century, yet the public's fascination continues to turn to the final years of his life when he took an epic mental and physical nosedive and his lieutenants went to war over control of his riches. With the deterioration of Hughes' condition in his last years, he no longer was able to dictate the course of day-to-day affairs of his many business enterprises. And executives working for Hughes had different ideas about how things should be done—and who should run the empire.

As Hughes gradually descended into darkness and drifted to the sidelines, top executives battled for control. Initially, Hughes entrusted Bob Maheu, based in Las Vegas, with primary decision-making authority. This move frustrated longtime Southern California executive Bill Gay, who felt he should be in charge. Meanwhile, New York attorney Chester Davis, too, had a large role in Hughes' affairs, especially his long-running legal battle over TWA.

Maheu maintained a high profile on Hughes' behalf, buying casinos and land in Las Vegas and handling political matters in Nevada and Washington, D.C. But Gay still controlled the coterie of aides who responded to Hughes' every want and need. Gay also controlled the doctors who cared for Hughes and provided him with a steady supply of pain-killing drugs.

Gay's control of the so-called Palace Guard gave him a distinct advantage when he and Davis made their move against Maheu in 1970. Evidence and testimony strongly support the contention that Gay and the aides persuaded Hughes to act in certain ways by increasing and decreasing his drug supply and censoring the information he received about his business affairs. They poisoned

Attorney Chester Davis participated in the scheme to get Bob Maheu fired. Courtesy of *Las Vegas Review-Journal* Archive.

Bill Gay oversaw the personal aides to Hughes and later ran the entire empire. Author's collection.

Hughes' relationship with Maheu, resulting in his firing, and talked Hughes into fleeing Las Vegas to avoid a legal confrontation with Maheu.

"They started telling him I was trying to steal his empire," Maheu recalled in a 2007 interview. "They were telling me I had either filed or was getting ready to file a lawsuit trying to gain control, which scared the hell out of him."

Hughes turned over control of his business affairs primarily to Gay and Davis. Ultimately, Gay, Davis, and the personal aides allowed Hughes' health to continue to deteriorate because this allowed them to run the companies without his interference.

One of the most straightforward summaries of this period of Hughes' life is contained in a legal memorandum filed in 1980 by the Hughes estate. The motion pulled no punches in outlining "an extraordinary scheme perpetrated upon Hughes and his companies by the 'Palace Guard' which surrounded Hughes for the last ten years of his life. These individuals . . . are charged with having seized control of Hughes' empire and having enriched themselves at Hughes' expense. They are alleged to have done so, in large measure, by taking advantage of Hughes' drug addiction, seclusion, and mental incompetency to run Hughes' enterprises—ostensibly in his name, but in fact for their own personal benefit—and by manipulating and controlling a virtually helpless Hughes."

According to the motion, the conspiracy scheme began while Hughes was secluded in the Desert Inn. "As in most conspiracy cases, many of the actions committed by the defendants may seem innocent in and of themselves. It is when they are taken in context that their role as integral parts of a wrongful scheme becomes apparent. . . . And when the evidence is viewed as a whole, it points directly to the conclusion that the defendants, their conclusory denials notwithstanding, did indeed conspire to gain control of Hughes' empire and to use it for their own advantage."

The motion argued that Gay, along with Nadine Henley Marshall and Kay Glenn, controlled the aides who surrounded Hughes. It contended they "served as a virtually impenetrable barrier between Hughes and the outside world, screening nearly all incoming and outgoing messages."

"Gay used his power over the aides to direct them not to deliver messages to Hughes which Gay did not want Hughes to receive and not to transmit Hughes' messages to others which Gay did not want transmitted. Aides who refused to follow these procedures were severely criticized by Gay, Glenn, or Henley Marshall, as well as by other aides." Further, the memo contended that they "cruelly took advantage of Hughes' physical and mental disabilities, his drug addiction, his eccentricities, and ultimately, his mental incompetency to help themselves to Hughes' wealth."

One form this took: "lifetime contracts" for selected executives, guaranteeing they would receive a regular paycheck from Hughes in perpetuity. As for Davis, he billed Hughes large sums for his legal services.

They controlled Hughes in large part by manipulating his drug addictions, according to the motion. "Beginning in 1961, and throughout the four years in Nevada, Dr. Norman Crane supplied Hughes with codeine and valium. He did so by writing false prescriptions in the names of the aides, primarily John Holmes, but also [Levar] Myler, [Roy] Crawford and [George] Francom. After Crane wrote the prescriptions, Holmes obtained the drugs and delivered them to Hughes in Nevada."

"Hughes regularly was under the influence of codeine, valium, and other drugs throughout the Desert Inn period," the memo stated. "He injected himself with codeine using syringes kept in a small metal box in the refrigerator in the aides' quarters outside his room." Indeed, Holmes and Crane were later convicted of conspiring to distribute codeine to Hughes.

The memo noted that Hughes' mental behavior also became stranger during the Desert Inn years. "Throughout the Desert Inn period, Hughes' behavior suggested severe mental problems as well. He was totally nude almost all of the time, only occasionally wearing a pajama top. He demanded that the windows be draped or closed and indicated no awareness of or concern with what the date or time was.

"Hughes required the aides to perform a series of bizarre rituals, many of which related to his unnatural fear of contamination by germs. He demanded that everything delivered to him be wrapped in Kleenex, and had a procedural manual which dictated among other things the specific numbers of Kleenex to be used for various actions. Other procedures were prescribed for washing one's hands, carrying and opening a can of fruit, etc. This fear of germ contamination was particularly anomalous when contrasted with his lack of personal hygiene and his use of an unsterilized syringe and needle to self-inject himself with large amounts of codeine."

The memo argued that Hughes led a very unhealthful lifestyle. "[His] physical condition also was appalling when he came to Nevada. He never brushed his teeth and had a foul breath odor. He seldom took a bath or shower. His hair was approximately shoulder length and his beard went down to approximately his chest. His eating habits were very poor. He was seriously underweight. He spent most of his time in bed, often staring blankly ahead, especially after taking large amounts of drugs. He often slept for lengthy periods, sometimes as long as twenty-four hours at a stretch. He suffered from chronic and severe constipation, often going two weeks without a bowel movement and requiring frequent enemas. When he did go to the bathroom, he often spent long periods of time there—as much as twelve hours."

In 1968, about two years after Hughes moved to Las Vegas, Gay approached Maheu twice about having Hughes committed and assuming control of his empire. Maheu refused to cooperate with the scheme.

Unable to team up with Maheu, Gay decided to poison Maheu in Hughes' eyes, according to the legal filing. During 1970, Gay began to limit Maheu's access to Hughes. "Gay, directly and through Glenn and Henley Marshall, directed the aides to withhold Maheu's messages from Hughes. As a result, Maheu's messages piled up without being delivered. . . . By late 1970, Maheu lost direct telephone contact with Hughes."

About that time, Hughes turned over control of the TWA litigation to Maheu, and Maheu fired Davis. "This set the stage for a power struggle which culminated with Davis and Gay seizing control of Hughes' empire," the memo stated.

On November 14, 1970, Gay and Davis obtained a proxy giving them nearly unlimited control over Hughes' Nevada operations. "At the time the proxy was obtained, Hughes was seriously weakened from the second in a series of bouts of anemia, complicated in November 1970 by pneumonia," according to the memo.

Dr. Harold Feikes testified that in 1968 Hughes was "critically ill" and anemic enough to be on the verge of heart failure. Dr. Crane later described Hughes as having "nearly died" from the 1970 bout of pneumonia. Hughes required frequent blood transfusions.

According to the motion, drugs used by Hughes shortly before the proxy "soared to among the highest levels of his life." "The November 14, 1970, proxy is a curious document indeed," the motion explained. "It gave Gay and Davis, acting together, absolute power—certainly a strange act from one who had expressed his dislike for Gay and who had authorized Maheu to fire Davis just a few months earlier."

"Proxy was procured by undue influence," the memo stated. "Davis used the proxy to get rid of Maheu, lest Maheu get rid of Davis. And Gay, too, was threatened by Maheu's rise to power."

With the proxy in hand, Gay and Davis persuaded Hughes to move out of Nevada, presumably so he wouldn't have to testify if Maheu challenged the proxy. On November 26, 1970, Hughes secretly flew from Las Vegas to the Bahamas. "He apparently had been convinced by the aides that it was necessary to leave to avoid a confrontation with Maheu," the memo stated.

Maheu was fired on December 3, 1970, and Gay and Davis traveled to Nevada to take physical control of Hughes' operations. Maheu filed a court action challenging his removal, but he lost, in part because Hughes was beyond the reach of the court's subpoenas.

Over the next six years, Hughes lived in numerous locations. The Bahamas: November 1970 to February 1972; Nicaragua: February 1972 to March 1972; Vancouver: March 1972 to August 1972; Nicaragua: August 1972 to December 1972; London: December 1972 to December 1973; the Bahamas: December 1973 to February 1976; and Acapulco: February 1976 to April 1976. He died on an airplane that left Acapulco headed for a hospital in Houston.

Although Gay had succeeded in removing Maheu, he faced one more obstacle to total control: Hughes Tool Company executives in Houston. To achieve this, he sold the tool division for $150 million in 1972, supposedly to raise money to settle the TWA litigation. Ironically, just days after the sale, the Supreme Court reversed the judgment and dismissed the case. In December 1972, Gay and Davis achieved total control. They filled the new boards of directors with their people.

Hughes' fragile health suffered another blow in August 1973 when he broke his hip. Dr. William Young, who X-rayed the hip, described Hughes' condition "as being in a stage of malnutrition comparable to that of prisoners of war in Japanese prison camps during World War II."

The billionaire never walked again. "For the rest of his life, he was bedridden and emaciated, with a body weight of approximately one hundred pounds, although he was originally six feet four inches tall," the memo stated. "He had increasingly long periods of unconsciousness, up to a day or more, and his days were spent sleeping, sitting in a semi-stuporous state, or watching movies, some of which he had seen dozens of times before, often dozing in mid-film. He was totally out of touch with the outside world and his business affairs. The aides continued and, indeed, encouraged his isolation."

At this point, at least two doctors had determined Hughes needed greater medical care than he was getting while sequestered in dark hotel rooms. Dr. Raymond D. Fowler testified that Hughes was mentally incompetent by August 1973. And in April 1974, Dr. Crane refused to continue supplying drugs to Hughes.

But instead of admitting Hughes to a world-class hospital where he could receive proper care, Gay and Davis had another solution: They brought in Dr. Wilbur Thain, Gay's brother-in-law from Logan, Utah, to supply the drugs, which he did until Hughes' death. In return, Thain was offered an employment contract and a high position with the Hughes medical institute.

Thain also helped to negotiate lifetime contracts for select employees, in part by threatening to withhold drugs, according to the memo. Summa Corporation's board of directors approved these contracts in September 1975. "The evidence . . . shows that Thain mercilessly manipulated Hughes, forcing him to give employment contracts to most of the defendants, not to mention himself, as the price of the drugs to which Hughes was addicted," the memo stated.

Gay and Davis came across another potential foe in 1974 when Hughes' longtime friend, Jack Real, was gaining a measure of influence with the billionaire and attempting to help him out of his mental and physical prison. In 1974, after Hughes suggested that he wanted Real to have substantial power in running his businesses, Gay and Davis instructed aides to isolate Real from Hughes.

"They literally locked Real out by changing the locks to the aides' office—which led to Hughes' room—without giving Real a key," according to the memo. "They held messages from Hughes to Real and from Real to Hughes. When Hughes asked for Real to visit him, the aides falsely told him that Real was unavailable."

After taking control of Hughes' businesses, Gay, Davis, and others began to feast at the trough. "Beginning at least as early as 1970, the defendants and their co-conspirators in fact treated themselves to lavish salaries, charged Summa with enormous personal expenses, and treated the company's aircraft, employees, houses, and other assets as available for their personal whim," the motion stated.

In 1972, Gay's salary was $111,000. In 1973, after taking control, his salary climbed to $412,000. Aides who essentially performed secretarial and nursing duties received salaries of $70,000 to $100,000—huge sums for the time. Why? Essentially, they were paid not to talk about Hughes' drug use, according to the memo.

In addition, they used corporate aircraft for personal trips. Gay and Davis, for example, flew to Europe in 1972 to find Hughes a new residence. "While there, they chartered a private jet and flew to Nice, France, to meet Gay's wife; to Zurich to look at a watch for Gay; and to Majorca so that Davis could visit his daughter there," the memo charged. Two houses in Miami were purchased and used by executives "for personal pleasure," according to the memo. Substantial improvements were made to Davis' offices in California and New York at Hughes' expense.

The legal memo also outlined Gay and Davis' mismanagement of Summa Corporation's Las Vegas casinos. "Neither Gay nor Davis had any experience in hotel or casino management, and apparently neither exhibited any understanding of the unique nature of the problems involved," the memo asserted. Gay, for example, "was personally involved in the hiring of entertainment" and imposed "arbitrary rules resulting in an inability to hire top entertainers for Hughes' hotels. As a result, the showrooms in these hotels were not filled and their revenues suffered a substantial decline."

Gay also allegedly mismanaged a Desert Inn expansion project, resulting in additional costs of $30 million. "He never had a comprehensive plan for the construction," the memo stated. "Rather, it was constantly being changed, depending on his whim. . . . At one point, Gay decided that one of the new buildings, which already had been topped out, should have an extra floor, on which he planned plush suites for himself. The building was altered to add the additional floor at a cost in excess of $1 million."

After Hughes' death in 1976, the Gay-Davis empire crumbled with the arrival of Hughes' cousin, Will Lummis. Lummis assumed control of the estate and eventually got rid of Gay, Davis, and the other alleged conspirators in his cousin's demise. The memo cited in this chapter listed Lummis as the lead plaintiff.

The Governors: *Dealing with Hughes*

About three weeks after Paul Laxalt was elected Nevada's governor in November 1966, he learned that Howard Hughes had moved to Las Vegas. At first, the Republican governor-elect took the news in stride. But it wasn't long before Laxalt and Hughes were inextricably linked in Nevada history.

When Hughes bought the Desert Inn, it presented Laxalt with a regulatory problem. In his autobiography, Laxalt explained: "Our gaming license people were in a quandary. On the one hand, it was welcome news that Hughes would buy the Desert Inn. The feds had suspicions about its ties to organized crime. On the other hand, what would we do about having Hughes adhere to our strict licensing requirements—such as fingerprinting, 'mugshots' and the like?"

Laxalt soon heard from Maheu, who asked that the usual requirement of a personal appearance be waived because of Hughes' ill health. "We decided to grant the waiver," Laxalt wrote. "After all, having Howard Hughes invest in Las Vegas in a casino was a huge plus for Nevada. His eccentricities aside, Hughes gave Las Vegas gambling a sort of 'seal of approval.' If Hughes, one of the world's shrewdest businessmen, didn't feel that he could conduct business in a legitimate manner in Las Vegas, he wouldn't touch it with a ten-foot pole."

Hughes then bought several more Las Vegas casinos, a trend that eventually concerned Laxalt. "We welcomed all the acquisitions—to a point," according to Laxalt. "We eventually became concerned about 'too much Hughes.' Our concerns were reinforced when we were advised by the U.S. Justice Department that they were concerned about the antitrust implications of Hughes' 'buying spree.'"

Facing pressure for Hughes to be treated like every other casino licensee, Laxalt met with Maheu and told him the time had come to "establish personal contact with Hughes." Maheu agreed to arrange it, and in a few minutes Hughes was on the telephone with Laxalt. "Hughes was very cordial, articulate, and spoke in a distinct Midwestern accent," Laxalt wrote. "He apologized for not having contacted me previously, calling it 'poor politics.'"

Laxalt told Hughes he thought a personal meeting would be beneficial. "During our conversation, Hughes said, 'I'd like to meet with you personally, but I look like hell.' He said that he was quite ill upon his arrival in Las Vegas and was still not feeling well." Laxalt told Hughes that he respected his privacy but had a "public responsibility to fulfill." Hughes responded that he hoped to feel better in a few months and would meet with the governor sometime after that. The conversation continued, with Hughes dissecting the 1968 presidential race and suggesting that Laxalt could be a good presidential candidate in the future.

Laxalt did not press Hughes further on making a public appearance before gaming regulators. He never met the billionaire, but he did speak to him on the telephone regularly thereafter. "He phoned me day or night," Laxalt wrote. "Constantly alone, in bed, and in semi-darkness, he clearly didn't know the difference between day and night." Finally, Laxalt explained that as the governor he led a very busy life and asked Hughes to call only during the day. "He apologized profusely and never called me late at night again."

Politics, not the gambling industry, was the main thing the two discussed. Hughes also spent a lot of time talking about nuclear testing. "I tried to assure him that all precautions were being taken so there would be no 'radiation leaks,'" Laxalt wrote. "He politely scoffed at what he must have considered my naiveté, stating that the underground tests would endanger the safety and health of Nevadans 'for generations to come' and that for certain our underground water was being contaminated."

While Laxalt occasionally talked with Hughes on the phone, he spent more time with Maheu. "Through all the 'Hughes years,' Bob kept us advised as to Hughes' plans," Laxalt wrote. "When he exhibited any interest relating to Nevada gambling, we knew about it first. . . . When the community college and medical school programs were in peril, it was Bob Maheu who called to say that Hughes wanted to help."

In 1970, when Maheu and two top Hughes executives, Bill Gay and Chester Davis, engaged in a power struggle, Laxalt traveled to Las Vegas to try to mediate the dispute, but soon realized he could be of little help. "It was clear to me there was little, if any, room for compromise," Laxalt wrote. "I doubted if there was any chance they could set aside their deep feelings against one another in favor of the 'greater good' of Hughes' Nevada operations and thousands of

Governor Paul Laxalt worked with Bob Maheu to ensure Hughes would invest heavily in Nevada. Courtesy of The Mob Museum.

employees." Laxalt joined Clark County District Attorney George Franklin and Gaming Control Board Chairman Frank Johnson at the Sands Hotel for a one a.m. conference call with Hughes. Unfortunately for Laxalt's friend Maheu, Hughes made it clear to the politicos that he supported Gay and Davis, and wanted Maheu fired.

Looking back, Laxalt remembered Hughes fondly: "From a personal standpoint, he was always courteous and fair in his dealings with me. His investing in Nevada gambling in the 1960s was enormously helpful, not only in terms of his capital contributions, but also the positive message his involvement conveyed to the business community worldwide. Without Howard Hughes, Las Vegas gambling, fickle animal that it is, could have easily suffered a severe recession, which would have jeopardized thousands of jobs. And without Howard Hughes, Nevada might not have created a community college system or a medical school."

After Laxalt announced in 1970 that he would not seek re-election, Maheu told him Hughes wanted to hire him. Laxalt declined the offer, in part because he wanted to avoid the appearance that his administration's cooperation with Hughes was a quid pro quo for a future job.

In his memoir, Maheu dismissed speculation that Laxalt benefited personally from supporting Hughes' Nevada investments. "There's been talk about payoffs and personal gain," he wrote. "Not a word of it is true. Laxalt never did anything that wasn't strictly kosher, and anybody who says differently is, quite simply, a liar."

Maheu argued that Laxalt saw Hughes, despite his eccentricities, as a big improvement over the mobsters who had controlled many Las Vegas casinos for two decades: "Laxalt believed—and I think rightly—that Hughes was just what Las Vegas needed. Hughes' arrival brought respectability to a city overrun by organized crime."

The banker E. Parry Thomas, who worked with Hughes and Maheu on some of their Las Vegas deals, had similar praise for the governor: "Laxalt knew that what Hughes was doing when he started buying hotels was in keeping with what everyone wanted to see happen. It was cleaning up the ownership of the Strip and it was infusing energy into the economy."

Laxalt, who went on to serve two terms in the U.S. Senate and was a close adviser to President Ronald Reagan, died in 2018. He was ninety-six.

Meeting with Hughes

Mike O'Callaghan was Laxalt's successor in the Governor's Mansion. Hughes had left Las Vegas by the time the gregarious Democrat took office, but rumors were circulating that Hughes had died or was very ill. O'Callaghan told reporters in 1971 that he had received a letter allegedly written by Hughes, but he did not believe it came from the billionaire himself.

"I refuse to get involved with the game playing by telephone and letter," O'Callaghan said. "I don't know the authenticity of it. And, furthermore, I am getting fed up with the intrigue that surrounds the matter. I'm tired of shadowboxing."

O'Callaghan demanded a face-to-face meeting with Hughes, threatening to revoke the billionaire's gaming licenses if he did not comply. O'Callaghan assigned his lieutenant governor, Harry Reid, to set it up. Reid spent three months negotiating with Hughes executives before securing a date and place. Hughes eventually consented, and O'Callaghan and Gaming Control Board Chairman Phil Hannifin got on a plane to London. The trip initially was kept secret. O'Callaghan told his staff he was going hunting in Southern Nevada. Reid, who years later would become the majority leader of the U.S. Senate, stayed behind to run the state.

Hughes' aides went to work cleaning him up in the hours before his late-night meeting with O'Callaghan and Hannifin on March 9, 1973. Hughes' barber, Mell Stewart, cut his hair and cleaned up his beard just before the meeting in Hughes' suite at the Inn on the Park. When the governor and gaming regulator arrived, they waited several hours before meeting with Hughes. Also present were Hughes executives Gay and Davis.

In *Howard Hughes: The Hidden Years*, James Phelan described the scene: "Hughes . . . received the two Nevada officials clad in a bathrobe. He used a hearing aid and after a few pleasantries got down to business, and the session lasted slightly more than an hour."

Back in Nevada, O'Callaghan declined to offer details of his conversation with Hughes, but he did report that the billionaire appeared to be in good health and in control of his business affairs. "During the meeting, which lasted more than an hour, O'Callaghan and Hannifin found Howard to be very lucid," wrote Jack Real, a Hughes friend, in his memoir, *The Asylum of Howard Hughes*. "They would report that he was very much in command of the

Nevada Governor Mike O'Callaghan demanded a face-to-face meeting with Hughes in London to make sure he could keep his casino licenses. Courtesy of *Las Vegas Review-Journal* Archive.

situation and knowledgeable about his interests in Nevada. They even reported that Howard said he was looking forward to returning to Las Vegas."

O'Callaghan and Hannifin agreed that Hughes could designate whomever he wanted to manage his Nevada casinos. "The Nevada men could not get over what a fine, articulate man Howard was," Real wrote. "As I had seen many times through the years, Howard was a charming man who could, when he wanted to, win almost anyone as a friend."

In a 2006 interview with *Las Vegas Sun* reporter Cy Ryan, Hannifin recalled that O'Callaghan and Hughes got into a shouting match during part of the meeting. "They were yelling at each other like two old bulls in a pasture," he said. "Gay and Davis were fluttering around, and I started to giggle." O'Callaghan and Hughes were arguing over whether to tell the press about the meeting. O'Callaghan wanted to do so; Hughes did not. "O'Callaghan kept pushing," Hannifin said. "He reminded Hughes that a Nevada gaming license was a privilege, and Hughes blinked."

O'Callaghan, who served two terms as Nevada governor, later served as executive editor of the *Las Vegas Sun*, owned by Hank Greenspun, who had championed Hughes' arrival in Las Vegas but later became his bitter foe. O'Callaghan died in 2004. He was seventy-four.

After Hughes died, Hannifin left the Gaming Control Board and became a casino executive for Summa Corporation. Only then did he learn that Hughes' aides had cleaned him up in preparation for the meeting. Hannifin was elected to the Gaming Hall of Fame in 2018.

Reid served one term as lieutenant governor. In 1977, O'Callaghan appointed him to the Nevada Gaming Commission. Reid was elected to the House of Representatives in 1982 and to the U.S. Senate in 1986. He was the Senate's majority leader from 2007 to 2015. In 2019, Reid recalled why O'Callaghan was so insistent on meeting Hughes in London.

"He always believed in following the law," Reid said. "Mike was the most honest person I ever met. He would not exceed the speed limit. That's how he was. A very, very honest man. He felt Hughes had evaded the law, and that was his frame of reference."

Bob Maheu, Part 2: *Aftermath of the Palace Coup*

After enjoying a high-powered, luxurious lifestyle as Hughes' right-hand man during the 1960s, Bob Maheu spent most of the 1970s in court.

His first legal foray occurred soon after Hughes quietly departed Las Vegas on Thanksgiving Eve 1970 en route to the Bahamas. Company executives announced on December 5 that Maheu had been fired. The press release stated, "Hughes Tool Company today announced the termination of all relationships with Robert A. Maheu and his organization. . . . "

Maheu responded with a press release of his own, distributed by famed odd-smaker Jimmy "The Greek" Snyder, who was working as his PR man. "My only concerns at this time are for Howard Hughes' personal welfare and for my responsibilities as steward of his Nevada investments. . . . Mr. Hughes placed with me responsibility for his Nevada properties. I shall continue to fight any attempts to remove me from that position of trust unless Mr. Hughes himself makes it known to me that he no longer wishes me to continue as chief executive of Hughes Nevada Operations."

With attorney Morton Galane at his side, Maheu charged into court, questioning whether Hughes had, in fact, authorized his termination. Galane obtained a temporary restraining order preventing Gay and Davis from ousting Maheu, then sought a preliminary injunction to prevent them from taking over the company's Nevada operations. Galane argued that Hughes' signature on the proxy giving the duo authority to fire Maheu and manage Hughes' companies was a forgery.

Maheu called in handwriting expert Charles Appel to testify. Appel, a former FBI agent who had testified in the Lindbergh kidnapping trial, declared the signature on the proxy to be a fraud. But Ralph Bradford, a handwriting analyst retained by the anti-Maheu forces, testified that the signature was genuine.

On the stand, Maheu related his experiences working for Hughes in Las Vegas, noting that the billionaire once told him they would be together "for the rest of our natural lives." Maheu said he found it strange that Hughes had not contacted him since his disappearance.

Amid the swirl of activity in the wake of Hughes' departure, Clark County Commission Chairman James "Sailor" Ryan wrote a letter to Hughes in which he asked for a face-to-face meeting. "By all means, we respect your right to privacy and are willing to accommodate your desires within our power to do so, but we do urgently need to meet with you to learn just who you want to run your casinos here in Clark County," Ryan wrote. "This is a licensing matter that has a great bearing upon our local economy."

That day, *Las Vegas Review-Journal* editor Don Digilio reported about a handwritten letter from Hughes to Gay and Davis that appeared to set the record straight on his intentions. "I do not understand why the problem of Maheu is not yet fully settled and why this bad publicity seems to continue," Hughes wrote. "It could hurt our company's valuable properties in Las Vegas and also the entire state." Hughes added, "I do not support Maheu or [security chief Jack] Hooper in their defiance of the Hughes Tool Company board of directors, and I deeply desire all concerned to be fully aware of this immediately."

On December 19, District Judge Howard Babcock ruled against Maheu, denying the preliminary injunction and upholding his firing. Babcock ruled that Hughes' signature on the proxy was authentic. Also, Hughes aide Levar Myler testified to witnessing Hughes sign the document.

Maheu was officially dethroned. He lost his job, $520,000-per-year salary, and unlimited expense account. He remained, temporarily, in his rent-free mansion, built by Hughes on the Desert Inn golf course. (A few weeks later, he was evicted. Within a week, he moved into a more modest house in the Paradise Palms neighborhood near Eastern Avenue and Viking Road. Maheu lived in that house, on what is now the Las Vegas National Golf Club, for the rest of his life.)

But Maheu told reporters he would "not rest comfortably until I am assured of [Hughes'] welfare." "Mr. Hughes I have known as a man of deep compassion, concerned about his friends and even his enemies," Maheu said. "I will not leave a stone unturned until I am thoroughly convinced that Mr. Hughes is well and that this is his wish. I have never been farther away than a phone call from him."

After mulling his plans over the Christmas holiday, Maheu returned to the legal arena on December 31, 1970, suing Hughes for $50 million in damages and character defamation. Maheu contended his termination violated an oral agreement with Hughes for lifetime employment.

Procedural motions and hearings dominated the case throughout 1971. When Judge Babcock denied Maheu's motion to force Hughes to testify, Maheu appealed to the Nevada Supreme Court (which later sided with Maheu). Behind the scenes, Maheu dropped into an emotional tailspin.

"For hours, I did nothing but sit and stare into space in a trancelike state," he said in his memoir, *Next to Hughes*. "I was a prisoner of my past, reliving past glories while retreating from reality." Maheu eventually pulled himself out of his depression, but his tribulations were just beginning.

On January 7, 1972, Hughes resurfaced, conducting a two-and-a-half-hour telephone interview with eight reporters, including the *Review-Journal*'s Digilio. Hughes spoke from his Bahamas hotel while the reporters were assembled in the Sheraton Universal Hotel in North Hollywood, California. The main reason for the interview was to confirm that author Clifford Irving's book, promoted as a Hughes autobiography, was a hoax. But during the interview, Hughes also spoke angrily about Maheu, and said he had fired him because he was a "no-good, dishonest son of a bitch and he stole me blind."

Hughes continued: "I don't suppose I ought to be saying that at a news conference, but I just don't know any other way to answer it. You wouldn't think it could be possible, with modern methods of bookkeeping and accounting and so forth, for a thing like this with Maheu [to] have occurred, but believe me, it did, because the money is gone and he's got it." Regarding Maheu's dismissal, Hughes said: "I specifically fired him, and I'm horrified when I think of the harassment this man has caused me."

Outraged by Hughes' comments, Maheu lashed out in the press. Journalist Ron Laytner interviewed him extensively, and the *Review-Journal* printed a series of articles in which Maheu struck back. "I've been extremely patient now for a year, but the Hughes forces, by innuendo and sheer lies, have attempted to destroy me and my family," Maheu said. "I feel there comes a point where even a former employer who has recompensed you well loses his immunity. As far as I'm concerned, the honeymoon is over."

In response to Hughes' statements during the interview, which were subsequently broadcast on national television, Maheu filed a defamation lawsuit in February 1972 seeking $17.5 million in damages. The complaint argued that Maheu's reputation was damaged by the comments. (Maheu eventually withdrew the $50 million lawsuit over his firing.)

The jury trial in the defamation case got underway in February 1974 in U.S.

District Court in Los Angeles. Maheu argued that Hughes besmirched his reputation by calling him a thief, while Hughes' attorneys claimed Maheu misappropriated $4.5 million in company funds.

The four-month trial featured astonishing stories involving some of the biggest names in Nevada and national politics. For example, Hughes attorneys contended that then vice president Hubert Humphrey never received $50,000 that Hughes told Maheu to give him during the presidential campaign in 1968. Hughes supported the Democratic candidate because of his opposition to nuclear testing in Nevada. Humphrey said in a deposition that he never received the money. Hughes' attorneys surmised that Maheu pocketed the cash.

But Maheu testified he delivered the money to Humphrey by leaving it in the politician's limousine, in the presence of others, at the Century Plaza Hotel in Los Angeles. Maheu noted that he also delivered $50,000 to Republican Richard Nixon and $25,000 to Democrat Robert Kennedy in '68. Those contributions were confirmed, but the Humphrey donation was in dispute.

Maheu, who was on the witness stand for fourteen days, testified that as far back as 1959, Hughes encouraged him to make elaborate billings for his contracted services so that he would give Hughes his full attention. "I told him he was imposing an increasing number of assignments to the detriment of my other clients and that the margin of profit in such assignments did not justify my giving him any additional time," Maheu said. Hughes "suggested that I be more liberal in my billings as justification for my giving him preference."

Hughes' attorneys charged that Maheu overbilled by an estimated $463,000 for security services at Hughes' Tucson, Arizona, properties. But Maheu said this was approved by Hughes as a way to pay Maheu higher amounts without letting other Hughes executives know how much he was making.

Hughes' attorneys called a $150,000 loan that Maheu received from *Las Vegas Sun* publisher Hank Greenspun a "kickback." They contended Maheu received the cash infusion for his services in helping arrange a $4 million loan Greenspun received from Hughes. But Greenspun testified that he made the short-term loan to Maheu because he desperately needed it.

During his testimony, Greenspun revealed that Hughes enlisted him, through Maheu, to help the billionaire buy the media empire of Donald W. Reynolds. Upset by news coverage in Reynolds' *Las Vegas Review-Journal*, Hughes wanted control of the newspaper's editorial content. Greenspun said he held an all-night meeting with Reynolds in a Washington, D.C., hotel, during which Greenspun suggested that Reynolds ask $21 million for his holdings. "I think you can get $21 million," Greenspun told Reynolds, "because I know Hughes doesn't want you around and he might be willing to pay it."

Greenspun said "Hughes went through the ceiling" when Reynolds said he wanted $31 million, and the deal fell through.

The Hughes-Maheu trial never lacked for big names and news-making testimony. A deposition from Moe Dalitz, a former owner of the Desert Inn, revealed that former Teamsters Union President Jimmy Hoffa interceded so that Hughes could extend his stay in the penthouse suite of the Desert Inn in 1966. Dalitz said he wanted Hughes and his aides out before the holidays so the luxury rooms could be rented out to high-rolling gamblers. But then Hoffa called on Hughes' behalf. "He asked me a personal favor to permit him [Hughes] to stay for a while—a month or two," Dalitz said. "I said, 'No, I'll let him stay till after New Year's." Hoffa said only that he had "personal reasons" for placing the call on Hughes' behalf, Dalitz said.

The suggestion that Maheu stole millions of dollars from Hughes was contradicted by Edward P. Morgan, a prominent Washington, D.C., attorney who brokered the Desert Inn sale to Hughes. Morgan said that after Hughes fired Maheu in 1970, he decided to advance him a $5,000 retainer because he was "virtually destitute."

Morgan said he had received a call from another Hughes executive, Francis Fox, who told him: "Eve Maheu [Maheu's wife, Yvette] was over to the house and in tears. She said the Maheu family was virtually destitute and I remember her specifically saying, 'Things are so bad, we can't even pay the grocery bill.'"

Maheu said that after he was fired, banks suddenly called in their loans and he had no money. Morgan sent Maheu the $5,000 retainer to "keep the firm informed on anything that might be of interest to us." Morgan said he later learned the $5,000 had saved Maheu's "economic life."

In a 2007 interview, Maheu admitted he never was good with money, and this was reflected in his dire straits after being fired. "I had loans out that were being called," he said. "I was building a yacht, at the request of Hughes, a beautiful yacht, by the way. I made some very stupid investments. I was not a good businessman."

Perhaps the most amazing testimony in the trial came from Maheu's son, Peter, who said he arranged to have his son born in Mexico to help Hughes, who had business interests there. "My child being born there would afford Mr. Hughes the opportunity to have control of a Mexican national for a minimum of 21 years," Peter Maheu said.

Mexican law at the time restricted property ownership and business activities to Mexican nationals. "Mr. Hughes desired to either move or to purchase

After he was fired by Hughes, Bob Maheu was involved in a range of legal battles in the 1970s. Courtesy of The Mob Museum.

property in Mexico, and he needed some form of protection in regard to any investments that he would make," Peter Maheu said. The issue came up at the trial because the Hughes lawyers questioned Maheu's use of company jets for three flights to Mexico City.

In a 2018 interview, Peter Maheu's wife, Rosemary, recalled her experiences having her first child, Jeff, in Mexico in 1970. As she remembered it, "Hughes was wanting to build a marina in Mexico, and I happened to be pregnant at the time, and the powers that be got together and said, gee, maybe Rosemary could have her baby in Mexico, and Jeff would have dual citizenship at that point, so that Hughes could own the land in Mexico. Don't ask me how they were going to make that work. It never came to fruition."

Rosemary said she insisted that her physician, Dr. Buckley, accompany her to Mexico City. "He went down there with Peter and I," she said. "But he could not deliver the baby. We had to have a Mexican doctor deliver the baby but they could all be in the room. They found a top gynecologist. I felt very safe, had very, very good care. I only got worried at the end when it was time to take the baby out of the nursery. There were so many documents. That's when I panicked. I thought, oh my gosh, what if they don't let me take him out of the country?"

Rosemary said her son has never had occasion to take advantage of his dual citizenship, but that it caused some delays when, as a teenager, he wanted to get a Social Security number in order to get a job.

On July 1, 1974, the jury ruled unanimously that Hughes had defamed Maheu. The jury returned in October to assess damages in the case. Maheu testified that Hughes' public allegations had "virtually destroyed" his reputation in the business world.

Eugene Maday, a Las Vegas taxicab company owner, testified that he hired Maheu in 1971. He said everyone he talked to had "high regard for Mr. Maheu." But after Hughes' remarks, Maday said, there was a complete reversal of opinion about Maheu. Maday continued to employ Maheu anyway.

Sidney Wyman, former chief executive of the Dunes Hotel, said Maheu was being seriously considered for a top job with the resort in 1971, but the hiring had to be dropped after Hughes' comments.

Attorneys for Hughes countered by arguing that their client's disparaging remarks were not widely distributed in the news media, and therefore the damages to Maheu were minimal. Hughes' attorney Norbert Schlei's closing argument to the jury included a surprising mea culpa:

"Everyone recognized that it was a mistake" for Hughes to accuse Maheu of stealing, he said. But he played down the significance of those comments, suggesting that the jury's verdict had already restored Maheu's good name. "You have vindicated Mr. Maheu and we do not begrudge him that vindication," Schlei said. But he asked the jurors not to let the lawsuit be used "as a massive club to beat someone who gets out of line and says the wrong thing."

Maheu attorney Galane urged the jury not to be swayed by Schlei's apologetic tone, which he called a "lawyer's technique, the kind of thing we studied in legal seminars." Galane noted that Hughes himself had issued no apologies for his comments.

On December 4, 1974—almost exactly four years after his ouster—Maheu was awarded $2.82 million. At the time it was one of the largest compensatory damage awards in judicial history.

But Maheu did not immediately collect. Hughes appealed the ruling, and in December 1977 the United States Court of Appeals for the Ninth Circuit ruled that U.S. District Judge Harry Pregerson had made statements too favorable to Maheu during the trial and therefore a new trial should be ordered. The appeals court said Pregerson offered a "glowing character reference," describing Maheu as "affable, intelligent, imaginative, articulate . . . a friendly man with important friends in high places."

After reading the trial testimony, the appellate court said it could not understand Judge Pregerson's endorsement of Maheu. In fact, the appellate court offered a brutal view of Maheu:

"He was flatly contradicted on many matters by many witnesses. His response, as to most of them, was that they lied. He was also contradicted by contemporaneous records. He repeatedly flatly contradicted testimony that he himself had given under oath either in other litigation or in his depositions. Some of his explanations were ludicrous. Sometimes all he could say was that he 'could see no conflict.' More than once, when he was floundering around for an explanation, the judge interrupted with a leading question embodying an explanation which Maheu gratefully adopted. Nothing can be more damaging to a cross-examination of a lying, prevaricating, equivocating, mendacious, dishonest, deceitful, untruthful, tergiversating witness. From our reading of all of his testimony, it can be persuasively argued that he was just that kind of witness, or at least the jury could have so found."

And so, the court ruled, "We have no choice but to reverse the judgment on the ground that the trial court's one-sided characterization of Maheu came close to directing a verdict in his favor, thus denying Summa a fair trial."

Instead of holding another, no doubt lengthy trial, the case was settled out of court in May 1979, with Maheu receiving an undisclosed settlement. In a 2007 interview, Maheu declined to reveal the settlement figure. "It was a very satisfactory amount," he said.

Pregerson, stung by the appelate court's reversal and commentary on his conduct, took the opportunity to issue a statement: "I think it is in order for me to remind all of us here that the jury believed that Robert Maheu had been defamed and it would seem to me that this settlement between Mr. Maheu and the Summa Corporation should vindicate him of any cloud that hovered over his head." (Later that same year, President Jimmy Carter nominated Pregerson to the Circuit Court.)

The Hughes/Summa forces had tried to ruin Maheu and failed. They had hired Intertel, a large private investigation firm, to conduct 525 separate probes of Maheu's activities and none came back suggesting he had done anything wrong.

This was the most high-profile court case in which Maheu was involved, but hardly the only one. In 1972, Maheu was called to testify before a grand jury investigating author Irving, who faked a Hughes autobiography. Maheu said Hughes executives had alleged that he fed information to Irving. Maheu said he did not know Irving, and observed that excerpts from the manuscript that he had seen were based on readily available information.

Also, Maheu testified extensively on behalf of Greenspun in his two legal battles with Hughes, and he was a defendant in litigation resulting from Hughes' purchase of Air West Airlines. And last but not least, Maheu wound up in court fighting the Internal Revenue Service, which President Richard Nixon had ordered to audit him.

"When they were done with their audit, they estimated my tax liability as $3.5 million, a figure that far exceeded my gross income for that period," Maheu wrote in *Next to Hughes*. "I spent the next fifteen years fighting that decision." A settlement finally was reached.

For Maheu, the IRS action negated any feelings of victory after the libel settlement. "I never got a penny out of that lawsuit," he said. "I never got a penny. Not even my expenses."

Looking back on his years with Hughes, Maheu lamented the times when he abused the power of his position. "Although I truly thought I was able to control power, power is very intoxicating," he said. "And in retrospect, there were a few instances where I misused it, and I'm not very proud of myself."

But Maheu insisted he never felt the need to grab more than Hughes had given him. "Could you go any higher than I was? I don't think so. But I breathe better at this altitude. I really do. I feel that I am at peace with myself, at peace with my family and at peace with God."

Maheu died in 2008, at age ninety, just a few months after the release of the first edition of this book. His son Peter, who was often by his father's side during the Hughes years, died in 2016. He was seventy-three.

In His Own Words: *The Hughes-Maheu Memos*

During his four years in Las Vegas, isolated in his suite on the ninth floor of the Desert Inn, Howard Hughes handwrote hundreds of memos, mostly to Bob Maheu, his top executive in Nevada at the time. Reading the memos provides fascinating glimpses into Hughes' approach to business dealings, his personal views, and his relationship with Maheu.

There is no central repository of Hughes memos, but batches of them can be found in the hands of various people and institutions. The Mob Museum in Las Vegas has photocopies of more than one hundred memos Hughes wrote to Maheu, as well as a few typewritten Maheu memos in which Hughes wrote comments in the margins. They were submitted as an exhibit in a court case, *Los Angeles Airways Inc. v. Hughes Tool Company*, in 1976.

The context of what Hughes writes to Maheu is not always clear, but understanding the background is often unnecessary to learn something about Hughes. For example, when he started actively expanding his gambling empire, he became intensely interested in buying William Harrah's casino properties in Reno. Harrah initially showed interest in selling, but the negotiations broke down. Hughes wanted Maheu to keep pressuring Harrah, while Maheu wanted Hughes to focus on acquiring Las Vegas casinos and forget about Reno. Their differences on this point apparently reached a boiling point. Hughes headlined the following memo as an "urgent message for Mr. Maheu":

"Bob, I am willing to forget there is a Northern Nevada, not for any reason you have advanced, but for entirely different reasons. However, only if you will consent to accommodate 3 requests.

1. That you and I find a way to lay aside any differences and attempt to return to the atmosphere of complete harmony and unity, and most important, enthusiasm that prevailed between us in the beginning of our Nevada activity.

2. That we plan to focus all of our concentration on the local area and attempt to put together the complex we planned before including the Stardust and [Silver] Slipper. The reason I have been so insistent about Harrah's facilities has been the fact that they are now, at present, laying off the profits we need. The Stardust-Slipper combination can only be fully productive with a lot of work. . . .

Hughes writes that he is willing up to "give up all my plans in the North and focus right here if you will revert to your old attitude of enthusiasm and accord that we had in the early stages of this operation." He continues:

At that time, I used to be able to communicate with you and not be frightened for fear each word I spoke or wrote might be the one that would cause you to get angry with me and wind up with my stomach tied up in knots. Please, Bob, let us go back to the environment of friendship that used to exist between us. That is all I ask. And if our differences are due to something I have said or failed to say in the past, or any other mistake I have made, I apologize most sincerely, and I hope you will accept this apology and let us put it all behind us.

This memo appears to reveal the vulnerability of Hughes in his relationship with Maheu at the peak of their Las Vegas partnership. Or it could show Hughes at his manipulative best. Either way, it reflects the intensity of the Hughes-Maheu relationship even though it played out only through phone calls and memos.

One of Maheu's memos, dated March 13, 1968, shows him doing the apologizing:

Your last two messages have really made me feel like the damn fool that I must be. It is obvious that I misinterpreted your instructions and I apologize for the tone of my unwarranted and unjustified memo. I can assure you, Howard, that it is never my intent to hurt you in any way whatsoever, and when I write one of these stupid things, I really wish you would attribute most of my contents to my blowing off steam but certainly with no deep-seated malcontent. I shall really strive to avoid this in the future, but the pressures in the last week to ten days have really been quite severe.

Hughes' response: "Bob, thank you deeply for your message. It makes me feel much better."

Nuclear testing sixty miles north of Las Vegas was a constant source of concern for Hughes. Through Maheu, Hughes worked aggressively to try to stop the tests. In one memo, he asks Maheu to find out more details about a nighttime nuclear test that rattled his hotel room.

"Please find out what in God's name went haywire at the Test Site. We just experienced the worst blast that I have felt since we came to Nevada. I am amazed. All tests in the past have been in the a.m., and when this large, preceded by heavy publicity. For this overpowering explosion to have occurred at night . . . certainly seems to have been the product of careless planning at best. Please get the story at once. A lot of people must have been taken by surprise and scared. . . . This may be the opportunity we have been waiting for to demand a real stop to this outrageous program!"

For Hughes, the nuclear tests were, among other things, a threat to Las Vegas. He believed they would deter people from visiting the city. "How can we expect to realize our full potential as a resort if we are scaring people away with bomb tests and earthquakes?" he asks Maheu.

The development of Circus Circus also drew Hughes' ire. He despised the casino's theme, which he thought would be a blot on the sophistication he desired for Strip resorts. In one memo, he outlines a scheme to damage Jay Sarno, the Circus Circus builder, using a local newspaper columnist, Paul Price of the *Las Vegas Sun*.

"I think you should make an all-out effort . . . to put Paul Price on the trail of 'wild man' Sarno. . . . Maybe you should persuade Price to interview Sarno, and to tell Sarno that he, Price, has some misgivings about the desirability of the Circus, or whatever type of remark is necessary to trigger Mr. Sarno off so that the 'wild man' will start raving and ranting and baring his teeth and threatening dire destruction to all who get in his path. If Sarno would just put on one of his standard performances in front of Price, we would have it made."

Circus Circus opened in 1968. Undoubtedly, if Hughes had visited Sarno's casino, he would have been appalled by the trapeze acts performing over the casino floor and an elephant parading among the slot machines. But Circus Circus has endured longer than any of the casinos Hughes owned, marking its fiftieth anniversary in 2018.

A few memos address Hughes' deep dissatisfaction with Bill Gay, a longtime executive in his Southern California operations office. Hughes essentially blamed Gay for not doing enough to help him save his marriage to Jean Peters. Hughes expressed anger when Maheu proposed helping Gay financially.

"I have read your message about Bill again, and the more I read it, the more angry I get. I certainly cannot get very sympathetic about Mary Gay being 'shook up' when Bill's total indifference and laxity to my pleas for help in my domestic area, voiced urgently to him, week by week throughout the past 7 to 8 years, have resulted in a complete, I am afraid irrevocable loss of my wife. I am sorry, but I blame Bill completely for this unnecessary debacle. And this is only the beginning. If I compiled here a complete list of the actions or omissions in which I feel he has failed to perform his duty to me and to the company, it would fill several pages."

Peters and Hughes divorced in 1971 after living apart for almost a decade. Ironically, Gay would play a role in Maheu's firing in 1970 and go on to run Hughes' operations in the 1970s.

Hughes fired Maheu because other executives persuaded him that Maheu was stealing from him. But not long before that happened, Hughes had such confidence in Maheu that he asked him to take on additional responsibilities beyond the borders of Nevada. In hindsight, Maheu would have been wise to decline those opportunities, because they led to the palace intrigue that resulted in his ouster. The following memo shows Hughes turning over the handling of his TWA litigation to Maheu:

"Bob, please understand one thing which I do not think you have understood heretofore: You have the ball on the TWA situation. You do not need further approval from me until such time as you are prepared to recommend to me a specific settlement at a specific sum of money. . . . I say again you have full authority to do what you deem best in this entire matter. All I want is information: no delays waiting for a decision from me. As I say, you have full authority."

Hughes gave Maheu reasons to believe he was destined to take control of the empire. This surely contributed to the shock Maheu experienced when his dream job suddenly evaporated.

Hughes and the Mob: *Arm's-Length Associations*

Howard Hughes was not in the mob, and there is no evidence he had any illegal entanglements with organized crime. But Hughes was acquainted with mobsters, and he wasn't above frequenting their establishments and doing business with them from time to time. Considering the mob's substantial influence in Hollywood and Las Vegas through the bulk of the twentieth century, it would have been difficult for Hughes to have avoided them entirely.

It appears that Hughes had some level of fascination with organized crime as a young film producer. His fourth film, 1928's *The Racket*, is a story of mobsters and political corruption in an unnamed city that looks a whole lot like Prohibition-era Chicago. The similarity resulted in the silent film being banned from Chicago theaters. *The Racket*, considered to be the first feature-length gangster flick, received a Best Picture nomination at the first Academy Awards. When Hughes acquired RKO Pictures, he remade *The Racket*, starring Robert Mitchum, in 1951.

After Hughes died, Summa Corporation donated his movie collection to the film department at the University of Nevada, Las Vegas. The first edition of *The Racket*, which had not been seen for decades, was digitally restored and broadcast on the Turner Movie Classics cable network in 2004.

Better known is the Hughes-produced 1932 classic *Scarface*, starring Paul Muni, George Raft, and Ann Dvorak. Hughes bought the rights to a 1929 novel called *Scarface* by Armitage Trail, a young writer who spent time around Chicago gangsters to research the novel.

Hughes wanted Howard Hawks to direct *Scarface*, but there was a problem: Hughes was suing Hawks at the time. Not long after Hughes produced *Hell's Angels*, Hawks made a World War I movie called *The Dawn Patrol*. Hawks had hired a lot of the aviation experts and cameramen whom Hughes had used to make his film, and Hughes claimed *The Dawn Patrol* even contained some of his *Hell's Angels* footage. Hughes agreed to drop the lawsuit if Hawks would direct *Scarface*, which he did.

Then Hughes landed the ideal screenwriter for the job: Ben Hecht. Hecht was a former crime reporter in Chicago who had a knack for crackling dialogue and fast-paced narratives like *Scarface*.

It was clear from the script that *Scarface* was going to be a very violent film by early 1930s standards, and Will Hays, the movie censor, refused to approve it. Hays demanded changes. He wanted less violence and for the story not to glorify criminals.

Hawks in particular refused to budge, but Hughes, having invested at least $600,000 in the movie, initially agreed to some changes, including changing the ending and the name of the movie to *Scarface: The Shame of the Nation*. But Hays still was not satisfied. Hughes was so frustrated that he ordered his team to restore the movie to the original version.

But Hays wasn't Hughes' only obstacle. He also had to contend with state movie censorship boards. Some states allowed the film to be shown, while others refused. Hughes sued several states that would not allow the movie. Multiple versions of *Scarface* were circulating around the country in an attempt to satisfy the censors.

The movie debuted in New Orleans and Los Angeles, and the reviews were enthusiastic. Hughes also received praise for fighting for free speech. He memorably declared:

> It becomes a serious threat to the freedom of honest expression in America when self-styled guardians of the public welfare, as personified by our film censor boards, lend their influence to the abortive efforts of selfish and vicious interests to suppress a motion picture simply because it depicts the truths about conditions in this country which have been front-page news since the advent of Prohibition.

Eventually, Hays relented and approved the movie, which opened across the country in April 1932. Interestingly, *Scarface* was still banned in Chicago until 1941, when it finally appeared there and set attendance records.

Years later, Hawks told interviewer Joseph McBride that during the filming of *Scarface*, representatives of Al Capone came out to California and told the director, "The boss wants to see the picture." Hawks told them Capone could

Scarface movie poster. Courtesy of The Mob Museum.

buy a ticket to see the movie in a theater like everybody else. They invited him to meet Capone in Chicago.

The fearless director and the mob boss met in a café. "When I saw Capone, we had tea, and he was dressed in a morning coat, striped trousers, a carnation, being a very nice man, saying how much he liked the picture. I was with him two, three hours."

Hawks said Capone saw the movie several times. "He had his own print of it. He thought it was great. He'd say, 'Jesus Christ, you guys got a lot of stuff in that picture! How'd you know about that?' I said, 'Look, you know how somebody can't testify if he's a lawyer? Well, I'm a lawyer.' And he laughed. He didn't give a damn."

Hawks, who made dozens of movies during his career, described *Scarface* as his favorite because he and Hughes did it without A-list actors or the support of a big studio. "Everybody was under contract to the studios," he said. "We couldn't get a studio, and they wouldn't loan us anybody, so we had to find a cast. They just didn't want independent pictures made in Hollywood. So we rented a little cobwebbed studio and opened it up and made the picture. It turned out to be the big picture of the year. We didn't get help from anybody."

Hughes was so possessive of *Scarface* that after its Chicago run in the early '40s, he locked it up in the basement of his offices and it was not shown again for almost forty years. After Hughes died in 1976, his estate sold the rights to Universal, which showed it at the New York Film Festival in 1979, then made it available as a home video. But the real benefit for Universal came a few years later. By purchasing the rights to *Scarface*, it was allowed to do a remake, which came in the form of the 1983 movie of the same name starring Al Pacino.

Billy Wilkerson

Hughes got to know Billy Wilkerson in the early 1930s after Wilkerson launched the *Hollywood Reporter* newspaper. As a movie mogul, Hughes regularly bought advertising in the *Reporter*. He was known to bail out Wilkerson by purchasing additional advertising when the publisher ran into money problems. Always obsessed with how he was portrayed in the press, Hughes talked Wilkerson into allowing him to preview news stories related to his affairs.

As W.R. Wilkerson III explained it in *Hollywood Godfather*, a biography of his father, "First Hughes would telephone to ask whether there was anything about him in the paper that day. If he decided there was reason for concern, he would arrive at the pressroom around eight o'clock as the paper was being put to bed. . . . The pressmen had received strict instructions to hold the presses while Hughes reviewed the plates in search of references to himself."

Billy Wilkerson, owner and editor of the *Hollywood Reporter,* had a close relationship with Hughes, who was allowed to control what was written about him in the newspaper. Courtesy of Wilkerson Archives.

Wilkerson also was an early procurer of female companionship for Hughes. Wilkerson played a role in Hollywood agent Walter Kane being hired to take over this duty. In the late 1960s, Kane became entertainment director of Hughes' Las Vegas hotels.

Wilkerson wasn't in the mob, but he had personal and business relationships with many racketeers dating to his days running speakeasies in Prohibition-era New York City. According to *Hollywood Godfather,* Wilkerson actively participated in the Hollywood studio extortion racket in the late 1930s and early '40s along with a number of Chicago mobsters, including Johnny Rosselli. But while those individuals were caught, convicted, and sent to prison, Wilkerson escaped prosecution.

In 1945, Wilkerson purchased thirty-three acres outside Las Vegas with a plan to build a luxury hotel-casino called the Flamingo. Needing investors to cover the estimated $1.2 million expense, Wilkerson approached his friend Hughes, who agreed to give him $200,000 in the form of a prepaid advertising contract. At the time, Wilkerson had already retained the services of the mob-connected Gus Greenbaum and Moe Sedway to run the Flamingo's casino.

Wilkerson may have been able to get the Flamingo built with some help from bank loans and friends like Hughes, but he had a big problem: He was a gambling addict. Wilkerson lost tens of thousands of dollars at the gaming tables down the road from the Flamingo construction site. With the project practically stalled, Sedway alerted his New York boss, Meyer Lansky, to the Flamingo crisis. Sedway convinced Lansky the Flamingo could be a financial windfall for the mob. Lansky and a few partners offered Wilkerson $1 million to finish the resort, with Wilkerson retaining creative and managerial control. This arrangement suited Wilkerson. But a month later, Lansky assigned a childhood friend of his to keep an eye on the mob's considerable investment: Benjamin "Bugsy" Siegel.

The rest of the story is well known. Siegel and Wilkerson started out as friendly collaborators, but Siegel took such a liking to the Flamingo that he pushed Wilkerson out of the picture. Threatened with his life, Wilkerson fled to Paris for a time. Siegel took full control of construction, and he ended up going several million dollars over budget to make the Flamingo bigger and more elegant than Wilkerson had envisioned. The Flamingo's casino opened on December 26, 1946, but its hotel rooms were not finished yet. Initially, the Flamingo suffered financially, and Siegel had to shutter it until the hotel rooms were ready. Arrogant and defiant, Siegel tested the patience of his partners seemingly at every turn. On June 20, 1947, Siegel was assassinated while sitting on the couch in his girlfriend Virginia Hill's house in Beverly Hills, California. No one was ever prosecuted for the murder, but the leading theory is that Siegel's partners decided the Flamingo would be more successful without him.

Twenty minutes after Siegel's death, Greenbaum and Sedway walked into the Flamingo and assured the staff that they were in charge and everything would be fine. The skilled operators turned the Flamingo into an iconic resort destination. One of the hotel's biggest customers in the late 1940s and early 1950s was Howard Hughes, who stayed in the bungalows for long stretches.

As for Wilkerson, he returned from Paris five days after Siegel's death. In the years to come, he would take a leading role, alongside Hughes, in the crusade to rid Hollywood of alleged Communists. Wilkerson and Hughes remained friends throughout the 1950s. Wilkerson's son remembered Hughes visiting their house: "When I was a young boy, Howard Hughes was a frequent caller at our home. I used to watch him drive up our driveway from my second-floor bedroom window. It always took him several minutes to park his car, using an arcane ritual—back and forth and back and forth. He was obsessed about parking it as close to the courtyard wall as possible."

Wilkerson III also remembered what Hughes looked like as he entered the house: "He always wore a tired gray Stetson, a black leather aviator's jacket, a white shirt untucked and unbuttoned at the collar, dark slacks, and an old pair of white sneakers with no socks. He entered through the kitchen door, but to avoid touching the handle, he tugged a white handkerchief out of his pocket and used it as a glove."

Sidney Korshak

Sidney Korshak was the Chicago Outfit's attorney in Los Angeles for several decades. In 1952, Hughes expressed an interest in selling RKO Pictures. Korshak put together a group of mob-associated investors to buy the movie company. Hughes signed the deal, but then the press started publishing exposés about the mob-tainted buyers. As the mobsters pulled out of the deal, Hughes took back control of the stock and kept the $1.25 million down payment he had received. As Gus Russo reported in *Supermob*, Hughes "ignited a lifelong feud with Sid Korshak that would play out over the next two decades in the Las Vegas gambling mecca." Korshak's particular issue with Hughes stemmed from his belief that Hughes had actually leaked disparaging information about the buyers to the press, setting up the scenario in which he kept the studio and pocketed the down payment.

Korshak believed he got the last laugh after Hughes moved to Las Vegas in 1966. Over the next four years, Hughes paid top dollar for six mob-connected Las Vegas casinos. Not only did Korshak's criminal compadres cash in on the casino deals, but they may have continued to skim proceeds from the casinos while Hughes operated them. An IRS audit in 1971 indicated that $50 million had disappeared from the Hughes casinos, which would explain why they were losing money.

Johnny Rosselli

When Hughes moved to Las Vegas, he wanted to make investments, but he did not plan to spend his money on casinos. That changed after Moe Dalitz, who ran the Desert Inn, where Hughes occupied the entire penthouse floor, wanted the billionaire to vacate the premises. Hughes balked. When Dalitz, a Cleveland syndicate boss, threatened to send the sheriff to physically remove the billionaire, Bob Maheu turned to an old friend, mobster Johnny Rosselli, to calm everybody down. Rosselli achieved this by contacting Teamsters Union boss Jimmy Hoffa, who called Dalitz and persuaded him to allow Hughes to stay.

But if Hughes wanted to stay in the penthouse permanently, he would have to buy the hotel. Maheu, with Rosselli's help, engineered that deal.

By all accounts, Rosselli was a good-looking, charming man. He had two nicknames: "Handsome Johnny" and "the Silver Fox." "He was a very charismatic character," said Bob Maheu's son, Peter, who knew Rosselli well. "There's something about people like that—when they walk into a room, everybody has to turn around and look at them. Johnny was one of those guys."

Bob Maheu threw lots of lavish parties that brought together politicians, business tycoons, and movie moguls. "My dad had one of his famous clambakes, and Johnny was there," Peter Maheu said. "The only way to really explain Johnny is that he sucked the air out of the room when he walked into it. He was so striking."

Bernie Sindler had similar memories of Rosselli, whom he knew well. They lived for a time in the same posh apartment tower in Los Angeles. "I used to have dinner with him at least once a week," Sindler said. "He always had a smile on his face. He was good company, very funny." Sindler remembered the quiet

Moe Dalitz, left, and Johnny Rosselli, third from left, were organized crime figures who played key roles in Hughes' purchase of Las Vegas casinos. Courtesy of The Mob Museum.

power that Rosselli possessed. "He was absolutely the boss, and what he said, that's what went down."

Most of the time, anyway. Rosselli's notable underworld achievements over the years were balanced by periodic errors in judgment. For example, in 1966, Rosselli was in Las Vegas when he received word that Clark County Sheriff Ralph Lamb expected him, as an ex-felon, to check in with the authorities. Rosselli arrogantly ignored the directive. Lamb decided the suave gangster needed a reminder of who was in charge in Las Vegas. He found Rosselli having lunch at the Desert Inn, yanked him over the table, and slapped him around. Then, just to make sure Rosselli got the message, Lamb escorted him downtown, where he was stripped and deloused.

An even dumber move was to get involved with a card-cheating scam at the Friars Club in Beverly Hills. In the mid-'60s, Rosselli was a regular at the exclusive social club. One of his friends there was Maury Friedman, an owner of the Frontier hotel-casino in Las Vegas. Friedman often played gin at the club alongside Hollywood aristocrats such as actor Phil Silvers and singer Tony Martin, as well as card sharps with underworld connections. Friedman gradually raised the stakes in the casual games, with thousands of dollars on the table at any one time. Losses for some players amounted to hundreds of thousands of dollars.

Little did the "pigeons" know that Friedman was cheating them. "Peepholes were drilled in the ceiling of the Friars Club, and a man posted in the rafters was rcading the cards of the well-heeled Friars," according to *All American Mafioso,* a Rosselli biography by Charles Rappleye and Ed Becker. "Signals were conveyed to the hustlers via a tiny radio transmitter strapped to the card cheat's midsection. If the game involved two-man teams, the hustler with the receiver would relay information through an elaborate voice code. A word or phrase beginning with the letter A meant to hold kings, B meant queens, C, jacks, and so on."

Rosselli rarely played gin, but when he learned about the scheme he demanded a cut of the winnings, to which Friedman agreed. In 1967, the FBI caught wind of the scam and raided the Friars Club. Agents seized the electronic equipment hidden in the rafters and convened a grand jury. Two months later, Rosselli was one of six men indicted. Rosselli worked the angles, from calling for a hit on one of the witnesses to talking with high-ranking friends in Washington to try to quash the case. It didn't work. After a complicated, six-month trial, Rosselli was convicted on December 2, 1968, and sentenced to five years. He served two years, nine months.

After many years representing Chicago Outfit interests in Hollywood, Rosselli was sent to Las Vegas in 1957. Rosselli had tinkered in Las Vegas before, but now he would be Chicago's main man there, replacing Marshall Caifano, who used intimidation and violence to get his way. Rosselli got more done with charm and guile.

Rosselli's first Las Vegas deal resulted in the Tropicana Hotel, which had hidden mob ownership interests from New York (Frank Costello), Miami (Meyer Lansky), and New Orleans (Carlos Marcello). Rosselli benefited from the deal by owning the parking and gift shop franchises, and booking the entertainment.

The Tropicana could have been a huge cash cow for everybody involved, but three weeks after it opened, Costello was shot in an assassination attempt orchestrated by power-hungry underboss Vito Genovese. Costello survived: The assassin's bullet only grazed his temple. But while doctors attended to Costello's wound, police officers went through his pockets and found a slip of paper that detailed the Tropicana skim.

Although the Tropicana skim soured for a time, Rosselli's influence in Las Vegas increased. Through his hidden interest in Monte Proser Productions, he controlled much of the entertainment booking in town. He arranged casino loans provided by the Teamsters Union's Central States Pension Fund. He orchestrated the Cleveland-Chicago mob takeover of the Stardust Hotel after its founder, Rosselli's old bootlegging partner Tony Cornero, died before it was finished. He even profited from the ice machine business on the Strip.

Las Vegas was an "open city," in mob parlance, meaning no single syndicate could gain a stranglehold on the Strip. But no matter who was involved, Rosselli coordinated nearly everything that happened. In their 1963 exposé of the mob's influence in Las Vegas, *The Green Felt Jungle*, Ovid Demaris and Ed Reid painted a colorful picture of Rosselli:

> "Rosselli is definitely of the new school—sharp silk suits, diamond accessories, swanky apartment, busty showgirls in full-length minks, big Cadillac, gourmet taste, sportsman golfer—the best of everything in the best of all possible worlds. . . . Rosselli spends his leisure hours (that is, all the waking hours of his day) at the Desert Inn Country Club. He has breakfast there in the morning, seated at a table overlooking the 18th green. Between golf rounds, meals, steam baths, shaves and trims, Twisting, romancing and drinking, there is time for little private conferences at his favorite table with people seeking his counsel or friendship. It may be a newsman, a local politician, a casino owner, a prostitute, a famous entertainer, a deputy sheriff, a U.S. senator, or the governor of Nevada."

With Dalitz threatening to physically remove Hughes, Maheu turned to Rosselli for help. Hughes, who knew Rosselli from his Hollywood days, approved. "Rosselli was like a key to the city, the ultimate mob fixer in the desert," Maheu wrote in his memoir, *Next to Hughes*.

Rosselli served as a key player in the negotiations for Hughes to buy the Desert Inn. For his services, Rosselli received a fee of $50,000. The Hughes buying spree coincided with Rosselli's Friars Club troubles, and he was frantic in his efforts to avoid going to prison. Rosselli wanted Maheu to appoint him manager of the Desert Inn casino, but Maheu adamantly opposed the idea.

"He came back after we got possession of the hotel and he wanted to run the casino," Peter Maheu says. "My dad got into a heated argument with Johnny. Dad said he wasn't going to have anything to do with the casino."

Despite that dustup, Rosselli also helped engineer Hughes' purchases of the Sands and Frontier hotels. For the Sands deal, Rosselli received a $45,000 fee. The Frontier was different: Instead of a fee, Rosselli was handed the lease for the gift shop, which netted him about $60,000 per year for the rest of his life.

As the mob's point man in Las Vegas, Rosselli was involved in all kinds of behind-the-scenes activity. Before Hughes purchased the Silver Slipper casino, it was owned by Shelby Williams and Jack Shapiro, the latter of whom was tied to the Detroit Mafia. Bernie Sindler said he was approached to buy a piece of the Slipper. "They came to me one day and wanted to see me. They said, we want you to buy three percent of the Silver Slipper for $30,000. But the deal was this:

You have to give one-third of it to Johnny Rosselli. He's going to be your partner. You are going to put up all the money, and he's not going to give you any money."

Sindler said the reasoning was that Rosselli was close to Maheu, who could be influential in persuading Hughes to buy the Silver Slipper. "It will be done at a good number, and you'll make a lot of money," Sindler was told. "But Rosselli is going to get a third of it."

Sure enough, Hughes bought the Silver Slipper, netting Sindler a healthy $231,000. But now he had to figure out how to give Rosselli one-third of the proceeds without drawing any law enforcement attention. "I was on the radar with the FBI all the time," Sindler said. "They wanted me to be an informant, and I wouldn't do it. So, how am I going to give Rosselli $77,000 without any trace of anything, no banks, no nothing?"

Sindler figured it out. He happened to be a very good—and lucky—gin rummy player, and he had stashed his winnings in shoeboxes in his closet. He paid Rosselli his share out of those shoeboxes. "I gave him his money, we shook hands, he went his way and I went my way," Sindler said.

Rosselli died four months after Hughes in 1976. Fishermen found his dismembered body in a fifty-five gallon steel drum floating in Dumbfoundling Bay near Miami. Nobody was ever arrested for Rosselli's murder, though it was widely speculated that the Chicago Outfit or Tampa Mafia boss Santo Trafficante Jr.—or the two in collaboration—were responsible. Rosselli had been testifying at congressional hearings, which was generally frowned upon in the underworld.

Stardust Hotel

As Hughes built his casino empire in Las Vegas, he negotiated a deal with Dalitz to acquire another mob-connected property, the Stardust, for $30.5 million. However, the U.S. Justice Department's Antitrust Division expressed concerns that Hughes was gaining monopoly control of the Las Vegas casino industry, and the deal fell through.

Considering what happened at the Stardust in the 1970s and early '80s, the Justice Department could have saved a lot of time and money if it had allowed Hughes to buy the resort. The Martin Scorsese movie *Casino* is a fictionalization of the mob's involvement with the Stardust, but it does a pretty good job of depicting what happened.

San Diego real estate investor Allen Glick's Argent Corporation purchased the Stardust in 1974. He obtained Teamsters Union loans to make the deal. At the time, the Teamsters were in league with the Chicago mob. Chicago initiated a skimming operation supervised by Frank "Lefty" Rosenthal and Tony

Spilotro. The Stardust skim generated millions of dollars for mob bosses in Chicago, Kansas City, and Milwaukee. State gaming regulators discovered the skimming operation, and Glick was forced out in the late '70s. Glick, who claimed ignorance of the skimming operation, was not charged with a crime. Instead, he became a cooperating witness against those who executed and benefited from the illegal siphoning of profits.

The Stardust was sold to new operators, Al Sachs and Herb Tobman. But the skimming continued, and Sachs and Tobman were removed. State regulators finally found an aboveboard operator for the Stardust, Boyd Gaming, in 1985. Boyd imploded the Stardust in 2007.

12
Hank Greenspun: *Media Friend, Media Foe*

During the 1960s, *Las Vegas Sun* publisher Hank Greenspun was among Howard Hughes' biggest fans. Greenspun helped make the arrangements for Hughes' secret move to Las Vegas in 1966. In his newspaper, Greenspun championed the billionaire's arrival and his investments in the city. He sided with Hughes in his campaign to stop nuclear testing. Greenspun said he installed an unlisted telephone in his home so Hughes officials would have instant contact if they needed him. Greenspun even traveled to the state capital, Carson City, to lobby on Hughes' behalf before Nevada gaming regulators.

In addition, Greenspun engaged in several financial deals with Hughes. The best-known transaction occurred in 1968, when Greenspun sold the KLAS Channel 8 television station to Hughes Tool Company (later renamed Summa Corporation) for $3.6 million.

But the friendship soured in 1970 when Hughes quietly left town and his chief executive, Bob Maheu, was abruptly fired. Greenspun took Maheu's side, and questioned in print whether the executives who ousted Maheu had kidnapped Hughes.

Hughes responded by demanding that Greenspun immediately pay back a $4 million loan made on September 20, 1967. Hughes had lent Greenspun the money—to build a newspaper plant to replace the one that had been destroyed by fire in 1963—at three percent interest. Greenspun was to pay back the note in large annual installments between 1970 and 1975. Greenspun secured the loan by putting up the Paradise Valley Country Club, 2,070 acres surrounding the golf course, and eighty percent of the *Sun* as collateral.

But in May 1969, Hughes and Greenspun reached a new agreement. Under this second note, Greenspun sold the Paradise Valley Country Club to Hughes for $2.25 million. The agreement also included the intention to sell the 2,070 acres surrounding the course to Hughes for $4.4 million. The deal modified the 1967 agreement so that Greenspun would not have to start paying back the loan until 1980 and in lower amounts over a longer period.

Greenspun received a check for the country club, but the rest of the deal was not completed. "For some reason not fully disclosed, Howard Hughes decided to rescind the whole transaction," according to a legal filing in the court battle.

Las Vegas attorney Ralph Denton, who represented Greenspun, recalled that Hughes became upset about buying the country club after he learned that the fairways were irrigated with treated wastewater. (Hughes was a notorious germophobe.) Hughes also claimed Maheu had struck the deal without his knowledge.

In retaliation, Hughes attorney Sam Lionel filed a motion against Greenspun, demanding immediate payment of the first note and placing a lien on the 2,070 acres. Greenspun countersued, to the tune of $142 million, arguing that the first note was no longer valid and that Hughes had reneged on the second agreement to buy the land surrounding the country club.

Hughes attorneys contended the second deal never went through and therefore the first note was still in effect. Hughes wanted Greenspun to pay back the loan immediately by defaulting on the land.

Greenspun argued that his public support for Maheu after he was fired sparked Hughes' change of heart on the loan. The decision to demand immediate payment, Greenspun contended, was a malicious attempt to ruin him and take over his newspaper.

The trial was held in Elko, more than four hundred miles north of Las Vegas, because of concerns that neither the plaintiff nor the defendant could get a fair trial in Las Vegas. When the trial began in March 1975, Greenspun sought to have Hughes, then living in the Bahamas, appear for a deposition. Naturally, Lionel vigorously fought the motion, as all of Hughes' attorneys had done in similar situations for decades. Lionel won that skirmish when Elko District Judge Joseph McDaniel ruled that Hughes did not have to appear. McDaniel wrote: "The court is mindful of the fact that Howard R. Hughes is an unusual person and that for him to appear for an oral examination would be oppressive." McDaniel ordered that Hughes must submit to a written deposition.

But then Greenspun questioned the validity of an unnotarized document, purportedly signed by Hughes, in which he answered questions in writing. Unsatisfied with the "vague and inadequate" answers, Greenspun tried to force Hughes to answer questions in the presence of a court reporter. That part of the case went to the Nevada Supreme Court, which decided the demand was "unwarranted."

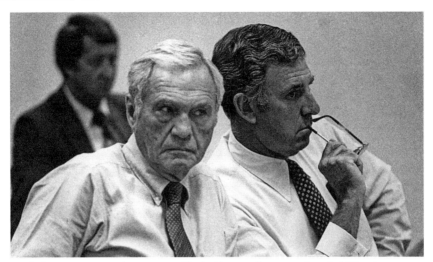

Hank Greenspun, pictured in 1982, was Hughes' biggest champion when the billionaire came to Las Vegas, but became one of his fiercest critics after he left. Courtesy of *Las Vegas Review-Journal* Archive.

The high court did order that written answers from Hughes be properly notarized. A new set of answers to sixty-seven questions, notarized by a Bahamian official, was filed on August 11, 1975. In the answers, Hughes basically said he didn't know anything about the dealings with Greenspun.

The trial did not resume until six months after Hughes' death in April 1976. Veteran reporter Cy Ryan wrote an amusing story remarking that this "high-stakes chess game" involving "two major forces from Las Vegas" was playing out in a small courtroom in remote Elko.

"It's like a World Series baseball game with no spectators," Ryan wrote. "Greenspun's wife, Barbara, and a couple of newsmen are the only steady courtroom spectators."

A real estate consultant testified that Greenspun had lost more than $11 million because Hughes had "clouded" title to the 2,070 acres. The consultant said American Nevada Properties Incorporated in Henderson, south of Las Vegas, was prepared to invest in Greenspun's plan to build an 8,400-acre community to be called Green Valley, but could not do so because Hughes had tied up 2,000 of those acres.

Maheu also testified on Greenspun's behalf. After the 1969 deal was made, Maheu said, he received a "frantic phone call" from Hughes, asking him to "bail out" of the deal. Hughes no longer wanted the golf course when he learned that recycled sewage water was being reclaimed for irrigation. Maheu said he told

Hughes that Greenspun "would let him off the hook about the land but that the golf course sale would have to stand."

On several occasions, Maheu's wide-ranging testimony generated banner headlines, particularly when he revealed that Hughes wanted to give then President Lyndon Johnson $1 million to stop nuclear testing in Nevada. According to Maheu, Hughes instructed him to set up a meeting with Johnson. Maheu dutifully set up the meeting at Johnson's Texas ranch, but he wasn't told the reason for the meeting until ten minutes before he got on a plane in Dallas to go see the president. Maheu said he did not deliver Hughes' message, because he did not want to subject Johnson to such a shady deal.

Also, Maheu related that Hughes believed he could buy or destroy anyone, and that he wanted to control the Nevada media. His goals, Maheu said, were to "control the editorial policies and so he could cut out any stories that were detrimental to his policies and put in any story that was beneficial."

Greenspun's case benefited from two other high-profile witnesses. Former Lieutenant Governor Harry Reid (later the U.S. Senate's Democratic majority leader) described a 1973 meeting held with Hughes executives Bill Gay and Chester Davis to try to reach a settlement of the case. Instead, Davis repeatedly called Greenspun an "SOB" and vowed he "was going to do anything he could to get him," Reid said.

Former Clark County district attorney George Franklin related a similar experience. Franklin said that in 1970 Davis said he would try to get rid of Greenspun and talked about taking over his newspaper. Franklin testified that Davis said, "As soon as we get rid of Maheu we are going to start on Greenspun." Franklin said Davis indicated "they had certain land transactions they would use against Greenspun."

Reid described Davis as "totally obnoxious" and "very foul-mouthed," while Franklin called the Hughes lawyer "a very abrasive man." Franklin's testimony was particularly compelling considering he was a longtime foe of Greenspun. Franklin, who once won a libel suit against Greenspun, was a reluctant witness.

Another witness, *Las Vegas Sun* photographer David Lee Waite, testified that Mint Hotel barber Jim Cullen, a part-time security employee for Hughes, asked him twice for a layout of Greenspun's office and where he kept a safe. "He told me they were going to get that son of a bitch and they wanted the newspaper," Waite said.

The photographer's testimony suggested a link between Hughes executives and a 1972 burglary of Greenspun's safe by Watergate conspirators G. Gordon Liddy and E. Howard Hunt. Liddy and Hunt were looking for a stack of memos between Hughes and Maheu that may have confirmed a $100,000 campaign donation Hughes had made to Nixon. Nixon also was interested in finding information to explain the link between Hughes and Democratic Party strategist Larry O'Brien.

Waite said he did not cooperate with Cullen. Hughes executive Gay testified that Liddy and Hunt approached the company about joining in the burglary scheme, but that he gave orders not to participate. Gay acknowledged that he did not notify the authorities or Greenspun about the plan. The burglary occurred, but the safe was not opened.

Greenspun's final witness hammered home the argument that Hughes wanted to act maliciously toward the newspaper publisher. Mell Stewart, who served as the billionaire's personal barber, testified that Hughes said of Greenspun, "We've got to get rid of him."

That day in court, Greenspun's side introduced a memo written by Hughes. In it, he directed Davis to "move immediately to buy Don Ray's [Donald Reynolds'] *Review-Journal*, etc." The memo also ordered, "Sell *Review* for five cents a copy" as a way to undercut Greenspun's *Sun*. Stewart said he recalled Hughes saying, "If we have to give the damn paper [the *Review-Journal*] away, we'll do so, but we have to get rid of this man [Greenspun]."

In another memo, Hughes ordered the hiring of ninety detectives to follow Greenspun twenty-four hours a day.

Hughes' attorney Lionel brought to the stand Calvin Collier, a company director from 1961-1972, who testified that Maheu lacked the authority to renegotiate Greenspun's $4 million loan and land deal with Hughes. Collier said Maheu needed the approval of the board of directors for the renegotiated loan to stand. Therefore, Collier said, the 1967 loan agreement was still in effect.

But Maheu testified that he served as Hughes' "alter ego" in Nevada and had full authority to negotiate on his behalf. Maheu produced memos in which Hughes had outlined this structure.

Davis testified that he never said he wanted to "get" Greenspun, and that he met with Greenspun on several occasions to try to settle the loan dispute.

Meanwhile, Lionel questioned economist Peter McMahon, hired by Summa to study the economic feasibility of Greenspun's Green Valley development. McMahon concluded that forty percent of the project's acreage could not qualify for FHA mortgages because it fell within airport noise zones. McMahon also argued that the land was too far from Las Vegas to sell.

(Hindsight is 20/20, of course, but this assertion must have been laughable even in 1977. Green Valley was the best-selling planned community in Southern Nevada for many years after the trial concluded.)

Greenspun countered with Paul Williams, who headed the development company and rejected McMahon's analysis. "I talked to FHA and they assured me there was no problem in insuring the housing in that area." Further, Williams testified to Green Valley's viability, noting that the average work commute from the area was only eight miles.

As the trial rolled through January 1977, *Review-Journal* reporter Jack Breger filed a story echoing Ryan's article marveling at the high-powered suits walking the dusty streets of Elko.

"In the summer, one is told, Elko is a busy place with tourists from southern Idaho and parts of northern Utah filling the hotels and motels, bringing life to the casinos. In January, however, it is bitter cold and the sidewalks become empty as soon as the sun goes down. Snow is piled up along the gutters and walking across the street can be a treacherous journey for a person without rubber-soled shoes. . . .

"Last Tuesday, tall, distinguished William R. Lummis, Howard Hughes' cousin from Houston, the board chairman of Summa, came to Elko as a witness. He strolled down Idaho Street that morning in his fine, wool three-piece herringbone suit—an imposing figure as he passed the general store, probably unnoticed by the kind, elderly Basque woman who is a clerk there."

The trial ended on January 20, 1977, with Judge McDaniel's decision pending the delivery of written legal briefs from both sides. In June, McDaniel ruled in Greenspun's favor, saying that Hughes "willfully and maliciously" permitted his board of directors to cloud title to the property and thereby prevent Greenspun from entering into a lucrative business partnership to develop the land.

The judge awarded Greenspun $53,204 in out-of-pocket expenses plus $1 million in punitive damages.

Summa appealed. In 1979, the Nevada Supreme Court initially voted 3-2 to uphold the judgment against Hughes, but throw out the $1 million in punitive damages. But in a mysterious twist, Denton recalled, he received a letter saying that four of the five Supreme Court justices had disqualified themselves from the case and that a new hearing would be conducted with four lower-court judges appointed by the governor. The newly constituted court reinstated the punitive damage award.

Paul Winn, a longtime aide to Hughes, said there was no mystery as to why the Nevada Supreme Court decided to rehear the case. "For eight or nine months, Greenspun went on a horrible diatribe in his newspaper against the members of the Supreme Court," Winn said. "He wrote terrible articles. He was a vicious guy. If he didn't like somebody, he could be incredibly vicious. He hammered those judges on the Nevada Supreme Court until they finally caved in."

Whatever the circumstances, after an eight-year battle, Greenspun won a complete victory.

Denton, interviewed in 2007, offered an interesting postscript to the case. The long delays in the case, he argued, worked in Greenspun's favor. "If Hughes had not died, we would have lost," Denton said.

Why? It wasn't until after Hughes died that many of his bizarre activities became common knowledge. Lacking those insights, the public perception of Hughes, especially in Nevada, was that he was some kind of saint. The things Greenspun was saying in court about Hughes didn't jibe with his image. "Everybody thought that he was the nicest man in the world, doing all these things for the state of Nevada," Denton said. "That was the attitude of the public."

Greenspun kept the land surrounding the Paradise Valley Country Club and combined it with several thousand more acres he purchased from the city of Henderson to build Green Valley. In the 1980s, Green Valley became the premier place to live in Southern Nevada, leading a suburban building boom that continued well into the twenty-first century. Greenspun was famous for his feisty newspaper, but was far more successful financially in the land development business.

The marathon court battle over the loan deal was not Greenspun's only legal fight with Hughes in the '70s. Greenspun also filed an antitrust lawsuit against Summa when its six hotel-casinos stopped advertising in the *Sun*. Greenspun accused Davis and Gay of pulling the advertising—one week after Hughes' death in 1976—in an attempt to put the *Sun* out of business.

The trial, held in federal court in Las Vegas, began on February 1, 1977—just a few weeks after the conclusion of the Elko trial. Greenspun's case, handled by his son Brian and former Lieutenant Governor Harry Reid, closely followed the script of the previous trial.

Attorney Walter Beebe, representing Summa, conceded that Greenspun's columns attacking Hughes and his top executives had upset his clients. He said Summa pulled the ads, for which the casinos paid a total of $8,000-$10,000 per month, for economic reasons, as well as the *Sun*'s editorial policy toward Hughes. But Beebe questioned Greenspun's claim that Summa advertising was a large percentage of the *Sun*'s revenue. He contended it was not enough to constitute an antitrust violation.

Contradicting the argument that the advertising was withdrawn primarily for economic reasons, several hotel-casino executives testified that they would have preferred to continue advertising in the *Sun*. And Perry Lieber, longtime publicity director for Hughes, said he recommended pulling the advertising on the day the *Sun* printed a story detailing a memo in which Hughes expressed his hatred for executive Bill Gay.

When Greenspun took the stand, he bluntly admitted he "prostituted" himself by taking loans from Hughes, but insisted he never lost sight of his obligation to tell the truth in his newspaper. Greenspun argued that when Summa boycotted the *Sun*, it influenced other businesses as well. Vendors doing business with Summa feared that if they continued to advertise in the *Sun*, Summa might drop them from its "preferred vendors" list.

Summa lawyers called just one witness in the trial. F.G. Baldwin, president of the Newspaper Advertising Bureau, testified that entertainment ads in the *Sun* were not a good buy because the *Sun* had fewer readers than the competing *Review-Journal*, yet the papers had the same advertising rates.

Trial testimony ended after five days, with visiting U.S. District Judge Warren Ferguson—a California judge who, oddly enough, had been born in Eureka, Nevada, and graduated from the University of Nevada, Reno—scheduling closing arguments for the following month. But before that could happen, Ferguson declared a mistrial. The judge said Greenspun had sent him a letter and *Sun* news clippings from the 1950s detailing Greenspun's battles with anti-Communist Senator Joseph McCarthy. Ferguson said he felt Greenspun sent the clippings to show that they shared political philosophies. "There can be no compromise or attempt to compromise my court," Ferguson said.

McCarthy had come up during the trial, and Greenspun apparently wanted to share the material with the judge. Brian Greenspun subsequently called the judge's secretary and asked her not to show the material to the judge. But it was too late. "I do not think Mr. Hank Greenspun intended anything wrong," Ferguson said. "But that letter and that phone call asking my secretary not to show me the material has compromised me to the decision that I must grant a new trial."

The case was rescheduled before U.S. District Judge Samuel Conti, who ruled in May 1977 in Summa's favor. He dismissed Greenspun's contention that Summa withdrew the ads in retaliation for negative news coverage.

That verdict contrasted with the result of an antitrust lawsuit Greenspun filed twenty-five years before. In 1952, Greenspun accused nine Las Vegas casinos and U.S. Senator Patrick McCarran of conspiring in an advertising boycott of the *Sun* in retaliation for critical news coverage. Greenspun won a preliminary injunction requiring the casinos to continue advertising in the *Sun*. Later, they reached a settlement in which the casinos paid Greenspun $80,500—enough to buy a new printing press.

Greenspun died in 1989 at age seventy-nine, after which his family entered into a joint operating agreement with the rival *Review-Journal* as a way to save the money-losing *Sun*. The Justice Department's Antitrust Division approved the agreement on grounds that it saved a "failing newspaper" and thereby maintained a diversity of voices in Las Vegas. The *Review-Journal* demanded highly favorable terms in the deal. The two newspapers maintained separate editorial staffs, but business operations were combined under the *Review-Journal's* management. The *Review-Journal* received ninety percent of the profits and the *Sun* received ten percent. Also, the *Review-Journal* continued to be circulated in the morning while the *Sun* was relegated to the less-attractive afternoon slot.

For fifteen years, the *Sun* survived but steadily lost ground in terms of readership, dropping to about 25,000 weekday circulation, a marginal figure in a metropolitan area approaching two million people. In 2005, the *Review-Journal* and *Sun* agreed to revise the joint operating agreement. The change transformed the *Sun* into a one-section newspaper included daily with the *Review-Journal*. The *Sun* was significantly downsized but its writers, especially editor Brian Greenspun, benefited from reaching a much larger readership.

In a 2001 oral history, Ralph Denton, Hank Greenspun's attorney in the real estate case, reflected on the seven-year legal battle:

"It always appeared to me if there had been anybody the least bit rational in the Hughes camp, the matter would have been resolved. But Chester Davis and those guys were so bitter. When they took over, Davis said they were going to bury Hank—*bury* him. Their threats were serious, and they should have known when they took on Hank, they weren't taking on a patsy."

Denton died in 2012. He was eighty-six.

John Meier: *Politics, Paranoia, and the Mining Scam*

John Meier was handed the rare opportunity to join Howard Hughes on the front lines of American history. But Meier's lies and frauds eventually caught up with him. Through a combination of chutzpah and deceit, he was embroiled in everything from a multimillion-dollar scam to the Watergate scandal.

Meier entered the Hughes organization in the mid-1960s when he went to work for Hughes Dynamics, a computer division launched by aide Bill Gay. The ambitious Meier was seen as a rising star. But Gay had created the computer division without Hughes' knowledge and when Hughes learned about it, he shut it down. Trying to help Meier, Gay asked Nevada Operations chief executive Bob Maheu to give him a job. It just so happened that Maheu had what seemed like an appropriate assignment: provide the scientific expertise Hughes needed in his fight against nuclear testing.

Meier embraced the mission, ingratiating himself with anti-nuclear groups around the country, meeting with politicians and government officials in Washington, D.C. and publicizing the dangers of nuclear testing. Maheu warned him not to involve Hughes, whose various defense contracts could be put at risk if he was associated with such organizations.

But before long, Maheu started hearing that Meier wasn't following instructions. Meier apparently had been telling people he was in regular contact with Hughes himself. "During my next conversation with Howard, I told him I wanted to fire Meier, and I told him why," Maheu said in his memoir, *Next to Hughes*. "Howard was adamant that Meier remain on the payroll. He told me that he was 'his man on underground testing,' and that I was never to fire him for any reason."

Meier had a second assignment: spearheading Hughes' interest in buying mining claims across Nevada. Hughes wanted to take advantage of rising gold and silver prices. Meier reported to Hughes (through Maheu) that a big profit could be turned from the venture. He estimated silver, lead, zinc, gold, and copper valued at $150 million could be dug out of Nevada's old mines. "John Meier has estimated the approximate net profit after development would be $50 million," Maheu said in a memo to Hughes.

Hughes excitedly gave Maheu and Meier the green light. Meier spent millions buying old mining claims on the Comstock Lode near Virginia City, in the gold and silver country of Tonopah (where Hughes had secretly married Jean Peters in 1957), and in other parts of the state. He plunked down $750,000 for the Mizpah Mine in Tonopah—the highest figure paid for a single claim. Most of the claims had not been mined in decades. The mysterious mining venture became national news, as reporters and mining experts alike wondered what Hughes was planning.

Asked to assess what Hughes was thinking, some scratched their heads. "Old-timers up here can't figure out what the deal is," Storey County Recorder James Gross said of a Hughes purchase near Virginia City. "There's other property might be more productive he could've gotten."

Another skeptic was Ralph Anctil, district geologist for the Union Pacific Railroad. "I just can't figure out what is going on," he said. "It doesn't make sense and this bothers me. I don't think there is a mining venture possible for the claims Hughes bought. . . . We don't consider most of the Hughes land to be potential mining property."

E.L. "Jack" Cleveland, a veteran miner and consultant to Meier, tried to explain to reporters: "The theory is that a major part of the silver is still there in those mines. We have 400 to 500 percent better methods of mining than they had in the boom days of those mines. The only advantage they had was cheaper labor."

Clarence Hall, another Meier consultant, said Hughes predicted a precious metals shortage in the 1970s that would send gold and silver prices skyrocketing. "It's a cinch that Nevada will become the nation's largest silver-mining state, although it may take years to develop the mines," he said.

Anctil also criticized Hughes for driving up the value of mining claims. "Union Pacific isn't a poor company, but we don't operate by paying for property without exploration," he said. "I personally know one man in Tonopah who was handed $375,000 by a Hughes representative for his property."

Hughes' mining investments generated excitement in rural Nevada communities longing for an economic boost. In Tonopah, where Hughes had purchased the original claims discovered by Jim Butler in 1900, some residents adopted a wait-and-see attitude, while others were confident Hughes would come through.

"I think it will result in a lot of good, solid economic activity here for a long time," J.L. Morrow, manager of Tonopah's First National Bank, told the *Los Angeles Times*. "We've had those three- to four-month booms before. This one I think will last."

Adding to the anticipation, Meier opened a Hughes Tool Company office in Tonopah, set up a mill there, and processed tailings from the nearby Manhattan mining district.

The scam unravels

Meier's house of cards started collapsing in November 1969.

Meier was a friend of President Richard Nixon's brother, Donald. They were involved in some real estate deals together—each profiting from their association with a powerful person. The president's close friend Bebe Rebozo, concerned about potential embarrassment for the president, called Hughes officials and asked them to keep Meier away from Donald Nixon.

Meanwhile, the White House tapped Donald Nixon's phone and had him followed, during which subsequent meetings with Meier were discovered, including trips to Switzerland and the Dominican Republic. When Meier refused to keep his distance from the president's brother, Maheu gave him the option of being fired or resigning. He resigned. The public was told that Meier was leaving to create an environmental foundation.

Meier did start a nonprofit called the Nevada Environmental Foundation. He used a broad brush to describe the foundation's goals. "This foundation will give me the opportunity to use what I have learned as an executive in the Hughes organization to analyze problems as diverse as the regeneration of natural resources to school dropout rates and causes," he said. The foundation gained a degree of clout because Meier was a member of Nixon's Citizens Advisory Committee on Environmental Quality.

But rumors swirled that the foundation was still associated with or funded by Hughes. Forced to publicly deny any link in July 1970, Maheu said, "There is no connection now, nor has there ever been a connection, between the Hughes organization and Mr. Meier's foundation." Also, students at the University of Nevada, Reno, dropped out of an environmental awareness program the foundation set up because they felt Meier was using the organization to advance his political career.

John Meier, pictured in 1973, was in charge of two projects for Hughes: buying mining claims and fighting nuclear testing. Author's collection.

After Meier resigned, Maheu assigned former FBI agent Dean Elson to investigate what Meier had been up to with the mining claims. Elson found serious discrepancies. "It proved to be the first snowflake of an avalanche that would hit me full force in time," Maheu wrote in *Next to Hughes*.

It eventually became clear that Meier had masterminded an intricate conspiracy in which he and several associates profited handsomely from selling the near-worthless mining claims to Hughes at inflated prices (Hughes paid out a total of $20 million for mining claims). Hughes' Summa Corporation sued Meier in 1972, alleging he had embezzled $8 million. Six years later, Summa won a $7.9 million judgment. But Summa never collected, as Meier had fled to British Columbia in 1972.

Bob Perchetti, a Tonopah native who operated a motel there, said the old mines Meier bought around Tonopah weren't all worthless, but would have been difficult to reopen. "There is good silver in those mines, but it's very, very deep," Perchetti said. "They would have had to dig 1,200 to 1,800 feet deep to find anything worthwhile."

In 1973, Meier was indicted on tax evasion charges. Prosecutors alleged he did not pay taxes on $2.5 million in income, much of it generated by the mining scam. Meier was arrested in Point Roberts, Washington, as he crossed the border into the United States, but he posted $100,000 bail and was allowed to return to his home in Canada. Meier did not appear for trial in Reno, his bail was forfeited, and a warrant was issued for his arrest. But since tax evasion is not an extraditable offense, he could not be jailed as long as he remained in Canada.

The house that Hughes bought

Howard Hughes' mining venture changed Frank Lewis' life. In the 1960s, Lewis was buying a lot of abandoned mining properties in Nevada. "I wasn't paying much for them, because nobody wanted them," he said. Almost no mining exploration was being done in the state at the time. "The gold price had been fixed since 1934, but the cost of everything else had gone up," Lewis explained. As a result, the prospectors had all flocked to South America.

Lewis sold some of his mining properties, mostly to hobbyists, and made a modest living doing it. But when he read newspaper articles about Hughes buying mining claims, he saw an opportunity. He put together a detailed package outlining all his mineral holdings and sent it to Hughes in care of the Desert Inn. "My letter came back with 'No such person at this address,'" Lewis said. "It was unopened."

Discouraged but determined, Lewis sent the package to the Hughes Tool Company in Houston. A Hughes Tool executive sent him a nice letter, but said the company wasn't interested.

"About two weeks later, a Nevada state mine inspector, Felix Traynor, who lived in Tonopah, called me on the phone and he wanted to take an option for thirty days on property I had in the Fairview District, east of Fallon," Lewis said. "I gave him a thirty-day option. In about a week or ten days, here came a letter in the mail saying my option had been assigned to the Hughes company, and they were going to pay cash."

Lewis hesitated. "I felt it was a fraudulent deal because they had not asked for any information on the property. They hadn't asked for any assays, no maps. I didn't want to do it, because I thought somebody was cheating Mr. Hughes and I didn't want anything to do with it." He called his attorney and told him about his misgivings. "He said, 'Wait a minute, if they have that option, you can't get out of it. They can sue you and charge you damages.' I said, well, okay."

The terms of the sale also raised red flags for Lewis. Hughes would pay about five times what Lewis thought the mining properties were worth. "You can see why I was suspicious," he said. "It didn't make sense." Because of his concerns, Lewis insisted that during escrow, every person involved, including Hughes, had to be notified of the sale terms. "At least I had done my duty as best I could."

So, the deal went through, and Lewis received the cash: $90,000 for twenty-two patented, deeded mining claims, plus twenty to thirty unpatented claims. Lewis promptly bought a big house in an exclusive neighborhood in Reno. It was a larger and nicer place than Lewis ever dreamed he could live in—until Hughes came along.

A few years later, federal investigators contacted Lewis. "I called my attorney," he recalled. "I was scared, you know? It was all over the newspapers. I knew my first instinct was true, that somebody was ripping off Hughes. I didn't know who, but I'd heard a lot of stories. They asked me who I'd paid off. I said I never kicked back any money to anybody. I showed them the books."

Lewis was not tainted by the investigation or the subsequent indictment of Meier. He lived in his Reno mansion for thirty-five years. Phillips Petroleum eventually acquired the claims he sold to Hughes, but later the U.S. Navy took possession of much of the Fairview mining district for use as a bombing range.

Victim of bad advice

Howard Hughes was known for hiring the best and brightest people in a particular field to help him with a project. This was best exemplified by his achievements in aviation. While Hughes was a tremendously important player in those triumphs, he had great people by his side the entire time.

Imagine, then, what might have happened if Hughes had hired the best and brightest to head up his Nevada mining venture. For example, what if he had hired John Livermore?

Livermore is a legend in the gold-prospecting field. In 1961, the Reno geologist discovered the Carlin Trend. Situated in northeastern Nevada, it's the source of more than thirty-five percent of all gold output in the United States. But unlike his nineteenth century predecessors, Livermore didn't just happen upon a rich ore vein. On the Carlin Trend, he identified "invisible gold"—microscopic gold that does not accumulate in rich veins. His discovery heralded an open-pit mining boom in Northern Nevada that continues to this day.

In a 2007 interview, Livermore remembered the days when Hughes was buying up old mining claims. Most of the claims were "pretty worthless," he said. But if Hughes had hired the right people, he just might have hit paydirt. In the '70s—just after Hughes left Las Vegas and abandoned the mining venture— there were several big gold discoveries in Nevada. Livermore found a new ore body about twenty miles north of Winnemucca in 1971. Hughes' "idea wasn't wrong," Livermore said, "he just didn't have the right people advising him."

And while buying old mines seemed to make little sense in the late '60s, it's a growing trend in the twenty-first century as the price of gold increased dramatically. "We're going back and looking at a lot of those old mines," Livermore said. "They keep going deeper and they find that this ore is good enough grade that they can mine it. At these prices it's profitable."

Livermore died in 2013. He was ninety-four.

Meanwhile, back in Tonopah . . .

When Hughes Tool Company opened its mining office in Tonopah, it hired Wally Boundy to do surveying work. Boundy grew up around the mining business in Ely, where his father worked as a millwright. He was White Pine

County's surveyor when he landed the job with Hughes. "It was kind of an opportunity for me, because everything was pretty slow where I was in Ely at the time," Boundy recalled.

Boundy traveled around the state surveying the thousands of claims Hughes had purchased. "They mostly bought old patented mines no longer in production," he said.

Hughes' buying spree generated substantial interest in Tonopah, but Boundy said there were skeptics. "A lot of people didn't really imagine a real big thing happening at the time." One reason, he said, was that Hughes' people "hadn't really been in the mining game."

Boundy noted that in addition to buying claims, Hughes Tool (later Summa Corporation) did some actual mine work. The company hauled ore from a mine in the Manhattan mining district, north of Tonopah, and put it through a refining process to make gold bars. "They made probably in the neighborhood of fifty gold bars," Boundy said, describing the bars as about five inches long and two inches square. "It was kind of a big experiment to them, I think."

No mining was done in Tonopah, where lower-valued silver was the dominant precious metal. "They'd taken a lot of samples of old tailings here thinking the price of silver would warrant [a new operation]," Boundy said. "But it just wasn't a profitable situation. There's still silver, probably a lot of it, but it's so far underground that it's just not feasible."

Boundy said he didn't recall meeting John Meier or the other men later accused of bilking Hughes. He said he didn't give it much thought at the time. "I kind of thought it was a funny deal. I was thinking, well, it would never last."

It didn't. But Summa did keep its Tonopah mining office going until after Hughes died in 1976. Boundy went on to become the Nye County surveyor and did independent surveying work. His office? The old Hughes Tool building. "He done some good in Tonopah," Boundy said of Hughes. "He put some people to work."

Summa Corporation eventually sold its Tonopah claims to Houston Minerals, which sold them to Tenneco. Echo Bay Mining bought out Tenneco, and then, in 1992, donated seventy acres of the claims to the town of Tonopah for a mining museum. The Tonopah Historic Mining Park opened in 1998. Yearly visitors to the park grew from 600 in 1999 to more than 7,000 in 2006. It is consistently voted one of rural Nevada's best museums.

One of the museum's biggest early supporters was John Livermore.

Meier's space odyssey

Meier's story might have ended with a quiet retirement in British Columbia, but he returned to the public stage numerous times.

In 1973, Meier played a bit part in the Watergate saga. Meier told Watergate investigators that he witnessed Hughes emissaries deliver $100,000 in cash to Nixon's close friend Bebe Rebozo. Meier said the money was intended to be a campaign contribution. Rebozo supposedly kept the cash in a safe in Florida for three years and ended up returning it to Hughes amid public scrutiny of the president's campaign activities.

Meier also told Watergate investigators that Hughes had close ties to the Central Intelligence Agency, primarily through Maheu. He claimed CIA agents were allowed to pass into foreign countries under the guise of working for Hughes.

Throughout the '70s, Meier maintained his innocence and contended that Hughes, the CIA, and President Nixon orchestrated his downfall. In 1975, the *Las Vegas Sun* published a seven-part series about Meier called "Invisible Government." An editor's note preceding the first part of the series described it as "a detailed description of how one man stood almost alone for six years against the Howard Hughes empire, CIA and a president, claiming his only crime was that he worked himself to the top of the Hughes empire and then quit with too much knowledge of the operation to be left alone."

Canadian journalist Gerald Bellett eschewed journalistic objectivity in summarizing his story: "Meier has been run out of the country, his reputation is in tatters, he's been branded an embezzler and a thief, and he's wanted for income tax evasion. Right now he is living in Canada with his family, a wanted man, a fugitive from justice."

Bellett related dramatic tales of agents for Intertel, the investigation agency closely associated with Hughes, ambushing Meier; efforts by Hughes and the White House to sabotage his campaign for a New Mexico U.S. Senate seat; and the CIA crossing the border to investigate him without alerting the Canadian government.

The articles described Meier as living "under a self-imposed house arrest" in the Vancouver suburb of Delta. "Afraid to go out at night, he will rarely if ever leave the house alone in broad daylight," Bellett wrote.

In 1978, Meier turned up in the Polynesian kingdom of Tonga, where he started a bank and planned to work on the expansion of the island's airport. But just a few months later, the king of Tonga told Meier he was no longer welcome and he returned to Canada.

A year later, Meier was deported by Canada to face trial in Salt Lake City on obstruction of justice charges. Federal prosecutors alleged that after Hughes died in 1976, Meier dispatched an accountant to Mexico to obtain copies of Hughes' files, which police had seized after Hughes died on a plane en route from Acapulco to Houston. Prosecutors said Meier forged Hughes' signature on documents to be used in his defense in his civil case with Summa. The documents said Meier was making mining claim purchases on direct orders from Hughes. Meier was convicted of the charge and sentenced to two and a half years in prison.

At the sentencing, Meier revealed his belief that Hughes did not die in Mexico in 1976, but seven years earlier. Meier claimed Summa Corporation officials were persecuting him for trying to prove this claim.

Meier's roller coaster did not end there. Just one day after being released from prison in 1981, he was indicted in Los Angeles on charges of conspiracy to commit murder. Meier and Gordon Hazelwood were accused of hiring William McCrory to kill a business partner, Alfred Wayne Netter, in 1974. Prosecutors alleged that Netter was stabbed to death at a Beverly Hills, California hotel to collect on a $400,000 "key man" life insurance policy. Hazelwood's company was the beneficiary. Denying any involvement in the killing, Meier said it was yet another case of powerful forces determined to destroy him.

After repeated delays in the case, in 1986 Meier pleaded no contest to a charge of being an "accessory after the fact to murder by harboring a suspect." Meier said he pleaded not because he was guilty, but "because it was the only way to just end this case." Meier was sentenced to two years in prison, but received credit for the three years he had already spent in custody. Hazelwood was granted immunity from prosecution and testified at Meier's preliminary hearing.

Although Meier always blamed outside forces for his troubles, it's clear from the record that he was more than capable of making his own trouble. In addition, as time passed, Meier's fertile imagination began to run wild. He even topped his claim that Hughes had died in 1969. In 1995, Bellett, the Canadian journalist who wrote sympathetically about Meier in the '70s, authored a book called *Age of Secrets: The Conspiracy That Toppled Richard Nixon and the Hidden Death of Howard Hughes*. The book's showstopper: Meier's claim that in 1976 he traveled to a secret location off the coast of Cuba, past armed patrols, and saw a cryogenic chamber containing Hughes' frozen corpse.

Finally, in 2005, retired FBI agent Gary Magnesen interviewed Meier for his book investigating Melvin Dummar's claim that in 1967 he picked up Hughes in rural Nevada and drove him to Las Vegas. Confirming Dummar's story, Meier told Magnesen, "Howard Hughes was with me and others in the Tonopah area. We were looking at mines. He went out on his own and got lost."

The fact that numerous reputable sources have disputed Dummar's—and Meier's—story probably doesn't matter a whole lot to someone who believes Hughes is resting comfortably in a cryogenic chamber.

Channel 8: *Hughes' Movie Source*

One bit of conventional wisdom about Howard Hughes is that while he bought casinos, airports, and thousands of acres of land in Las Vegas, he didn't really build anything there. But there's one big exception: the KLAS Channel 8 television station. After buying the station, Hughes made major improvements that boosted the CBS affiliate at a critical time in its history.

Las Vegas Sun publisher Hank Greenspun and seventeen partners founded KLAS and began broadcasting at 7:05 p.m. on July 22, 1953. Governor Charles Russell pulled the switch that put Nevada's first television station on the air.

Greenspun sold the CBS affiliate to Hughes on March 28, 1968, for $3.6 million. Channel 8 caught Hughes' interest not because he saw an opportunity to make a bundle of money, but because he wanted to control the late-night movie schedule. As a chronic insomniac living in his Desert Inn suite with the windows blacked out, Hughes often was awake at night and would watch movies for hours.

An oft-repeated story is that Hughes became annoyed that Channel 8 would sign off when he was ready to watch more movies. He repeatedly complained to Greenspun, who told the authors of *Empire*: "The man wanted the station open all night long, and he wanted certain pictures to be shown. Every night it was a call at my home like that. If Mr. [Bob] Maheu wasn't calling me to put a certain picture on, then Mr. [Dick] Gray was asking me to do it."

Finally, Greenspun told a Hughes executive that if Hughes wanted to control the late-night schedule, he would have to buy the station. Which he did. Hughes retained Washington, D.C., attorney Edward P. Morgan, who also was an old friend of Greenspun, to grease the wheels of the Federal Communications

Commission. Hughes was able to avoid making a personal appearance before the commission to obtain a license by having one of his top execs, Raymond Holliday, technically serve as the party responsible for the station.

While it was no secret that Hughes would call the shots, his primary goal was to keep the movies going all night, as well as dictate which ones would be shown.

Mark Smith, Channel 8's general manager at the time, said in a 2007 interview that the popular story about Hughes buying the station is partly in error. At least six months before Hughes bought the station, Smith said he was already running movies through the night. The reason? "Greenspun wouldn't spring for a new transmitter," Smith said, "and I couldn't turn the damn thing off, because if I did, it wouldn't come back on again."

After Hughes bought the station, one of the billionaire's top aides, Nadine Henley, helped Smith purchase new transmission facilities—at a cost of about $100,000. A two-hundred-foot-high tower was erected atop Black Mountain, south of Las Vegas, improving reception across the valley.

"It was a big event," recalled Bob Stoldal, who was a KLAS reporter at the time and later served as the station's vice president in charge of news. "It gave us a much clearer signal." But Stoldal said the investment had a more important effect: "It was really a signal from Howard Hughes that he was involved with the station, that we weren't just another landscape that he purchased. It meant a lot to the people at the station that we were part of his future."

Smith said it's true that when Hughes bought the station, his primary interest was selecting the late-night movies. Every day, Smith's staff would prepare a list of the movies the station had available to air that night. A runner would deliver the list to Hughes at the Desert Inn. Hughes would peruse the list and select the three he wanted to see—back to back, with no commercial interruptions.

At times, Channel 8's late-night schedule in the late 1960s, dubbed the "Swinging Shift," must have left viewers scratching their heads. Hughes was a fan of Westerns and airplane pictures, as well as movies he had produced or directed, Smith said. And if he fell asleep in the middle of a movie, he sometimes would order the station to start the movie over. "People who were watching at night must have thought we were crazy."

Hughes occasionally tried to meddle in the station's affairs. For example, Smith recalled that one early morning, when the station planned to cover a live NASA landing, Hughes wanted a movie shown instead. "We didn't listen to him all the time."

The best way to counter Hughes was to mention the FCC. "I always had a fall-back," Smith said. "I would go to Ray Holliday and tell him, if he does this kind of

Mark Smith managed KLAS Channel 8 during the time when Hughes picked the late-night movies. Author's collection.

thing, we'll risk our license. The FCC was the only thing I ever had to block him, because if you let him run rampant like that, you really risk losing your license."

In *Citizen Hughes*, based on a large cache of Hughes' handwritten memos from his Las Vegas years, author Michael Drosnin cited numerous instances of Hughes instructing the station's managers. In one memo, he complained—and rightly so—about the volume of commercials:

"I am fully aware of the pressure from advertisers to keep the volume of their commercials up in order to blast through the many viewers who use their remote control to squelch the commercial. However, for every one viewer who squelches the volume at every commercial, there are ten or maybe fifty who do not carry the remoter around in their pocket and who are not so trigger-quick as to be able to squelch out a commercial like the Dunes that pops in with a blast that almost shatters the nerves."

Knowing enough about filmmaking and electronics to be dangerous, Hughes also complained about picture quality. "For the last three days, approximately, the transmission has been technically deficient in a manner that has resulted in the screen being periodically darker than any normal value," Hughes wrote. "So dark in fact, that, in the Bette Davis film 'Stolen Life,' and in the RKO film 'Half Breed,' the screen was almost black throughout its entire area for long periods of time."

Hughes saw these lapses as a black mark on his reputation, considering his ownership of Hughes Aircraft Company. "I suggest you tell the station manager that the ownership of the station is publicly known to rest with the Hughes Tool Company, and that the Hughes Tool Company is known to have available to it the assistance of the Hughes Aircraft Company, probably the foremost organization engaged in advanced electronics in the entire world." If Channel 8 engineers couldn't fix the problem, Hughes suggested, he would dispatch a Hughes Aircraft team from California and "damn well have this station operating satisfactorily."

Hughes nitpicked all sorts of decisions by station managers, from which ads to accept to which shows to air. But he reserved most of his attention for the late-night movies. Because he made last-minute decisions on which movies to show, the "Swinging Shift" lineup could not be published in newspapers or TV guides. And at times the lists of movies Hughes received from the station failed to deliver anything he wanted to see. "There are simply no pictures on this list that I consider satisfactory," Hughes wrote. "I am familiar with every one of these movies—I even made quite a few of them—and there are not enough to fill out the package of three needed for tonight."

Hughes also took issue with some of Channel 8's daytime programming. He was particularly incensed by programs about African Americans, especially a morning program called *Black Heritage*. In a memo quoted in *Citizen Hughes*, Hughes wrote, "Isn't there any safe way to get rid of this TV academic program on *Black Heritage* which CBS is carrying every morning? As you know, this program was commenced without my permission. Since then I have been forced to squirm under the intense displeasure of watching this program every morning—I have to watch and listen every morning while the only academic program on KLAS pours out such propaganda as: 'Africa is the mother and the father of the world.'"

It turned out Hughes did not have to cancel *Black Heritage*. The NAACP voiced objections to the show as well, and it was canceled two months later without Hughes' involvement.

(This was not the first time Hughes revealed his racial bias. In the late 1950s, he kept a screening room at Goldwyn Studios. He frequently would watch movies there. When Hughes learned that *Porgy and Bess*, a 1959 film featuring an all-black cast, had been made on the Goldwyn lot, he complained and never returned to the Goldwyn screening room.)

Smith pulled no punches when describing Hughes: "The guy was insane. I always said, if anyone would get me out of the television business, it would be Hughes, because he'd just drive you nuts if you let him." Smith's troubles ended when Hughes left town in 1970. "I breathed a sigh of relief and got a full night's sleep."

In terms of the news, Stoldal doesn't remember Hughes trying to censor or direct Channel 8's coverage. "There were never—zero—times that Hughes or one of his aides came down and said we would like the story done this way," Stoldal said. "I always felt comfortable talking to the Hughes people, that they understood that the news department was separate from the corporate."

One thing Hughes *would* do is ask the news department to provide him with more information about stories he saw. "I'd get these calls from one of

Bob Stoldal was a reporter at KLAS Channel 8 when Hughes owned the station in the late 1960s. Courtesy of *Las Vegas Review-Journal* Archive.

his aides requesting more information," Stoldal said. "Mr. Hughes would like more information about this story or that story. It could be anything, such as stories about atomic energy."

Working for Channel 8 at that time was a unique experience in television. "We always felt that Hughes was watching us," Stoldal said. "That was always intriguing. There was something special about this billionaire looking down and watching everything we did."

Fortunately for Channel 8, Hughes' departure from Las Vegas did not mean the station was neglected. On the contrary, Hughes made a second major investment in the station in the form of a state-of-the-art $2 million broadcast center. Ground was broken in 1975 for the 31,000-square-foot facility, and employees moved in the following year.

The location, just off Desert Inn Road east of the Strip, is adjacent to a small house that Hughes occupied in 1953-54 and kept sealed until his death. The so-called Green House still stands today, and Channel 8 uses it occasionally for meetings and receptions.

Stoldal said when Hughes was in Las Vegas, it was an exciting place to be a working journalist. "He was a newsmaker, and the town was excited about that," he said. "From a news standpoint, it was just one major story after another."

After Hughes' death and the settlement of his estate, Summa Corporation gradually liquidated many of its holdings, including KLAS. Landmark Communications purchased the station in 1978. Landmark owned Channel 8 until 2015, when NextStar Broadcasting acquired it for $145 million. Channel 8 still operates out of the same building, since expanded, that Hughes built.

While in Las Vegas, Hughes' media interests extended far beyond Channel 8. He wanted to own all the television stations, radio stations, and newspapers in Nevada. But his expansive plans were unsuccessful. For one thing, Donald Reynolds, who owned the *Las Vegas Review-Journal*, *Nevada Appeal* in Carson City, and *Ely Times*, didn't want to sell.

Hughes also coveted a much bigger media property: the ABC television network, then a distant third among the big three networks. But in this case,

Hughes wasn't interested in choosing the late-night movies. He wanted a bigger voice in national politics.

His surprise 1968 bid met stiff opposition from ABC's board of directors, which sued to block his hostile takeover. A judge rejected ABC's motion and ruled that Hughes could proceed, but then the Justice Department piped up, suggesting there could be antitrust implications from Hughes' bid. Furthermore, the FCC announced that if Hughes wanted to own the network, he would have to make a public appearance to be licensed. That was the deal-killer. Hughes bailed out. He was willing to spend $150 million to control ABC, but appearing before the FCC was out of the question.

Despite the anguish associated with the failed ABC bid, Hughes continued to explore ways to expand his media empire. He purchased Sports Network Incorporated, which syndicated live and taped sports events, and renamed it the Hughes Television Network. But HTN never developed into Hughes' vision for a fourth national network to compete with ABC, NBC, and CBS.

All things considered, Hughes would not have been a happy network owner anyway. He couldn't stand most of the programming. After watching episodes of *The Dating Game* and *The Newlywed Game*, Hughes dashed off a memo to Maheu: "I just got through watching ABC's 'Dating Game' and 'Newlywed Game' and my only reaction is let's forget all about ABC." Hughes was particularly bothered that a black male contestant had selected a "very beautiful and attractive white girl" to accompany him for an all-expenses-paid trip to Rome. Hughes didn't realize that the "very beautiful and attractive white girl" was in fact a light-skinned African American.

Part 3:

After Death

Melvin Dummar: *Good Samaritan or Teller of Tales?*

It was 2007, and Melvin Dummar sat in a chair behind a small table in his room at the Clown Motel in Tonopah, Nevada. He stayed at the motel—eerily decorated with thousands of clown dolls, statues, and pictures—every three weeks or so. It was owned by longtime Tonopah businessman Bob Perchetti, who gave living folk heroes like Dummar a special rate: twenty-five dollars a night.

Dummar, who lived in Brigham City, Utah, traveled through rural Utah and Nevada selling frozen meat. He drove a pickup truck with freezers strapped into the bed. When he stopped at night, he would run an extension cord out to the truck to keep the freezers humming. The brochure for Dummar's Premium Food lists an array of steaks, pork products, seafood, chicken, and pies.

Sitting in the dimly lighted motel room, Dummar was an older, bulkier, and more weathered version of the gregarious young man people remember seeing on TV in the late 1970s. His hair was receding and his forehead was deeply creased. His belly hung over his blue jeans. His eyes, once sparkling with endless good humor, reflected decades of emotional wear and tear. Yet Dummar was not sullen. He smiled easily and was quick to laughter. But it also didn't take much to make him cry.

Dummar was asked to tell his story of picking up Howard Hughes in the Nevada desert almost forty years earlier. He didn't seem to mind telling the tale for the thousandth time.

"I'd split up from my wife, my ex-wife Linda, and come to Nevada in late December of '67," Dummar said. "I was over in Gabbs and I wrecked a motorcycle and went to the hospital in Hawthorne. After I got out of the hospital, Basic Incorporated, the mine in Gabbs where I was working, told me to take a week or two off to let myself heal up. So, since I was chasing after my ex-wife all the time, I decided to go to California and see if I couldn't find her. I left Gabbs that day, came through Tonopah and cashed my check at the Mizpah [Hotel]. I stayed there for a little while. I used to like to play cards, 21. I remember that night I didn't really win anything, didn't lose anything. I think I was there for two or three hours or so and broke even and thought I better get out of here. After I left there, I was gonna drive down through Las Vegas and then on to Southern California. I just passed the Cottontail Ranch, which takes forty-five minutes or an hour from here to drive there, and I passed it a few miles."

Dummar explained that he had recently returned to the location where he said he picked up Hughes and it's actually about seven miles south of the Cottontail. The brothel, now gone, was about one hundred and fifty miles north of Las Vegas at a highway intersection called Lida Junction.

"I had to stop and relieve myself, and so I just slowed way down and I seen a little dirt road taking off to the right. So I said well, I'll just pull up this road a little ways so I'm not right on the highway. I drove up the road, I don't know, maybe two or three hundred yards. It wasn't too far. And what I noticed was a guy, a body, just laying in one of the ruts of the dirt road. At first I thought I'd found a dead person because he was just laying there. I stopped, and I was contemplating what I should do. I was thinking about, well, I better go back to Goldfield or didn't even know how far I was from Beatty. I was contemplating where I should go because I was going to go get the sheriff or somebody and come back and show 'em this body, you know, show 'em where it was at. And I wasn't there very long, probably just a few seconds, and then I seen him moving. I thought, well, whoever this person is, at least they're not dead. So I was relieved.

"I got out of the car, and I went over and helped him up. The headlights and everything was on him. He had blood and stuff on his face, looked like on his shoulder and stuff. I thought he was hurt. I didn't know how bad, but I helped him up to his feet, and then I kind of halfway carried him over to the car and put him in the car and asked him if I could take him to a doctor or a hospital or if I should just take him to the police. And the only thing I could get out of him was, 'No.' You know, everything I'd ask him, he'd just say, 'No.'

"I said, 'Well, I can't leave you here. You're going to die, you're going to freeze to death,' you know. 'Cause he didn't have a coat on. He just had a shirt and these baggy old pants. . . . I said, 'Well, I got to take you to town or somewhere, You can't lay out here. You about froze to death already.' And so he just asked me if I could take him to Las Vegas. I said, 'Well, yeah, I'm going that way anyway. I'm going to go through there, so I'll drop you off in Vegas.'"

Melvin Dummar, pictured at the Clown Motel in Tonopah, Nevada, in 2007, always stood by his story of picking up Hughes in the desert and driving him to Las Vegas. Author's collection.

Dummar described what the old man looked like. "He had blood on his left side—the side facing me when I was in my car. I thought he was bleeding out of his ear. . . . He had kind of long hair. His hair wasn't super-long, but it was shoulder-length hair. He had a beard, not a real long beard. It looked kind of scraggly too."

In the movie *Melvin and Howard*, Dummar is depicted driving a truck, but in fact, he says, he had a 1966 Chevrolet Caprice, "two-door, blue in color. California license plate JFK 007."

"I put him in the front seat and he just kind of hunched over and was just shaking, just trembling. I didn't know whether it was just because he was so cold or he was afraid of me or whatever. At the time I picked him up, my face was just one big scab from the motorcycle wreck. I probably scared him as much as I was scared he was gonna die.

"I drove him on down to Las Vegas. But he kept asking me, it seemed like the same thing over and over again. That was after a while. At first he didn't say hardly anything, probably the first hour or so. After we'd got past Beatty and we were going on down toward Indian Springs, he kind of stopped shaking so much and then he started asking me who I was and where I was from and what I was doing and where I was going and just all kinds of questions. So I told him that I worked in the mine. I remember telling him that I hadn't been up here very long because I'd been in the Air Force and I loved flying and I told him when I got out of the Air Force I'd tried to get a job in the aircraft industry, and that I was down in California and I'd went around to Douglas Aircraft and Hughes Aircraft, there in Fullerton. And when I mentioned Hughes Aircraft, that's when he told me he was familiar with it. And then he went on to elaborate and said that he owned it and he was Howard Hughes. And I thought, aw, c'mon. I thought he was a bum. I thought he was just a wino or a bum, like you'd find on skid row somewhere. I don't remember saying anything to offend him like I do in the movie. In the movie they have Paul Le Mat telling him, 'Well, I believe anybody can call themselves anything they want.' But I didn't say anything like that.

"We got there to Vegas and I asked him where he wanted to go, and he told me he wanted to go to the Sands Hotel. Then Las Vegas Boulevard, you could just pull right off the Strip and drive into the parking lot and everything. I remember I drove in the parking lot and he acted like he was scared, like he was scared to death. He was telling me, 'No, no, no, you want to go around back.' He didn't want to be close to the building or anything. I said okay, so I drove him around to the back there. It seemed like there was some kind of a parking structure, like carports. He told me drop him off there, and just when I was stopping there, he asked if I had any money and that's what kind of gave me the impression he was a bum. I gave him some change, and he thanked me and got out of the car. And as soon as he got away from the car, I left and never seen him again. I just drove off, and I don't know where he went or anything."

The old man never told Dummar how he ended up on a dirt road in the middle of nowhere. "I don't think he mentioned how he got there or what he was doing. I really don't know. . . . My impression of where he was and the condition he was in, I have always felt that somebody took him there and dumped him. I've always been under the impression that somebody dumped him and thought nobody'd ever find his body or something. Maybe left him for dead. . . . It appeared to me that somebody had hit him upside the head. But I don't know if that was the case."

Dummar estimated he picked up Hughes about midnight. "Got to Vegas around three o'clock in the morning. It was only about eight or eight-thirty when I got down to my in-laws' place in Cypress, California, and it takes about five hours to get there from Vegas." When he arrived, he said he told his father-in-law, Wayne Sisk, about picking up the old man in the desert. "I told him, 'Hey, guess who I picked up on the way down here? The old guy said he was Howard Hughes.' And Wayne, his comment was, 'Well, why in the hell didn't you take a picture of him? Nobody's seen him in fifteen years.' He kind of harassed me a little bit, but that was his first comment."

This is the first chapter of Dummar's famous story. It's simple and easy to digest. The second chapter is more difficult to comprehend. In 1973, Dummar married his second wife, Bonnie, and a year later they moved to Willard, Utah, where he leased a gas station. "When Hughes died in '76, I was working the station, and under the G.I. Bill I was going to Weber State College. I guess about two weeks after he died, LeVane Forsythe—I didn't know who he was at the time—he come in the station there and started asking me all kinds of questions about Hughes and if I'd ever met him and what I thought about him dying and all that, and I hadn't seen him before so I didn't know really what to make of it. But everybody was talking about him [Hughes]. He asked me if I'd ever met him and stuff. I said, 'Well, I picked up some guy one time who said he was Howard Hughes, but I don't know if it was him or not.

"He was there for a while. I was in the station and he followed me around in the station and I thought he was actually a little weird for a minute or two there. But then . . . another customer came into the station and I remember telling him if he could excuse me, because I had full service, so I went out and was pumping some gas for—I remember it was a girl. I put some gas in her car and wash her windows and check the oil. I used to do all that crap. And when I came back in the station, this Forsythe was gone. I didn't even see him leave. I didn't know where he went or what he was driving or anything. I've seen reports that said he was driving a blue Mercedes and all that, but I don't know where they came up with that. I don't remember ever telling anybody that. Because I didn't see him leave.

"After the lady left and everything, what I was doing, I was studying for one of the classes that I had up at Weber State. I had the books open and stuff. When I went back to the books, there was this envelope sitting right on my books. It said, 'Dear Mr. McKay, please see that this will is delivered after my death to the Clark County Courthouse.' It was signed 'Howard R. Hughes.' I picked it up and said, what kind of joke is this? Then I kind of looked around and I said, where did this guy go? But he'd gone. We had a bell if they ran across in front of the pumps. But he walked in. He didn't run across the bell."

Inside the envelope Dummar found a handwritten "last will and testament" signed by "Howard R. Hughes." The will left one-sixteenth of the billionaire's estate—later estimated to total $156 million—to "Melvin Du Mar of Gabbs, Nevada."

"I looked at this envelope. At first I thought, why is this here? Why did this guy leave this here? Because I knew it had to have been him. I was curious, you know, and I shouldn't have but I had to see what this is all about. I had a frying pan there and turned it way up and got it hot and steamed the envelope open. It wasn't addressed to me but I wanted to see what it was all about. I opened it and read it, then it just scared the living daylights out of me. I think it was being more confused than anything. I didn't know why it was left with me in the first place, or who the guy was. I couldn't answer any of those questions. I'm thinking, oh my God, what am I going to do with this? It was like somebody handing you a hot potato, and it started scaring me. I didn't know if it was somebody's idea of a joke or if it was real. What am I going to do? I read it several times, and David O. McKay I knew was president of the church but

I didn't think he was still the president of the church at the time. At that time I'm Mormon but not real active. Because it was addressed to David O. McKay, I thought, well, maybe that's where I should take it, take it to church and give it to the president of the church, because that's who it was addressed to.

"I went to Salt Lake, and I didn't know where to find the president of the church. I knew where the visitors center was, the temple. I went in there, and one of the guys working in the visitors center kind of cornered me and wanted to tell me the whole history of the Mormon Church. I kept asking him, must have asked him a dozen times, I've heard this before. All I want to know is where I can find the president of the church. I have something important. I want to find the president of the church! The guy just kept telling me about Joseph Smith and Brigham Young and finally I just, I don't know if I was rude to him, I said all I want to do is know who the acting president is and where I can find him. Then the guy finally, it hit him and he says, 'Oh, that's right next door. See that big tall building over there?' I think we went outside and he pointed and said that's the world headquarters of the church. I didn't know.

"So I went over there and went in and asked. They had security guards there, and I asked where I could find the president of the church and I think they said his office is on the twenty-fifth floor. I went and got on the elevator and some lady got on the elevator with me and I asked her, too, where is the president at, [and she said] on the twenty-fifth floor. She got off somewhere around the twentieth floor and I went on up to the twenty-fifth floor, got off the elevator and as soon as I got off, there was a security guy there and a secretary at a desk. I went over and asked them if I could see the president of the church. They started telling me no, he was in a meeting, that I had to bring my bishop and I had to make an appointment and I had to, I can't even remember it all, they had a list of things I had to do. I just couldn't walk off the street. So what am I going to do, you know?

"When I was at the visitor center, the guy there, he asked me if I wanted some souvenirs or anything about the church, so basically all I took was an envelope, church stationery, that this guy who was there gave to me. I put the will, I had to fold it because that envelope was bigger than the church envelope. In the movie I think they've got me stuffing it in a big manila envelope, but it wasn't the case. It was a smaller envelope like you put a letter in. I put it in it and I found out that Spencer Kimball was the president and I just put Spencer Kimball on there and just left it on the desk and walked out. But I didn't try to hide it or anything. I just laid it on the desk. Right in the middle of the desk."

It didn't take long for the will to hit the news.

"I went into Ogden, and I heard it on the radio about Howard Hughes' will being found in the Mormon Church headquarters," Dummar said. "And that some mysterious woman had delivered it there. I don't know where they came up with that. I thought, if they think a woman delivered it, I really didn't want any part of it."

Initially, Dummar didn't tell anyone, even his wife, that the will had been left at his gas station or that he had delivered it to the church headquarters. But after his fingerprints were found on the envelope, he admitted he had lied about that part of his story. "I think the reason was, there were so many unanswered questions. I didn't know why it was brought to me. I thought it was somebody's idea of a joke. I was scared to death. If they think some woman delivered it, I'm just going to go along with it."

In the meantime, the news media caught Melvin Dummar fever.

"The day after I heard it on the radio, I was going back to the station and the phone rang for a week after that. You couldn't even hang it up, and it would be ringing again. Reporters and people wanting money and long-lost friends, supposedly, and just everybody. The letters started pouring in from around the world. It turned into a nightmare."

Mormon Will case

The discovery of what came to be known as the Mormon Will on April 27, 1976, just a few weeks after Hughes' death, generated a firestorm of news coverage and legal activity. The will, handwritten and containing numerous spelling errors, described how Hughes' estate should be divided upon his death, including one-fourth of his assets going to the Howard Hughes Medical Institute in Florida, one-eighth divided among three universities, one-sixteenth to the Mormon Church, and one-sixteenth to the Boy Scouts. The document, dated March 19, 1968, also mentioned one-sixteenth going to "Melvin Du Mar of Gabbs, Nevada."

At first glance, the will appeared to be an obvious fake. The most telling sign was the mention of the "spruce goose," the famous giant wooden airplane that Hughes built in the 1940s. Hughes called his flying boat the H-4 or *Hercules*, not the "spruce goose," a derogatory nickname concocted by the press. Also, Hughes didn't actually own the airplane at that time; the U.S. government owned it. The will also stated that one-sixteenth of the estate should go to "William Loomis." Hughes surely knew the correct spelling of his cousin's last name was Lummis. Adding further doubt to the will's authenticity, it listed Noah Dietrich as the executor. Hughes had fired Dietrich, his longtime top executive, in 1957.

Melvin Dummar answers questions from reporters during the Mormon Will case in 1977. Courtesy of *Las Vegas Review-Journal* Archive.

Despite these glaring problems, the court took the Mormon Will seriously enough to hold a trial. Lawyers representing an array of interests, from Hughes' heirs on one side to the universities standing to benefit on the other, converged on District Judge Keith Hayes' Las Vegas courtroom for the proceedings.

When Dummar took the stand, he admitted he had lied and that he was the one who had delivered the will to the Mormon Church headquarters. He testified that a man (later identified as Forsythe, who allegedly had worked as a secret courier for Hughes) had brought the will to him at his gas station in Willard, Utah.

Forsythe, meanwhile, said Hughes himself had given him the will in Vancouver, British Columbia, in 1972 for safekeeping until his death. About three months before Hughes died, Forsythe said, someone who knew about his work for Hughes called him and instructed him to deliver the will to Dummar.

The trial lasted seven months. Sixty-nine witnesses testified. Proponents of the will argued that the handwriting matched that of Howard Hughes. Contestants suggested that Melvin Dummar's second wife, Bonnie, had forged the will and that Dummar's desert encounter with Hughes could not have happened because Hughes was inside the Desert Inn the entirety of his four-year stay in Las Vegas.

Eleven handwriting analysts took the stand, with those solicited by the will proponents testifying it was clearly Hughes' handwriting and those brought in by the opponents testifying it was a clever forgery.

An array of Hughes' personal aides testified that he never left the Desert Inn between 1966 and 1970. Gordon Margulis, who helped take care of Hughes' personal needs for many years, testified that it was impossible for Hughes to slip out of the hotel without being noticed by his aides. He also expressed dismay at the inconsistency of testimony from his former colleagues. "All I know is there is a lot of lyin' going on here," he said.

A man named Edwin Daniel offered some support for Dummar's story when he testified about seeing agitated Hughes aides at the Mizpah Hotel in

Tonopah around the time of Dummar's alleged encounter, and that they said they were looking for Hughes. Another man, John Henderson, testified that he saw and talked to Hughes while the billionaire was walking along a desert road near Virginia City in late 1967.

After eleven hours of deliberation, the jury ruled in June 1978 that the will was a forgery. As a result, Hughes' heirs, led by cousin Will Lummis, took control of the estate.

Robert List, Nevada's attorney general at the time, played an important role in undermining the Mormon Will. After the will was filed, List said two attorneys for the Hughes estate, James Wadsworth and Bill Morse, came to see him in Carson City. They told him they believed the will was a forgery and that Dummar had done it. List sent his chief investigator, Bruce Greenhalgh, to Salt Lake City. In the offices of the Mormon Church's law firm, he found the envelope in which the will had been delivered to the church. List sent the envelope to the FBI, which found Dummar's left thumbprint in the lower-left corner. The discovery of the fingerprint forced Dummar to change his story, generating grave doubts about his credibility.

The attempted revival

After the jury's ruling, few had any interest in exploring the case further. Dummar wanted to appeal but couldn't find a lawyer to take the case on contingency. Legal files were stored away, potential leads were dropped, and Hughes' estate was placed firmly into the hands of his family heirs. But over the years, Dummar kept telling his story to anyone who would listen. Occasionally, a reporter would run across him and write about what he had been up to lately, and Dummar would dutifully tell the story of his desert encounter.

It took almost twenty years for someone to take up Dummar's cause again and pursue new evidence to support his story. Gary Magnesen, a retired FBI agent, was that someone. Magnesen detailed his research in a 2005 book, *The Investigation: A Former FBI Agent Uncovers the Truth Behind Howard Hughes, Melvin Dummar, and the Most Contested Will in American History.* In 2015, he published a second book, *Stolen Justice,* that offered a few more circumstantial tidbits he believed bolstered Dummar's story.

Magnesen served as an FBI agent investigating organized crime in Las Vegas. He "worked the underbelly of the sprawling place for sixteen years," he wrote. His career brought him into contact with an array of colorful characters, from a "degenerate gambler" to a "washed-up showgirl" to a "wealthy ex-state senator" who was "dark and corrupt, a miserable excuse for a public official." (He was referring to the late state senator Floyd Lamb, a longtime politician convicted of taking a bribe in an FBI sting.) He once interviewed a "top-heavy dominatrix" whom he found "creepy." She eagerly showed off her dungeon, complete with "shackles, chains, ropes, pulleys, a four-foot-high wooden stock, and several leather whips." He was not impressed: "I felt like I needed a shower." But Magnesen said he also came into contact with many "ordinary people" in Las Vegas. He separated the place into "two towns," one the Strip, a "plastic world of make-believe," the other the normal place where people "live their lives."

Magnesen's primary responsibility in Las Vegas was to root out the remnants of the mob in a city that had become a "corporate enclave, controlled by accountants and gaming officials." His mission was "to take them down, one at a time, by finding a crime to charge them with."

In retirement, in 2002, Magnesen met Dummar. The former agent came into the meeting with the impression that Dummar was a "kook." Dummar told him he simply wanted people to know he wasn't a "fraud or a crook." Based on his years of experience as an investigator, Magnesen said he did not detect that Dummar was lying and decided to pursue the case further.

A legitimate will?

Magnesen concluded the Mormon Will is legitimate based on several factors, including that it was written on yellow lined paper (Hughes' preferred medium for memo writing), that some handwriting experts testified that Hughes wrote it, and that aides testified Hughes frequently told them he had a secret will.

But what about the misspellings and general sloppiness? A doctor testified during the trial that Hughes' kidney disease could have hampered his ability to concentrate. "I have seen similar errors in the handwriting of patients with uremic poisoning," the doctor said. What's more, some handwritten memos Hughes wrote to top aide Bob Maheu in the 1960s contain spelling errors.

Magnesen argued that the key to the case is not handwriting, it's whether to believe Dummar's story of picking up Hughes in the desert. Magnesen tracked down Dummar's attorney during the trial, Roger Dutson, who was a judge in Ogden, Utah. Dutson said he strongly believed Dummar picked up Hughes in the desert and the will was authentic. He recalled that Forsythe, who delivered the will to Dummar, did not testify at the trial because he had received a death threat. Instead, his sworn deposition was read into the record, which did not have the same impact on the jury.

Linda Acaldo, who served as a secretary for Dummar's trial attorney, Harold Rhoden, told Magnesen that a key piece of evidence not presented at the trial could have bolstered the case. She said records for the Desert Inn show a significant drop-off in outgoing phone calls and room service charges from December 27-30, 1967—the period when Dummar says he picked up Hughes.

However, Paul Winn, who was the director of corporate records for Summa, says the suite where Hughes lived had outside telephone lines. The calls did not go through the Desert Inn switchboard, so Alcaldo could not have seen any records relating to outgoing phone calls from Hughes' suite. Further, he points out that the food provided to Hughes and his aides on the ninth floor did not go through room service.

Providing some balance to his book, Magnesen says he interviewed Kay Glenn, one of Hughes' top aides, who insisted Hughes never left the Desert Inn while he was living there. And he interviewed George Francom, a longtime Hughes personal aide, who said Hughes would have been too weak to leave the hotel.

Surprisingly, Magnesen employed pure speculation—offering little or no evidence—to accuse Hughes' longtime attorney, Chester Davis, of participating in a "dark mission" to prevent the will from being deemed authentic. Magnesen accused Davis of knowing the will was real, destroying evidence, threatening witnesses into refusing to testify, and convincing others to lie on the stand. Unlike most of his other investigative work, Magnesen had no basis on which to make these allegations, except that Davis was a notorious schemer. Davis died in 1983.

The desert road

Magnesen quoted an anonymous man "associated with the Hughes corporation" who said he knew someone who said he saw Hughes in Tonopah when he was supposed to be in the Desert Inn. Magnesen was unable to locate the man who said he saw Hughes. The author went even further down desperation road: Apparently, Dummar's sister-in-law once received a phone call from an obviously drunk woman who said her ex-husband was a Hughes aide. He once told her that Hughes had left the Desert Inn and Dummar had picked him up in the desert. Again, Magnesen was unable to locate the mysterious caller.

Magnesen decided to take a look at the scene where Dummar said he picked up Hughes in an effort to figure out why this titan of business would have been in this desolate place at all. He met Dummar at the Cottontail Ranch, and they went together to find the site: a dirt road leading west from U.S. 95 about seven miles south of the brothel. Unfortunately, the desert excursion yielded no clues.

Still seeking reasons for Hughes to leave the Desert Inn, Magnesen explored Hughes' mining claim purchases in the late '60s, the project headed by John

Meier. Magnesen eventually reached Meier by telephone, and Meier endorsed the claim that Hughes was at the Mizpah Hotel in Tonopah and had come up to the area to look at mining claims. "He went out on his own and got lost," Meier said in support of Dummar's story. Although the conversation was brief, Meier assured Magnesen they would talk again. Meier, however, never spoke with Magnesen again before the book went to press, leaving many of his questions unanswered.

A visit to the Esmeralda County Recorder's Office in Goldfield proved fruitful. Magnesen discovered that Hughes purchased several mining claims near the end of the dirt road where Dummar had found him lying on the ground. Magnesen speculated that Hughes had come out to the area to look at the claims and bought them upon his return to Las Vegas.

The pilot's tale

The Melvin Dummar mystery turned in a new direction for Magnesen when he got a call from Robert Deiro, a pilot and longtime Las Vegas businessman who worked for the Hughes operation at what is now the North Las Vegas Airport in the '60s. Deiro alleged that he talked to Hughes about airplanes and flying and was sent out on flying missions to test takeoffs and landings, presumably in preparation for building a supersonic airport near Las Vegas.

Deiro said Hughes often accompanied him on flights, always at night. These adventures allegedly were orchestrated by aide Howard Eckersley. Flying a Cessna 310, Deiro said, they would check out possible airport locations and talk about flying. Sometimes, he said, Hughes would fly the plane. These alleged night flights took a new turn when Hughes decided to take advantage of Deiro's side business: flying customers to Nevada brothels. Hughes asked to be taken to a brothel in late summer or early fall of 1967. First, Deiro said he took him to the Ash Meadows Ranch, about one hundred miles northwest of Las Vegas in the Amargosa Valley. Then, around Christmas of that year, Deiro said he flew him to the Cottontail Ranch farther north.

During the brothel's lineup ritual, Deiro said, Hughes chose a woman named Sunny who had a diamond embedded in her tooth. Deiro waited in the bar. And waited. And waited, eventually falling asleep in the kitchen. When he awoke about five a.m., he was told that his friend had left with someone. Deiro took off and flew around the area looking for signs of Hughes, but didn't find anything. He returned to Las Vegas, he said, and never heard anything more about the incident. It turned out to be his last encounter with Hughes. No more flying chitchat, no more nighttime flights over the Nevada desert.

Deiro continued to work for Hughes at the former Alamo Airways, adjacent to McCarran International Airport, and eventually became vice president of administration for Golden West Airlines, run by Hughes' friend C. Arnholt Smith, a prominent San Diego businessman and friend of Richard Nixon. It was a job Deiro believed Hughes quietly helped him get.

Helen Holland, Deiro's secretary during the time of his alleged flights with Hughes, told Magnesen that she transferred calls from Hughes to Deiro but didn't know what they talked about. She also claimed she took dictation from Hughes regarding the operation of the North Las Vegas Airport.

For years, Deiro said he didn't make a connection between Dummar and his secret flights with Hughes. Somehow, he didn't pick up the signs during the blitz of news coverage of the Mormon Will case that the two incidents could be related. "He considered Dummar a fool, and his understanding was that Melvin had reported finding an old man at his gas station in Northern Nevada," Magnesen wrote. "He never associated Dummar with the Cottontail Ranch. None of the publicity he was aware of rang any bells in his head."

Deiro said his memory was jogged in 2004 when he saw an Associated Press report in which Dummar recounted his story and mentioned the Cottontail Ranch. But is Deiro's story believable? Magnesen is convinced that it is. "He is a very successful man," he wrote of Deiro. "He isn't the kind of person who would concoct such a remarkable story. He has nothing to gain and has asked for nothing in return for his disclosure to me or anyone else."

Others acquainted with Deiro, however, say he's just the kind of guy who might concoct such a story to attract the spotlight. Curiously, Deiro came forward with his story the year after the death of Eckersley, the Hughes aide he claims facilitated the flights.

In 2008, I met with Deiro to quiz him about the story he had told Magnesen. He recounted basically the same tale. But he also handed me a copy of a twenty-five-page typed document that goes into even greater detail about his alleged flying adventures with Hughes.

Deiro says that before Hughes would fly with him, he instructed his security chief, Jack Hooper, to investigate his credentials and background. His flying experience checked out, but he said Hooper expressed concerns about some of his ancillary activities, such as partying on the Las Vegas Strip and running "'Midnight Special' charter flights" to brothels in rural Nevada.

"These associations and activities were not conducive to the image that a buttoned-down Hughes Tool Company executive should have and normally would have resulted in the personnel department passing on hiring me in any capacity," Deiro wrote. "But, and I'm sure to Hooper's amazement, Hughes had immediately approved my employment. A good argument could be made from what happened next that Howard knew exactly how he was going to use my legitimate, and my questionable, talents."

Deiro says his first assignment to fly with Hughes came in early 1967. The mission was to explore the Mormon Mesa area, about sixty miles northeast of Las Vegas, for a possible supersonic airport. Standing next to the Cessna 206 they would be flying, Deiro watched as a black sedan approached. "A tall, shadowy figure exited the sedan with an audible grunt and walked slowly toward the passenger side of the dual-control airplane. It was Hughes. Relief that he was apparently going to let me fly almost overcame my excitement at seeing the legendary man."

According to Deiro, Hughes was thin but looked healthy. "Dressed in a light-colored, long-sleeved shirt buttoned at the neck and the sleeves. No hat, tie or jacket even though at altitude the temperature was in the mid-sixties. His baggy gabardine trousers were dark and pleated like they went with a 1940s-era suit. There was a brown leather belt with the end hanging several inches out of the gold-colored buckle. He wore old-fashioned low-top white deck shoes." However, a lack of basic hygiene was evident: "He reeked of body odor and when he spoke it was obvious his breath wasn't something one wanted to smell either. . . . It was apparent he hadn't shaved for at least a week. His thinning hair was unkempt, gray and 'hippie' length."

Deiro says he and Hughes flew around Southern Nevada three more times, including over Eldorado dry lake, Jean dry lake, and the Pahrump Valley. Small talk was not part of the equation. "No hail fellow well met pilot camaraderie," Deiro wrote. "Strictly business. No compliments, thanks or handshakes."

On their next night-time flight, in the summer of 1967, Hughes instructed Deiro to fly to Ash Meadows, the main feature of which was a brothel called The Annex. As they climbed out of the plane, Deiro said he noticed that Hughes was carrying a black satchel "not unlike an old-fashioned doctor's bag." Upon entering the brothel, they were presented with a lineup of seven women in evening gowns. Hughes selected a woman named "Sunny." Deiro says he recognized the woman, and that he thought she "had worked in Hollywood."

Deiro sat down in a chair and waited. "Within thirty minutes Hughes re-entered the front room and without saying anything crossed quickly to the door clutching the black bag to his chest. He kept his head down while waiting for the barkeep to round the bar and open the door. He looked about furtively and walked quickly to the plane." Another trip to the Ash Meadows brothel occurred a couple of weeks later, according to Deiro. This time, he said, Hughes was with Sunny for more than an hour and left happier than the time before.

The Cottontail Ranch brothel, operated by Beverly and Howard Harrell, opened in November 1967, and Beverly enticed Sunny to relocate. According to Deiro, Hughes must have gotten word of Sunny's move, because "on a night between Christmas Day and New Year's Eve, Eckersley called me to set up the flight." When they walked in, Hughes immediately waved Sunny out of the lineup. This time, Hughes was gone much longer, and Deiro asked the madam if he could rest his eyes in the kitchen. He fell asleep. A maid awakened him about four a.m. When Deiro inquired about Hughes, the bartender said he had left and insisted it was time for him to go too. Deiro looked around outside and then circled the brothel in the Cessna. Seeing nothing, he flew back to Las Vegas. Deiro claims he heard nothing from Eckersley or anyone else. But he was never asked to fly with Hughes again.

So, what happened to Hughes at that brothel? Deiro speculates that perhaps when he had finished with Sunny and didn't see Deiro in the front room, he found another ride home. "Hughes, who to any human predator would look like an easy victim, could easily have been trick-rolled and left beaten and penniless in the desert." Or, Deiro guesses, maybe Hughes had a conflict with Sunny and was thrown out of the brothel. He didn't have the keys to the plane, so he could not have flown away. "Walking away from the brothel's lights and into the pitch black desert, he could have fallen and injured himself before being found by Dummar."

The Cottontail Ranch madam, Beverly Harrell, died in 1995, but Magnesen tracked down her husband, Howard, in California. Howard Harrell said his wife told him that Hughes had visited the Cottontail and she wanted to come forward about it during the Dummar case. "She wanted to go to the cops in Las Vegas and tell the story about Hughes when we heard about the trial, but I talked her out of it," Harrell said. "I told her it would bring her nothing but trouble. There were too many powerful people involved, and I thought she would be in danger."

Magnesen said he "began this journey as a skeptic but finished as an advocate." He concluded that Dummar's story holds up and that only Hughes could have written the Mormon Will. He said that in the Mormon Will case, "the trial process failed and justice was denied." Magnesen's book relies heavily on the testimony of Dummar, Meier, Deiro, and Howard Harrell—a motley crew by any measure. But if nothing else, Magnesen raises some intriguing questions about the longstanding conventional wisdom that Hughes never left the Desert Inn during his four years in Las Vegas.

"The world's perception of Melvin Dummar needs to change," Magnesen wrote. "He made mistakes, but he's not a fraud. . . . Society owes Melvin an apology. There also is a great deal of money owed him and the other beneficiaries."

Back to court

The Investigation renewed media interest in Dummar's story, and based on new details in the book, Dummar filed a federal lawsuit in June 2006 in Salt Lake City. Since securing a piece of the Hughes estate was no longer a realistic goal, Dummar told reporters he simply wanted to set the record straight and rescue his reputation.

The validity of Dummar's new claim rested heavily on Deiro's shoulders. But Deiro was not the ideal person on whom to hang a court case. "For Hughes to go anywhere like that, it would be such a big deal that we all would have known about it," said Paul Winn, who worked in Hughes' Operations Office in Los Angeles when the incident allegedly occurred. "We knew every second what was happening up in that suite. He could not have gotten out of there without anybody knowing it."

Winn added: "Hughes had no clothes at that time. When he came here [to Las Vegas], he was naked. What did he wear?"

Also, Winn questioned why Deiro would be singled out to fly Hughes. "He's not going to go flying with Bob Deiro, who he never heard of, when he had a crew out at Hughes Aircraft Company. He had people. He's not going to take on some guy he didn't know anything about or never been around. No way. *The Wizard of Oz* is much more believable than these stories about Bob Deiro."

Interviewed in 2007, Gordon Margulis reiterated his Mormon Will testimony that Hughes was too sick to leave the DI without substantial assistance. "If you had seen the man, you would know it was impossible," he said. "He was not in the condition to walk down the fire escape and walk back up. I mean, come on."

In January 2007, U.S. District Judge Bruce Jenkins threw out Dummar's lawsuit, arguing that it had been "fully and fairly litigated" in 1978. Undeterred, in April 2007, Dummar filed a new lawsuit in state court in Las Vegas, suing Will Lummis and Bill Gay, whom he accused of acting fraudulently to invalidate the Mormon Will.

Dummar hoped the new evidence and witnesses Magnesen had dug up would persuade a judge to order a new trial. "I honestly believe that if a judge will hear it and schedule it for trial and if it goes before a jury, I think we have a better chance of winning now than we did thirty years ago," Dummar said. "Because thirty years ago, nobody was saying nothin'. It was all on me. I knew that some of these guys were lying, but everybody was calling *me* a liar. How do you get around that?"

The case went nowhere.

Was Dummar duped?

Dan Newburn suggested another possible chain of events involving Dummar. Newburn is a longtime Las Vegan and former chairman of the Clark County School Board. He came to Las Vegas in 1971 to be the pastor of a Baptist church and help start a Christian school. He also hosted an interview program, *Vegas Scope*, on KVBC Channel 3 (which was KORK back then, KSNB today), and later served as news director at KLVX Channel 10. Through the school project, Newburn met Dick Gray, a lawyer for Hughes, and became friends with Gray and his wife, Linda.

When Gray died in 1975, Hughes' Summa Corporation was engaged in a legal battle with *Las Vegas Sun* publisher Hank Greenspun. Gray had put together a loan to Greenspun that was the focus of the lawsuit. Newburn learned from Linda Gray, who was miffed at Summa because it would not hand over some lounge chairs she had purchased from the Sands Hotel, that her husband had papers relevant to the Greenspun-Hughes battle. Newburn took the papers to Greenspun. "Those lounge chairs ended up costing Summa a million dollars," Newburn said.

Meanwhile, Greenspun, impressed by Newburn, asked him, "How'd you like to come work for me and learn the newspaper business?" Newburn handled "special investigations" for the *Sun* from 1976 to 1981. In this unique position, Newburn took his orders directly from Greenspun. Typically, he would investigate news tips and then, if they panned out, turn over his research to a *Sun* reporter such as Gary Thompson or Jim Barrows who would do the actual writing. Sometimes, Newburn's assignments from Greenspun had nothing to do with researching a news story. For example, Greenspun, fearing somebody was listening to office conversations, once directed Newburn to "debug" the newsroom.

When the Mormon Will trial started, the plaintiff's attorney, Harold Rhoden, needed examples of Hughes' handwriting to compare with the handwriting on the alleged will. Newburn knew where to go: his friend Linda Gray, whose late husband had kept Hughes' memos dating from the time the will presumably was written.

While the Mormon Will trial was unfolding, Newburn said dozens of people came into the *Sun* offices with stories they hoped would result in them getting a piece of the Hughes estate. Newburn talked to many of them, unimpressed with most of their obviously tall tales. But as the trial was wrapping up, a man came to the office with a story that caught Newburn's attention.

The man, whose name Newburn does not remember, said he had a friend named Robert Newton. They had worked together at the Gabbs mine where Dummar also worked. When Newton wasn't working, he was an amateur prospector. Out prospecting in the desert one time, he had fallen down and gotten scratched up. Newton said Dummar picked him up and took him to Las Vegas. Newton, the man said, was a notorious practical joker. When Dummar asked him his name, he said, "Howard Hughes."

Later, the man said, he saw Newton writing a fake will "to mess with Melvin Dummar." Before the Gabbs job, Newton had worked as a security guard in Long Beach, California, where Hughes' flying boat was kept, so he knew a little bit about the reclusive billionaire. "He writes up the will, puts it in an envelope and leaves it for Dummar, laughing all the way," Newburn said.

Newburn's efforts to verify the story were complicated by the fact that Newton had died. But Newburn contacted people who knew Newton and confirmed a few things: Newton was indeed a frequent practical joker, and he always used yellow legal pads to write letters to his family. Newburn found Newton's son in Sacramento, California, and convinced him to send evidence of Newton's handwriting. "A couple of weeks later I get a packet of letters, Xeroxed copies, written on legal tab paper," Newburn recalled. "The writing is remarkably similar" to Hughes' writing.

Newburn took his research to Greenspun and suggested the newspaper print a story, but Greenspun declined, fearing it would only further confuse the Mormon Will case. As a result, the Robert Newton practical joke scenario never saw the light of day. Years later, Newburn remained intrigued by it. It's more plausible, he said, that Dummar *believed* he picked up Hughes than that he actually did. Newburn sides with the camp that insists Hughes never left the Desert Inn. He noted that Hughes' aides "could control him any time he would get rambunctious."

Newburn questioned two other parts of Magnesen's story attempting to validate Dummar and the will. Newburn said he knew the brothel madam, Beverly Harrell, and if Hughes had been a customer, "she would not have been able to shut up about it." And as for Deiro's story of flying around with Hughes, Newburn argued that "Howard would have wanted to fly himself."

"Of all the stories, and I saw hundreds of explanations, [the most plausible] is that Dummar got a hold of something he thought was a will," Newburn said. "I don't think Dummar was smart enough to write the will. But he was naïve enough to believe the one he had was real."

Newburn called Dummar and the Mormon Will "one of the greatest untold scenarios" of our time. Like the Kennedy assassination, the true story may end up being one of those mysteries that is never completely revealed.

His extensive journalistic work on Hughes left a deep impression on Newburn, so much so that when he was elected to the Clark County School Board in 1987, he pushed for a new school to be named for Lummis, Hughes' cousin and the executor of the Hughes estate, who is credited with rescuing the company from impending ruin. William Lummis Elementary School is located at 9000 Hillpointe Road in Summerlin, the master-planned community built on Hughes' land.

Another rumor containing an ounce of plausibility is that the man Dummar picked up in the desert was actually Jimmy Vernon, a public relations man in Las Vegas who did work for Hughes for many years. According to the story, Vernon, a heavy drinker, was with a group of Hughes lawyers and aides in Tonopah involved in one of those infamous mining deals. During the night, Vernon disappeared, perhaps headed for the Cottontail Ranch. Those who knew Vernon say it would not be surprising if he told Dummar that he was Howard Hughes. Vernon, in fact, had some physical similarities to the billionaire. Furthermore, Vernon apparently kept a suite at the Sands Hotel, so it would make sense that he would ask Dummar to take him there. Unfortunately, Vernon died at roughly the same time as Hughes, so the story could never be verified.

The verdict

The Melvin Dummar story, as improbable as it is, seems to have eternal life. Dummar's earnest demeanor and the consistency with which he told the story over the years—at least since his initial deception about the will—lead those who have not carefully studied Hughes' life to believe it just might be true. It's human nature to root for the little guy. Just as we cheer the truck driver who wins the lottery, we want Dummar to collect a piece of the Hughes fortune.

We also are uneasy about the idea that a man as adventurous as Hughes never left the top floor of a hotel for four years. Hughes was a man of action. He made epic movies, flew airplanes at record speeds, and dated Hollywood's most beautiful women. He was known for disappearing acts, such as in the early '30s when he took an assumed name and landed a job as a junior airline pilot. Why would he remain cooped up when he had all the money in the world to do anything he wanted?

The inconvenient truth is that when Hughes was at the Desert Inn, he was no longer the great aviator, the ladies' man, the rugged industrialist of his younger days. He was terribly sick, heavily dependent on pain-killing drugs, and losing his battle with obsessive-compulsive disorders. He had highs and lows while in the DI penthouse, but he was rarely if ever in good enough condition to sneak out of the hotel and fly around rural Nevada at night. Most of the time, he could barely stand up.

Furthermore, Magnesen's speculation that Hughes was walking in the desert looking at mining claims is hard to swallow. First of all, Hughes took only a meager interest in his ill-fated mining venture. He had many other business and political interests at the time that took greater priority. And what exactly would Hughes have expected to learn from wandering around central Nevada? He was not a mining expert, and a firsthand look at old mines would not have yielded significant information.

Oh, and speaking of the Nevada desert: Hughes was deathly afraid of nuclear testing. In the 1950s, he ordered his aides driving cross country to avoid Southern Nevada. In the late '60s, he lobbied all the way to the White House to try to get the underground explosions stopped. Would a man so worried about radiation exposure have eagerly flown into close vicinity of those testing areas, then walked around in the radiation-infused dust? Not likely.

Finally, the notion that Hughes partook of the services of a prostitute at the Cottontail Ranch makes little sense. First of all, the drugs Hughes was hooked on practically eliminated any sexual urges or abilities he once possessed. Second, his fear of germs certainly would have kept him away from a rickety rural brothel, as well as the women working there. Third, if he wanted female companionship at that time, he probably could have arranged for his wife, Jean Peters, to join him in Las Vegas. Failing that, he could have ordered up an attractive woman in Las Vegas to meet him on the ninth floor.

And so it is practically impossible to reconcile Dummar's story with everything we have heard about Hughes at that time of his life. Even if we want to believe Dummar, familiarity with Hughes and his organization breeds doubt, if not outright incredulity.

And yet, any individual who believes he knows with absolute certainty the entirety of Hughes' affairs is kidding himself. Hughes was one of the most complex men in history—enigmatic, unpredictable, and prone to secrecy, even within his small circle of aides and confidants. That doesn't mean Dummar's story is true. But it justifies leaving the door open just a crack.

Back at the Clown Motel

For Dummar, the Good Samaritan act of picking up an injured old man in the desert was more curse than blessing in his life. After the high-profile trial, he had trouble getting jobs. "I've had employers say, 'Oh, Melvin Dummar, you're a con man, you're a crook, you're a thief, you're a liar. We don't want nobody like you around here.' That's what kind of hurt me. It's not only me, it's my whole family." As a result, Dummar said he opted for self-employment and gradually fell into a depressive state that lasted twenty years.

"Even though outwardly I was cordial to people and tried to treat everybody with respect and kindness and stuff, I was hurting inside, and I never got close to anybody. Because right at first, even some of the good church members, they wouldn't let their kids play with our kids. And it hurt. Then people saying you're a liar and a con man, so I just kind of shied away from people. Consequently, I have very few friends. I mean, I have acquaintances and customers now, but it's not that I get close to anybody. . . . I used to be real outgoing. I loved to go out and party—I didn't like to drink and all this, but go to parties and have good times and go fishing and hunting with all these guys and different things. And almost the last thirty years I've been almost a loner. I do my own thing. I try not to step on anybody's toes."

During our more than two-hour interview at the Clown Motel in Tonopah, Dummar spoke freely and in great detail about many aspects of his life, but his most poignant comment exemplified the duality of his saga. He said of Hughes: "I'd have been further ahead if he'd never remembered me." If you believe Dummar's story, you might be inclined to commiserate with his plight. But if you're convinced he made up the story, it's hard to feel sorry for a guy who suffered for two-thirds of his life as a result of his own lies.

At the time of the interview, Dummar had heart trouble and had recently survived two bouts with non-Hodgkin's lymphoma. He wore an orthopedic sleeve on his enlarged right arm to treat a blood clot in his shoulder. He was sixty-three—just a year older than Howard Hughes was in 1967 when Dummar says he picked him up in the desert.

Death and legacy

Melvin Dummar died from complications of cancer on December 9, 2018, at his home in Pahrump, Nevada.

The news immediately thrust me back to that interview, twelve years earlier, when Dummar told me his story, my microcassette recorder positioned on the table between us. As we talked, not once did I sense that he was putting on a show. He had told these stories to journalists, lawyers, and others hundreds of times by then, but his words did not feel rehearsed or polished to advance a particular agenda. I'm no expert at identifying whether people are telling the truth, but my impression was that Dummar was being honest—that he genuinely believed everything he told me.

His apparent candor in that Tonopah motel room does not, however, mean that his version of what happened holds up to scrutiny. It's possible that what he said was truthful as far as it went, but that he didn't tell me the whole story. It's also possible that Dummar's memory of what happened was faulty, a challenge all of us deal with. And finally, it's possible that he was a con man who, although he never got rich from it, stuck to his story to avoid the shame of admitting it was made up.

I do not support the latter option. Dummar, I believe, picked up *somebody* on his fateful drive between Tonopah and Las Vegas in 1967. It just wasn't Howard Hughes. The evidence overwhelmingly indicates that Hughes never left the penthouse floor of the Desert Inn between 1966 and 1970. If Hughes had left the DI during this period, his coterie of personal aides would have known about it and been at his side the whole time. That's just how it was in Hughesworld.

While I can believe that Dummar picked up *somebody* in the desert, his story about the will being dropped off at his Utah gas station is harder to digest. It's possible he was merely a pawn in a scheme to introduce the fake will. I'd like to believe that, because the man as I knew him seemed incapable of masterminding such an elaborate flimflam. But it's also difficult to imagine Dummar being completely oblivious to such an elaborate enterprise unfolding around him. Still, the fact that he stuck to the story to his death—that he never ratted or confessed despite the hardships he suffered as a result—leaves open the option that he was, to borrow a word associated with another great conspiracy theory, a patsy.

One of the most interesting threads of the Dummar story is that he had many supporters, people who believed—who still believe—that he was cheated out of his rightful share of the Hughes fortune. Dummar was a gentle and friendly man. During his endless travels selling frozen food across the rural West, he befriended many people who had little trouble believing that larger forces had used their power to discredit him and deprive him of his windfall.

The Oscar-winning movie inspired by Dummar's story contributed to this sentiment. When *Melvin and Howard* was released in 1980, its screenwriter, Bo Goldman, summarized the story as "a meeting of one of the richest men in America and one of the poorest." The film helped transform Dummar from a fraud into a living folk hero, a regular guy whose shot at the American dream was thwarted by more powerful forces. It's human nature to take Dummar's side —the side of the underdog, of FDR's forgotten man.

After Dummar died, I engaged in a few discussions about him on social media. People asked me whether his story was true, and I expressed my doubts. This didn't go over well with one friend, who commented, "I don't know why you want facts to ruin a good story." I understand the feeling, even as I recoil at its larger implications.

I don't know the whole story of Melvin Dummar, Howard Hughes, and the Mormon Will. Perhaps nobody does, or ever will, especially now that its protagonist has passed on. But I believe the more complicated version—the version that pokes holes in his story, that asks more questions than it answers—is more interesting than the unexamined legend.

16

The Estate: *Will and the Wills*

Howard Hughes' money is almost as intriguing as the man himself. Money provided Hughes with opportunities out of reach for 99.9 percent of the human population, from making big-budget movies to building experimental airplanes to owning airlines and Las Vegas casinos. It also helped open the bedroom doors of many Hollywood actresses. But as James Phelan and Lewis Chester note in their 1997 book *The Money: The Battle for Howard Hughes' Billions*, money not only failed to buy Hughes happiness, it "bought him an inordinate amount of misery." Especially in the last thirty years of his life, which were characterized by drug addiction, seclusion, and mental and physical illness.

What happened to Hughes' money after he died in 1976 is another interesting story, a drama with high stakes and a huge cast of characters, ranging from the comedic Melvin Dummar, who claimed to have saved Hughes' life and later came into possession of Hughes' long-lost will, to the heroic William Lummis, the Houston attorney who took charge of his cousin's estate and steered it admirably for a decade.

When Hughes died, what his estate contained was unclear: how much his companies were worth, how much property he owned, how much money he had. Because of severe mismanagement of some of his companies in his final years, he could have been much less wealthy than his public reputation suggested. Phelan and Chester determine that, in fact, he was much richer than many had thought. They estimate he was worth more than $6 billion, putting him well ahead of J. Paul Getty, long considered the world's richest man. (Getty died in June 1976, just months after Hughes, at age eighty-three, so they were near contemporaries.)

Hughes could have eliminated much of the drama by leaving a will. But an eccentric to the end, he did not do so, or if he did, it was lost, destroyed, or hidden by individuals within his organization who saw greater benefits for themselves if it did not surface. With no legal instructions for the administration of his estate, a free-for-all ensued. "More than a thousand people would hit the Hughes greenback trail, staking claims of heirship to the fortune," Phelan and Chester write. "This fever of greed, fantasy, and legal contention was fueled not only by the magnitude of the money, but by the sense that much of it was up for grabs."

In short, everybody with any possible link to Hughes—and some eager beavers with no identifiable ties whatsoever—wanted a piece of the action. "Heirship claims clogged the judicial system with a horrendous tangle of litigation for more than a decade after Hughes' death," according to Phelan and Chester. "The throng included purported wives and mistresses, purported business partners, self-proclaimed children and self-described bastards, and any number of people asserting undying intimacy with the reclusive billionaire."

Arelo Sederberg, a press liaison for the Hughes organization in the 1970s, remembered the deluge of claims on a piece of the billionaire's fortune. "People with the remotest past association with Hughes held hopes that the eccentric rich man had somehow blessed them," Sederberg wrote in *Hughesworld*, a memoir of his years working for Hughes. "For each of these there were a dozen opportunistic pretenders. Since mine was an open phone, I got the calls. Some were kooks with labored breath or weird giggles. Others had smoother approaches, intelligent and sincere. I listened and passed on the information, no matter how deranged, to the will searchers."

About two weeks after Hughes died, Sederberg was asked to place classified ads in newspapers in forty cities that Hughes had visited. The ad read: "Howard Robard Hughes Jr., son of Howard Robard Hughes Sr. and Allene Gano. Born Dec. 24, 1906. Died April 5, 1976. Anyone having information regarding this death, please call 213-986-7047." (Sederberg's classified ad had Hughes' birth date wrong by a year and a day.)

The ad ignited a firestorm of press coverage and calls. "Few advertisements in the history of American ballyhooing produced the mileage of this little one," Sederberg wrote. "It was reproduced in front page news stories and resulted in more than a thousand calls. Many were from news reporters wondering what it was all about. When they asked me, I had a fair answer. The ads were nothing more than a legal formality, necessary before investigators could ask banks to search their records to see if Hughes might have had a safe-deposit box in their vault. A few leads in the

Will Lummis, a Houston attorney, took over his cousin's estate in 1976. Courtesy of *Las Vegas Review-Journal* Archive.

will search developed from the experiment but all of them were dead ends."

Just days after Hughes died, his cousin Lummis was officially named temporary administrator of his estate. Lummis, who had met Hughes only twice as a child, would be in charge until a will was located. Lummis moved to Las Vegas and began the task of sorting out what was happening within the sixteen divisions of Summa Corporation, the company that operated Hughes' casinos and other enterprises.

He discovered that many operations were either not doing much or not making money. The company had lost $131 million in the five years since Hughes left Las Vegas. The ranching division consisted of one ranch operated by a man who had trouble getting anyone to pay attention to his modest needs. The mining division had purchased hundreds of worthless claims and had no plans to do anything with them. The casino division was mysteriously losing money, while its Las Vegas competitors were cashing in.

Lummis soon ran into conflict with the three individuals who had been running the company, Bill Gay, Nadine Henley, and attorney Chester Davis, who figured they should continue their unorthodox and Machiavellian ways. Lummis learned of Gay's lavish executive perks, such as flying with his family to Europe on corporate jets and fixing up a Miami Beach home at company expense. As for Davis, Lummis came to see that he had little handle on the vast array of lawsuits filed against Hughes and refused to cooperate with efforts to resolve them.

Since no will had been found and therefore the estate's fate remained unclear, Lummis decided to start slowly in his efforts to right the Summa ship. He sold the thirty airplanes that Hughes had stored in hangars all over the country. Some of them had never been used. This saved the company two million dollars a year in hangar and maintenance fees alone. He also cut the corporate jet fleet to one and flew commercial himself.

These and other minor corrections were not going to be enough to save Summa, though. Lummis knew that much more invasive surgery was needed.

Battle for Summa

In the summer of 1977, Lummis reached the breaking point with the old guard members of the Summa board, who routinely stood in the way of his plans to fix the company's financial problems. Lummis removed Davis, John Holmes, and Levar Myler from the board. He then appointed Phil Hannifin—the former Nevada Gaming Control Board chairman who had met Hughes in London in 1973—to head Las Vegas casino operations. This severely diluted Gay's responsibilities, and before long Gay and Henley resigned from Summa. Finally, Davis was fired as the company's general counsel.

However, Gay, Henley, and Davis weren't out of the picture yet. The three continued to sit on the board of the Howard Hughes Medical Institute, which owned and controlled Hughes Aircraft, the biggest piece of Hughes' business. Davis believed that when a proper will was found, it would direct Hughes' money to the institute. In other words, Davis and Gay believed they remained in prime position to control the company and cash in. Davis and Gay enhanced their public standing by significantly increasing the amount of money the medical institute dedicated to research.

Lummis was in a tough spot, but new information about Hughes' physical and mental condition in his final years turned the tide in his favor. X-rays and autopsy information about Hughes after he died revealed the full extent of his physical deterioration and drug addiction. Extensive research revealed Hughes' unstable mental state. The information validated the many rumors that Lummis had been inclined to dismiss. When it became clear that Hughes was not in charge of his own affairs in his later years, Summa was able to resolve many lawsuits with much lower judgments than it previously feared it would have to pay.

In addition, the revelations about Hughes' condition led to criminal investigations. On March 16, 1978, a federal grand jury in Las Vegas indicted aide John Holmes and Dr. Norman Crane on charges of illegally supplying drugs to Hughes for nineteen years. Crane wrote the prescriptions in the names of some of Hughes' aides, and Holmes made sure the supply was always available for Hughes. Crane also taught Hughes how to inject himself rather than taking the drugs orally. In 1974, Crane became uncomfortable with being Hughes' drug supplier and Dr. Wilbur Thain took over the duty. Thain was also indicted.

Crane and Holmes pleaded no contest and agreed to testify against Thain. They were sentenced to probation. Thain pleaded not guilty and went to trial in his home state of Utah. During the trial, Thain did not deny supplying drugs to Hughes, but he justified his actions by arguing that the billionaire needed the drugs to deal with chronic pain and discomfort. Despite several other doctors disagreeing with his assessment, Thain was acquitted.

In the wake of the revelations about Hughes' final years in the Thain trial, in 1979 Lummis filed a lawsuit on behalf of the estate seeking $50 million in damages from the individuals he considered responsible for his cousin's demise: executives Gay and Davis, doctors Crane, Thain, and Homer Clark, and aides Holmes, George Francom, Howard Eckersley, Levar Myler, Chuck Waldron, Jim Rickard, and Kay Glenn. The strongly worded complaint outlined a scenario in which they took advantage of Hughes to further their personal interests. Parallel with filing the lawsuit, Lummis instructed Summa to stop paying the "lifetime contracts" they had secured while Hughes was on his deathbed.

The clever Davis, however, filed no less than nine countersuits in different states, presenting Lummis with the expensive proposition of having to defend each of them, and Davis was also still pursuing another legal action—the so-called lost will case on behalf of the medical institute and the paternal heirs. In that case he delivered a witness, Jack Pettit, who said in a lengthy deposition that he had seen Hughes' will while in Davis' office in 1962. He said he was shown the will by Raymond Cook, whose office was next door to Davis and worked for the firm of Andrews Kurth—the very firm for which Lummis worked and which was handling the estate. Pettit said he recalled that the will left everything to the medical institute. Cook was not alive to corroborate Pettit's story.

The Nevada Supreme Court ruled in 1980 that while there was evidence Hughes had drafted wills during his lifetime, under Nevada law two credible witnesses were needed to legitimize a lost will case. The court did not deem the witnesses provided by the plaintiff sufficient.

The Graves will

In 1981, another Hughes will surfaced. Martha Jo Graves came forward with a five-page will that she said Hughes drafted in 1960 while living at the Beverly Hills Hotel. She said she found the will while going through the effects of the late Los Angeles attorney Earl Hightower, for whom she had worked for ten years. Graves said the will was inside a metal lockbox. The will left twenty percent of Hughes' fortune to the Acme Mining Company. To no skeptic's surprise, Graves was the president and major stockholder in this mining enterprise.

Graves decided to deliver the will to a Houston attorney she trusted, but during her flight, she said the airline lost her luggage containing the original will. Fortunately, she had made copies before she left. The lack of an original will did not end the case immediately. In fact, it was a clever ploy, because having only a copy eliminated key investigative techniques such as examining the paper and ink.

From the perspective of Lummis and others, the problem with the Graves will was not whether it was real—to them it clearly was a fake—but that it could take years for the case to course through the clogged California court system.

Fortunately, in the meantime, the Los Angeles District Attorney's Office launched a fraud investigation of Graves and her partners, a doctor and a businessman who claimed they were witnesses to the will signing in 1960. The doctor, Stanley DuBrin, fearing criminal prosecution, changed his story. He said Graves had forged the will in 1981 and he had decided to sign it as a favor to the businessman, Harold Mallet. Then DuBrin convinced Mallet to tell the truth, and Mallet agreed to be wired to catch Graves. Graves ended up serving a year in prison for her tall tale.

The other secret wedding

Neither of Hughes' wives nor their heirs placed a claim on his estate. Hughes had settled amicably with each of them when they were divorced. Ella Rice and Jean Peters each remarried, and both lived comfortably. But during his lifetime, Hughes had been a busy womanizer, and it was perhaps inevitable that other women in his life would bubble up during the distribution of the estate.

But only one proved to have even a halfway legitimate claim: Terry Moore. Moore was a young Hollywood actress in the late 1940s—starring in *Mighty Joe Young*—when she met Hughes. Although he was twice her age, they had an affair that was documented in the tabloid press. Moore contended she secretly married Hughes on his yacht off the Mexican coast. A sea captain conducted the ceremony, which was witnessed by two people for the groom and two for the bride. But the couple did not obtain a marriage license and Hughes swore everyone on board to secrecy on grounds that it would hurt Moore's career.

Moore and Hughes returned to their working lives but met often and talked constantly on the telephone. But when Hughes became less and less available to her, Moore became suspicious and caught Hughes in a lie. He said he was working on his flying boat in Long Beach, but the operator revealed to her that the phone call had originated from Las Vegas. With the help of a detective, she tracked him down to the Desert Inn, where he was spending time with another woman.

Soon, Moore was dating football player Glenn Davis and married him in 1951—without revealing her alleged secret marriage to Hughes. But their marriage fell apart, and she returned to Hughes. In 1953, she contended, she and Hughes planned a public marriage at a Tucson, Arizona, ranch, but another fight over his philandering canceled the event.

Many parts of Moore's case could be verified, but at the time she laid claim to Hughes' estate, only one witness to the secret marriage was still living: her mother. And in legal terms, the fact that she had married Davis without divorcing Hughes left her with a weak case. In 1981, Judge Patrick Gregory threw out her claim. But Moore was not done. She appealed the ruling, which could have meant several more years of uncertainty about the settling of the estate.

Lummis and his attorneys pursued a settlement, and in 1983 Moore held a press conference to announce that her claim of being Mrs. Howard Hughes had been acknowledged and she had been awarded an undisclosed sum. She did not reveal the amount, but said it was "more than five figures and less than eight figures," or between $100,000 and $1 billion. Other sources later put the figure at $350,000.

The Medical Institute and the IRS

Hughes' maternal relatives, most living comfortably in the Houston area, constituted the bulk of the individuals who ultimately would receive the inheritance. On the paternal side, people claiming blood lineage introduced a variety of intriguing stories in court, but in the end just five paternal heirs were approved. Howard Hughes was close to none of them.

Once the heirs were determined in 1981, that didn't mean big checks would be coming in the mail. Lummis still had numerous hurdles—taxes, lawsuits—to clear before any cash could be distributed. The highest remaining hurdle was how the Howard Hughes Medical Institute, run chiefly by Davis and Gay, would fit into the estate. In 1983, a Delaware judge dissolved the executive committee run by Davis and Gay and appointed nine trustees to manage the institute, including Gay and Lummis.

That year, the heirs saw their first paychecks, $16 million, split among twenty-two people. It was a relatively small amount considering the size of the estate, but it was a clear sign that Lummis' years of effort were starting to bear fruit. The heirs would divide another $75 million in 1985.

Next on Lummis' seemingly endless agenda was settling with the Internal Revenue Service and the states claiming a piece of the estate. He faced the very real prospect that if certain decisions didn't go his way, the bulk of the estate could end up in the hands of tax collectors. Initially, Lummis wanted a determination that Hughes was a Nevada resident rather than a Texas or California resident, because the tax burden would be substantially lower (Nevada has no inheritance tax). More than anything, he wanted to avoid being taxed by more than one state.

Hughes was born and raised in Texas, but he had not lived there since he was a very young man and he last set foot in the state in 1949. He lived in California for nearly forty years of his life, mostly in hotels and, early on, a few more permanent houses, but it could be argued that he never really settled down. He lived in Nevada for one year in the early 1950s and for four years in the late 1960s, making the claim of residency fairly slight, though Las Vegas was his last permanent residence.

The final decision, made by a court-appointed mediator in 1984, established residency in both Texas and California—so they both would get a chunk of money. Texas would get $50 million and California $119 million.

Meanwhile, the IRS worked diligently to determine the value of the Hughes estate so that it could deliver its bill. Previous estimates had put the figure somewhere between $168 million and $1.1 billion. The IRS came up with $460 million, which would mean a federal inheritance tax of $275 million. Lummis appealed the figures. In 1984, Summa and the IRS finally settled on a figure: $361,704,267. The tax bill: $147 million.

Paying that kind of money might have ruined Summa in 1976, when the company was a mess. But by 1984 it was a different company, significantly more valuable and able to sustain such a financial blow. "Not only could it face what looked like enormous tax bills with equanimity, it could stay in business and make the heirs rich beyond any normal dream of avarice," Phelan and Chester wrote.

The key was Lummis' reorganization of the company and prudent decisions to increase its value. As executor, he could have simply held a fire sale to pay the tax bills and dole out what little was left to the heirs. Instead, he operated Summa with the intent of growing the business. He sold off low-performing or stagnant properties, improved the bottom lines of other operations, and developed new projects. For example, instead of unloading the money-losing Hughes Helicopters, he put Jack Real in charge, secured a lucrative government contract, and fulfilled the contract (to produce the AH-64, or Apache, helicopters used heavily during the Gulf War). He was able to sell the division to McDonnell Douglas in 1984 for $470 million, realizing a $300 million profit.

Lummis also put new men in charge of the Las Vegas casinos, and their bottom lines improved. Subsequently, he was able to sell the properties at better prices. The Landmark, which had never done well, sold for a respectable $12.5 million. The Silver Slipper went for $11.5 million, and the Castaways for almost $50 million. Meantime, Summa invested in the Desert Inn, Frontier, and Sands to help those larger resorts improve their earnings.

Bill Friedman, who ran the Castaways and Silver Slipper casinos from 1976 to 1989, described it as the best period of his life. "They kept me separate from all the corporate politics," he said. "And they treated me like a prince." Friedman was said to be the first person of Jewish heritage to reach department head level within the Hughes empire, which, knowing Hughes' views, may have been true. "I always said, if what they are doing to me is discrimination, I want all of it I can get," Friedman said. "Not a month went by that somebody didn't offer me more money to leave. But I always told them I'm happy. They were the greatest bosses."

Summa sold its large land holdings around Tucson for $75 million, but it kept the 25,000 acres west of Las Vegas that Hughes had purchased in the early '50s. That land was master-planned and Summa sold it off piece by piece to builders. The resulting Summerlin community today is one of the most attractive addresses in Las Vegas. Summa also developed large tracts in three other parts of Las Vegas for commercial and industrial projects.

In the second half of the '80s, Lummis accelerated the sales of Summa properties with the goal of giving the heirs the rest of their money. He sold the Desert Inn, Sands, and Frontier hotel-casinos in Las Vegas and Harolds Club in Reno. By decade's end, the heirs had received a combined $400 million from the estate, with regular payments still arriving every quarter thereafter.

The final piece of the puzzle was the Howard Hughes Medical Institute. Freed from its connection with Hughes Aircraft, the new board moved the headquarters from Florida to Maryland, settled with the IRS, and worked to improve the institute's bizarre, secretive image. By the mid-'90s, HHMI was among the most revered research organizations in the world, focusing on biochemistry and spreading its funds to other continents.

Will Lummis retired in 1990, no doubt comfortable in the knowledge that he had done a fine job of managing Hughes' enormous estate. The tax agencies got paid, the heirs received much more than they could have realistically expected, the companies and resources were either sold at a profit or put to their best possible use, and the medical institute was transformed into an international bastion of philanthropy. Howard Hughes and Will Lummis were cousins, but they were very different men. It took Hughes to build the empire, but Lummis was required to save it.

Lummis died in 2017. He was eighty-eight.

Legacies: *Hughes in Hindsight*

And so we come to this question: How should Howard Hughes be remembered in Las Vegas? What is his rightful place in the city's history? Is he a pioneer or simply a spicy anecdote for historians to tell before getting to the main course?

In his bicentennial history of Nevada, Robert Laxalt (brother of Paul Laxalt, the former Nevada governor and U.S. senator) offered a concise assessment of the Hughes effect: "He could not have arrived in Las Vegas at a more opportune time. The town had been caught up by overbuilding, both in resort hotels and private construction. It was an open secret that several of the hotels were in dire financial straits. Huge construction, service, and supply bills were owing, and the possibility loomed large that some of the troubled hotels might have to close their doors, with devastating impact on the Las Vegas economy." Hughes "solved all the problems," Laxalt wrote, by investing hundreds of millions in the city and clearing a path for respected corporations to come to town.

Burton Cohen was president and chief executive officer of the Desert Inn for a brief period while Hughes was living upstairs. That put him in an ideal position to see what impact his boss was having on Las Vegas. "He accelerated the departure of the old guard to bring in the new guard," Cohen said in 2007, using "old guard" to refer to the organized crime bosses who once ran Las Vegas. "When you buy the Sands, the Frontier, the Desert Inn, and the Castaways, which were four hotels owned by the old guard, you gotta say that he accelerated that departure."

And when Hughes bought a casino, money-handling procedures changed and skimming diminished greatly, if not entirely. Cohen didn't buy the oft-repeated claim that the mob continued to skim after Hughes bought casinos. "I think it's bullshit," Cohen said. "The executives he had running his casinos at the time were top drawer, the cream of the crop. At the Desert Inn, there was no skimming, because everything was checks and balances, the cage, the whole ball of wax."

Before Hughes came to town, Cohen said, the "blue-noses"—lawyers, doctors, insurance companies, etc.—refused to hold their conferences and conventions in Las Vegas. That changed after Hughes spurred corporate ownership of Strip resorts.

Bill Friedman, a casino management consultant and author, ran the Castaways and Silver Slipper casinos for Summa Corporation from 1976 to 1989. He acknowledged that Hughes pushed organized crime out of the casinos he purchased, but not those properties he did not control. "Hughes had an impact," Friedman said. "But I wouldn't go so far as to say he cleaned it up. The feds were still busting serious mobsters here into the 1980s."

James Phelan was skeptical that Hughes even managed to push the mob out of his own casinos. "When Hughes moved to Las Vegas, hid himself away on the top floor of the Desert Inn, and began buying up great chunks of the town, he set off a fresh flood of stories, long on sensationalism and short on facts," Phelan wrote in *Scandals, Scamps, and Scoundrels: The Casebook of an Investigative Reporter.* "A popular thesis was that he was on a federally approved mission to rid the gambling industry of its long-entrenched mob influence by buying up Mafia-infested casinos. It was a thesis that matched the public perception of Hughes as a kind of innovative, offbeat Daddy Warbucks endowed with the insight, connections, and vast resources that could enable him to do what the Justice Department and the FBI had been unable to accomplish in twenty years. . . . Hughes, however, did little or nothing to purge mob-connected figures from the casinos he purchased. He retained many of them as casino pit bosses and gambling overseers because of their invaluable experience."

Taking a larger view, Bob Maheu said the billionaire "changed the image of Las Vegas. If you went to central casting and tried to find one person, under the conditions that existed, who could do it as fast as he did, you'd be hard put." Maheu noted that U.S. Attorney General Robert Kennedy had concluded the only way to push organized crime out of Las Vegas would be to purchase the casinos. Other ways would take too long. "Now you've got a bunch of people who are old and know they are in trouble and want to get their affairs in order, and the buying market is limited," Maheu said. "So here comes a man who has instant recognition not only in Nevada, but throughout the world."

But Hughes wasn't perfect. "Hughes was a buyer, not a builder," Maheu said. "He was a buyer, not a seller. Once he owned something, he never wanted to part with it. But he'd do nothing with it."

As a result, Hughes made few improvements to his casinos or developed his vast land holdings in Southern Nevada—two knocks against his importance to Las Vegas history. But Maheu offered a nuanced addendum. "When people try to pay a compliment and say you and Hughes are the ones who made Las Vegas, I correct them. We did not make Las Vegas. We got it ready."

Paul Winn, a longtime Summa Corporation executive, said Hughes' arrival changed the city's fortunes. "When he came here in 1966, there were housing tracts that were empty," Winn said. "The fact that Howard Hughes came here, the mystique of the Howard Hughes name—you cannot overestimate the value of that alone in getting this place started into what it has become."

When Hughes moved to Las Vegas, his Operations Office in Los Angeles started receiving one large mailbag per day of letters from Las Vegas. "They would just write 'Howard Hughes, Las Vegas,'" Winn said. "We hired a group of people to answer that mail. Most of them wanted money. You never read so many sad stories in your life as used to come in those mailbags. 'You've got so much money and if you'd only give me a little bit . . .' There was so much of that."

Bob Stoldal, who was a television reporter for KLAS Channel 8 when Hughes owned the station, said the billionaire played an enormous role in shaping modern Las Vegas. "He put his signature on the community, saying this is a viable, real community, a real place for investments, this place has a future. He was always coming up with these plans, telling people that Las Vegas was the city of the future."

But David G. Schwartz, author of *Roll the Bones: The History of Gambling* and former longtime director of the Center for Gaming Research at the University of Nevada, Las Vegas, said Hughes' impact on the city tends to be overstated. "I don't think he's as significant to gaming as is commonly believed," Schwartz said. "At the time, in the 1960s, because of his stature in the business community, it was a big step as far as legitimacy goes for the casinos. But in retrospect, you can see that the ground had already been laid. Del Webb had already been involved in Nevada gaming by that time, and he owned the New York Yankees. He was about as mainstream as you can get."

Furthermore, Schwartz sees a disconnect between Hughes and the notion that he ushered in the corporate era in Las Vegas. "I always thought he was against the corporations. He viewed himself as the last bastion of individual enterprise. It's a mistake to think that because he was respectable, he was corporate." The corporations were inevitable, Schwartz said, because the industry needed more capital to build bigger resorts.

Schwartz also echoed the sentiment that Hughes wasn't a builder or innovator in the casino business. He designed great airplanes, but he didn't have much feel for the gaming floor. "I don't think Howard Hughes had any vision of how casinos should run," said Schwartz, who pointed to Las Vegas legends such as Jay Sarno, Jackie Gaughan, and Steve Wynn as casino operators who brought something new to the industry.

Indeed, Hughes' grand visions of Las Vegas growing into a city the size of Houston were contradicted by his actions. He did not expand his casinos or build new ones on the vast tracts of Strip land he owned. In addition, Hughes actively tried to dissuade Kirk Kerkorian from building his International Hotel (now the Westgate), failing to suppress his ego long enough to grasp the long-understood maxim that competition fuels the casino industry's growth.

Another uncharitable view of Hughes came from John L. Smith, the former *Las Vegas Review-Journal* columnist and author. In his 2005 book *Sharks in the Desert: The Founding Fathers and Current Kings of Las Vegas*, Smith castigated Hughes for treating Las Vegas like a "banana republic." "Howard Hughes broke all his promises to the people of Nevada," Smith wrote. "Although the tremulous local media uttered few words of criticism of him during his Las Vegas tenure, outside investigative reporters gradually began to ferret out the truth about the man and his vastly corrupt machine."

Hughes' greatest legacy in Las Vegas, it turned out, had nothing to do with the glittery Strip. It was assembling the land that would become Summerlin, the largest master-planned community in Nevada and one of the most admired in the country.

Order out of chaos

The job of developing Hughes' land fell to his cousin, Will Lummis, who assumed control of the estate after Hughes' death in 1976. Lummis proceeded to revive failing divisions and sell off oddball assets. More than anything, Lummis and his new executive team, led by John Goolsby, established a clear mission for the company. It was not a mining or ranching company, so it sold the mining claims and ranches. It was not in the television business, so it sold KLAS Channel 8. It was not in the airport business, so it sold the airport. It didn't want to be in the gambling business either, so it sold the casinos. The company didn't have a need for a large compound on the shores of Lake Tahoe or a gun club near Reno, so those were liquidated.

But Lummis held on to Hughes' extensive land holdings in Las Vegas. Summa Corporation would be in the real estate development business. Lummis orchestrated a long-term plan to develop those properties, resulting in impressive profits for the heirs as well as several popular, useful, and enduring facilities for the growing community.

Ron Brooks was involved with most of those developments as an executive for Howard Hughes Properties, a Summa subsidiary, from 1979 to 1996. He remembered his years with the company very positively. "It was a great company, well-managed," he said. "It was extremely profitable with many, many loyal employees."

Brooks said the company sometimes had to cope with old perceptions about Hughes and the strange mix of executives who ran his Las Vegas operations before he died. The new men in charge, led by Lummis, shattered those perceptions by operating a highly ethical company. "I had never worked for a company with such a high level of ethics," Brooks said. "There were situations where we did things based on ethics that a lot of companies wouldn't do."

Sometimes this meant Summa was perceived as difficult to deal with. "We had a level of arrogance," Brooks acknowledged. "We sold property the way we wanted to sell it. We always achieved the highest values and sold property in a way that best protected the company."

Strip projects

Summa eventually got out of the casino business, but that didn't mean it eliminated its presence on the Strip. It was involved with two major non-gaming projects on Las Vegas Boulevard: the Fashion Show Mall and the Wet 'n Wild water park.

The Fashion Show Mall, on the northwest corner of Spring Mountain Road and the Strip, stands today as the largest and most popular indoor shopping mall in Las Vegas, frequented by tourists and locals alike. It has undergone a couple of major expansions since Summa's tenure, and now boasts eight department stores, twenty-five restaurants, and almost two million square feet. Since it opened in 1981, it has been the community's first stop for high-end retail shopping. The prime location at the intersection shared by the Palazzo, Wynn, and Treasure Island resorts provides a steady source of foot traffic within the sprawling mall.

Summa partnered with the Hahn Company on the mall project. The Rouse Company took over the mall in 1996 when it bought Summa's successor, Howard Hughes Corporation. General Growth Properties acquired Rouse in 2004, and Brookfield Property Partners acquired General Growth Properties in 2018.

For Wet 'n Wild, on twenty-seven acres next to the Sahara Hotel, Summa partnered with George Millay, founder of the SeaWorld parks, and they built what became a popular summer attraction for local kids and the children of vacationing gamblers. Brooks said the high cost of insurance liability made Wet 'n Wild less profitable than Summa anticipated when it opened in 1985. Summa eventually sold the park in 1998, and it went through several owners before it closed in 2004. The skyrocketing value of land on the Strip simply made the park a marginal use compared with a resort or a high-rise condo project. Ironically, several proposals for hotels and arenas on the site have never come to fruition.

Steve Wynn's start

The Strip's explosive expansion in the 1990s can be traced in part to Hughes-related transactions in 1972 and 1987. In 1968, a company co-owned by banker E. Parry Thomas sold Hughes a narrow one-acre strip of land at the northwest corner of Las Vegas Boulevard and Flamingo Road. Hughes paid about $500,000 for it. Hughes leased the land to Caesars Palace, which used it for parking. A couple of years later, a young entrepreneur named Steve Wynn took an interest in the property and approached Hughes' real estate man, Herb Nall, about selling it. According to Wynn, Nall advised him to forget about it, because Hughes "doesn't sell. He buys."

Wynn was undeterred. He went to Thomas, who urged Hughes executive Bill Gay to unload "that strange piece of property next to Caesars." Thomas made his case and asked Gay to think about it. According to Wynn, "A couple of days go by, and it's now Sunday morning. My home phone rings. I'm at the pool with [my family]. I run into the den and I pick up the phone, and it's 'Hello, Steve, this is Herb Nall. I hope I'm not calling at a bad time. I got your number from Parry.'"

Nall told Wynn that Hughes would in fact sell the property. They agreed on a price and a condition, imposed by Hughes himself—there could be no advance publicity about the sale or the deal would be off.

"I remember putting the phone down," Wynn recalled, "and like Steve McQueen in *The Thomas Crown Affair*, I danced around on my bare feet on the travertine floor because I knew on the spot that I had just made my first big deal."

Wynn announced plans to build a hotel-casino, called The Godfather, on the tiny parcel, effectively increasing its value. Naturally, Caesars didn't want a competitor in such close proximity. Less than a year later, Wynn sold the property to Caesars Palace for $2.25 million, pocketing a handsome profit.

"That purchase from Howard Hughes still ranks as the most thrilling business deal of my life," Wynn said. "That's number one, and it's a long way down to number two."

The transaction triggered Wynn's rapid rise in the gambling world. At age thirty, he took control of the Golden Nugget downtown and transformed it into a Strip-quality resort. Buoyed by that success, Wynn set his sights on the Strip. In 1987, he paid Hughes' heirs $50 million for the seventy-five-acre Castaways site and built The Mirage, the first modern megaresort. The opening of The Mirage in 1989 marked the beginning of a resort boom in Las Vegas that did not slow down until the Great Recession.

Off the Strip

Beyond the resort corridor, Summa officials early on identified three large blocks of property well-suited for commercial development.

- The Hughes Center, along the west side of Paradise Road near Flamingo Road, was built on the old Sands golf course. The centerpiece of this corporate office park is the eighteen-story First Interstate Bank tower, now the Wells Fargo Bank tower. The Hughes Center also hosts the exclusive Park Towers high-rise condominiums, built by longtime local developer Irwin Molasky, as well as several restaurants, including Gordon Biersch Brewery.
- The Hughes Airport Center, south of McCarran International Airport, provides office and warehouse space for an array of commercial and industrial companies. However, the center's best-known resident is probably the U.S. Postal Service, which maintains its busy regional post office on Sunset Road.
- The Hughes Cheyenne Center is north of the North Las Vegas Airport. Summa sold the airport to Clark County, which today operates it as well as McCarran. But Summa retained land north and east of the airport and developed it into a distribution and manufacturing center that serves as the northern counterpart to the Hughes Airport Center in the southern valley.

Summerlin

Summa's commercial and industrial centers are landmarks within the valley, but in terms of overall impact, they pale in comparison with the Summerlin master-planned community.

Hughes acquired the 25,000-acre property from the federal government in the early 1950s. Under the Taylor Grazing Act, he acquired 73,000 acres in five rural counties. He exchanged this land for the large parcel west of Las Vegas. The rural land Hughes offered was worth $1.25-$1.50 per acre. The Las Vegas land was worth $3 per acre. But Hughes ended up getting the better deal, because the U.S. Department of the Interior did not factor in the potential of Las Vegas' future growth.

Hughes dubbed the land Husite and planned to use it to test "new and improved radar control and guided missile devices" for the military, ostensibly because a West Coast location was too vulnerable to attack.

At the time, Hughes Aircraft was based in Culver City, California. But Hughes was spending a lot of time in Las Vegas, and he got the idea to move his aircraft company to the desert. He also saw tax advantages.

But Hughes Aircraft executives put up stiff resistance to Hughes' relocation plan—Las Vegas was a dusty, remote outpost at the time—and eventually he abandoned it. When he moved to Las Vegas in 1966, Hughes pondered the idea of building a supersonic airport on the Husite property, but it never materialized. Thus, Husite sat vacant for more than thirty years after his acquisition.

Lummis, however, saw its potential for a large planned community. Summa executives started thinking about developing Husite about 1981, but their nebulous plans didn't reach outside ears until 1984. Local environmentalists reacted quickly, decrying the potential impact of a large population so close to the natural beauty of Red Rock Canyon.

In 1988, Summa completed a two-part land swap. First, the federal Bureau of Land Management paid $2.8 million to Summa for 439 acres adjacent to the Red Rock visitor center. And second, Summa gave the BLM 4,863 acres near Red Rock in trade for 3,767 acres south of Husite. Longtime Las Vegas environmentalist Jeff Van Ee said the land swap was a huge benefit to Red Rock Canyon, which became a heavily visited national conservation area. Van Ee, however, was particularly encouraged by Summa's open-minded approach to development. "In response to public concerns, they listened and they were proactive," he said. This was something new in Las Vegas: a company that had more on its mind than short-term profits. "They recognized that Red Rock is an asset for Summerlin and for the rest of the Las Vegas Valley, and they had a responsibility and a duty to protect it."

Husite was renamed "Summerlin"—the maiden name of Hughes' grandmother—and infrastructure work began in 1989, along with construction of the Tournament Players Club golf course. Meanwhile, Summa generated cash flow by selling off pieces of acreage to other developers. (Those parcels eventually became The Lakes, Sun City Summerlin, and Desert Shores.) Home building at

Summerlin began in 1990, and by 1992 the development was a runaway success story. Between 1991 and 2001, more than 18,000 houses were sold in Summerlin.

Summa, now called Howard Hughes Properties, agreed to a second land swap in 2002, trading 1,071 acres in the Red Rock foothills for 998 acres south of the community. Again, the developer exhibited an environment-first philosophy, as the foothill acreage offered the opportunity to sell view lots at premium prices.

In addition to the land swaps, Summerlin was the first Las Vegas development to embrace the arid Mojave Desert environment. Rather than planting vast expanses of water-wasting grass, it landscaped public spaces with drought-tolerant trees and bushes.

Bisected by the Las Vegas Beltway, Summerlin is a shopping and entertainment destination for residents across the valley. Downtown Summerlin is a high-end shopping mall, anchored by Macy's and Dillard's. It is also home to the practice facility for the Golden Knights, the city's National Hockey League team, and a minor-league baseball stadium, home of the Las Vegas Aviators (an homage to Hughes).

Summerlin also is an education hub, with twenty-six schools. The four largest private schools in Las Vegas—The Meadows, Faith Lutheran, Milton I. Schwartz Hebrew Academy, and Bishop Gorman—are located there. What's more, Summerlin has more than one hundred parks, one hundred fifty miles of trails, and ten golf courses.

Summerlin was not the first master-planned community in Las Vegas, but it was the first to take a holistic approach to community building, said Robert Fielden, a Las Vegas architect and urban planner who designed the Summerlin Library and Performing Arts Center. "It was the environment that created the market and demand for the land," he said. "The landscaping, pathways, and open space created an environment for living."

When Summerlin is fully developed, probably about 2030, it will be home to an estimated 200,000 people.

The benefactor

Hughes' philanthropic works in Nevada were decidedly modest, and they were primarily tools to earn political points. Nevertheless, two contributions he made served key roles in the creation of important state institutions.

Hughes' donation toward the establishment of the University of Nevada School of Medicine in Reno helped get the fledgling project off the ground in the late '60s. Hughes' pledge of $200,000 per year for twenty years convinced the 1969 Nevada Legislature to move forward with the medical school.

When Governor Paul Laxalt campaigned across the state before his election in 1966, he heard again and again about the lack of doctors in rural Nevada. He made establishment of a medical school in Nevada a top priority, but he could not convince state lawmakers to fund it. When Hughes read about the political fight over the medical school, he offered to help by making his pledge. "It changed the momentum of the whole effort and permitted us to take the next step and go to the Legislature," Laxalt said.

Hughes bailed out the financially strapped Elko Community College. The college, started in 1967 by local civic leaders, had grown to five hundred students in 1968, but it faced closure because of a lack of funding. Governor Laxalt sought help from Hughes, who provided $125,000 for one year's operation and another $125,000 for a study of creating a community college system in Nevada. State funding for the Elko college began in 1969. Since then, the community college has grown into Great Basin College, offering four-year degrees, and Hughes' generosity formed the basis for the growth of the state's other community colleges as well.

Howard Hughes Medical Institute

Hughes' greatest philanthropic legacy, the Howard Hughes Medical Institute (HHMI), is international in scope but had a Las Vegas connection.

The institute's origins date to 1925, when Hughes, then just nineteen years old, hired his late father's Houston lawyer, Frank Andrews, to help him draft a will. In addition to including a few family members and friends in the will, he said his assets should go to an entity to be called the Howard R. Hughes Medical Research Laboratory, which would be "devoted to the discovery of ways, means, antitoxins, and specifics for the prevention and curing of the most serious diseases with which this country may from time to time be afflicted."

After Hughes died in 1976, a massive search for the signed original of this 1925 will turned up only an unsigned copy, which was not legally binding. Hughes wrote new wills in 1929 and in 1938, both of which also dedicated most of his money to medical research. Alas, neither of those original, signed wills was found either.

Hughes finally created the Howard Hughes Medical Institute in 1953 in Miami. Hughes' lawyers advocated for the nonprofit institute's creation as a way to reduce his federal tax burden. Hughes hated taxation, so this undoubtedly played a role in his decision to move forward when he did. But it is also clear that his long-standing desire for his money to contribute to medical science was on his mind as well. Language in the press release reflects this: "For more than twenty-five years his will has provided for the creation of such an institution and the transference to it of the bulk of his estate, but five years ago he made the definite decision to create this foundation during his lifetime."

Hughes founded the institute, then turned over the assets of Hughes Aircraft to the charity. This, in effect, made Hughes Aircraft a tax-exempt organization. Biographers Donald Barlett and James Steele elaborated: "For several days early in 1954, working on yellow legal tablets in a suite at Las Vegas' Flamingo Hotel, Hughes laboriously drafted and polished the document, then had it typed on hotel stationery. Still not satisfied, he began to write in changes." The finished press release said HHMI would "provide millions of dollars for medical research to combat disease and human suffering." Lofty missions aside, the short-term benefit of HHMI was to cut Hughes' 1953 tax bill by $2 million.

The institute started without an endowment and in fact had an $18 million debt to repay. Between this funding shortfall and a lack of focus, the organization started off sluggishly, operating out of leased space at the University of Miami. When Hughes died in 1976, HHMI's fate hung in the balance as it became a pawn in the legal battles over his estate. But in 1985, General Motors bought Hughes Aircraft for $5.2 billion and HHMI suddenly had a huge endowment. HHMI relocated to Chevy Chase, Maryland, and its research work grew exponentially.

"In 1984, there were fifty-four HHMI investigators in eighteen institutions, and the annual budget was $36 million," Purnell Choppin, the organization's president emeritus, wrote in 2011. "By 1986 there were 132 investigators with an annual $230 million. . . . By 2000, the number of investigators had grown to 330 at more than seventy institutions."

In the twenty-first century, HHMI has evolved into a major force in biomedical research with a $20 billion endowment. It opened a second research campus in Virginia in 2006. Twenty-eight HHMI scientists have been awarded Nobel Prizes.

Globally speaking, HHMI is arguably Howard Hughes' greatest legacy.

Las Vegas legacy

If I had to vote on the single most significant legacy of Hughes' involvement with Las Vegas, I would choose Summerlin. It was and remains the most vibrant and attractive address in the Las Vegas Valley. Summerlin's emergence in the 1990s represented a giant leap forward in the maturation of the community.

Of course, we must place an asterisk by that vote, because Hughes neither envisioned Summerlin nor built it. He was the one who secured the 25,000 acres west of town in the early '50s on which Summerlin is being built. He saw the area's long-range potential fifteen years before he moved into the Desert Inn, and almost forty years before the city's collective consciousness realized Las Vegas could become what the late historian Hal Rothman called "the first city of the twenty-first century."

But Summerlin, for all its lasting value, doesn't encapsulate Hughes' importance to Las Vegas. Assessing Hughes' legacy in Las Vegas forty years after his death, it's interesting to note that his impact was obvious even while it was happening. Al Freeman, a longtime publicist for the Sands Hotel, was interviewed for the March 1969 issue of *Esquire* magazine. Nobody before or since has described Hughes' impact on the city better:

"Hughes has changed all this Mafia bullshit because The Man has a tremendous reputation for integrity! He is beautiful for the image of this town, which you New York writers are always putting down. Business has been fantastic and it's all due to the man's public image. Now when somebody makes reservations for a room or a show, he can feel secure it will be honored. That's the man's reputation, right? That's his code—integrity. I mean the man's famous for his word. His name carries a lot of equity. I'll tell you what I think. I think Howard Hughes is the biggest thing that's happened to Las Vegas since, I'd say, Bugsy Siegel."

It wasn't really what Hughes did in Las Vegas that mattered. It was who he was—and the hype that followed his every move. Hughes did not follow through on most of the big-picture projects he promised the town, such as the supersonic airport or the Sands megaresort. But his mere presence in Las Vegas—a place yearning to go legit—made all the difference.

Part 4:

Industry

18
TWA: *The Airline That Got Away*

Howard Hughes was the most famous owner of TWA, but he neither created the airline nor had any involvement with it during its first ten years of operations.

In 1928, four men—Paul Henderson, Chester Cuthell, Clement Keys, and Charles Lindbergh—joined forces to create an airline that would transport people from coast to coast. At the time, airplanes could not safely transport passengers at night, so the plan was to combine air and rail service to move people from coast to coast as quickly as possible. Although the airline was incorporated as Transcontinental Air Transport, it was publicly known as "the Lindbergh Line," because of the world-famous aviator's involvement.

Lindbergh provided the technical expertise to the enterprise. "All decisions by the board of directors were subject to the approval of Lindy's committee if they involved technical or operational matters," writes Robert Serling, author of *Howard Hughes' Airline: An Informal History of TWA*.

With a $5 million budget, Lindbergh mapped out the airline's routes, established weather stations across the country, and selected the best airplane model for the job—the Ford Trimotor, known as the Tin Goose. In some cases, TAT had to build or improve airports—runways, hangars, and terminals—to accommodate its plans for transcontinental travel. The next task was to scout the country for good pilots. Most of them came from the military or from other airlines flying the mail.

Lindbergh had one more invaluable contribution, according to Serling: "Lindbergh insisted on equipping the aircraft with a newfangled device: two-way radios. The transmitters were installed in the rear of the cabin and reception was erratic. Static interference was frequent, but the sets were the best available and TAT was the only airline to have them."

Transcontinental Air Transport's debut trip occurred on July 7, 1929. A combination of trains and planes traveled east to west, with Lindbergh piloting the leg from Winslow, Arizona, to Los Angeles. The trip took about forty-eight hours.

Early passenger flight was not particularly comfortable. Passengers frequently got air sickness, and the motors were so noisy that the airline handed out cotton to plug one's ears. In the age before pressurized cabins, passengers sometimes passed out when planes climbed as high as 16,000 feet to fly over mountain ranges.

TAT was not an immediate success. Accidents and weather-related cancellations took their toll, and the public had not yet embraced the notion of routine transcontinental air travel. Furthermore, during the Great Depression, fewer people had money to fly. Air mail service kept the airlines afloat.

In 1930, TAT merged with Western Air Express, changing the name to Transcontinental and Western Air and becoming known by its initials: TWA. Among other assets that came with the merger was a young pilot and manager named Jack Frye, who would become the second-best-known figure associated with TWA's history.

Airplane technological advances occurred rapidly during the 1930s, and TWA took advantage. It started using Douglas DC-1s in 1933, DC-2s in 1934 and DC-3s in 1936, with the DC-3s finally fulfilling the promise of providing passengers with a safe and comfortable experience.

As TWA president, Frye was ambitious and forward looking. He saw all kinds of opportunities to grow the airline. Despite the growth of air travel, by 1937, only one percent of the U.S. population had taken a scheduled flight. But TWA's board of directors did share Frye's desire to invest heavily in larger airplanes and better equipment.

Determined to change the dynamics within TWA leadership, Frye paid a visit to Howard Hughes. They had known each other for several years. Frye explained his conflicts with his board of directors. After exploring a range of possible ways to work together, Hughes finally suggested that he buy TWA. By the end of January 1939, Hughes had acquired about twelve percent of TWA's stock, equal to what the board chairman, John Hertz, owned. Hertz then sold his stock to Hughes, giving him twenty-five percent. Hughes eventually acquired almost eighty percent of TWA stock.

Hughes' main interest in TWA always revolved around buying new airplanes. Hughes was intensely interested in advances in aviation technology, and

Hughes and Jack Frye, president of Trans World Airlines, depart from a TWA Constellation in 1944. Courtesy of Howard Hughes Public Relations Photo Collection, Special Collections and Archives, University Libraries, University of Nevada, Las Vegas.

he wanted TWA to have the latest, best aircraft. In 1939, Frye and Hughes made their first big investment with Lockheed to develop a four-engine plane capable of crossing the United States in less than ten hours. They agreed to buy forty Constellations for $18 million. However, the financially struggling TWA did not have the money, so Hughes Tool Company paid for the planes and would be paid back over time.

The development of the Constellation for TWA was cloaked in secrecy. Only a handful of people knew about TWA's deal to buy the airplanes or even were aware that the aircraft was being developed.

Hughes did not design the Constellation, as some publicists and chroniclers have claimed, but he played a significant role in many of its features, from the cockpit layout to the curtains covering the sleeping berths. Hughes even had specific ideas about the passenger seats. Lockheed President Bob Gross once described Hughes' role in the project:

"We had our ups and downs. But as the project moved along, we began to respect some of his ideas and he ours. Howard had more in-born engineering ability and know-how about systems and instruments than anyone gave him credit for, and he had a human-engineering touch that gave the plane a lot of personality. He gave a lot more to the effort than the dollar sign."

World War II delayed the introduction of the Constellation to the public until April 17, 1944, when Hughes and Frye took turns piloting the "Connie" prototype from Burbank, California, to Washington, D.C., in six hours and fifty-eight minutes—a record.

In 1945, the Constellation became the first commercial transport plane with a pressurized cabin. This greatly reduced delays and flight cancellations, because pilots could fly above bad weather.

The next frontier for TWA was international travel, and it started with a name change suggested by Hughes: In 1945, TWA now stood for Trans World Airlines. Frye was able to work his magic in the nation's capital to secure several international routes, despite opposition from Pan American's Juan Trippe, who wanted his airline to have a monopoly on international travel. TWA's first international flight, in a Constellation, departed Washington, D.C., on February 5, 1946, and landed in Paris.

Then the relationship between Hughes and Frye began falling apart. Frye was blamed for a debilitating pilots' strike, a precipitous drop in TWA stock value, and some questionable expenditures. Frye's primary opponent was not Hughes himself but Hughes' top executive, Noah Dietrich, who had a seat on the TWA board and, at the time, enjoyed considerable influence with Hughes.

Hughes, either in person or through Dietrich, fired Frye in February 1947. Although Frye left TWA, he and Hughes continued to talk, and Frye remained a defender of his former partner. According to Serling, when a colleague once said something critical of Hughes, Frye responded: "There's something I want you to remember about Howard Hughes. No one must ever write that man off. He has without question one of the most brilliant minds I've ever encountered. In fact, I would describe him as being on that fine line between sanity and insanity just because he's so brilliant. That's why so many people don't understand his peculiarities."

With Frye's departure, TWA was firmly in Hughes' grip. One of his most frustrating habits was ordering the airline to give special treatment to his Hollywood friends. For example, celebrities liked TWA because it offered sleeping berths on transcontinental flights. Hughes required the airline to block out several berths on every eastbound flight in case Hollywood people wanted to fly at the last minute. Hughes often bumped regular passengers off scheduled flights to make room for VIPs. He ordered flights to be delayed to wait for one of his movie industry friends.

In the mid-1950s, aviation technology leaped forward with the emergence of jet propulsion. America's first jet transport plane, the Boeing 707, debuted in 1954. A year later, Douglas debuted a jet of its own, the DC-8. Pan Am, seeking a competitive advantage, quickly ordered twenty-five DC-8s and twenty 707s.

The timing of Pan Am's order was a blow to Hughes' reputation: He had just made a $50 million commitment to buy twenty-five propeller-driven Lockheed Model 1649 Constellations. It wasn't a case of Hughes being behind the times, though. In fact, the jets Pan Am was buying would not be ready for a few years. TWA needed good, fast planes as soon as possible.

The fatal flaw in the relationship between Howard Hughes and TWA was his insistence on retaining complete control of airplane acquisition. As Serling put it, "He would not take the airline into his confidence. He foisted equipment on it that TWA neither wanted nor needed, and he insisted on one-man control in an area begging for consultation."

As the jet age approached, Hughes became interested in the Convair 880, a much smaller jet than the Boeing 707 or DC-8 but suitable for TWA's short and medium routes. Hughes was heavily involved in the 880's development—so much so that he ignored concerns raised by engineers about its engines.

Hughes ordered thirty Convair 880s, thirty-three Boeing 707s, and 300 Pratt & Whitney jet engines. The combined price tag exceeded $400 million. While he was intent on making TWA competitive as the jet age loomed, he had a problem he had rarely encountered in his life: He was strapped for cash. A few years before, Hughes had turned over Hughes Aircraft to the Howard Hughes Medical Institute, a nonprofit research foundation. As a result, he could not tap Hughes Aircraft for money. More troubling, Hughes Tool Company, always a cash cow for Hughes, did not have $400 million to spend.

Most companies would obtain long-term financing to make such large purchases, but Hughes did not like the strings attached to bank loans. And he no longer had longtime financial adviser Noah Dietrich at his side: He had fired Dietrich over his demand to become a minority stockholder in Hughes Tool.

Hughes cooked up a series of byzantine financial maneuvers to secure delivery of the first two Boeing 707s, but he had no plan to acquire the remaining sixty-one jets on order. As Serling reports, "So on March 20, 1959, TWA gallantly entered the jet age with exactly one jet." With another series of intricate financial moves, Hughes was able to take possession of a total of fifteen 707s for the TWA fleet.

TWA was making good money on the international flights, but it remained behind Pan Am and American, which had more jets in the air. Hughes continued to work out financing schemes to buy more jets. This was good for TWA, but not good for Hughes. Incredibly, in the midst of this critical period, Hughes committed to spend another $85 million to buy thirteen Convair 990s, an upgraded version of the 880. TWA executives didn't want the 990s. Neither did they want the forty Lockheed Electras that Hughes was planning to buy.

The plans to buy the Convair 990s and the Lockheed Electras were nixed when Hughes couldn't come up with the money. But Hughes' problems were only mounting. In 1960, his banks cut off his credit. And without financing for more jets, TWA was at risk of going under.

A power struggle ensued between Hughes and TWA President Charlie Thomas, and Thomas resigned. Lenders demanded that Hughes give up control of TWA and place his stock in a trust. Hughes refused. But then the banks seized the accounts of TWA and Hughes Tool for debt default. With both companies on the verge of bankruptcy, Hughes finally agreed to sign over his stock to a voting trust on December 29, 1960. Only one of the three trustees would be a Hughes loyalist: Raymond Holliday, Hughes Tool vice president. The other two were appointed by the banks.

"For the first time in twenty years, Howard Hughes no longer controlled TWA's destiny," Serling wrote. Jack Real, Hughes' closest friend in the latter part of his life, concluded:

"Howard would not have liked to hear me say this, but he would never have lost TWA if he hadn't fired Noah Dietrich. Noah didn't know anything about airplanes, but he knew how to put a financing deal together. Howard didn't. He was afraid of bankers."

Although Hughes was out of the day-to-day picture at TWA, he remained the majority stockholder, and he soon started scheming to take back the airline.

In 1961, lawsuits came from both sides. TWA sued on grounds that Hughes had seriously injured the airline by monopolizing control of aircraft purchases. Hughes countersued, claiming the current TWA management was damaging the airline.

Two years later, Hughes was ordered to testify in person. Deep in seclusion by this time, he did not show up, and the judge dismissed his lawsuit. The case was appealed to the U.S. Supreme Court, where the default judgment was allowed to stand.

But the legal battle was far from over. Hughes' attorney Chester Davis, took his case to the Civil Aeronautics Board, which, without conducting an investigation or holding any hearings, ruled that Hughes should regain control of TWA. TWA appealed, and the Court of Appeals ruled that the Civil Aeronautics Board must hold hearings to determine whether giving TWA back to Hughes was in the public interest. Naturally, TWA would demand that Hughes testify at the hearings. Rather than facing that prospect, Hughes dropped his pursuit of the airline through the Civil Aeronautics Board.

While all these legal battles were playing out, TWA's performance was improving substantially. In 1962, its stock value was $7.50 per share. By 1965, it had risen to $86 per share. Hughes recognized an opportunity, selling all his shares and receiving a check for $546.5 million. "He may have lost most of the battles," Serling wrote, "but in monetary terms, at least, he had won the war."

The proceeds from selling his TWA stock became the nest egg Hughes used to make his investments in Nevada, including real estate, mining claims, airports, and casinos. But Hughes could have gone another direction with his money. Real said that during the four years Hughes lived in Las Vegas, he devised all kinds of plans to get back into aviation. In 1967, for example, he wanted to take over Lockheed and Douglas and merge them into one big aircraft manufacturing company. Douglas ultimately merged with McDonnell. Later, in 1970, Hughes revived his pursuit of Lockheed but it didn't work out. Real was more successful helping Hughes acquire Air West, a regional airline, although it proved to be a horrible investment.

As for TWA, it thrived into the 1980s, but suffered through two Chapter 11 bankruptcies in the 1990s. Amid a third bankruptcy filing in 2001, American Airlines acquired TWA. The final flight before TWA was absorbed by American occurred on December 1, 2001, and it traveled between St. Louis, the airline's hub, and Las Vegas.

Today, TWA's heyday is remembered in the form of a 500-room hotel and conference center at Kennedy International Airport in New York City. Developers have renovated the TWA Flight Center, which opened in 1962, retaining its iconic midcentury design elements. A museum tells the story of the jet age, TWA, and midcentury design. A restored 1958 Lockheed Constellation shipped to the hotel site has been transformed into a bar and restaurant.

19
Hughes Aircraft: *Hands-Off Success*

When one considers the aviation achievements of Howard Hughes, the focus invariably turns to the airplanes he helped design in the 1930s and the speed records he set piloting them. He was arguably the world's most famous person in 1938 after he flew around the globe in record time. A decade later, the *Hercules* flying boat—the Spruce Goose—became another highlight of the Hughes narrative. While those accomplishments cannot be ignored, a strong case can be made that Hughes' greatest contributions to aviation, and its younger cousin, aerospace, came years later—and without his direct involvement.

Hughes established Hughes Aircraft Company in 1932 in Glendale, California, on the heels of the production of *Hell's Angels*, his World War I flying picture. He hired Glenn Odekirk as the company's general manager. Their first project was to design and fabricate the H-1 *Racer*. Innovations such as flush rivets and retractable landing gear helped Hughes set a world speed record (352 miles per hour) in 1935. Then Hughes put longer wings on the H-1, allowing him to set the transcontinental speed record in 1937.

In 1941, Hughes Aircraft relocated to 1,300 acres in Culver City, California. A giant hangar was built there to accommodate the H-4 *Hercules*, the wooden flying boat that Hughes and his team were designing to transport troops across the Atlantic Ocean. The flying boat was not completed until after the war, but Hughes successfully flew it in Long Beach Harbor in 1947.

Another wartime project was the XF-11, a fast, long-range photo reconnaissance plane. But the war ended before the XF-11 was ready, and the government canceled a contract for Hughes to build one hundred of them. Hughes famously crashed an XF-11 into the Los Angeles Country Club in 1946, suffering life-threatening injuries.

During the war, Hughes Aircraft also did work for other defense firms, and had six thousand employees in 1944. But after the war, Hughes Aircraft was at a crossroads. The company was ill-equipped to compete with well-established companies such as Boeing and Lockheed to earn military contracts to produce airplanes. In response, Hughes pivoted the company to focus primarily on military aviation electronics. Delving into radar, air-to-air missiles, and other cutting-edge technologies, Hughes Aircraft prospered. Hughes' reputation as an innovator and maverick helped to attract talented engineers, even though he had little to do with the company's defense contracts. Hughes did not have security clearance because he refused to be fingerprinted.

Changing leadership

By the early 1950s, it became increasingly clear that Hughes himself was impeding the aircraft company's potential growth. He was either meddling or unreachable. He was spending most of his time in Las Vegas, where he ignored the pleas of Hughes Aircraft executives for decisions on important matters. Military officials were growing wary of his eccentricities. "With the Soviet Union on everyone's mind, the fear grew at Hughes Aircraft that production schedules could not be met because of Hughes' antics," wrote biographers Donald Barlett and James Steele. Adding to the misery for Hughes Aircraft leaders, Hughes' right-hand man, Noah Dietrich, was scrutinizing the books and making life difficult for engineers creating cutting-edge technology to win the Cold War. Yet another conflict revolved around Hughes' idea to move the aircraft company to Las Vegas, where he had just acquired 25,000 acres. The executives strongly objected, arguing that, among other things, it would be difficult to convince the nation's best scientists and engineers to move to what was then still a small, remote desert town.

Four top Hughes Aircraft executives met with Hughes in a bungalow at the Beverly Hills Hotel in September 1952. They urged him to get Dietrich off their backs. Nothing was settled during the meeting. Eleven months later, the company's top two executives, Simon Ramo and Dean Wooldridge, resigned. Others followed them out the door. Concerned, U.S. Air Force Secretary Harold Talbott traveled to Los Angeles to meet with Hughes. Talbott told Hughes that if he didn't straighten things out at the aircraft company, the Air Force would cancel all its contracts. He gave Hughes ninety days.

In response to the crisis at Hughes Aircraft, Hughes came up with an innovative—and surprisingly selfless—solution. Literally on day ninety, he created the Howard Hughes Medical Institute, a nonprofit dedicated to medical research, and then he gave Hughes Aircraft to the institute. In effect, he gave up control of Hughes Aircraft. His last significant act was to hire Pat Hyland to run the company.

In his memoir, Hyland described his early frustrations with Hughes. It started with his hiring. Hyland was invited to Los Angeles for a face-to-face meeting with Hughes, but several days went by and the meeting was not scheduled. Frustrated, Hyland told Hughes aide Nadine Henley that if the meeting did not occur within twenty-four hours, he would return to Detroit, where he led Bendix Corporation. Henley pleaded for forty-eight hours, and Hyland reluctantly agreed. The meeting finally occurred at the Beverly Hills Hotel. The two hit it off, and Hughes said an employment contract would be drafted.

Hyland returned to Detroit, expecting the contract to arrive in short order. But after hearing nothing for two weeks, he called Henley. She said the contract had been prepared, but Hughes was out of town. Three days later, Hyland called again. Henley said Hughes was back in town but was very busy and hoped to get to the contract soon. His patience exhausted, Hyland said that if the contract was not in his hands by midnight two days later, the deal would be off. Having heard nothing as he and his wife, Muriel, went to bed on that Friday night, Hyland assumed he would be staying in Detroit. But at eleven thirty p.m., the doorbell rang. A TWA captain was standing there, holding a brown envelope.

"He left and Muriel opened the envelope," Hyland wrote. "There was the contract signed 'Howard R. Hughes.' I was to report for duty November 22, 1954."

After Hyland started work, he soon experienced the pitfalls of working for Howard Hughes. The biggest issue was procrastination. When Hyland wanted to do something that required Hughes' approval, such as buying real estate, he often found himself waiting long periods for an answer. Hyland solved this problem by concluding his memos to Hughes with this sentence: "If I do not hear from you in three days, I will consider that you have approved this issue." This "silence means acceptance" strategy worked.

Competitive advantages

The growth of Hughes Aircraft benefited greatly from its relationship with the Howard Hughes Medical Institute. The private ownership of Hughes Aircraft took the profit demands of shareholders out of the equation. As a result, the company's profits that did not go to the medical institute could be plowed back into research.

"The lack of outside pressure for dividends allowed senior executives to adopt a 'big picture' philosophy," wrote D. Kenneth Richardson in *Hughes After Howard*, a detailed company history. "Decisions could be predicated on anticipated long-term results, on nurturing an unusually large number of science and engineering professionals, and on investing in new high-technology exploitation."

Richardson, who worked for Hughes Aircraft for forty years, said the company operated more like a research institute than an industrial firm. "Dominant was the concept of 'laboratories' conducting experiments in science," he wrote. "Individuals were stimulated to try where others had failed. A new product line usually was not the inspiration of a senior officer; it often came from an engineer who had individually made a unique device."

Electronics projects

Hughes formed a "Radio Department" in 1944 that became the basis for almost everything that followed. The rise of the Cold War spurred massive increases in defense spending, and Hughes Aircraft took full advantage. Its transition into aviation electronics started with the development of radar systems for military aircraft.

The company then became involved with air-to-air guided missiles, resulting in the Falcon missile, which the Air Force started using in 1956. While constantly improving its work on radar and missiles, Hughes expanded into other areas as well, including infrared systems, sonar-guided submarine torpedoes, lasers, and communication satellites. The public experienced the value of Hughes night vision technology during Operation Desert Storm in 1991, when CNN broadcast stunning video of U.S. nighttime attacks on Baghdad.

A Hughes satellite provided the first wireless international telephone conversation when President John F. Kennedy spoke with Nigeria's prime minister in 1963. The following year, a Hughes satellite delivered real-time transmissions of the Tokyo Olympics to the United States.

Years later, Hughes Aircraft created a subsidiary, Hughes Communications, and introduced its satellite technology into the commercial sector. At first, it sold its service to cable television companies, including HBO, Disney, Cinemax, and Showtime. Then, in 1994, it shifted to selling its satellite service directly to consumers in the form of DirecTV.

Ramo, one of the Hughes Aircraft executives who resigned in frustration in 1953, marveled at "the evolution of a relatively obscure firm in California into what many proclaimed was the world leader in military electronics, and which later became the dominant developer and operator of communication satellites."

Space race

The government's formation of NASA in 1958 created yet another opportunity for Hughes Aircraft. It developed the *Surveyor* spacecraft, which, in 1966, became the first man-made object to land on the moon. Television networks covered the landing live from the Jet Propulsion Laboratory in Pasadena, California, where cheers and applause erupted when scientists reported that it had landed perfectly. CBS News correspondent George Herman summarized the achievement: "The *Surveyor* program has successfully done, in this one shot, something that it took the Soviet Union nine tries, nine lunar firings, to accomplish—a soft landing on the moon."

After the *Surveyor* landed successfully, its probes measured the soil chemistry and its cameras surveyed its surroundings.

"*Surveyor I* responded to 158,000 instructions from the Earth station and transmitted 11,500 photographs of the moon's surface," Richardson wrote, noting the "firsts" accomplished by the *Surveyor* project: "precise guidance to a predetermined landing spot far from Earth; autonomous control of a remote object; radar reflectivity data about a hitherto unknown surface; and a radar-controlled soft landing. Also notable were long-distance microwave performance in space conditions; flawless data transmission to and from the moon; and remote chemical analysis of materials collected by the soil probes." Four more *Surveyors* landed on the moon and conducted various tasks over the next two years.

The only knock on the *Surveyor* project was its ultimate price tag. Hughes Aircraft originally estimated that it would cost $60 million. In the end, NASA spent $360 million. But considering the project's success amid the space race with the Soviets, few people complained.

Hughes was involved with a number of other space projects over the years, including the *Pioneer Venus* vehicle, which measured the atmosphere of Venus, and the *Galileo Probe*, which explored the atmosphere of Jupiter.

'Black' projects

Naturally, Hughes Aircraft was involved in a number of highly classified military projects, and in some cases that meant working at Area 51, the secret air base sixty miles north of Las Vegas. Considering that Hughes specialized in radar and infrared detection, it makes sense that the military would look to Hughes to figure out how U.S. aircraft could *evade* radar detection. Major stealth aircraft developed at Area 51 have included the SR-71 *Blackbird*, the F-117 *Nighthawk*, the F-22 *Raptor*, and the B-2 *Spirit* stealth bomber.

Richardson, author of *Hughes After Howard*, confirmed that Hughes Aircraft was involved to varying degrees in the development of all these aircraft. But he is intentionally vague about much of the company's work, because it remains classified.

Sale to General Motors

After Howard Hughes died in 1976 and left no will, the Internal Revenue Service began pressuring the Howard Hughes Medical Institute to sell Hughes Aircraft. In 1985, it sold the company to General Motors for $5.2 billion. The sale provided a great windfall for the medical institute, which was able to dramatically expand its medical research in the years that followed. However, General Motors was unable to either retain Hughes Aircraft's research-focused creative spirit or take advantage of its know-how to build better cars. As Richardson described it, "After that divestiture, we became another publicly owned enterprise, with onerous demands for short-term flashy results and a higher priority on profit. The opportunities to remain at the front edge of worldwide electronics technology using R&D investment also began to fade."

At its peak, Hughes Aircraft—the name changed to Hughes Electronics under GM—employed 84,000 people, 22,000 of whom were scientists and engineers. It occupied multiple buildings and campuses across Southern California, as well as a large plant in Tucson, Arizona, and facilities in several other states. It also had offices and facilities in Canada, Scotland, England, Mexico, and other countries.

In the 1990s, GM started selling off Hughes Aircraft piecemeal. The biggest chunk of the company went to Raytheon for $9.5 billion in 1997. Three years later, Boeing acquired three other pieces of Hughes Aircraft for $3.75 billion. And in 2003, Rupert Murdoch's News Corporation purchased DirecTV and other satellite interests for $6.6 billion.

In 2015, AT&T purchased DirecTV for $67 billion. Today, DirecTV has thirteen satellites serving more than twenty-one million subscribers.

The only piece of the Hughes Aircraft empire that retains the Hughes name is Hughes Communications, which provides satellite television and internet services under the name HughesNet. Most of its customers are in rural America.

The *Hercules* hangar today

The massive hangar where Hughes built the *Hercules* flying boat remains a central feature of Playa Vista, the Los Angeles neighborhood where Hughes Aircraft Company was located from 1941 until 1985.

In the twenty-first century, Playa Vista, just north of Los Angeles International Airport, has become the Silicon Valley of Southern California, home to an array of prominent tech companies. But it didn't happen right away. After Hughes died, the flying boat moved first into a geodesic dome in Long Beach, then to an aviation museum in Oregon. McDonnell Douglas Corporation continued to use the Hughes Aircraft facilities for aviation work until 1985.

Almost immediately after McDonnell Douglas moved out, movie production companies moved in. The 450,000-square-foot hangar was used to film big-budget action movies, including *Titanic*, *Transformers*, *Avatar*, and *Iron Man*.

Film production continues to be the focus today, but now there's a distinctly digital emphasis. Tech behemoth Google leased the hangar in 2016 and commenced major renovations. The building houses thousands of employees and has large soundstages for its video subsidiary, YouTube, to produce original programming.

YouTube is an internet juggernaut. Its worldwide audience is estimated at 1.8 billion people. Two-thirds of the video content viewed digitally comes from YouTube. YouTube started out hosting videos created by others, but it later expanded into creating original content, investing hundreds of millions of dollars to produce movies and television series. Much of that content is being produced in the old *Hercules* hangar.

Google has transformed the hangar into a four-story structure, although the building's original wood skeleton has been preserved. "Each layer of the building is stepped back from the last, allowing for lots of light to flow through the cavernous space," wrote Bianca Barragan for Curbed Los Angeles, an urban planning website. "Where the new and old architecture meet throughout the building, the new elements are always set back to allow the older elements to take center stage."

Interpretive signs throughout the building explain its historical significance. A sculpture consisting of 2,800 steel balls hangs from the atrium, and when it is viewed from a certain angle, it has the distinctive shape of the Spruce Goose.

Howard Hughes was one of the twentieth century's great innovators, particularly in the field of aviation. In the twenty-first century, the hangar where he did arguably his finest work lives on as a major hub of creative endeavor.

20

The *Glomar Explorer: Partnering with the CIA*

On March 8, 1968, while Howard Hughes was living in a penthouse suite at the Desert Inn in Las Vegas, a Soviet submarine equipped with three nuclear ballistic missiles sank in the Pacific Ocean. The Soviets spent six months searching for the submarine, but had no luck and gave up.

The United States knew its Cold War enemy had lost a submarine in the Pacific and wanted to find it. U.S. military and intelligence agencies could gain untold advantages from the opportunity to examine a Soviet submarine and its nuclear missiles. Using data from seismic sensors, U.S. officials pinpointed the sub's location 1,560 miles northeast of Hawaii. It was three miles beneath the ocean's surface.

The technology to retrieve a 328-foot-long, three-million-pound submarine from the bottom of the ocean did not exist in 1968. It had to be developed. And that was only half the challenge. The other half was to conduct the operation without the Soviets knowing it was happening. President Richard Nixon assigned the project, codenamed Azorian, to the CIA, which had been successful spearheading development of the U-2 and A-12 Blackbird spy planes.

While the CIA enlisted the aid of the nation's finest marine engineers to figure out how to lift the submarine, others went to work coming up with a cover story. A simple but ingenious plan was concocted. The giant ship being developed for the project—the *Glomar Explorer*—would be built in plain sight in a Philadelphia shipyard. The public was told it would be used to conduct deep-sea mining operations. The entrepreneur behind this expensive, ambitious undertaking? Howard Hughes.

It was the perfect cover, as author Josh Dean explains in *The Taking of K-129: How the CIA Used Howard Hughes to Steal a Russian Sub in the Most Daring*

Mining of manganese nodules was the cover story for the top-secret *Glomar Explorer* project. Some of these nodules were retrieved from the ocean floor and given out to officials and news media as souvenirs to bolster the cover story. Author's collection.

Covert Operation in History: "Hughes Tool was a private corporation that didn't have to explain its activities to investors. Even better, it was a private company owned by a reclusive billionaire industrialist who was famous for investing in risky ventures and had no apparent concern for his public image."

The "black contract" operation was set up so that Hughes Tool Company would secretly receive money from the government and then disburse it to the various contractors involved in the project. The contract between the CIA and Hughes Tool was signed on November 13, 1970.

Hughes established an office near Los Angeles International Airport and hired a man named Paul Reeve to serve as the project's public face. Reeve announced the project to the press in November 1972, explaining, falsely, that Hughes had conducted extensive research before embarking on the venture and had been involved in deep-sea mining since "the early 1960s."

What would this deep-sea mining operation hope to find? Manganese nodules attached to the seabed. The nodules are known to contain valuable minerals such as nickel, copper, and cobalt. To bolster the cover story, Hughes attorney Chester Davis offered the idea of retrieving a large number of manganese nodules from the ocean floor and distributing them to the press and everyone involved in the project. CIA officials agreed. If the cover story was going to work, there had to be a work product to show people.

Of course, the real operation had nothing to do with collecting nodules. The *Glomar Explorer* was going to lift a Soviet submarine three miles from the ocean floor and quietly haul it away to be studied. The ship itself was public knowledge, but the "claw" needed to grab and lift the submarine was perhaps the government's biggest secret at the time.

Lockheed was selected to build the claw—dubbed Clementine—at a secure facility in Redwood City, California, south of San Francisco. Designing the device was a daunting task because of what it was being asked to do. According to Dean, it "had to be remotely controlled from a ship three miles above, by men who needed to have a live, well-lit picture of the target and its surroundings. It had to be strong enough to endure the crushing pressure of that depth—almost eight thousand pounds per square inch—as well as the impact with the seafloor; dexterous enough to navigate forward, backward, and from side to side . . . and delicate enough to grab and hold the object without damaging or dropping it."

"What Clementine had to do required technical precision of a kind that would be difficult to accomplish on the surface, considering the size of the machines in question, but to do it under the ocean—three miles from the men who'd be operating the machine—would require the most advanced technologies on the planet."

While the claw was being built in California, the ship was being constructed across the continent outside Philadelphia. When it was ready, in July 1973, the massive ship embarked on a two-month, 12,700-mile journey around South America to Long Beach, California. It pulled up to a pier in Long Beach Harbor next to the hangar where Hughes kept his giant World War II-era flying boat.

A crew of 178 was assembled to operate the *Glomar Explorer*, and after an extensive flurry of tests and sea trials, it was ready to fulfill its mission within the "good weather window" during the summer months of 1974. All it needed was a "go" signal from Washington, D.C. The debates in the nation's capital were intense—officials weighed the odds of the project being successful and what would happen if the Soviets found out what they were doing. Finally, with President Richard Nixon's approval, the *Explorer* headed out to sea on June 20, 1974.

Thirteen days later, the ship reached its destination—40 degrees latitude and 180 degrees longitude. Bad weather slowed the process of sending the claw down to the ocean floor, but it finally reached the submarine. "After more than four years of preparation, and twenty-six days of struggles and stresses at the target site, the claw was in position over the submarine it had been designed to grab," Dean wrote.

The claw successfully got a grip on the sub, but that was just the first step. Now the crew needed to pull the three-million-pound, ballistic missile-equipped submarine up with 16,500 feet of pipe. It was a slow and perilous process, the equipment strained to the limit. Just when some in the crew thought the slow process was becoming a bore, the ship was jolted. Peering at the cameras monitoring the lift, it became clear that tines on the claw had broken off and two-thirds of the submarine was gone.

The crew was devastated, but it pulled up what was left of the sub, completing the task on August 6, 1974. Next came the dismantling of what remained of the sub and its ill-fated inhabitants. The human remains were gathered carefully.

One of the most interesting discoveries about the Soviet submarine was its

The *Glomar Explorer* was used to find and retrieve a Soviet submarine from the bottom of the Pacific Ocean. Author's collection.

shoddy workmanship. Many experts thought the Soviet Union had a more advanced submarine program than the United States did, but the K-129 suggested otherwise. One of the most important discoveries was a handwritten journal that one of the Soviet officers had kept.

With the recovery completed, the *Glomar Explorer* headed for Hawaii. The cover story was back in action, as Reeve greeted the ship's arrival in the port at Lahaina. Journalists dutifully reported that the *Explorer* had returned from its first ocean-mining voyage, undoubtedly weighted down by piles of precious manganese nodules.

The *Glomar Explorer* crew had one remaining task: to bury the remains of the Soviet submariners at sea. Six intact bodies and many body parts were placed in a large red box, and a somber, formal ceremony was conducted before the box was dropped into the water and sunk.

The ship soon returned to Long Beach, and the boxes containing the submarine parts were placed on trucks, believed to be headed for Area 51, the secret military installation sixty miles north of Las Vegas.

The CIA had every intention of gearing up for a second voyage of the *Glomar Explorer* to recover the rest of the Soviet sub. But then the cover story started leaking facts. On February 7, 1975, the *Los Angeles Times* published a story about the submarine recovery effort. A number of details in the story were wrong, such as saying that the operation had occurred in the Atlantic Ocean. When other reporters started following up on that report, CIA Director William Colby successfully convinced the *New York Times*, *Washington Post*, and several other newspapers and magazines to hold off on the story in the national interest.

But a month later, Colby's efforts to bury the story were rebuffed by investigative reporter Jack Anderson, who, on March 18, 1975, exposed the project to a nationally syndicated radio audience. When Anderson broke the story, all the other press outlets were free to follow suit. The news coverage ended the project for good. The *Glomar Explorer* was mothballed. It later was used for a real deep-sea mining venture and for off-shore oil drilling. In 2015, it was cut up and sold for scrap.

Some writers have questioned whether Howard Hughes knew about the *Glomar Explorer*'s secret mission. But the weight of the evidence suggests he was well aware of the project's true nature. In the end notes of *Citizen Hughes*, author Michael Drosnin reports that he interviewed Hughes Tool chief Raymond Holliday, who said he had told Hughes about it by telephone and later sent him a detailed memo about it. "I discussed it with him extremely thoroughly," Holliday told Drosnin. "I told him the true mission was the submarine-raising, which is what the CIA told me, and Hughes approved of our involvement long before the contact was signed."

As for Reeve, affable front man for the *Glomar Explorer*'s cover story, he continued to work for Hughes, eventually moving to Summa Corporation's Las Vegas offices. In the late 1970s, he oversaw the sale of the 1,500 mining claims Hughes had purchased across Nevada.

RKO Pictures: *How to Wreck a Movie Studio*

In 1925, a Wall Street banker named Joseph Kennedy got into the movie business by buying FBO, Film Booking Offices. Under his ownership, the studio produced low-budget Westerns and thrillers, churning out as many as one per week. FBO gained a reputation for its silent Westerns, starring actors such as Fred Thomson and his white horse, Silver King, as well as Tom Tyler, Bob Steele, Bob Custer, and, for a while, Tom Mix.

Two years later, in an effort to compete in the fledgling talking movie business, Kennedy's FBO joined forces with David Sarnoff's radio company, RCA. A year later, Kennedy took control of two other movie concerns, Keith-Albee-Orpheum and Pathé. A few months after that, the company was renamed RKO, for Radio-Keith-Orpheum, and set up as an RCA subsidiary. A considerable Hollywood empire was born.

RKO's first sound pictures, released in 1929, were Broadway-style musicals: *Syncopation*; *Street Girl*, starring Betty Compson; and *Rio Rita*, starring Bebe Daniels. The latter two drew positive reviews, with *Rio Rita* rated among the year's best films. But the song-and-dance form soon grew stale, and the studios turned to that old favorite, the Western. RKO dove in with a big-budget retelling of Edna Ferber's popular novel *Cimarron*, about the Oklahoma land rush. Starring Richard Dix and Irene Dunne, the film, released on January 26, 1931, was a huge critical success, garnering three Academy Awards, including Best Picture.

RKO had arrived.

Kennedy soon dropped out of the Hollywood game. After his failed efforts to partner with actress Gloria Swanson to make big, successful pictures, his swan song was to sell Pathé to RKO and return to Wall Street.

In 1931, Sarnoff brought in the young maverick David O. Selznick to run RKO, and he had a brief but profoundly important tenure with the studio. Selznick quickly went to work producing a string of intriguing, if not brilliant movies, including *What Price Hollywood?*, a searing portrait of the movie game, and *The Lost Squadron*, about cinematic stunt fliers.

Selznick's big achievements, however, were still to come. He discovered Katharine Hepburn on a Broadway stage and gave the twenty-three-year-old the starring role in *A Bill of Divorcement*, which drew critical raves, and initiated work on *Little Women*. Meanwhile, he gave the green light to his executive assistant, Merian Cooper, to make an action picture the likes of which had never been seen, *King Kong*.

King Kong was a financial lifesaver for RKO, which had struggled financially amid the Depression. "Audiences agreed with the critics that Merian Cooper's *King Kong* surpassed any horror picture that had gone before, and they were enchanted by its beauty-and-the-beast theme as interpreted in Ruth Rose's fairy-tale dialogue," writes Betty Lasky in *RKO: The Biggest Little Major of Them All*.

When Selznick left RKO for MGM in 1933, RCA chief Sarnoff chose Cooper to take his place. One of Cooper's early moves was to pair dancer extraordinaire Fred Astaire with the young actress Ginger Rogers. Their first movie together, *Flying Down to Rio*, and their follow-up, *The Gay Divorcée*, were huge hits.

Hepburn, meanwhile, soon earned an Academy Award for her role in the otherwise unremarkable *Morning Glory*, and drew huge audiences with her performances in *Little Women* and *Alice Adams*. Another young actress, Bette Davis, made a splash starring in the RKO filming of the classic W. Somerset Maugham novel *Of Human Bondage*.

In the late 1930s and early '40s, RKO produced an array of memorable pictures: the epic *Gunga Din*, starring Cary Grant and Douglas Fairbanks Jr.; the comedy *Vivacious Lady*, introducing Jimmy Stewart and starring an Astaire-free Ginger Rogers; and *The Hunchback of Notre Dame*, starring Charles Laughton and Maureen O'Hara. But the studio may be best remembered for hiring a twenty-four-year-old creative genius, Orson Welles, under a contract that gave him almost total freedom. Before long, Welles was hard at work on *Citizen Kane*, which was released in 1941, despite intense pressure from media mogul William Randolph Hearst, whose life story inspired the script. In the coming decades, *Citizen Kane* would be widely considered the greatest movie ever made.

The war years proved to be stable and profitable ones for RKO. Popular young crooner Frank Sinatra made his RKO debut in 1943 with *Higher and Higher*. Gregory Peck also arrived in Hollywood via RKO with *Days of Glory*.

And in 1945, RKO produced one of its most enduringly beloved movies, *The Bells of St. Mary's*, starring Bing Crosby and Ingrid Bergman.

In 1947, RKO executives made a bold move, hiring screenwriter Dore Schary as vice president in charge of production. Schary was interested in "new approaches and new styles." He wanted to take some chances to draw what he believed was a more sophisticated audience than the movies were generally given credit for. One of his first efforts in this vein was *Crossfire*, a dark study of anti-Semitism on the homefront starring Robert Young, Robert Mitchum, and Robert Ryan. The movie did well, encouraging Schary to explore more challenging themes.

However, Schary's ambitious plans were derailed by the rising Red Scare. In 1947, the House Un-American Activities Committee leveled contempt charges against ten Hollywood writers and directors for refusing to cooperate with the committee and denouncing its mission. The so-called Hollywood Ten were promptly fired by the studios and sentenced to one year in prison. Two of Schary's top men, producer Adrian Scott and director Edward Dmytryk of *Crossfire*, were members of the Hollywood Ten. But while other studio heads such as Jack Warner, Louis B. Mayer, and Walt Disney joined the anti-Communist crusade, Schary strongly defended Hollywood.

After the committee hearings, the studio honchos gathered in New York and collectively decided on a strong anti-Communist policy that included firing any suspected Communists they employed. Rather than quitting in protest, Schary decided to go along and vowed to work against blacklisting from the inside. When *Crossfire* won various awards in the ensuing months, Schary had to accept them without Scott and Dmytryk at his side. *Crossfire* was nominated for five Academy Awards but won none, perhaps because of its Communist ties.

Schary had another big success in 1948 with *I Remember Mama*, starring Irene Dunne as the head of a Norwegian immigrant family. But in the meantime, RKO was on the brink of another change. While 1946 had been the studio's most financially successful ever, 1947 showed a much more modest return. "The company was heading down a perilous road again—at its end loomed a corporate graveyard," Lasky wrote. Enter Howard Hughes. While RKO executives were looking to sell out before the studio tanked, Hughes was ready to buy. For one thing, he wanted access to RKO's 124 theaters for his own films, including the censorship-challenged *The Outlaw*. On May 10, 1948, Hughes bought RKO for $8.8 million.

Initially, Hughes told RKO executives and Hollywood skeptics that he did not intend to meddle in the studio's business. Even Schary, the creative leader, agreed to stay on. But just a few weeks later, Hughes ordered Schary to stop production on three movies, among them the World War II picture *Battleground*. Schary promptly resigned (and soon was hired by MGM).

(Reflecting the complexity of Hughes' character, Schary told this story after Hughes' death: They no longer worked together, but Hughes kept in touch with Schary over the next few years. When Schary injured his back and was confined to a hospital bed in New York, Hughes heard about it and offered to fly him back to Hollywood in a plane equipped with a hospital bed riveted to the floor and with a nurse to care for him. "The plane would land on his private field and be met by an ambulance," Schary recalled. "All of this would be done as a gift to me. I remember saying to him that if I wasn't already on my back, I would be floored by the invitation." Once Schary returned home, he was ordered to remain in traction for four weeks. Hughes heard about this as well and showed up on Schary's doorstep one day, offering whatever help he needed.)

Soon, Hughes ordered massive layoffs, reducing the payroll from 2,500 to 600, and installed his own people in the executive suites. What's more, RKO announced a change in philosophy: no more "message pictures." The new plan was to make movies with the highest box office potential.

Hughes meddled in all aspects of RKO business. He initiated a movie project of his own, *Jet Pilot*, starring John Wayne and Janet Leigh. Hughes envisioned an updated version of his 1930 epic *Hell's Angels*, featuring dramatic airplane stunts. But Hughes, distracted by other interests and displaying his increasingly antisocial behavior, frustrated his fellow moviemakers with delays and bizarre diversions. The movie was not released until 1957.

In 1949, the first full year with Hughes in charge, RKO planned to release forty-nine movies. Instead, it released twelve. But Hughes managed to pull off a coup the following year, hiring top producers Jerry Wald and Norman Krasna away from Warner Bros. With Hughes busy on other matters, Wald and Krasna, dubbed "the Whiz Kids," were assured of freedom to work their magic at RKO.

It didn't work out that way. Wald and Krasna had twelve pictures they wanted to produce in short order. In 1951, only two of them were released. They either clashed with Hughes or couldn't get in touch with him to make decisions. The duo left RKO a year later.

Hughes supported the anti-Communist hunt, but apparently he didn't notice that RKO had hired screenwriter Paul Jarrico in 1951 to rework the script that became *The Las Vegas Story*, starring Jane Russell. Although not one of the Hollywood Ten, Jarrico was a vocal Communist Party activist. While he was completing work on the script, the House committee voted to subpoena Jarrico. "When he arrived at RKO the following day to make revisions on *The Las Vegas Story* script, he was turned away at the gate," historian Larry Ceplair wrote in

The Marxist and the Movies, a biography of Jarrico. "He was not even allowed to go to his office to pick up his personal papers and his whiskey bottle."

Although he now was unwelcome at RKO, Jarrico still expected to receive a writing credit for the script. However, RKO had decided to give sole credit to a man named Earl Felton. Felton had changed much of the film's dialogue but the story remained the same.

Jarrico asked the Screen Writers Guild to arbitrate the matter. It concluded that the credit should read, "Screenplay by Paul Jarrico, Harry Essex, and Earl Felton. Based on an original story by Jay Dratler." But Hughes refused to honor the Guild's ruling, arguing that Jarrico had violated the morals clause in his contract. *The Las Vegas Story* was released in February 1952 without mention of Jarrico's contribution to the script.

RKO then filed a lawsuit seeking a judgment that would strip the Screen Writers Guild of the right to determine screen credits. After a trial, Superior Court Judge Orlando Rhodes ruled for the studio, supporting Hughes' assertion that Jarrico had violated the morals clause in his contract because of his Communist Party activities. An appeals court upheld the ruling.

Blacklisted in Hollywood, Jarrico became a leader of an effort to produce films outside the established studio system. During a family vacation in New Mexico, he learned about a strike of Mexican-American miners. When a judge ordered the miners back to work, their wives stepped in to keep the picket lines in place. The miners' story became the basis for a movie called *Salt of the Earth*. During its production, the film was attacked mercilessly by mainstream Hollywood, including Hughes, who publicly urged movie industry people not to help the blacklisters in any way. The movie was completed nonetheless, and it premiered in 1954 at a theater in New York City. It played for nine weeks, drawing good audiences and receiving favorable reviews. But no mainstream distributors would take it on. After the New York run, it played for a couple of weeks at a time in a few other cities around the country, and had a long run in the Soviet Union.

Salt of the Earth saw a revival in the 1960s as it became a popular film among student activists, feminists, Hispanics and labor groups.

As for Jarrico, he continued to work as a screenwriter, although his income dropped precipitously after he was blacklisted. He died in 1997 when he fell asleep while driving and hit a tree.

While Hughes was rooting out Communist sympathizers within RKO, the studio flailed financially, losing more than $10 million in 1952. Hughes was ready to cut his losses. He accepted a $1.25 million down payment from a group of Midwestern investors whose links to organized crime were revealed in the press.

RKO executives jumped ship, and minority shareholders raised complaints. Unable to turns things around, the shady investors resigned from their board positions and returned control of the company and their stock to Hughes. Under terms of the deal, Hughes kept the down payment, prompting speculation that he had leaked the mob ties story to the press in order to pocket the down payment.

Hughes was back, but shareholders remained unhappy with his management of RKO, and numerous lawsuits were filed contending that he was wasting money and ruining the studio. Hughes' response was a bid to buy out all the shareholders and obtain total control. And, in March 1954, that's exactly what happened: Hughes wrote a personal check for $23.5 million.

But while Hughes had managed to eliminate most of the internal dissension, he was left in 1955 with a badly ailing studio. Hughes sold RKO for $25 million to Thomas F. O'Neil, the General Tire and Rubber Company heir, who was building a television and radio empire and wanted RKO's ample film library.

Hughes effectively parted ways with the movie industry at that point, falling into deep seclusion. The only threads still connecting him to Hollywood were the actress Jane Russell, who received a regular paycheck from him until the early '70s, and his wife, Jean Peters, who dropped out of acting shortly before she married Hughes in 1957.

While Hughes created havoc at RKO, the studio produced a few decent movies during his five-year tenure, including *The Big Steal*, starring Robert Mitchum; *Born to Be Bad*, starring Joan Fontaine; *Flying Leathernecks*, starring John Wayne; *Affair with a Stranger*, starring Victor Mature and Jean Simmons; and *Underwater!*, starring Russell.

But there also were some giant duds, highlighted by *The Conqueror*, starring Wayne as Genghis Khan. *The Conqueror* was filmed in southern Utah, where hundreds of local Shivwit Indians served as Mongol and Tartar tribesmen. Beautiful desert settings and photography could not compensate for the ludicrous notion of Wayne, with a Fu Manchu mustache, in the starring role. *New York Times* film critic A.H. Weiler, writing in 1956, blasted the movie's "childish dialogue and rudimentary romance," and warned that it would elicit "unintentional laughs."

The Conqueror was more than a bad film. It may have been deadly. Radioactive ash from nuclear tests in Nevada had drifted directly over the set location, in Snow Canyon State Park near St. George, not long before filming commenced. A high percentage of those involved in making the movie later died of cancer, including stars Wayne, Agnes Moorhead and Hughes' one-time girlfriend Susan Hayward. Hughes may have contributed to the problem by shipping some of the irradiated dirt to the Hollywood studio to reshoot certain scenes.

It's worth noting, however, that Wayne, Moorhead and others involved in the movie were heavy smokers—four packs a day in The Duke's case. It's possible that some, most or all of the cancers developed by the cast and crew of *The Conqueror* may not have been caused by their relatively brief time in the Utah desert. It's a different story for the thousands of "downwinders" in southern Utah who were exposed for more than a decade to fallout from Nevada's aboveground nuclear tests.

Part 5:

People

Uncle Rupert: *The Renaissance Man*

Howard Hughes was famous while he was alive and remains almost as well known more than forty years after his death. His uncle, Rupert Hughes, was almost equally famous during his life, but has been all but forgotten in the sixty years since his death.

Rupert Hughes was, first and foremost, a writer. But he did not limit himself to a particular style or genre. He wrote poems, plays, short stories, novels, biographies, screenplays, speeches, songs, and essays. He delivered weekly radio commentaries and wrote for and appeared on television. He directed movies and crusaded against movie censorship and for women's rights.

Rupert is perhaps best remembered today for two things: 1) introducing his nephew to the movie business, and 2) writing a groundbreaking three-volume biographical study of George Washington. But Rupert was an incredibly prolific writer who authored more than sixty books and had fifty movies made from his novels, plays, and stories. Roughly between 1910 and 1950, he was among the best-known and respected cultural figures in America.

So, why has Rupert Hughes been relegated to the dustbin of history? It's primarily because, with the exception of academia's lingering interest in the Washington books, Hughes was not responsible for a "masterpiece" that entered the film or literary canon. Unlike a contemporary such as Ernest Hemingway, Hughes produced no novels that continue to be read today. Many of the movies with which he was involved were very popular in their day—and featured major stars—but never achieved the lasting appeal of, say, *Casablanca* or *Gone With the Wind*.

Still, it's unfortunate that Rupert Hughes has been neglected while his eccentric nephew continues to fascinate millions. Rupert deserves to be better known today as one of the great renaissance men of American letters.

Rupert Hughes was born in 1872 in Lancaster, Missouri, three years after his brother, Howard Robard Hughes. The family soon moved to Keokuk, Iowa, on the Mississippi River. Rupert was a bookish child. He read voraciously and wrote poems and plays. At age fourteen, he attended a boarding school in St. Charles, Missouri, where he produced plays that he wrote and in which he acted. He published his first short story in the school newspaper at Adelbert College in Cleveland, after which he did postgraduate work in literature at Yale.

His first job was as a reporter for the *New York Journal*, but he soon left the day-to-day world of journalism to work as a freelance writer and editor of literary magazines. The twenty-three-year-old produced his first Broadway musical, *The Bathing Girl*, in 1895. It was a disaster, closing after only one performance.

But Rupert soon found success with a popular series of short stories about boys. First serialized in magazines, they were collected in book form as *The Lakerim Athletic Club* in 1898. Rupert also found success during this period by writing about American composers, eventually compiling a two-volume music encyclopedia in 1903.

Rupert wrote many short stories and novels. Among his most popular and critically praised novels: *The Gift Wife* (1910), *Excuse Me* (1911), *The Old Nest* (1912), *What Will People Say?* (1914), *Clipped Wings* (1916), *The Unpardonable Sin* (1918), *Within These Walls* (1923), *The Golden Ladder* (1924), *Destiny* (1925), *Love Song* (1934), *Stately Timber* (1939), *City of Angels* (1941), and *The Triumphant Clay* (1951). As well-received as many of his works were when they were published, he did not win any major literary prizes such as the Pulitzer. He had literary ambitions, but most of his novels were better suited to movie adaptations than to literary immortality. As a result, they are all out of print today, and difficult to find even in secondhand bookstores.

A major player in the silent film era, Rupert wrote, directed, and produced films that achieved major box-office success. Arriving in Hollywood in 1919, Rupert worked with film mogul Sam Goldwyn and palled around with Charlie Chaplin. Many of his short stories and novels were adapted for the screen, including *Johanna Enlists* (1918), *The Unpardonable Sin* (1919), and *The Old Nest* (1921). In 1921 alone, Rupert was associated with seven released movies.

Rupert made several movies starring actress/dancer Colleen Moore, who was considered the nation's top box office attraction during the early '20s. Later, Moore would be the first screen flapper and launch the bobbed hair craze.

And in 1923, Rupert garnered widespread acclaim for *Souls for Sale*, a positive look at the movie industry, designed as a response to the negative publicity surrounding the Fatty Arbuckle murder scandal. Arbuckle, a silent screen

Rupert Hughes, uncle of Howard Hughes, with his wife, Adelaide, in the early 1920s. Prints and Photographs Division, Library of Congress.

star, was charged in the mysterious death of a young actress named Virginia Rappe with whom he and two other men were partying in San Francisco in 1921. Two trials resulted in hung juries, and Arbuckle was acquitted by a third jury, which issued a written apology to the actor.

During this period, Rupert regularly invited his nephew, who was attending a boarding school in Ojai, California, to his movie sets, sparking the boy's interest in filmmaking. Young Howard also accompanied his father to parties at his uncle's home, where the teenager became enamored with Hollywood starlets.

"Rupert's Hollywood Sunday brunches were an institution," according to Donald Barlett and James Steele's *Empire: The Life, Legend, and Madness of Howard Hughes*. "Famous actresses, actors, and directors met and mingled on the grounds to eat, drink, and talk about motion pictures. Hughes Sr. was a regular participant and he usually brought Howard along."

The mentoring relationship between uncle and nephew collapsed when Howard Sr. died in 1924 and his eighteen-year-old son moved aggressively to take control of his father's lucrative drill bit manufacturing business. Rupert wanted to act as the teenager's guardian while he finished his education and until he turned twenty-one, but Howard resisted. Bitter arguments over how to proceed left Howard alienated from Rupert and other family members.

Howard eventually received a long, pointed letter from his uncle. Biographer James Kemm notes that if Howard had heeded his uncle's mix of advice and criticism, he might have had a happier life. In any case, Rupert accurately described his nephew's character:

"You have good looks, wit and much magnetism. You had as a child and as a younger boy an extraordinary intelligence and imagination and ingenuity. Those last three qualities I have not found so marked in recent years.

"Two faults you seem to have which are splendid in moderation but dangerous in excess: selfishness, and a sense of thrift which tends to run almost to miserliness, with occasional outbursts of recklessness as is common to people who are not inclined to be over-economical.

"You were a most lovable child and still have very lovable qualities, but then, as now, you have showed a tendency to give the least possible and take the maximum."

Rupert expressed surprise and dismay that Howard Jr. did not appear to mourn his father's death. "To my horror I have never seen an indication that the hour was tragic or in the least important to you. Since your father's death I have never heard you say one word in his praise, make one suggestion of a memorial to him or show any desire to emphasize his greatness or the importance of his splendid achievements."

Further, Rupert criticized Howard Jr.'s "grasping determination" to obtain full control of his father's business. In his father's will, Howard Jr. received three-quarters of the estate, leaving the remaining quarter to other family members (not Rupert). Howard Jr. pressured those heirs to sell their shares to him for less than they were worth.

"Dishonesty on your part in carrying out your father's expressed wishes, grasping determination to wrest from other people money that belongs to them, and a terrible reluctance to be generous can only result in robbing your life of friendship, love, and passion and all the things that make life beautiful and worth while. . . ."

Rupert had pegged the traits that his nephew would carry with him throughout his life. Obviously, the young Howard Hughes did not take the frank assessment to heart.

The most ambitious project of Rupert Hughes' life was still to come. Based on exhaustive research, in 1926 Rupert published the first volume of a biography of George Washington. The book was distinctive for its warts-and-all approach. Rupert debunked myths about Washington and presented new evidence that he was not a perfect human being. Some attacked the book for raising less-than-flattering aspects of the beloved first president's life, but it received critical acclaim and big sales. The second volume followed in 1927 and the third in 1930. Both were equally praised. Rupert anticipated writing two more volumes about Washington, but because of a variety of distractions, professional and otherwise, they never materialized.

Despite his earlier criticism of Howard Hughes Jr., Rupert celebrated his nephew's flying exploits in the 1930s. He wrote several long magazine articles that lauded Howard's aeronautical skills. Predictably, Howard did not appreciate the articles, threatening his uncle with legal action if he wrote about him again.

In most ways, Rupert and Howard Hughes could not have been more different people. Rupert was a man of letters, an artist, and a scholar, a beloved figure of good sense and good humor. Howard was strictly a man of business, brilliant but uncultured, with few friends, only employees and business associates.

Rupert and Howard, however, had several things in common. They both worked tirelessly at their various endeavors. Rupert was a hard-working writer who considered sleeping a waste of valuable time. When Howard latched on to a project, whether it was a new airplane design or a movie, he was known to work day and night to see it to fruition.

They both fought movie censorship. Rupert was an early proponent of film as a legitimate art form and opposed efforts to cleanse movies of controversial or provocative material. Howard constantly battled with movie censors who thought his movies were too sexually explicit.

They both were hard of hearing, widely believed to be an inherited defect known as otosclerosis. Rupert Hughes even appeared in a newspaper advertisement for a hearing aid company shortly before his death.

They both were staunch anti-Communists. Both men worried about the Communist influence in Hollywood after World War II and sought to clear out alleged infiltrators. Rupert's criticism and naming of alleged Communists in Hollywood contradicted his long-standing advocacy of free expression, but he also was a diehard patriot throughout his life, and the postwar anti-Communist fervor got the better of him.

Rupert Hughes died in 1956 at age eighty-four. Biographer Kemm notes that the news of his death appeared on the front pages of many newspapers. The *Los Angeles Examiner* described Rupert thus: "for more than 50 years a towering figure in the literary life of the nation." The *Los Angeles Times* editorialized that Hughes was "an extraordinary American and he made a mark on his times."

Kemm argues that history has unjustly neglected Rupert Hughes. "After reading his books, stories, essays, articles, poems, and letters, and listening to some of his music and viewing his films that are still in existence, it becomes obvious that he is entitled to a lasting place in the history of literature and the arts in America."

(One small sign that Rupert Hughes was remembered: The Maui Writers Conference sponsored an annual Rupert Hughes Prose Contest, in which a $5,000 first prize was awarded for excellence in unpublished writing. Rupert Hughes descendants Barbara Cameron and her daughter, Kimberley Cameron, a literary agent who was active in the Maui Writers Conference, granted the award. However, the annual Maui Writers Conference ended in 2010 after seventeen years.)

Howard Hughes might have benefited from maintaining a closer relationship with his uncle, who could have served as a wise mentor. Just imagine what they might have accomplished together if their skills had been combined on a movie set. Instead, Howard chose throughout his adult life not to trust his family and to keep his own counsel.

When Rupert died, Howard's right-hand man, Noah Dietrich, asked him whether he wanted to send flowers to the funeral. According to Hughes biographer Richard Hack, Hughes replied: "I never liked Rupert, and he never liked me. I think it's a little late to care, don't you?"

Jack Real: *Hughes' Last Friend*

In the last twenty years of Howard Hughes' life, his best friend was Jack Real, a pilot and aviation industry executive.

Real was born and raised in Michigan. After earning a bachelor's degree in mechanical engineering in 1937, he almost immediately went to California to work for the Lockheed Aircraft Company. Soon he was developing jet fighters in the company's research division, popularly known as the "Skunk Works."

Real met Hughes in 1957, when Lockheed dispatched Real to persuade him to buy its new turboprop airplane, the L-188 Electra, for TWA. This seemingly routine mission ended up occupying much of Real's time for years. "For the next four years, I would be on the phone with Howard Hughes nearly every day," he wrote in his memoir, *The Asylum of Howard Hughes*. "He just loved to talk aviation. By now, we were talking for two or three hours every day—about flying characteristics, fan engines, jet engines, split compressors, split turbines, and turboprops."

In addition to phone conversations, Hughes and Real sometimes met at Real's office. "He would arrive in the evening, and we would take a tour through the factory, or part of the factory. Sometimes he would sit in the Electra and do some paperwork, and then have couriers come and pick it up to be delivered somewhere. Then, late at night, or maybe early in the morning, I would drive him home to the Beverly Hills Hotel." Real and Hughes also flew together during those years, including occasions in which Hughes would fly the Electra.

Real never did manage to sell a fleet of Electras to Hughes, largely because Hughes became embroiled in a huge fight with TWA executives over his handling of company affairs. Hughes was the majority shareholder, but

Jack Real was a business associate and friend of Hughes who tried unsuccessfully to help him in his final years. Author's collection.

he held no actual position with the company. Yet he treated TWA like he was the sole owner-operator. When he wanted to buy a fleet of Electras, TWA President Charles Thomas, in a show of independence, balked at the deal. After years of litigation, Hughes eventually sold his TWA stock. Although Hughes would have preferred to remain involved with the airline, the $546 million check he received in 1966 provided him with the means to make huge investments in Las Vegas.

During Hughes' four years in Las Vegas, he and Real never met in person, but they talked at least weekly on the telephone, and sometimes daily. Many of those discussions revolved around the idea of merging Hughes Aircraft and Lockheed. Hughes also contemplated buying Douglas Aircraft Company and merging it into this proposed new aviation monolith. The latter plan fell apart when Douglas merged with McDonnell, forming McDonnell Douglas in 1967.

With his aviation initiatives going nowhere, Hughes turned much of his attention to Las Vegas investments. He did manage one more airline purchase: Hughes bought a small, troubled airline called Air West, which became known as Hughes Air West. During his Las Vegas years, Hughes also became heavily involved in the production of military helicopters, which paralleled Real's evolving role at Lockheed.

Real arranged the transportation—a Lockheed Jet Star—when Hughes secretly moved from Las Vegas to the Bahamas in 1970. Real was asked to monitor the weather to find a day when the winds were no more than ten miles per hour. "Howard was concerned about leaving the hotel to board the aircraft when the wind was more than ten miles per hour, because he feared coming in contact with dust that had been contaminated by radiation from the nuclear tests that were conducted at the United States government's Nevada Test Site," Real wrote. Finally, on November 25, Hughes' aides carried him out of the Desert Inn on a stretcher and took him to the Jet Star, which was parked at Nellis Air Force Base. They flew to the Bahamas.

A year later, Raymond Holliday, chief executive of Hughes Tool Company, came to Real with an offer: to become the number two man at the company, with full intentions of assuming the top position when Holliday retired. Real accepted the offer and gave notice at Lockheed. But soon after, Real was approached by Bill Gay, the head of Hughes' communication center in Los Angeles. Real wrote: "Bill Gay would quickly become the villain in my life. . . . Gay apparently had no intention of sharing any of the power he had shrewdly acquired through the preceding quarter century."

Gay cooked up a new organizational chart for the Hughes companies that put himself at the top and Real effectively into a subordinate role in which he was primarily involved with aviation matters. Real naively accepted this proposal. Real says he was unprepared for Gay's "bitter animosity" toward him. "This was the result of his jealousy of my long-standing friendship with Howard, and his fear that whatever authority I might take on would only diminish his power."

Actively working to make sure messages from Hughes did not get to Real, Gay instructed an aide to tell Hughes the lie that Real had quit and was living in Europe. "Howard had instructed them to hire a private detective company to find me," Real wrote. "They never did. They didn't need to. I was at the Encino office every day."

In 1972, Hughes ran into trouble in the Bahamas. The government wanted to kick him out. Hughes called Real for help, and Real recommended a move to Nicaragua. Hughes endorsed the idea, and Real called his friend, Nicaraguan President Anastasio Somoza, to reserve the top floor of the Intercontinental Hotel in Managua for Hughes. Aides slipped Hughes out of his Bahamas hotel and carried him down the fire escape on a stretcher. Then he traveled by boat and plane to Nicaragua.

But Hughes quickly became uncomfortable with the political situation in Nicaragua. Somoza's critics said he was going to take advantage of Hughes. Arrangements were made to move Hughes to Vancouver, but before he left, he met with Somoza. Aides cleaned up Hughes' shaggy appearance, and the titans of business and politics met at two a.m., enjoying each other's company as they teased about who was the richest man and who was the best pilot.

After just a few months in Vancouver, Hughes was informed he would have to pay taxes if he stayed any longer. He decided to move back to Nicaragua, where Hughes and Real worked on several business deals. But on December 23, 1972, an earthquake struck Nicaragua, with ten thousand people killed and

Managua suffering widespread damage. The Intercontinental Hotel, where Hughes was staying, sustained some damage, but because it was a newer building it did not crumble. Hughes, a longtime Californian, remained calm throughout the event.

Hughes was flown to Fort Lauderdale, Florida, where U.S. Treasury Department agents detained his plane because they wanted to talk to Hughes about the TWA litigation. But his fast-talking aides managed to avoid a confrontation, and plans were made for Hughes to go to London. The brief stop in Fort Lauderdale in 1972 would mark the last time Hughes ever set foot in the United States alive.

Throughout his foreign travels during the '70s, Hughes had no passport, but his aides always were able to convince customs and immigration officials that he was a special case.

In London, Hughes decided he wanted to return to his greatest love—flying airplanes—something he hadn't done since about 1960. Aide Howard Eckersley called Real to make the arrangements.

Real, however, says he was not well-received by Hughes' aides, who had become downright hostile to outsiders. "They had become the architects and builders of the bubble of isolation that surrounded Howard, and they feared that I was the bridge to the outside world that would disrupt their inside world," he wrote. In London, Gay instructed the aides not to allow Hughes to watch television or read newspapers. As a result, he lost touch with the happenings of the outside world. When he did get hold of a newspaper, he was amazed by what he had been missing, particularly news of the Watergate scandal.

Meanwhile, Real was looking for the right airplane and the right airport outside London for Hughes to resume his flying. He and Hughes eventually agreed on a Hawker Siddeley HS-748, a forty-seat turboprop.

Preparing Hughes involved buying him a suit of clothes. Since he had been staying in hotel suites for so many years, he didn't really have any clothes, so Real and Gordon Margulis went shopping.

On June 10, 1973, Hughes decided it was time to fly. Real and aide George Francom helped Hughes out of bed and they slowly advanced to the elevator, descending to a waiting Rolls-Royce, which took them to Hatfield airport.

Aboard the airplane, Hughes took the left seat and pilot Tony Blackman sat down next to him. Real was in the jump seat between them. Soon, the plane was airborne, with Hughes in control, but with Blackman ready with advice and the ability to manipulate the plane if necessary. They took off and landed several times until it got dark.

For Hughes to stay in London, aides determined he needed to leave the country and come back. This would buy him six more months in England without having to obtain a passport and visa. Real arranged a flight to Belgium, and despite bad weather, they took off on June 27. Forced out of the pilot's seat by the bad weather, Hughes slept in the cabin for much of the flight.

A month later, Hughes flew again, this time in a nine-seat business jet, the HS-125. It was the most satisfying flying experience yet for Hughes. "The flying was obviously doing his physical condition a great deal of good, especially since he was up and around more than he had been in years," Real wrote. "The summer of 1973 was turning out to be the best that Howard had experienced in years. He was relaxed, and he just told me that he was going to start living again, and I could really see it. Six weeks earlier, he could barely walk down the hotel hallway."

Hughes flew four times in England, with ten hours logged in the pilot's seat. He had been eagerly planning more flights when, on August 9, he fell and broke his hip. Hughes underwent surgery at the London Medical Clinic to insert a metal pin. The accident reversed the progress Hughes had made in returning to something resembling a normal life. "His world would once again become a medicated haze," Real wrote. "Before the accident, he was self-medicated out of habit, but now, like in 1946 when it all had started, he seemed to be using drugs to fight the pain. Before we started flying again, he had been sedentary out of choice. He was now truly bedridden."

In the weeks before and after Hughes' hip injury, he and Real, along with attorney Chester Davis, worked on a complicated deal to bail Lockheed out of a financial bind and ultimately buy the aircraft company. Owning Lockheed was a long-held dream for Hughes, and the timing seemed right to finally make it happen. On September 13, marathon final negotiations ensued, with aides having to wake up Hughes several times to read papers and approve conditions. The two sides finally signed a memorandum of understanding on September 15.

Lockheed did not end up completing its deal with Hughes. In the months after the signing of the memorandum, the energy crisis erupted and oil prices skyrocketed. This prompted a recession that hit the aviation industry hard, and with orders for new planes canceled, Lockheed no longer needed Hughes' money.

In the fall of 1973, Hughes' aides began preparing for a move back to the Bahamas. With no penthouse floors available to rent in popular Bahamas vacation spots, Real helped negotiate the purchase of a hotel, the Xanadu Princess, in Freeport. Real also made the arrangements for Hughes' departure on December

19. When the plane landed in the Bahamas, government officials were waiting with a red carpet and a marching band. Real was the first person to exit the plane, and the dignitaries thought the tall, thin man was Hughes. Real did not disabuse them of this notion, shaking hands as he quietly walked down the carpet. "I didn't say anything, I just shook hands with them and let them think I was Howard Hughes," Real wrote. "Because it was raining, they all got back in their cars and drove away as soon as I had worked my way through the line. I went to find a bathroom while Gordon Margulis and the aides unloaded the real Howard Hughes."

As the entourage settled into the hotel, Hughes told Real of his intention to resume flying, and the two talked often of their plans. But the reality was that once Hughes entered his sealed-off suite, he didn't leave it for three years.

Meanwhile, Hughes created an "Eastern Division" and put Real in charge of it, with the primary goal of pursuing business opportunities in the Bahamas. Real bought real estate there. He also investigated buying a television network and an island, ultimately recommending against each investment. Real pursued a promising plan to brew Coors beer in the Bahamas, but Hughes turned down that idea, ostensibly because he didn't want to contribute to the delinquency of native Bahamians. Hughes was more enthusiastic about the idea of buying an airline. They considered buying Bahamas Air, Bahamas World Airlines, and International Air Bahamas but no deals came to fruition.

Hughes and Real had ambitious plans for the Eastern Division. But Gay and his aides thwarted them, routinely sabotaging communications between the two and actively working to keep them apart. At one point in 1975, they changed the locks that led to Hughes' suite, forcing Real to communicate with Hughes through memos, many of which were not delivered. When Hughes started wondering why Real wasn't coming to see him, he ordered his aides to give Real a key to the new locks.

Gay's efforts to gain greater control of the Hughes empire accelerated in August 1975 when he tried to have Hughes declared mentally incompetent, with Gay, naturally, to be placed in charge of his holdings. Hughes got wind of Gay's plans, however, and declared that Real, not Gay, was in control of his affairs.

Hughes left the Bahamas in February 1976, going to Acapulco, Mexico, yet another move that Gay and his allies engineered in defiance of Real's authority. The traveling road show moved into the Acapulco Princess Hotel.

Even as his health deteriorated to the point that he couldn't walk across a room, Hughes talked with Real about getting back into the pilot's seat. Real made preparations for that to happen, renting a hangar at the airport and having a plane brought in, but he knew it wasn't going to happen. "By now, the drugs that had ruled Howard's life for so long had taken it over almost completely," Real wrote. The high dosages of codeine left him constantly groggy and had the side effect of eliminating his appetite. Always thin, he was reduced to skin and bones. "He was just wasting away," Real wrote, estimating that Hughes weighed less than ninety pounds.

Real began working on plans to get Hughes into a hospital. He made arrangements for a private room on the top floor of a facility in Bermuda and found someone to handle the flight on short notice. But those were the easy parts. Real could not convince Hughes' aides to go along with the plan without obtaining approval from the man who signed their paychecks, Bill Gay, who undoubtedly would nix any plan he orchestrated.

In the meantime, Hughes' condition worsened. Doctors inserted an intravenous feeding tube and hooked him up to an oxygen tank. Hughes complained that he couldn't see clearly, a sign of kidney failure.

When aides reached Kay Glenn, Gay's right-hand man, he insisted that if Hughes were to go to a hospital, it should be in Houston or Salt Lake City, not Bermuda. And when they finally reached Gay, he insisted that Hughes' "lead doctor," Gay's brother-in-law Wilbur Thain, look at him before any decisions were made to move him. Thain was in Miami, and a private plane was arranged for him to fly to Acapulco the next morning.

That night, Hughes tried to inject himself with codeine, but he couldn't complete the task and began whimpering for help. Later that night, doctors determined that Hughes had slipped into a coma. A Mexican doctor, Victor Montemayor, urged that Hughes be taken immediately to a good hospital in the United States. Real found a LearJet at the local airfield and arranged with the owner for it to be used to transport Hughes to Houston. When Real returned to the hotel suite, he said he found Dr. Thain focused on shredding papers rather than attending to his patient.

Hughes was loaded onto the LearJet and it took off for Houston at 11:45 a.m. on April 5, 1976, landing in Houston a few hours later. Hughes died in the air. At Methodist Hospital, an autopsy concluded that Hughes had died of chronic renal failure: His kidneys had stopped working, a byproduct of his codeine abuse.

Hughes' death sparked widespread speculation about his will and who would get control of his estate. It was known that he had prepared at least three wills in his lifetime, one signed and later destroyed, and two others never signed. A massive search ensued, with Gay, attorney Chester Davis, and Real traveling all over the place in hopes of locating a will. Real wrote that he believed Hughes had a will but that it must have been destroyed, leaving only an array of fake wills to be adjudicated in the months after Hughes' death.

Will Lummis entered the picture after Hughes' death. Lummis was Hughes' cousin and a Houston attorney. He was named administrator of the estate and joined the search for a will. Real allied himself with Lummis, who eventually fired all of Hughes' personal aides, as well as Gay, Davis, and Nadine Henley.

Real stayed with the company, serving as executive vice president of Summa Corporation. He focused on aviation matters, including running the helicopter division and selling off the array of airplanes Hughes had purchased over the years.

Lummis, meanwhile, faced the daunting task of improving the results at the struggling Hughes operations. He brought in new management of the Las Vegas casinos, and in 1979 he put Real in charge of turning around Hughes Helicopters, which was on the brink of bankruptcy. The company was developing the AH-64 Apache helicopter for the U.S. military, but the project had bogged down because of design problems and political games. Real put his engineers to work seven days a week resolving the design flaws and set a tight deadline to have the helicopter flying. As the project moved forward, Real moved the company out of Southern California to a new assembly facility in Mesa, Arizona, where test flights could occur over less populated areas. The first Apache was delivered to the Army in 1983. With the helicopter company in good shape, Lummis decided to sell it to McDonnell Douglas, which made Real president of its new helicopter division. Real retired from McDonnell Douglas in 1988. The Apache was first used in combat in Panama in 1989, and subsequently saw action in Iraq, the Balkans, and Afghanistan.

In 1990, the Aero Club of Southern California honored Real with its annual Howard Hughes Memorial Award.

Real closed out his career by helping to move Hughes' flying boat from Long Beach, California, to the Evergreen Aviation & Space Museum in McMinnville, Oregon. He served as the museum's president and chairman from 1995 to 2001. Real died in 2005 in Mission Hills, California. He was ninety.

Paul Winn: *Secretary to Hughes*

For Paul Winn, Howard Hughes is more than a black-and-white face in a documentary or a larger-than-life character in a book or movie. Unlike most people alive today, Paul Winn knew Hughes and remembers him as a flesh-and-blood human being.

Winn, retired in Las Vegas, started working for Hughes in the summer of 1957. Born and raised in rural Idaho, Winn dreamed of escaping to the city and becoming a lawyer. After a stint in the Army during the Korean War, he was attending Brigham Young University and working as a legal secretary in Provo, Utah, when a friend encouraged him to apply for a job with Hughes. He traveled to Los Angeles and was interviewed by Nadine Henley, one of Hughes' top aides in the Operations Office at 7000 Romaine Street. "I was making three hundred dollars a month in that law firm in Provo, and they offered me two hundred and twenty-five dollars a *week*," Winn recalled. "So I said I'd try it for a year."

The Operations Office, run by Bill Gay, employed an array of security guards, drivers (including the actor Wilford Brimley), and office workers, as well as a few aides who worked directly with Hughes. A large number of the Operations Office employees were Mormons, including many, like Winn, recruited from BYU. "It wasn't all Mormons," Winn explained. "There were quite a few because Bill Gay was a Mormon. I think everybody does this. They tend to hire people they know. There were a lot of people there who were related to each other."

A shorthand and typing whiz, Winn was hired as a secretary. After getting settled in, he took dictation from Hughes over the phone. Before long, Winn was assigned to what was dubbed the Shubert Project.

Yvonne Shubert was one of Hughes' starlets—young women he identified as having potential to become actresses or singers. Hughes would provide the

Paul Winn was a personal aide and secretary for Hughes who later became a Summa Corporation executive. Courtesy of Paul Winn.

women with places to live, acting classes, security, entertainment, basically whatever they needed. (Unlike most of the others, Shubert actually spent time with Hughes, including, she says, having sex with him.) Shubert joined the starlet ranks in 1955 when she was just fifteen years old. A few years later, Winn was one of six men assigned to the woman who in Hughes circles was known as "the Party." He described some typical duties:

"Picking up the maid in the morning and taking her to the house. Taking the maid shopping. Taking the two poodles to the poodle groomer once a week. [Shubert] had a Chrysler convertible and two guys had to go with her wherever she went. She had voice lessons, she had acting lessons, she had a hair appointment. She would go for fittings. She would go shopping and spend a lot of money."

Winn remembered picking up Shubert's parents and brother to have dinner with her, and taking her to see movies in a screening room at Goldwyn Studios. "I remember one time she went to an art thing over in Pasadena and she wanted to buy a bunch of art, and I went and we took about $250,000 in cash to buy these art pieces. She picked out the ones she wanted and then we went over and bought them."

As time passed, Shubert chafed under Hughes' strict rules and would lash out at him and his aides with foul-mouthed tirades. She started breaking the rules by sneaking out on her own. Her lifestyle changed abruptly after she was involved in a shooting that left her boyfriend dead. He and Shubert had gone to a firing range for some target practice with a handgun. The boyfriend was examining the gun when it accidentally went off and shot him between the eyes. Hughes subsequently "terminated" Shubert, directing all his employees who had contact with her, including Winn, to treat her as a "total stranger."

"I was probably the last guy, with Chuck Waldron, to deal with her," Winn recalled. "We helped her move back to Santa Ana."

In Operations, Winn was ensconced in the elaborate system to track communications within the Hughes empire. "When somebody called and wanted to talk to Hughes, we kept what we called the call sheet," he said. "We'd take down the message that they wanted to leave and the time they called, that sort of thing. Then we would post it to a posting sheet of that person. So, for example, if Del Webb called, we knew all the times that he had called from the time they started keeping the system."

The Operations staff came to know intuitively which calls to pass on to Hughes and which ones to ignore. Gay often would decide whether a message should be forwarded to Hughes. "If it was something urgent, he'd say give it to Hughes. Volunteer it the next time he called. When Hughes would call, he often would say, 'Don't volunteer anything. I don't want any calls.' He'd say I want you to do whatever. I want you to call somebody and tell him so and so. And when he got ready to hang up, we'd say, 'Mr. Hughes, so and so called,' and he would sometimes get furious! 'I told you I didn't want any calls, now you've upset me.' It was a constant battle over this kind of thing. He'd get all over you, curse you. Hughes was tough to deal with."

Winn came on board at a very busy time for Hughes—in the early stages of his battle for control of TWA. "When I first started he was extremely active. He was making all kinds of calls, he had a lot of things going. It was a very, very busy place. I remember I would come in at four in the afternoon, and often the day shift wouldn't leave until after six o'clock. We were just going wild in there."

Hughes got his first look at Winn when the aide was assigned to go to Lockheed, where Hughes was going to fly a new plane called the Electra with his friend Jack Real. Winn was sent to pick up another aide, Howard Eckersley, who was driving Hughes to the air field and leaving the car. "I drove down there, and I was there early. I stand there at the gate talking to Jack Real. Eckersley drives up with Hughes and they drive through the gate over to the airplane and Hughes gets out and gets in the airplane and Eckersley parks the car."

Nothing special. But Real later told Winn that when he got into the plane, Hughes asked him, "That one of your boys?" "I said, 'No, that's Paul Winn from your office.' Hughes got up and looked out through the windshield and said, 'He's a big son of a bitch, isn't he?'"

"So that was the first time Hughes had seen me physically," Winn said. "Of course, he knew who I was, he knew my name, because I'd been talking to him on the telephone."

Hughes and Winn soon developed a closer relationship. In December 1960, Hughes moved with his wife, Jean Peters, to a big house in Rancho Santa Fe, a suburb of San Diego. The house, however, was not completely finished and lacked a conventional telephone hookup. A phone in the cabana by the pool was used by the construction crews, but the phone inside the house, the one

Hughes used, could not dial out. So he needed someone to man the cabana phone to get him in touch with the outside world.

Enter Paul Winn. Hughes called the Operations Office, and Winn answered. Hughes told him to get in his car right away and drive down to the Inn at Rancho Santa Fe. He did. "Hughes had a system," Winn explained. "When somebody was going to work with him, you went into isolation for some period of time. Isolation meant they sent you home, and you stayed home. You didn't go anywhere. You didn't go to church, you didn't go to the grocery store. You didn't have any contact with the public at all other than your own family."

Winn was at the hotel for a few days—isolated—when he was called to help install a new television in the bedroom of the house. "The next night Hughes called me up there. Johnnie [Holmes] took me up there in the bedroom with a flashlight. We're standing by Hughes' bed. They slept in twin beds. Mrs. Hughes is asleep in the other bed. Johnnie leaves, and Hughes begins to dictate to me in the dark! Oh my goodness. I remember that the memo went to [lawyer] Raymond Cook. When I got out to the telephone, I could read it [the dictation] fine. I was amazed at how straight I had written by shorthand across the page."

Winn began spending much of his time at the house, primarily taking dictation from Hughes. "Hughes would never let me talk," he said. "I never spoke in his presence at all. If you ever notice when you are talking and the light is just right, you can see that there's stuff coming out of your mouth, and Hughes wanted none of that. So I never spoke to the man except on the telephone."

While in the house, Winn was required to have Kleenex always at hand. "I had to use Kleenex to open the doors, to touch things," he said. "You don't ever barehand a door or anything like that." When Winn had written messages to deliver to Hughes, the papers would be clipped to a clipboard. "When I'd give them to him, he'd take the corner of the paper and I'd release the clip so he could pull the paper out. I did not barehand the paper to Hughes."

Verifying the legend that Hughes wore Kleenex boxes for shoes, Winn explained that Hughes preferred to use a toilet near the home's indoor swimming pool. "The thing plugged up and flowed over on the floor, and he got his shoes wet," Winn said. "Hughes always wore a pair of wingtip shoes without laces. He had me call Roy Crawford to get some new shoes. Roy handled anything to do with Hughes' clothes. But in the meanwhile, he just kind of took a pair of Kleenex boxes and stuck them on his feet." Winn believes this was a unique incident and that Hughes did not make a habit of wearing Kleenex boxes on his feet.

Waiting for Hughes in the house, Winn sat in a specific chair. "I had a chair that was assigned to me," he said. "I couldn't sit just on any chair in the house.

Hughes instructed aide Paul Winn to sit in this chair outside his bedroom door in his Rancho Santa Fe, California, home. Courtesy of Paul Winn.

That was my chair, and it was just outside the bedroom door." At some point during his time at the Rancho Santa Fe house, Winn took a picture of the chair sitting in the middle of a room with a desert landscape visible outside floor-to-ceiling windows.

Peters did not suffer under the same restrictions as Hughes' aides. "She could do anything she wanted," Winn said. "She could touch anything. She didn't have any rules."

Winn said Hughes and Peters had a great relationship while in Rancho Santa Fe. "I can tell you right here and now that those two people loved each other," he said. "I saw them interact together, and they did love each other. She loved that old man. They had some really nice, light moments." Winn remembered Peters fondly. "She was magnificent. She had more class in a minute than most women have in a lifetime. And she was very kind and nice to all of us who worked in the house. She put up with us being there all hours of the day and night, which most women wouldn't. They'd put a stop to that kind of nonsense."

The flurry of messages between Hughes and his executives and lawyers over TWA kept Winn extremely busy. "How I handled this was I got a teletype machine installed in my room at the Inn. Hughes would have had a fit if he had known that, because they are fairly easy to wiretap. So, during the day when these messages would come in, they would go to Romaine Street. Those guys would take it in shorthand and put it on the teletype. Then I had a typewriter in my room and I would take it off the teletype and type it up, so I would never hand Hughes a teletype. It was a good system."

Hughes liked to push his aides to see how far they would go. Winn had his limits. "I always kind of had the feeling that he liked me because I would only go so far," he said. "I would stand up to him. For example, we had food restrictions. We were not supposed to eat pork, onions, that kind of stuff. He would have loved it if we had just eaten New York steaks and vegetables and salads. And we pretty much, but not always, complied. Well, he didn't have a watch, and remember, I couldn't talk to him, and he'd say, 'What time is it?' I'd put my arm out and let him look at my watch. Now, he knew that the lunch period at the Inn was very short, because it's a small place. From 12 to 1:30 or so. He'd say, 'Okay, I guess it's lunch time.'"

A few days later, Hughes would check the time and it would be a little later before he would let Winn go for lunch. Then a little later. And a little later, until Winn found himself missing his midday meal. "I said to myself, you are never going to have lunch again, fella. This is it. So I went out to the phone, called Fred Jayka, and asked him to go to a hamburger place, get me a hamburger and load that sucker with onions. I want more onions than hamburger on it. And bring it up to me. I ate the hamburger, and the next time I went in there I breathed onions all over Hughes. He knew I'd had my lunch. From that day forward, at lunch time, he'd say, 'I guess it's time for your lunch.' That's the way you had to handle him."

Another time, Winn was taking dictation and Hughes took a break to go to the bathroom. "He motions for me to follow him, and I do," Winn said. "He gets to the bathroom door and I shake my head no, I'm not going into the bathroom."

Winn also fired back at Hughes one time in anger. "If he didn't like what you had to say, he'd say, 'Oh, that's a bunch of shit.' So, one day he wanted me to get Raymond Cook on the phone. I called Operations, and they said he went out to dinner. 'Where is he?' 'We don't know.' Hughes picks up the phone and says, 'Hello, Raymond?' 'No, sir. They don't know where he is.' 'You guys, for God's sake. I don't understand it. You don't give a damn about me and my problems, but oh, you don't want to bother Raymond Cook.' I said, 'Mr. Hughes, that is a bunch of shit. You can question my methods all you want but now you're questioning my motives, and you don't think I have your best interests at heart. If you don't think I have your best interests at heart, then I will get in my car right now and drive back to Los Angeles, because you should not have me here. And here I am, working seven days a week, twenty-four hours a day, never get home to my family, and now you're telling me I don't have your best interests at heart? That is a bunch of shit, and I will not tolerate it.'"

Hughes backpedaled. "Well now, Paul, I realize that you've put in a lot of time and trouble. It's been hard for you. I'll get Roy [Crawford] down here. And if you are unhappy with your pay, take it up with Bill Gay.' That was the way it worked."

Winn recalled a time when Hughes appeared to be ill. "Jean was really concerned about him. He got sicker by the day. He was weak. I called Bill Gay, and I said I was concerned. I was up there at the house, and she was wiping his forehead and so forth and so on. I'm standing there, and she goes to the kitchen or wherever. He says, 'Is she gone?' He wasn't sick at all! He had faked the whole thing. Oh my gosh, I almost fainted on the floor. He had her convinced that he was on his death bed." Winn said he never learned Hughes' motivation for faking the illness.

Perhaps the most amusing story of Winn's tenure at the Rancho Santa Fe house revolved around Peters' cat, Nefertiti. The cat went missing, and Peters was worried. When Hughes got wind of it, he expected everybody but the National Guard to join the search. Winn was on a weekend trip when it happened, and when Hughes learned that Winn was gone, he erupted. "He was absolutely livid," Winn said. "He was furious that I would leave in a time of crisis like that." Hughes called aide Kay Glenn and told him to fire Winn. In addition, Hughes told Glenn, "I want you to call [attorney] Greg Bautzer and I want you to sic Bautzer on him and I want you to see to it that he can't get a job anywhere." Glenn then informed Hughes that Bill Gay had approved Winn's weekend trip. Hughes switched gears, realizing that his beef was with Gay, not Winn. "You tell Paul to get his ass back down here," Hughes said.

When the Romaine Street aides didn't find the cat, and didn't seem too concerned about it, Hughes unleashed his wrath in a recorded call to Glenn:

> I want somebody who is an expert in the ways of animals of this type and who would know where to look and how to look and how to go about this line. I mean, for example, directly, dogs get a cat treed up a tree and the cat just stays there, afraid to come down, and the dogs rush around in the vicinity somewhere. . . . If we can find some evidence . . . the cat's body, or somebody who heard the episode. . . . Now, it just seems to me that if Bill [Gay] gave a goddamn in hell about my predicament down here he would have obtained from somewhere, from some place—I don't know where—from Los Angeles or someplace, he would have got some expert in the ways of animals, cats in particular, and had him come down here and then put about eight or ten of [Bob] Maheu's

men at his disposal and they would have conducted an intelligent search based upon being instructed by somebody who knows the habits and ways of an animal of this kind. But, instead of that, so far as I have been able to make out, not one thing has been done. . . .

Hughes went on like this for several more minutes, arguing that if it were a "dangerous animal escaped from some zoo or circus" that was on the loose, it would have been found quickly. "I consider the loss of this particular animal and the consequences it has had to my wife to be just as important."

The cat strolled back to the house a few days later.

Peters loved the Rancho Santa Fe house, which was a welcome change after living in the Beverly Hills Hotel. "Hughes had told her that he had bought the house and that it was hers," Winn said. "She set up the guest house for her sister, who had a couple of little kids. Jean herself built bunk beds for the kids. She had a loom. She had her kiln there and did pottery work. She worked in the garden, planted flowers."

This idyllic scene came crashing down when a sheriff's deputy showed up to post a lien on the garage door. Winn said:

> One day, I got a call at the Inn from Romaine Street saying get up to the house quick, there's a sheriff's deputy trying to serve papers. So I jump in the car and race up there. The guy who had done the terrazzo work apparently had not been paid. The house was built by [fishing rod mogul] John Heddon and anyway, there had been some spat over the terrazzo. Unfortunately, a week or two before, Hughes had begun to worry about process servers and he pulled our regular people off the project, people who would have died and bled on the driveway rather than let the sheriff in. He called Bob Maheu and said I want you to take over security. Bob Maheu did like Maheu would do and he called some detective agency in San Diego, so we had some detective who didn't really know what was going on, and this stupid detective let the sheriff in. When I got there the sheriff had just driven in and was at the garage door. I told the guy, look, we're tenants here in this house, we're just renting this thing. It's owned by John Heddon, who lives in Palm Springs, so there's no sense posting a notice on the garage door because he's not going to see it. Well, unfortunately, Jean was in the garage working on the loom and heard the whole damn thing. I had no idea she was even around.

The deception about the house's ownership, combined with the fact that Hughes would not allow plumbers inside to make repairs, prompted the move to a new house in Bel Air. With the move to Bel Air, Winn returned to the Operations Office. But he also was itching to fulfill his sidetracked dream of becoming a lawyer, so he switched to the midnight shift at Operations and took classes during the day. Winn eventually earned his law degree from the University of Southern California.

Winn recalled another cat story from when Hughes and Peters were living in Bel Air. An old tomcat came up from the canyons around the house and starting eating the cat food, so Peters put out extra food for the stray. She told Hughes about the old cat and how beat up it was. "He'd been in a fight and he'd had part of an ear torn off and she was concerned about the cat," Winn said. "Hughes, of course, wanted the cat caught and taken care of."

Guards caught sight of the cat going into the garage of the house across the street. "Somehow they got the garage door shut, but the cat was so wild and vicious that they had to go in with those blankets you move furniture with," Winn said. The guards managed to capture the cat, tranquilize it, and take it to a veterinarian. Eventually Hughes had the cat put up at Black's Hotel for Cats, a feline boarding house. A Hughes employee was ordered to stay with the cat to make sure it was all right. "Tom Lashley spent eight hours a day there for a while," Winn recalled. "We did this for a while, and Hughes would inquire about the cat. But eventually the cat was forgotten by Hughes and everybody else."

When Hughes died—about fourteen years later—staffers were going through things and discovered monthly bills for Black's Hotel for Cats. "The invoices were still coming in and being paid on a regular basis," Winn said. "That old cat probably had died years before."

Winn also was familiar with Hughes' peculiar eating habits. According to Winn, when Hughes was living in a bungalow at the Beverly Hills Hotel, he would call the Operations Office and announce that he was ready to eat. Operations then would contact the cook, who was located in a separate bungalow. "Hughes would say that he wanted to eat in thirty-three minutes," Winn recalled. "He would never round up or down—it was a precise time."

Hughes typically ate one meal per day, and he ate it around one o'clock in the morning. For weeks at a time, he would eat the same thing every night. He would have, say, beef stroganoff over and over, then all of a sudden change to chicken day after day.

Steak and peas was one of his favorite meals. This could be frustrating for his cook. The cook would prepare a steak to be ready in thirty-three minutes—only

Paul Winn, pictured at his Las Vegas home in 2007, stands beside a painting of Hughes depicting his appearance in the early 1950s. Author's collection.

to find that Hughes was on the phone or busy with something and could not eat at that time. If there was a prolonged delay, a new steak would have to be cooked. "This might happen multiple times in one night," Winn said.

After Hughes moved to Las Vegas, his contact with the Operations Office all but stopped, as Maheu and aides at the Desert Inn handled his needs. Hughes also took to writing his memos in longhand, a change probably prompted by the lack of a good shorthand-taker among the Las Vegas aides.

When Hughes left Las Vegas and Maheu was ousted in 1970, Gay rose to power and made Winn, now a lawyer, the executive assistant in his Encino, California, office. In this position, Winn became the official custodian of records for the company, which meant he often was called to testify in legal matters. And after Hughes died in 1976, Winn survived Gay's firing. Now relocated to Las Vegas, he became a senior officer under the direction of Hughes' cousin, Will Lummis. Winn retired in 1989 after thirty-two years.

"Will Lummis is probably the finest guy in the whole world," Winn said. "He looked like Hughes. It was scary. After having seen Hughes and been around him, it was kind of spooky to be around Will."

While Winn was not a central figure in the Howard Hughes saga, he had a front-row seat for much of it. But he never sought the spotlight shone on individuals who spoke publicly of their experiences with Hughes. His name pops up five times in Barlett and Steele's *Empire*, still considered the definitive Hughes biography. He also makes a couple of brief appearances (with his last name misspelled) in Ron Kistler's *I Caught Flies for Howard Hughes*. An affidavit by Winn shows up in *The Money*, James Phelan and Lewis Chester's examination of the battles over Hughes' fortune. But Winn did not choose to be involved in any of those books. He said Michael Drosnin, author of *Citizen Hughes*, called him repeatedly for an interview, but he refused to talk with him.

Today, Winn is long retired and eighty-eight years old. He keeps busy with his passions for travel, tennis, and substitute teaching. But his life's work for Howard Hughes is far from forgotten. In addition to a shelf full of books about Hughes, he has a portrait of the billionaire on the wall in his living room and a photograph of the flying boat over his desk. As one of the last surviving people who knew Hughes, Winn has become a relentless fact-checker for journalists, historians, and others dealing with the Hughes story.

For years, Winn has lived in Sun City Summerlin, a seniors-only planned community in northwest Las Vegas. His house sits on land once owned by Howard Hughes.

Clifford Irving: *The Hoax and the Interview*

The seeds of the greatest literary hoax of the twentieth century germinated in the desert sands of Las Vegas.

Clifford Irving was a modestly successful author searching for a way to break into the big time. In 1970, he identified his ticket to fame and fortune: Howard Hughes. Irving, residing in Ibiza, Spain, read in the papers about the struggle for control of Hughes' empire after the reclusive billionaire fled Las Vegas and moved to the Bahamas. Hughes' chief executive, Bob Maheu, had been fired, contending his demise was orchestrated not by Hughes, but by two other Hughes execs: Bill Gay and Chester Davis. The controversy was the talk of the town in Las Vegas, but it also attracted international media attention. And when Hughes' handwritten memos were leaked to the press and appeared in *Newsweek* and *Life* magazines, Irving figured out his play.

"Irving reasoned that the Vegas conflict had whetted the public appetite for a Hughes book, and there were indications of a large fallout of new Hughes material which could—if they laid hands on it—be incorporated in such a volume," wrote the authors of *Hoax: The Inside Story of the Howard Hughes-Clifford Irving Affair*.

Based on the handwriting from the published memos, Irving forged a few pieces of correspondence from Hughes and showed them to the editors at McGraw-Hill, who were especially excited by the third letter, in which Hughes suggested he might be agreeable to the writing of an authorized biography. They took Irving's bait.

The editors' only concern was that the eccentric Hughes would end up backing out of the deal. To that end, they drafted a contract for Hughes to sign. Irving was to deliver the contract to Hughes. Naturally, he brought it back with a signature.

Irving and McGraw-Hill signed their contract on March 23, 1971. Irving would receive a $100,000 advance, another $100,000 upon completion of his research, and $300,000 when he turned in the manuscript. He would split the proceeds with Hughes fifty-fifty. Irving also would receive a percentage, or royalty, on book sales.

But the gravy train was still rolling. McGraw-Hill then contacted *Life* magazine, offering the lucrative rights to print excerpts from the Hughes book. *Life* agreed to pay $250,000. Paperback rights and Book of the Month Club rights promised hundreds of thousands more for the publishing house—and Irving.

Irving and his partner in crime, fellow author Richard Suskind, set to work on the research. The duo traveled to Washington, D.C., Houston, Las Vegas (where Suskind perused the *Las Vegas Sun*'s library of news clippings), and the Bahamas. All the while, Irving told his editors he was conducting interviews with Hughes.

Then Irving delivered a message from Hughes to his editors: He wanted a more lucrative contract, double the original amount, or $1 million. McGraw-Hill agreed to $750,000 after Irving indicated the interviews were going so well that he thought the book actually would be an autobiography instead of a biography.

The publisher was comforted by language in the contract that precluded a Hughes-related firm, Rosemont Enterprises, from getting involved with the Irving project. Rosemont Enterprises, incorporated in Nevada, was well-known for suppressing books about Hughes. Bulldog attorneys Chester Davis in New York and Greg Bautzer in Los Angeles worked tirelessly to shut down book projects. The rationale was that Rosemont owned the exclusive rights to Hughes' story and was preparing an authorized biography.

Rosemont did, in fact, conduct voluminous research on Hughes. Paul Winn, a longtime Hughes aide, described the firm as a "clipping service." It gathered news clippings about Hughes from all over the world and kept them in scrapbooks. The material also was preserved on IBM punch cards. All this presumably was done to make the material available to a writer retained to craft the definitive Hughes bio. It never happened.

Meanwhile, Rosemont delayed distribution of a Random House-commissioned biography by John Keats. Rosemont ultimately lost the case, with the court ruling that Hughes was a public figure who could not control every published word about him. The aggressive legal action, however, deterred other publishers from writing about Hughes.

Except for Lyle Stuart. The feisty New York publisher, responsible for numerous books about Las Vegas, wasn't going to bow to Rosemont's threats. Amid a spate of litigation, Stuart published two books about Hughes: *The Bashful Billionaire* by Albert Gerber and *Howard Hughes in Las Vegas* by Omar

Garrison. (Stuart later tangled in court with Las Vegas casino mogul Steve Wynn over a biography written by John L. Smith. Promotional literature for the book suggested Wynn had ties to organized crime.)

When Irving delivered a rough manuscript to the editors at McGraw-Hill, they were pleased with their investment. The thousand pages, including long question-and-answer transcripts, delivered on the promise of the Hughes story as told by the man himself. *The Autobiography of Howard Hughes*, with introduction and commentary by Clifford Irving, was prepared for publication.

A complication arose: a competing sort-of autobiography of Hughes edited by Robert Eaton. Irving settled McGraw-Hill's worries by appearing to have Hughes send the publisher a letter disavowing the Eaton book (see Chapter 29 for more on this book).

Life Editor Ralph Graves, however, suggested a precaution, perhaps the first feeling of doubt at the publishing house: have a handwriting expert look at the letter and verify that Hughes wrote it. Alfred Kanfer, who had examined Hughes' handwriting before, declared the letter authentic.

McGraw-Hill issued a press release about the book on December 7, 1971. Investigative reporter James Phelan, arguably the most knowledgeable Hughes-watcher on the planet, got the news while sitting in the office of *Las Vegas Sun* publisher Hank Greenspun. Phelan was skeptical about the book's legitimacy, but he also knew how unpredictable Hughes could be. He offered his services to McGraw-Hill editors to determine the book's authenticity, but they said that would not be necessary.

Phelan got in touch with another respected Hughes-watcher, Frank McCulloch, a longtime *Time* magazine editor and reporter who was the last journalist to interview Hughes in person in 1958. Although *Life* and *Time* were sister publications, McCulloch had not been told about the book or brought in to check it out.

These two journalistic skeptics should have been ready to quickly declare the book a fake, but experience with Hughes compelled them to keep an open mind. Why had the denial of the book's authenticity come from Hughes Tool Company and not Hughes himself? Did this suggest that Hughes had participated in the book without informing his underlings? This certainly would not be unprecedented with Hughes, who was known for secret operations.

Phelan had another reason to believe the Irving book might be legitimate. Phelan had been working on a book with Noah Dietrich, Hughes' chief lieutenant for thirty-two years until 1957. But the project screeched to a halt in 1971 when Dietrich decided he was not happy with Phelan's work. Dietrich selected a different writer, but they were having trouble finding a publisher. Phelan reasoned that Hughes was working behind the scenes to see that Dietrich couldn't land a publishing contract. And, so the theory went, Hughes was delaying Dietrich so he could get his memoirs out first.

It turned out Phelan's theory wasn't sinister enough. In fact, while Hughes was indeed keeping tabs on the Dietrich book, the bigger story was that Phelan's unfinished manuscript had made its way into Irving's hands and formed the basis for his fake autobiography. If the McGraw-Hill editors had agreed to show Phelan the manuscript when he asked, the hoax could have been exposed much sooner than it was.

In the days after the book was announced, Hughes did not issue a denial, and this bolstered the McGraw-Hill editors' confidence that all was well. But over at *Time* and *Life*, doubt was nagging at some of the hard-nosed journalists there. Then, on December 16, McCulloch learned that Hughes would be calling him that afternoon to talk about the book. McCulloch took the call and recognized Hughes' voice. With witnesses listening in, Hughes said the book was phony and that he'd never met Clifford Irving.

Yet McCulloch did not immediately dismiss the Irving book. After he read portions of it, he was impressed. "The style, the pace, the earthiness of the language all sounded so true to Hughes' form that when he went into the office the next day he was able to inform Graves that he was a convert," according to *Hoax*. He was particularly convinced when he came across details of an off-the-record Hughes interview with a *Time* reporter that only McCulloch and Hughes would know.

With McCulloch supporting the manuscript, the *Life* editors decided Hughes' phone call must have been a case of him changing his mind or a ploy of some kind to generate further publicity for the book.

Still, the editors ordered a second handwriting analysis. A respected firm compared Irving's letters with correspondence in the possession of the Nevada Gaming Control Board. Amazingly, Irving's forgeries passed muster again.

Irving then submitted to a lie-detector test. But, insisting he had to catch a plane, he walked out before the test could be completed. The administrator detected inconsistencies in Irving's story, but refused to write a report because the test was incomplete.

Hughes' attorney, Chester Davis, was frustrated by the publishers' refusal to take his denials seriously. So he finally produced the heavy artillery: Hughes himself.

Hughes' public relations team handpicked seven journalists who had known Hughes in the old days to come on January 7, 1972, to a conference room in the Sheraton-Universal Hotel in Los Angeles. The conference room was connected to a Hughes Tool Company switchboard in Miami and then to the Bahamas hotel where Hughes was staying at the time. The authors of *Hoax* set the bizarre scene: "Seven grown men, clustered around an electronic box, frantically posing questions to a disembodied voice, while television cameras recorded the whole charade."

The first goal of the press conference was to confirm that it was truly Hughes on the line. The journalists, several of whom were old aviation writers, started quizzing him about aircraft designs and flying feats. It turned out Hughes was not able to successfully answer some of the test questions—he had trouble remembering names—but it was soon clear to all concerned that the voice on the telephone was indeed that of good ol' Howard Hughes.

Hughes finally got around to the point of the press conference: Clifford Irving. "I don't know him," Hughes said. "I have never even heard of him until a matter of a few days ago when this thing first came to my attention." Hughes said he had not left the Bahamas to go to any of the places Irving claimed they had met.

Then Hughes, using careful language, suggested there might be more than meets the eye behind the Irving caper. The implication was that Hughes' former chief aide, Bob Maheu, with whom he was embroiled in a legal battle, might have been behind the bogus book.

An eighth journalist also was in the room: *Las Vegas Review-Journal* editor Don Digilio. Digilio sat on the sidelines for the event, but he fed a fateful question to the reporters who got to speak with Hughes: Why had he fired Maheu?

When Hughes replied, "Because he's a no-good, dishonest son of a bitch who stole me blind," Maheu sued Hughes for libel and eventually won an undisclosed settlement (see Chapter 10).

During the two-and-a-half-hour press conference, Hughes freely answered questions about his physical appearance, his health, and his old penchant for wearing tennis shoes with formal wear. The latter question prompted a long dissertation on the kind of shoes he wore and why. He also vowed to return to Las Vegas, although he was clearly exasperated by incessant litigation.

In hindsight, the Hughes telephone interview should have been the death knell for Irving's hoax. But amazingly, it only served to confirm for many observers that Hughes had in fact cooperated with Irving and was now disavowing it on the advice of his lawyers.

McGraw-Hill announced that it was standing by the book, while Irving claimed that it was not Hughes on the telephone hookup. Irving also was interviewed by Mike Wallace for *60 Minutes*, and some of his answers raised eyebrows about whether he was telling the truth. But Wallace had read the manuscript and was convinced of its authenticity.

Unable to convince the publishers that Irving was a fraud, Davis took the issue to court, demanding that McGraw-Hill be prevented from publishing the book on the grounds that it infringed on Rosemont Enterprises' exclusive rights.

In defense of the book's authenticity, McGraw-Hill produced the financial records of payments to "H.R. Hughes" having been deposited in a Swiss bank.

The McGraw-Hill and *Life* magazine defense, filed January 18, 1972, also included affidavits from top editors vouching for Irving and the book. Even McCulloch went out on a flimsy limb for Irving:

"I am convinced beyond reasonable doubt as to the authenticity of the Howard Hughes autobiography. This conviction is based upon my long-standing personal familiarity with Howard Hughes, my readings of the manuscript, and my interviews with Clifford Irving. My belief in that authenticity is not shaken by denials of that story, nor is my belief in the authenticity of the autobiography shaken by the denials which I have heard from a man I believe to be Howard Hughes."

The key to unmasking Irving was not to be found in evaluations of the manuscript, but by following the money. The Swiss bank, alerted to a possible problem by a visit from Davis, started doing some checking, and it came to learn that the "H.R. Hughes" making deposits was a woman named "Helga."

Committed to secrecy and not wanting to invite negative publicity, the Swiss bank did not volunteer the discovery of this scam to the world. But it didn't take long for others to start making inquiries. McGraw-Hill and *Life* lawyers flew to Zurich to investigate, but they were one step behind Robert Peloquin, president of Intertel, a legendary private investigation firm that Hughes had long kept on retainer. Peloquin brought his evidence to the Swiss police and they started asking questions at the bank. The bank cooperated and the fraud was revealed, including an indication, not yet made public, that Irving's wife, Edith, was the "Helga Hughes" who had handled the deposits and withdrawals.

McGraw-Hill suspended publication of the book, acknowledging publicly that the financial irregularities needed to be addressed. But incredibly, the publisher reiterated its belief in the authenticity of Irving's autobiography.

Irving was ready for the onslaught. Meeting in New York, he made his case to McGraw-Hill and *Life* officials that the mystery woman in question likely was a "loyal servant" of Hughes. Meanwhile, Swiss authorities had tracked down Edith Irving in Ibiza, Spain, and questioned her about the bank activity. Before Clifford Irving flew back to Ibiza to aid his wife, he underwent yet more questioning by McCulloch. Irving once again put on an Oscar-worthy performance, offering fascinating details of his secret meetings with Hughes.

Reporters from all over the world flocked to the story, and the Irvings entertained many of them in Ibiza, laughing off suggestions of any foul play on their part. Meanwhile, Irving's undoing, in the form of the U.S. Postal Inspection Service, was gearing up for action across the Atlantic. Working with reporter Bill Lambert, the

Inspection Service tracked the letters Irving supposedly had sent to a Hughes intermediary in Miami. And using Irving's detailed descriptions of his meetings with Hughes, they followed his footsteps and discovered discrepancies in his story. These concerns were relayed to McCulloch in New York, who immediately stopped the presses on the latest edition of *Life* containing excerpts from the book.

Then, instead of staying in the relative peace and safety of Ibiza, Irving returned to New York. The authors of *Hoax* surmised that Irving, confident as ever, felt the need to be "back in the middle of the action." More than one hundred reporters and photographers met Irving at John F. Kennedy Airport and shouted questions at him as he hustled to a waiting car.

A strange case of mistaken identity led to Irving admitting the hoax—or at least part of it. McCulloch came to suspect that Irving's go-between with Hughes was John Meier, who worked for Hughes in the 1960s. But when Irving heard the last name, he confused it with that of Stanley Meyer, who *was* integrally involved in the hoax. The jig was up, he thought, and he told the district attorney and McCulloch that his wife was "Helga Hughes."

Irving's story started to collapse. First, a mistress, the Danish folk singer Nina Van Pallandt, exploded his tale of interviewing Hughes in Mexico. During the dates in question, Irving had been with her. Then another mistress, Anne Baxter, described a fun-filled trip to the Virgin Islands with Irving during which he was supposed to have interviewed Hughes.

Two grand juries were impaneled—federal and state—and investigations kicked into full gear. One line of questioning, prompted by Davis, suggested that ousted Maheu was the mastermind and Irving simply a stooge. Davis conjectured that Maheu was trying to force Hughes into the public so he could be confronted in Maheu's wrongful firing lawsuit. Maheu testified before the grand jury that he knew nothing about Irving.

Meantime, excerpts from Irving's manuscript started leaking out—on purpose to test their authenticity—and journalist Phelan came across a familiar anecdote from the manuscript that was reprinted in the *New York Times*. He recognized it as something he had written for his defunct Dietrich memoir. He flew from his home in Long Beach, California, to New York, and the two manuscripts were scrupulously compared. Eerie parallels popped up.

"In most cases Irving had diligently rewritten and rephrased the Phelan material, rather than plagiarizing it directly," according to *Hoax*, but in a few cases he had cribbed Phelan's words almost exactly. Most importantly, in several instances Irving had Hughes relating stories that he couldn't possibly have known about, including a couple that Phelan had dug up on his own.

At long last, McGraw-Hill and *Life* editors admitted, on February 11, 1972, that Irving's manuscript was a hoax. *Time* magazine's next cover story featured the headline, "Con Man of the Year."

So, how did Irving obtain Phelan's manuscript? Through Stanley Meyer. A low-level Hollywood mover and shaker, Meyer had been involved with Phelan's work on the Dietrich memoir. But instead of helping Phelan and Dietrich, he tried to derail their project by leaking it to Hughes attorney Bautzer, who naturally did everything in his power to kill it. He then ensured the project's doom by driving a wedge between Phelan and Dietrich. Meyer recruited Irving to take Phelan's place and rewrite the manuscript. Irving did not want to take on the rewrite job, but Meyer sent him a copy of the manuscript anyway. (Dietrich's memoir was later written by journalist Bob Thomas, based largely on Phelan's research, and, in the wake of the Irving hoax, found a publisher eager to release a legitimate book about Hughes.)

As for the identity of the forger of the Hughes letters, speculation ran in all directions. But everyone agreed on one thing: Whoever did it was an expert in the deceitful trade. But federal investigators studying the forged letters came to an unlikely conclusion: The forger was Irving himself.

Clifford and Edith Irving and Richard Suskind were indicted on forgery, perjury, and conspiracy charges in state court in March 1972. Then a federal court indicted the Irvings on mail fraud charges. Three days later, the Irvings pleaded guilty to the federal charges. Clifford Irving was sentenced to two and a half years in prison. Edith Irving was sentenced to two years in prison in Switzerland. They also had to pay back the $750,000 received from McGraw-Hill. Suskind was sentenced in state court to six months in prison.

While awaiting sentencing, Irving drafted a book about the hoax. He originally planned to call it "The Book About the Book," but he later changed it to *The Hoax*. The memoir is a fast-paced narrative that may be the best thing Irving had written to date.

In January 1974, after a tumultuous seventeen months in three different prisons, Irving, age forty-three, was released. He was deep in debt, and his wife wanted a divorce. He returned to writing, authoring a half-dozen novels. In 1999, he made *The Autobiography of Howard Hughes* available for purchase on the internet.

In April 2007, Miramax released a movie, *The Hoax*, about Irving's caper. Richard Gere starred as the author, Alfred Molina as accomplice Richard Suskind, and Marcia Gay Harden as Irving's wife. Before the film was released, Irving, age seventy-five, told the *New York Times*, apparently without irony, that the screenplay played fast and loose with the facts. "The movie is basically fiction," Irving wrote on his website. "You could call it a hoax about a hoax."

The movie does, in fact, deviate from the historical record in several respects, often simplifying the story in the interest of achieving the fast pace and narrative clarity demanded by Hollywood studios. That said, *The Hoax*, directed by Lasse Hallström, is an intriguing depiction of the Irving story. *New York Times* critic A.O. Scott called it "briskly entertaining" and gushed about Gere's "brilliance" in the lead role. Kenneth Turan of the *Los Angeles Times* said it's a "smart" film in which Gere delivers a "mature" and "convincing" performance.

Interviewed by the *Village Voice*, Irving gave the film a mixed review. "I enjoyed a lot of it," he said. "I think it's fast moving. And I think Richard Gere is terrific in it, even though the character that he plays is not me. If I was that guy, I'd shoot myself, because that guy is desperate." Unlike the character in the film, Irving said, he was not "broke, desperate, and washed up." In fact, Irving was quite successful. "I wasn't burning the world down, but I had a four-book contract at the time," he said. "I owned a big house in Spain, I owned a boat and a Mercedes, and my wife had a private income. We were very well off, and it's harder to grasp why someone like that goes off on an absurd, zany experience than why the character in the movie does."

It's even difficult for Irving to describe why he did what he did. He told the *Voice*: "It's hard to dig deep as to motivation in your own life. I was talking to Richard Gere the other day and we kind of honed in on something that not many people have talked about thus far, which is that the climate of the late 1960s and early '70s was a climate of happening and events. And where I lived, on the island of Ibiza, that was a community of anything goes. It was sex, drugs, and rock 'n' roll. It wasn't the real world. And that was a very important part of what happened that, unfortunately, is not included at all in the movie."

Irving died of cancer in Sarasota, Florida, in 2017. He was eighty-seven. After his death, a friend, the historian Beldon Butterfield, wrote that Irving once told him, "I don't want to be around people who don't have some larceny in their DNA." Irving's home at the time, in San Miguel de Allende, Mexico, was full of Modigliani paintings. "They look so authentic," Irving told Butterfield. "The forger signed the back of these paintings, making them quite valuable, though, of course, not as much as the originals."

26

Jane Russell: 'Two Good Reasons to See The Outlaw'

Jane Russell described her relationship with Howard Hughes as a "platonic love affair." It was one of the few of its kind for the actress-obsessed Hughes.

After graduating from high school in Los Angeles, Russell attended a couple of acting schools and did some modeling, but for the most part she led a slacker's life, drifting from one menial job to the next, almost as if she was waiting for something big to happen. And then it did: She answered an ad in the entertainment industry newspaper *Variety* seeking an unknown actress for Howard Hughes' next movie. She sent in a photo that emphasized her ample cleavage. When Hughes saw the picture among hundreds that were sent in, he decided Russell was the one he wanted. Hughes reportedly told his advisor, Noah Dietrich, that Russell had "the most beautiful pair of knockers I've ever seen in my life."

Howard Hawks was slated to direct Hughes' next movie, *The Outlaw*. Hawks gave Russell the script of a rape scene from the movie and told her to study it in preparation for a screen test at Hughes' headquarters, 7000 Romaine Street. Russell and three other women auditioned. The following week, Russell was called to meet again with Hawks, who told her Hughes had seen the test and wanted her to be in the film. In 1940, she signed a contract paying $50 per week and promptly went out and bought a car.

Shooting of *The Outlaw* started in November 1940 in remote Tuba City, Arizona, on the edge of the Navajo Nation. Russell was photographed extensively for publicity purposes, but never actually acted in any scenes there. Long before the movie was finished, billboards across the country promoted it. The signs featured Russell and told motorists about "Two good reasons to see *The Outlaw*."

Hughes, unhappy with how things were going on the Arizona set, ordered everyone back to Los Angeles. Hawks, whom Hughes had left alone to direct the classic *Scarface*, quit after heated talks with Hughes, who complained that there weren't enough clouds in the desert scenes and wanted Hawks to wait for the right conditions. Ten years earlier, Hughes had insisted on waiting for the ideal cloud formations when producing his flying movie *Hell's Angels*, but Hawks didn't share Hughes' meteorological obsessions. He wanted to finish *The Outlaw* in an efficient time frame so he could move on to other projects, specifically *Sergeant York* starring Gary Cooper.

Soon, Hughes called Russell to meet at his Romaine Street office and told her he was going to direct the film himself. During the shooting, now in a Hollywood studio, Hughes was "always very kind and soft-spoken," Russell said, but he insisted on dozens of takes for each scene. For one scene, there were 103 takes. Russell didn't know this was unusual, but some of the more veteran actors became exasperated.

Hughes famously decided he was going to design a bra for Russell. "When I went into the dressing room with my wardrobe girl and tried it on, I found it uncomfortable and ridiculous," she wrote of the metal contraption. "Obviously he wanted today's seamless bra, which didn't exist then. It was a good idea—as usual, he was way ahead of his time—but I wasn't going to do 103 takes on this subject. So I put on my own bra, covered the seams with tissue, pulled the straps over to the side, put on my blouse, and started out. Emily, my wardrobe girl, was terrified. What if they found out? I assured her they'd never find out from me. Everybody behind the camera stared, and Howard finally nodded okay and filming proceeded. I never wore his bra, and believe me, he could design planes, but a Mr. Playtex he wasn't."

The Outlaw took several months to shoot, substantially longer than the usual six to eight weeks for a movie at that time. Besides Hughes' obsession with shooting scenes dozens of times and working at night, he had many other business affairs that took him away from the set. In the meantime, Hughes turned Russell into one of the best-known actresses in Hollywood—and she hadn't even made a picture yet.

"An extraordinary publicity campaign was well under way," wrote John Keats in his biography of Hughes. "Photographs of Miss Russell were appearing everywhere; news of her tastes, opinions and activities were channeled into gossip columns. . . . And she was scheduled for rounds of personal appearances at Army camps. Hollywood considered it a patriotic duty to display its beautiful women to the troops. Presumably the morale of the soldiery would

Jane Russell starred in Hughes' 1943 movie *The Outlaw*. Courtesy of The Mob Museum.

be uplifted by visions of that which was denied them. More to the point, personal appearances were good publicity. Miss Russell found herself paraded before the troops by day and before the cameras by night."

But the film's famous saga was just beginning. Once Hughes finally had *The Outlaw* ready in late 1942, he couldn't get a seal of approval from the Hays censorship office. The original verdict was that 108 scenes had to be cut. After intense lobbying, the film board reduced its objections to three scenes. But Hughes still wasn't satisfied. Russell recalled that she knew Hughes had shot one of the scenes from another angle and could have used that instead, but he welcomed the censorship battle. "He was stubborn and knew damn well that people would die to see something they were told they couldn't," Russell wrote.

Russell was under contract with Hughes, but didn't live the same life as many other young women. "The girls who were under contract to Howard were provided with a house and a couple for companionship, plus a driver to take them shopping," she wrote. "I met two who practically never heard from Howard—and were in no way mistresses—even though some wished they were. They were simply being kept from the 'wolves.' That wouldn't have been a lifestyle for me—I'm much too independent."

On February 5, 1943, *The Outlaw* finally debuted in San Francisco. Hughes spent huge amounts of money on publicity. "The press was flown up en masse at Mr. Hughes' expense and put up in the finest hotels," Russell wrote. "I would have hated to pay the bills for the phone calls, let alone the booze, food, and the rest." Hughes also had a huge billboard erected near the theater featuring a sexy shot of Russell and the lines, "Sex has not been rationed" and "The picture that couldn't be stopped." Hughes also decided that Russell and co-star Jack Buetel would perform an added scene onstage before each showing of the film. Critics savaged *The Outlaw* (and rightly so), but it played to packed houses during a ten-week run across the country. Mysteriously, Hughes then yanked the film out of theaters, never offering an explanation.

Hughes had intended to roll out the film with Russell as part of the tour's entourage. But Russell refused. Instead, on Easter weekend in 1943, she drove to Las Vegas and married her longtime boyfriend, UCLA quarterback Bob Waterfield. Soon after, Waterfield was sent to Officers' Training School at Fort Benning in Georgia. Russell decided to go, too, suffering through a summer in the South without air conditioning. Waterfield's military tenure was cut short by a knee injury, which earned him an honorable discharge.

After graduation, his knee back in shape, Waterfield signed a contract with the Cleveland Rams, and Russell became a player's wife, rooting for her husband from the stands. There was a lot to cheer about: Waterfield was named the NFL's Most Valuable Player in 1945, and his team won the championship.

Meanwhile, *The Outlaw* sat in an airtight room in the Romaine Street offices, waiting for Hughes to figure out his next move.

Hughes loaned out Russell to United Artists for *Young Widow*. When the movie was completed, Hughes made a deal to distribute the movie, with *The Outlaw* distributed alongside it, in 1946. This time, Russell agreed to be part of the traveling production, which involved nine shows a day, on the condition that she be allowed to sing. Hughes was skeptical, but Russell pulled it off, effectively launching her singing career.

When Hughes decided to re-release *The Outlaw*, it quickly resumed its box office success. The censorship debate followed the picture in city after city and fueled public interest in what officialdom didn't want it to see. "*The Outlaw* earned more money in Atlanta than the previous record holder, *Gone With the Wind*," according to Keats. "In all, *The Outlaw* earned $5,000,000—double its cost—before Hughes once again withdrew it from distribution and locked the film in the lead-lined room at 7000 Romaine Street."

By today's standards, *The Outlaw* would barely require a PG rating. But even in the mid-'40s, it could not be classified as a dirty movie. Its historical significance lies in Hughes' willingness to take on the dictatorial Hays censorship office. His efforts were historically important in helping to open the door for other filmmakers to explore more mature sexual themes.

In 1947, when her first contract with Hughes ended, Russell agreed to another seven-year deal with him. A year later, she visited Hughes' house for a party that included Ava Gardner, who was palling around with Hughes at the time. The party ran late, and Hughes urged Russell to stay the night rather than drive home. She agreed, but after Hughes' publicity man, Johnny Meyer, aggressively came on to her, chasing her around her room, Hughes invited her to sleep in his room, where there were two beds. She agreed, figuring she was safe with Hughes. But in the night he came to her bedside, claiming he was cold, and asked if he could sleep with her. She reluctantly agreed, insisting on no

The Outlaw movie poster. Courtesy of The Mob Museum.

funny business. Before long, however, Hughes put his hand around her waist. She told him to get out of the bed. He agreed, but on his terms: "All right. I'll go. But let me get out when I decide. I don't like people telling me what to do. I won't touch you again. I promise."

"What a funny, stubborn man," Russell wrote. "That was Howard. He'd give in but only on his terms. I knew he always kept his promises, so I turned over and went to sleep. The next thing I knew it was noon and he was gone."

Russell says she finally realized the drama involving Meyer was a ruse: "The whole act was set up with Johnny so Howard could come to my rescue, thereby getting me into his bedroom under proper pretenses. If I hadn't been so sleepy, I would have remembered Billy the Kid in *The Outlaw* and Rio climbing in the bed to warm him up."

On loan to other movie companies, Russell made a couple of successful comedies with Bob Hope and then another film with Hughes, *The Las Vegas Story*, released in 1952. *The Las Vegas Story* was a bomb at the box office, but Russell's next movie was a different story. She co-starred in 1953 with Marilyn Monroe in the highly successful *Gentlemen Prefer Blondes*, directed by Howard Hawks, the original director of *The Outlaw*. Once more it was back to work for Hughes on *The French Line*, and Hughes wanted Russell to wear a bikini that he had designed—in 3-D.

"At the time bikinis were only worn by a few naughty girls in the south of France," Russell wrote. "No one in America wore them. I stood before my horrified camera crew, feeling very naked. I went back to the designer Michael Woulfe and said forget it." Woulfe came up with a clever alternative: a suit with teardrop-shaped holes in it, above and below the waist, but one piece.

"Well, the shit hit the fan again," Russell remembered. "Censors screamed. Howard couldn't get a seal of approval." Which was just what Hughes wanted, even if Russell publicly agreed with the censors.

The French Line was far more overt in its sexuality than *The Outlaw*. Charles Higham, author of *Howard Hughes: The Secret Life*, describes one scene: "The farce reaches its nadir as Russell engages in a bump and grind, throwing her crotch into the audience in one 3-D close shot after another— the roughest entertainment outside of a stag show in Hollywood's history to that date."

The film was released on December 29, 1953—again without film board approval—in St. Louis. An advertisement placed in the *St. Louis Post-Dispatch* made Hughes' intentions clear: "J.R. in 3-D. It'll knock both your eyes out!" The large Catholic population of St. Louis had fits, its church leaders urging a boycott, and readers castigated the newspaper for running the ads. Despite negative reviews, crowds flocked to *The French Line* to get a look at Russell's censorship violations.

In 1955, Hughes sold RKO Pictures for $25 million, and Russell's second contract with him was expiring. Other movie companies such as MGM and Warner Bros. wanted Russell to work for them, but she still felt loyal to Hughes. In the end, Hughes worked out a complicated twenty-year contract that paid Russell $1,000 per week and allowed her to do pretty much whatever she wanted.

In 1957, Russell received an offer to perform a nightclub act at the Sands Hotel in Las Vegas. "I was in Las Vegas for four weeks, doing two shows a night with no day off," Russell recalled. "It was totally different from the pictures. You worked at night, went to bed at dawn, and slept until three in the afternoon. I got tired, especially with no days off, but the hours seemed to come more naturally to me. I was never a morning person."

Through the early '60s, Russell had singing stints on the Strip at the El Rancho Vegas, Riviera, Sahara, and Tropicana.

After a bitter divorce from Waterfield, Russell met the man who would be her second husband, the stage actor Roger Barrett, while doing a play with him in Chicago in 1968. Hughes did not attend the wedding, as by then he was ensconced on the top floor of the Desert Inn. But he did send a nice wedding gift.

"Howard Hughes, whom I hadn't seen or heard from in years, sent giant baskets of flowers and a huge box with an enormous bow on it, so big that Roger and I had to get up on a chair in order to reach and untie the ribbon," Russell wrote.

"'I bet it's one of his airplanes,' Roger cracked.

"It turned out to be an octagonal Spanish coffee table with a hibachi sunk in its center. We loved it. It was so thoughtful of Howard; I was really touched."

Sadly, Barrett died of a heart attack just three months after they were married. He was forty-seven. Hughes again sent a large number of flowers to the mortuary.

In 1974, Russell's last contract with Hughes ran out, which meant she needed a new source of steady income. She had money coming in from her Playtex bra commercials and from real estate, but she still performed in stage productions to pay the bills.

Around the same time, Russell was watching television when the news of Hughes' death was reported. Her reaction mixed disbelief with anger:

"How could they have waited so long to get him some real help? What had really happened? I knew he was stubborn, but if any of his old guard had been there, they wouldn't have listened to him. He would have been in a hospital long before. Howard had the ability to forge lifelong friends; I knew many of them and knew they wouldn't have let him die. They'd have laid down their lives for him. Where were they? But none of them had seen him in years. I wish to God I'd been there. I'd have outshouted him and anyone else and he would have been in a hospital on a kidney machine."

Russell remembered what Hughes had meant to her life: "I thought back to the first time I had ever seen Howard and what he had been in my life, how he had changed it, what a good friend he had been, how loyal and 'as good as his word.' I loved him."

In 1985, Russell published her autobiography, *My Path and My Detours*. The book's cover features a publicity shot from *The Outlaw*. The nineteen-year-old is lying in a pile of hay, one hand behind her thick black hair, low-cut blouse dropping off her shoulder, her other hand gripping a revolver. The picture is both ridiculous and sensual.

Many Hollywood observers believe Russell's movie career could have been more successful if she had not been tied to Hughes in her prime and if producers generally had appreciated her acting talents as much as her cleavage. Her career essentially peaked in 1953 playing second fiddle to Monroe in *Gentlemen Prefer Blondes*, a movie Hughes did not make.

"The truth is that, more often than not, I've been unhappy about the pictures I've been in; that is, the final results displeased me," Russell wrote. "Howard Hughes was a good and fair boss, but he lacked the artistic taste to do the kind of films I really would have liked to be in, with parts I could get my teeth into. He wasn't the man I needed if I was to have developed into a serious actress."

Russell, ever kind to Hughes in her memoir, could have been more pointed. Hughes was a lousy filmmaker and ran RKO Pictures into the ground. If Russell had not been allowed to make pictures for other studios, her career might have ended with her first movie, *The Outlaw*. But Hughes was eternally loyal to Russell, even after he abandoned the movie game, and his weekly paychecks no doubt maintained Russell's comfortable lifestyle for decades.

In the years after her movie career ended, Russell lived in Sedona, Arizona, and Santa Barbara and Santa Maria, California. She died in 2011 at age eighty-nine.

27
Terry Moore: *Hughes' Secret Wife?*

Terry Moore was the Drew Barrymore of her era, a child star turned girl-next-door starlet. She achieved blockbuster fame playing opposite a gorilla in *Mighty Joe Young* and earned an Oscar nomination for *Come Back, Little Sheba*. Moore also famously palled around with future icons Elizabeth Taylor, James Dean, and Marilyn Monroe. But while Moore chalked up a respectable acting career, she is best remembered for her "secret" marriage to Howard Hughes.

It's a saga with numerous Las Vegas connections.

Moore has written two books, both focused on her years with Hughes. In the first, *Beauty and the Billionaire* (1984), she offered a breathless summary of her stormy relationship with Hughes: "He was my lover, my adversary, my father, and my husband. From the moment we first met, an eternity ago, my life has been inextricably wound around his like the spirals of a double helix."

The second book, *The Passions of Howard Hughes* (1996), is a series of dramatized vignettes telling Hughes' life story based in part on conversations she had with him during their years together.

Moore, whose real name was Helen Koford, was born on January 7, 1929, in Los Angeles. She made her film debut in 1940 in *Maryland*, starring Walter Brennan. She appeared in several more movies during the '40s, including *Son of Lassie* and *Gaslight*, before her big break in 1949's *Mighty Joe Young*.

She met Hughes in 1948. At the time, she thought the meeting at the Beverly Wilshire Hotel was happenstance, but she later learned it had been carefully orchestrated by Hughes, who wanted to meet her after seeing her latest film, *The Return of October*. Her first reaction? "I found him utterly repulsive." Moore wrote that Hughes' incessant stare left her uneasy. "All the time he talked, he

Actress Terry Moore claimed she was secretly married to Hughes in 1949. Author's collection.

devoured me with his eyes. Those deep brown, penetrating, unescapable eyes. His eyes would analyze a person from head to toe, inside and out. They seemed to reach inside me. I was growing more and more nervous."

Despite Moore's anxiety, the meeting ended with a date the following night to fly in Hughes' airplane. Moore flew several more times with Hughes, but at the time she was not interested in any kind of relationship with the much older man. Moore thought she was off the hook when she embarked on a cross-country tour to promote *The Return of October*, but Hughes started showing up at stops along the tour route.

Returning home, Moore found her family's house full of flowers sent by Hughes. Eager to be rid of him, Moore decided to invite Hughes to her Mormon parents' home in Glendale, California, thinking this might convince him to pursue women of a less wholesome nature.

Instead, Hughes charmed Moore's mother, who was his age, and earned the respect of Moore's no-nonsense father. Moore and Hughes would talk on the phone every night, and finally she agreed to go on a date with him. Moore was embarrassed that her parents insisted she be home by midnight, but she says the situation delighted Hughes. "He was living a part of life he'd missed," she surmised.

As the relationship developed, Hughes invited Moore and her family to watch movies with him at the Goldwyn Studios, and the odd couple often went to a neighborhood bowling alley, where Hughes was unlikely to be recognized.

Moore became aware that Hughes was dating other women, including his future wife Jean Peters, and angrily confronted him, but Hughes was always able to sweet-talk his way out of it. For a while, Moore said, Hughes agreed to her demand to spend nights on the sofa in her family's house so she would know he wasn't out with other women.

Before long, Moore wrote, Hughes was talking marriage. Moore said she played along, but didn't take him seriously at first. But then Hughes took her on a long drive along Mulholland Drive and they conducted a "spiritual" marriage, reciting their vows under the stars. Hughes presumably concocted the event be able to take Moore back to his bungalow at the Beverly Hills Hotel, but Moore still resisted.

In the fall of 1949, Moore wrote, Hughes agreed to marry her in a more traditional, legal manner, but with a catch: Hughes wanted the ceremony and their marriage to be a secret—for the good of Moore's career, of course. The couple and Moore's chaperoning mother traveled to San Diego, where they climbed aboard a large cabin cruiser. After they ate Nathan's hot dogs that Hughes had flown in from Coney Island, Moore claims the couple exchanged vows in international waters off the coast of Baja California.

"The ceremony on the boat was like a dream while it was happening," Moore wrote. "Only Howard's voice seemed real when he said, 'I do,' and he whispered, 'Forever.' Then his kiss brought me back, and around my neck he placed the very same string of valuable pearls his father had given his mother on their wedding night."

The secret marriage consummated on the boat, Hughes and Moore returned to their lives—Moore making movies, Hughes running his companies. In the evenings, they often hung out together, flying airplanes, visiting Cary Grant, screening movies, and staying overnight in his bungalow at the Beverly Hills Hotel.

But after a few weeks Moore was a bundle of anxieties. Hughes had borrowed her from Columbia Pictures to star in a movie at his RKO studio. Moore was initially excited, but soon realized she was badly miscast starring opposite Victor Mature in *Gambling House*. "My whole world was falling apart," she recalled. "I was making a movie in which I was treated like a leper on the set and my own husband wouldn't let me off the picture. I was married but couldn't tell a soul, and now I had good reason to suspect my husband was cheating on me. . . . I was confused and miserable." Moore eventually decided to move back home to Glendale with her parents. But she and Hughes continued to see each other regularly, often flying out of town to Palm Springs or Las Vegas.

While Moore heard persistent rumors of Hughes' cheating ways, she finally caught him red-handed. In a phone conversation, he told her he was working late on the flying boat at his aircraft facility in Culver City, but at one point the operator came on and revealed that Hughes' call was emanating from Las Vegas. Moore's father contacted a friend in Las Vegas, a former FBI agent, who tracked down Hughes at the Desert Inn. Moore and her parents traveled to Las Vegas to catch Hughes in the act.

Which they did. Moore was seated at the table next to Hughes' reserved table in a DI restaurant—hidden behind a newspaper—when he came in with an eighteen-year-old beauty, her mother, and the publicist Walter Kane. The group was admiring some bathing suits Hughes had picked out for the teenage girl. Finally, Moore walked up to the table and confronted Hughes. "Suddenly Mr. Big became Mr. Little," she wrote. "He seemed to shrink before my eyes. Howard did not know whether to invite me in the party or whether to die on the spot." Moore handled the whole thing with a painted-on smile, but she was brokenhearted. She and Hughes were finished—at least for a while.

Moore's rebound date was football star Glenn Davis, who had previously dated Moore's friend Elizabeth Taylor. In contrast to her secret relationship with Hughes, Moore and Davis were a Hollywood sensation, showing up at public functions and having pictures taken together. Davis and Moore planned to marry, even though Moore said she still loved Hughes. Up to the minute of exchanging wedding vows with Davis, Moore said she expected Hughes to show up dramatically and announce that he was ready to go public with their marriage at sea. But it didn't happen, and she and Davis married on February 9, 1951.

Hughes wasn't giving up, though. In football's off-season, Moore and Davis moved to Texas, where Davis was trying to break into the oil business. Before long, Moore got a call to come back to Hollywood to star in another RKO movie called *High Heels*. Hughes orchestrated the whole thing, and Moore quickly fell for him again. (The movie was not made.)

Soon, she asked Davis for a divorce. With Davis refusing to cooperate, Hughes flew Moore and her friend Mary Jane to Las Vegas. From there they drove northwest out of the city to Tule Springs Ranch (now Floyd Lamb Park). Moore and her friend adopted fake names, as did Hughes when he visited, with the intention of living in Nevada for six weeks so Moore could secure a divorce.

Moore and Mary Jane typically would ride horses in the morning, eat lunch with the ranch hands, then swim in the ranch's large pool in the afternoon. In the evening, Hughes would show up and give Moore flying lessons. Moore said Hughes enjoyed his times at the ranch. "Howard was more at home than I'd ever seen him, and he was thoroughly enjoying himself, laughing uproariously at his own jokes," Moore wrote. "He was like a Will Rogers spinning his yarns and telling stories about a Hollywood of the past."

Hughes, Moore, and Mary Jane took a road trip to Mount Charleston, west of Las Vegas, and the car overheated on the way back. They coasted down the hill, but they were stranded in the desert sun until Hughes flagged down a passing car and asked the driver to get word to Las Vegas of their plight. Hours later, they returned to the rustic comforts of Tule Springs Ranch.

To make up for the mountain mishap, Hughes took the young women on a boat trip down the Colorado River. The trip lasted hours longer than expected, and the boat was running low on fuel. Fearing the worst, Hughes' people had alerted the authorities to go looking for the boat. "It was three o'clock in the morning when the search boat led us into the dock," Moore remembered. "A crowd of people were gathered in front of the boathouse. We had been reported lost about six hours earlier, and Hughes' people from Vegas and others who had flown in from Los Angeles had sent out boats and planes. They were just about to launch a major search when we appeared."

Before the six-week residency period was over, Moore's attorney called off the plan. He said Davis was not going to agree to a quickie divorce and wanted big money to go away. The saga resembled Hughes' misadventure of 1931, when he and actress Billie Dove lived on a remote ranch in Nevada, under assumed names, while she established residency to get a divorce. That effort, too, ended prematurely, and Hughes paid off Dove's husband to secure the divorce.

Moore believes the short stay at the ranch was "one of the best times of Howard's life. He laughed more often and more deeply than I've ever heard him laugh, and he knew without a doubt that these people loved him for himself."

Back in Los Angeles, Hughes set up house with Moore to keep her away from Davis until the divorce could be finalized. Moore took flying lessons from one of Hughes' pilot friends, Glenn Odekirk, and Hughes bought her a plane, a Cessna 140. She soon received her pilot's license.

Hughes' refusal to be monogamous with Moore led to another split. Hughes invited Moore and her parents to Palm Springs, California, for Thanksgiving 1951. But Hughes also was celebrating the holiday with women at two other Palm Springs eateries, a fact that eventually reached Moore's ears.

Her rebound man this time around was Nicky Hilton, ex-husband of Elizabeth Taylor and the son of hotelier Conrad Hilton. She also dated other stars of that era, all of whom made Hughes jealous.

Hughes finally arranged Moore's divorce from Davis in 1952 by employing a dirty trick: He engineered a deal in which Davis would star in a movie but he had to be single to do it. Davis fell for the ploy, and after the divorce was finalized, he was dumped from the movie.

With the divorce completed, Moore wrote, Hughes allowed their relationship to become more public, including frequent trips to Las Vegas. Moore said Hughes also started talking about moving to Las Vegas. She said he was attracted in part by the clean air and privacy. Moore reconstructed a conversation from that period that suggests Hughes had plans for Nevada long before he started buying casinos in 1967.

"'I'm going to buy Nevada," he said.

"'That's nice," I quipped. "How much is it selling for?"

Hughes explained to her that Nevada has the same number of senators as any other state. "Nevada is controlled by gambling. If I buy up the casinos and move my operations there, I'll have two senators in my pocket, a governor, and the next president of the United States."

Moore said Hughes was motivated politically by the imbroglio he had a few years earlier with Senator Owen Brewster of Maine, who conducted a congressional investigation of his defense contracts. Hughes' dramatic testimony before the investigating committee essentially ended the probe's momentum.

After a jealous blowup in Las Vegas—Moore was miffed that Hughes was teaching fellow starlet Debbie Reynolds to gamble—Moore started dating other men, including Nicky Hilton and Greg Bautzer, the famous Hollywood attorney who worked for Hughes. But her goal was to get back at Hughes, and before long she was back with him.

Then, during the filming of the Elia Kazan film *Man on a Tightrope* in Munich, Germany, Moore collapsed. Her mother discovered her in a tub full of bloody water. She was rushed to a hospital, where she said she delivered a premature baby—allegedly Hughes' baby—which died twelve hours later. Moore said Hughes steered clear of the scene, and Moore finally started to see what he was really all about.

"I had my first real misgivings about Howard," she wrote. "Why isn't he here? I kept asking myself. Why isn't he by my side? He should be holding me in his arms. It was his child, too, and he doesn't even care enough to be here. I almost wanted to die of shame. I had lived for this man who tried to con me out of my virginity on Mulholland Drive, this man who demanded our legal marriage be kept a secret, this man who continued to see other women after I married him. This was the man who, I saw now, had allowed me to go through with an illegal marriage to Glenn Davis; this was the man who let me pay seven thousand dollars of my own money so he could have me back. He knew I'd be crushed by my loss, and yet he wasn't here." Despite these realizations, through 1953 and '54, Moore kept seeing Hughes, who continued to promise a public wedding.

Between films, Moore was offered the opportunity to perform at the Flamingo Hotel in Las Vegas. One problem: She couldn't sing. But Moore was determined. For five months in 1954, she took singing and dancing lessons. The work paid off with a well-received three-week run in the Flamingo showroom.

Later that year, Moore learned she was pregnant again, and Hughes convinced her to fly with him from Las Vegas to Tucson, Arizona, to get married. A ferocious dust storm kept planes grounded in Las Vegas, however, and they planned to stay over at the Desert Inn. But Moore's old paramour, Nicky Hilton, showed up, drunk, and confronted Hughes. Hilton revealed to Moore that Hughes had several other actresses stashed at other Las Vegas hotels. Moore went home with Hilton. Back in Los Angeles, training for a dance picture with Fred Astaire, Moore started having cramps and was rushed to the hospital. Three months pregnant, she lost another baby.

The Las Vegas incident soured Moore's parents completely on Hughes, but somehow she still loved him and retained a lingering hope that they would be publicly married. Time apart, however, allowed Moore to be more accepting of the flirtations of other suitors, and the eventual winner was Gene McGrath, a World War II hero, international businessman with ties to the CIA, and resident of Panama.

Hughes kept calling her, asking why she was cheating on him. "It became monotonous and depressing," Moore wrote. "I wanted to have fun. All I could think about as Howard repeated himself over and over was how many times he'd cheated on me and lied to me and the countless hours of pain and tears he'd caused me. I wasn't going to cry or fall for his sentimentality and go running back to him."

Moore married McGrath in a Las Vegas wedding chapel on New Year's Day 1956. They divorced in 1958. A year later, she married Stuart Cramer, the ex-husband of Jean Peters, whom Hughes had married in 1957. They had two children together, but divorced in 1971.

After Hughes died in 1976, Moore became embroiled in the court battles over his estate. Revealing her secret marriage to Hughes and their premature baby that died, she laid claim to a piece of the fortune. Sitting in the Houston law firm of Andrews, Kurth, Campbell, and Jones surrounded by dapper lawyers, Moore could have been excused for being nervous. Instead, "her deposition had the atmosphere of a Mary Kay Cosmetics party," wrote Suzanne Finstad in *Heir Not Apparent*. "Not in the least daunted by the imposing circle of legal talent that surrounded her, firing questions, she prattled on, happily drawing doodles, relaying inside Hollywood scoop during breaks in her interrogation. Without missing a beat, she would occasionally pull out a full-sized makeup mirror, set it up on the conference table, and touch up her face."

Moore's tale of her marriage at sea was seemingly impossible to prove. The ship's logs had been destroyed, and the only living witness to the event was her mother. But witnesses did confirm she spent a lot of time with Hughes. Odekirk, one of Hughes' closest friends, said: "She was with him quite a lot then. However, I spent a week with her and her mother in New York. In fact, it happened to be at the same time, and I was there and Howard had me teach her to fly, preliminary part of teaching her to fly, so he went with her quite a while."

She eventually received a cash settlement, believed to be $350,000, in 1983. She said the payment validated her claim to being "Mrs. Howard Hughes," while others said the heirs settled simply to get her out of their hair. Either way, the resulting publicity was good for Moore: The next year, at age fifty-five, she appeared nude in *Playboy*.

Moore's second book about Hughes, co-written by husband Jerry Rivers, is less compelling than her memoir. It's essentially a speculative narrative of key moments in Hughes' life and offers no new information. The book includes several explicit sex scenes, including one involving Moore herself. *The Passions of Howard Hughes* ends, however, with an eloquent and moving summation of the billionaire's anguished final years, during which his greedy executives and aides controlled his life.

"Most of them," Moore wrote, "were good men, very good men—no dope, no booze, no gambling, no womanizing, church-going men—but the lure of money, Howard Hughes' money, was too great to resist. Absolute greed, like absolute power, corrupts absolutely. They could have saved him. They controlled all communication to and from Howard Hughes. They watched as his life spun out of control, they watched as he took more and more drugs to kill the pain. They even procured the dope for him, kept him in a stupor, under their control, neither dead nor alive, just stood there and let it happen. They watched and waited until Howard began to die. They watched and waited and did nothing as one of the greatest men of the twentieth century, a visionary, an innovator, a king maker, one of the richest and most powerful men on Earth, the world's first billionaire, whose charmed life had survived five airplane crashes, finally died of malnutrition, dehydration and—worst of all—of a broken heart."

Terry Moore continued to work in movies and television well into her eighties. In 2014, she landed a role in an episode of HBO's critically acclaimed series *True Detective*. In 2016, she was in an episode of Showtime's *Ray Donovan*.

28

Close Encounters: *Memories of Howard Hughes*

Jimmy "The Greek" Snyder will go down in history as an itinerant gambler, the best-known bettor in the country in the 1960s and '70s, and for a controversy related to his appearances on television. But Snyder's day job was public relations, and his most famous client was Howard Hughes.

Raised in Steubenville, Ohio, Snyder grew up fast after his mother died when he was nine years old. As a teenager during the Great Depression, Snyder started running bets for illegal bookmakers, and then dealing craps at a nightclub. Along the way, he became a skilled horse player as well.

But Snyder soon abandoned the racetrack ("too many variables") in favor of gambling on team sports, especially football. He was a diligent researcher, foreshadowing the statistics-crazed handicappers of today. His prowess briefly drew the attention of the Kefauver Committee, the U.S. Senate panel that in 1950 and 1951 investigated corruption in the gambling industry.

After failed efforts to strike it rich in the oil business, Snyder decided to concentrate on what he knew best: gambling. And where better to do that than Las Vegas? He moved there in 1956.

Snyder was immediately smitten with the town. In his 1975 memoir *Jimmy the Greek*, he recalls:

"There is a feeling you get, once inside a Vegas casino going at full blast, that is guaranteed to make your adrenalin pump. . . . I have seen people transformed by that music, as though they had walked through a veil. It is contagious. In their hearts, everyone is a high roller. The bellmen bet on which way an elevator is going. A housewife who once could have been pacified with a book of trading stamps will break your arm if you so much as approach the nickel slot machine

Jimmy "The Greek" Snyder was a public relations consultant for Hughes in the late 1960s. He was better known as a sports bettor. Courtesy of *Las Vegas Review-Journal* Archive.

she is saving, after she finishes this one. A Las Vegas judge, Myron Leavitt, once performed a wedding ceremony in front of the keno booth at the Horseshoe, because the happy couple was in a lucky streak and didn't want to leave."

Snyder says he particularly enjoyed Monday through Thursday in Las Vegas, because that's when the town "belonged to us, the professionals." That changed, he says, as the city grew and the corporations took over. "The casino hotels became attuned to the masses, instead of the elite, and for me the place lost something."

Myths, Snyder notes, fueled the Las Vegas mystique. Tales of mobsters and prostitutes did wonders for Las Vegas tourism numbers. "When I was handling PR for Caesars, whenever reservations slowed down, we'd send out another note or news release denying the Mafia rumors, and the hotel would fill up in three days," he says.

After several years of ups and downs as a high-stakes gambler, including a run-in with Robert Kennedy's Justice Department, Snyder in 1963 started writing a weekly handicapping column for the *Las Vegas Sun*. While the column helped make Snyder the "oddsmaker to the world," his day job was public relations. Soon, he snagged the PR account for a newly opened resort, Caesars Palace, and went to work courting the world.

A few years later, Snyder also handled PR for Howard Hughes. Snyder never met with Hughes, but said "his presence was everywhere." Snyder took his orders from Bob Maheu, whom he described as "the second most powerful man in the state."

Hughes' presence "gave Las Vegas a new image and a new vitality," Snyder said. "You could sense it everywhere. . . . Gambling and tourist income increased more than twenty-five percent a year, twice the rate before he came. Suddenly, more people *trusted* Las Vegas. The place was damn near respectable."

Snyder was doing publicity for Hughes, but more often than not, that meant his job was "to keep his name *out* of the news." Soon after being hired,

Snyder was handed a challenging task: stop the large nuclear explosions in the Nevada desert. He was told that Hughes didn't want the tests to happen, but that his name must not be associated with Snyder's efforts.

"It was a touchy assignment," Snyder said, and one of his employees initially was reluctant to participate on the grounds that it was unpatriotic. But Snyder suggested that maybe Hughes was right about the dangers of nuclear testing, and that they needed to do some research first.

"We didn't have to dig very deep," he said. "Radiation had affected some cows, ruined their milk, poisoned some babies. Measurable amounts were found in the water. There was concern about an earthquake. The more we researched it, the more we came to believe in our opposition to nuclear testing."

Snyder flooded science writers with copies of articles that raised questions about the tests. "In no time, we were sending out packages as thick as a phone book," Snyder said. "Within six months, the Atomic Energy Commission announced that it was halting its megaton-plus testing in Nevada."

Snyder's work alone did not determine the outcome of the battle between Hughes and the federal government over nuclear testing. Hughes and Maheu attacked the issue in a variety of ways, including appealing directly to President Lyndon Johnson. Ultimately, the government continued to conduct large nuclear tests in Nevada until a moratorium in 1992.

The only time Snyder's PR work prompted a reaction from Hughes himself was when Snyder employed artist LeRoy Neiman to paint a portrait of Hughes, showing what he would look like twenty years after his last known photograph was taken in 1947. "Neiman did a masterful job," Snyder said. "Gray at the temples, a little salt and pepper in the moustache. A few lines for character. It was a handsome portrait and I was delighted."

Snyder gave it to Bob Maheu's son, Peter, to get it approved. Weeks passed. "I kept asking about the portrait. Finally, Pete said, 'Come on over. I have your answer.' I went to his office and there, on his desk, was the painting, with an original comment by Howard Hughes: an X slashed across the face."

Snyder said his research into Hughes' past suggested that he picked up and left a place every four years. "You could set your calendar by him," Snyder wrote. But when Snyder alerted Maheu to this phenomenon in 1970, Maheu didn't buy it. "'Jimmy,' he said, reassuringly, 'Mr. Hughes is going to spend the rest of his life right here in Las Vegas. Your job is secure.'"

But Snyder proved prophetic. It wasn't long before Hughes quietly slipped out of Las Vegas, on Thanksgiving Eve 1970, exactly four years after his arrival in Las Vegas. Hughes' departure coincided with the firing of Maheu, which meant

Snyder no longer had his lucrative PR job with the billionaire. But Snyder wasn't bitter, even after Hughes' executives refused to pay him every dollar he was owed: "On final reflection, I would have to say that it was one of the more interesting periods of my life."

Snyder later would rise from moderately famous to household name when, in 1976, he landed a job as a professional football analyst for CBS. Snyder offered his streetwise oddsmaker's wisdom to a national audience on the network's *NFL Today* pre-game show. But Snyder's television celebrity ended in 1988 after an offhand comment about black athletes—that they benefit from selective breeding practices during slavery. Snyder, the expert oddsmaker and veteran PR man, didn't know what hit him. What seemed to him a fact of life generated a furious response, and CBS yanked him off the air. He died in 1996 at age seventy-seven.

Ralph Pearl

Ralph Pearl wrote an entertainment column for the *Las Vegas Sun* for four decades. He also hosted a weekly television talk show. In his 1973 memoir *Las Vegas Is My Beat*, Pearl offered a positive but always realistic portrait of the place he had called home for twenty years (he continued to work and write in Las Vegas until his death in 1992 at age eighty-one). Pearl noted that Las Vegas had a high percentage of Mormon residents who rarely participated "in the luxuries of drinking and gambling" and who "proudly emphasized the fact that Las Vegas has more than 150 churches, two synagogues, and almost two hundred Boy Scout troops." But, he noted, they don't mention "the hookers, hustlers, and whores (there's a difference) who ply their wares in the casino hotels."

Pearl first came to Las Vegas in the mid-'40s and helped a New York law school buddy, Hank Greenspun, publish a magazine. But the magazine folded, and Pearl left Las Vegas after Bugsy Siegel's murder in 1947. He returned in 1953, starting work as a columnist for Greenspun's newspaper, the *Las Vegas Sun*. Pearl reveled in the Vegas heyday of lounge entertainment, when boozy ham Joe E. Lewis was performing at the El Rancho Vegas and "had the town and the millions who came here in his hip pocket." Pearl provides eyewitness testimony to 1960's famed "Summit at the Sands," Frank Sinatra's three-week gathering of the Rat Pack in the Copa Room, calling the series of shows "psychopathically funny." Over the years, Pearl sparred with numerous entertainers, from Dean Martin to Shecky Greene, who were stung by his "unfavorable notices." Pearl will forever hold a place in Vegas lore for being in the chorus of local critics when Elvis Presley first performed in Las Vegas in 1956. Presley was paid $8,500 per week for a two-week stint. Pearl wrote: "When I first caught Elvis Presley on the Frontier stage, I told the bosses, 'Fellers, you overpaid Presley $5,000 a week.' Wisely, I had reported earlier, 'Presley belongs in a Nashville theater where his young followers would come eagerly and in large crowds. Las Vegas showrooms are out of his league."

Pearl recalled the early '50s when Howard Hughes hung out on the Las Vegas Strip, usually with a Hollywood starlet by his side. "The gaunt, poorly attired gent with the flashing black eyes and nervous manner sat in the booth in the back of the showroom at the Flamingo Hotel one June night in 1954 with a bosomy blonde who had a ravenous appetite. He seemed out of place in those surroundings . . . as Zsa Zsa Gabor might have been at an outdoor rally of the Daughters of the American Revolution in Pasadena."

Naturally, Pearl saw his mission: to get an interview with the elusive Hughes. Noticing Hughes at a Tony Martin show at the Flamingo, Pearl watched him closely and sprang into action when he observed Hughes getting up to leave. Pearl caught up with Hughes in the parking lot and persuaded him to answer a question.

"What is the question, Mr. Pearl, and please make it fast," Hughes said.

"Well, sir, is there a possibility that you are at this time planning to move your aircraft business from the West Coast and settle here in Nevada—or maybe Las Vegas?" Pearl asked.

"No, Ralph, there's absolutely no truth to such a rumor," Hughes replied. "I have no plans to move my aircraft plant to Las Vegas or Nevada." After a pause, Hughes added, "The gaming casinos and never-ending supply of free whiskey to the gamers would make it highly impractical. Especially if those gamers were employees of mine. I'm not about to compete with blackjack, craps, and the slot machines at their easy disposal."

That was the extent of Pearl's interview, which took up half of his column the next day. In fact, Hughes did at one time want to move his aircraft research facilities to the outskirts of Las Vegas, on the land where his heirs built the Summerlin master-planned community after his death. But Hughes' aircraft company executives balked at the idea, and the showdown represented one of the few times that Hughes listened to his employees.

Hughes later returned to Las Vegas, living for four years on the top floor of the Desert Inn. Instead of building an aircraft plant, he bought hotel-casinos, but Pearl contended that bad management decisions by Hughes and his right-hand man, Bob Maheu, put his casino operations in the red.

"He had a staff who belonged in the driver's seat like Truman Capote belonged in the Green Bay Packers' backfield," Pearl said. "Bob's idea that Hughes hotels could be run like General Motors, U.S. Steel, and RCA had proved to be utterly disastrous. His idea of doing away with free booze, lodgings, junkets to the gamblers, and operating on the practical theory of profit and loss had fizzled."

Pearl said an "asinine move" was hiring ex-FBI men to oversee hotel operations. "As soon as it leaked out, many high rollers in the Sands, Desert Inn, Frontier, and Landmark gambled elsewhere. One thing they certainly didn't want was an ex-FBI man looking over their shoulders when they were splurging with the big black chips in enormous quantity on that green felt table."

But Pearl acknowledged that Hughes' presence in Las Vegas was positive for the city as a whole. "Much was written in newspapers and magazines all over the world about Howard Hughes' coming to Las Vegas to invest many of his millions in that legalized gambling hotel industry. Locals were tremendously pleased. They felt it would enhance the economy—also create more jobs. As for some of the gaming owners who'd been taking a beating from the boys in Washington who were out to get them, they hoped Hughes would be the answer to their troubles."

To some extent, he was. Governor Paul Laxalt proclaimed that Hughes gave Las Vegas the "Good Housekeeping Seal of Approval," and he was right. When Wall Street saw Hughes investing hundreds of millions of dollars in Las Vegas, it signaled the beginning of the end of the mob-controlled casinos, and the idea of mainstream companies getting involved with Las Vegas suddenly wasn't so foreign to their sensibilities.

Louella Parsons

For the legendary Hollywood gossip columnist Louella Parsons, "'the first to know' were the most beautiful words in the dictionary." And during her four decades on the Hollywood beat, Parsons often was the first to report on Howard Hughes' activities, especially as they pertained to his pursuit of glamorous movie actresses.

In her book *Tell It to Louella*, published in 1961, Parsons devoted a chapter to Hughes. She led with an amusing story about Hughes calling her in 1957 to inform her that he had married Jean Peters.

"'What a story!' I shouted. 'It'll make page one in every paper in the United States.'

"'Not page one. Either you'll handle it the way I tell you or there won't be any story.'

"'But—' That was as far as I got.

"'Louella, I'm making a bargain with you. If you put the story on the front page, I'll deny it. Write it the way I want it and you can have it, not otherwise.'

"I wrote it the way he wanted it. Nobody that I know has ever been able to have it his own way with Howard Hughes."

Parsons published a brief column item about the marriage, flying in the face of journalistic reason. But at least she was the first to know.

Hughes was known for being secretive and mysterious, but Parsons had a different perspective. "I have never regarded him as mystery man or spook. I have known him since he was a boy of twenty-one and I realize that he is reticent, wary of strangers, and secretive because that is the way he feels he can best protect himself and his interests. He is my friend. But oh, what an exasperating friend he can be for a newspaperwoman who wants to put everything she learns in print!"

Parsons says that unlike those who complained that they couldn't reach Hughes, she never had any trouble getting him on the phone. But that didn't mean he was forthcoming with publishable information. "My business is getting news about important people into the paper. Howard feels that there shouldn't be any news about him in any paper at any time."

As a young man, Hughes had a different personality, according to Parsons. "He was quite young; a tall, lean, good-looking man with a lopsided, ingenuous smile. He was more gregarious at that time, too."

Parsons offered several examples to show that Hughes was a giving, caring man, not the misanthrope of public lore. When he crashed an airplane and was rescued by a Marine, some reports indicated that Hughes never rewarded the hero. "I know how generously rewarded the boy was," Parsons wrote. "But that was another story Howard would never let me write."

While defending Hughes on many fronts, Parsons admitted she didn't know the whole story. "I have heard him described as Dracula, Bluebeard, and Satan. I have heard stories about him that I know are completely untrue and read others equally false. And yet I know that I do not know the truth, the whole truth and nothing but the truth about him. I'm not sure that anyone does. He is so complex that there must be times when he is a stranger even to himself." Parson died in 1972 at age ninety-one.

Frank McCulloch

Frank McCulloch was the last reporter to interview Howard Hughes face to face. It happened in 1958, and the circumstances were just as unusual as you would expect.

McCulloch was the son of a pioneer Northern Nevada ranch family. He was born in Fernley, about thirty miles east of Reno. He graduated from Reno High School and the University of Nevada, Reno, where he edited the student newspaper, the *Sagebrush*. His first reporting job was for United Press International in San Francisco. After a stint in the U.S. Marines during World War II, he returned to Reno, reporting for the *Reno Evening Gazette*. But McCulloch was destined for the national journalism stage, going to work as a reporter, editor and bureau chief for the Time-Life News Service.

McCulloch was Time-Life's Los Angeles bureau chief in 1958 when his editors in New York assigned him to secure an interview with Hughes, who was having trouble raising money to buy jets for TWA. It was a tough assignment. By this point in his life, Hughes was increasingly reclusive and not granting interviews. In an article for *Time* magazine in 1970, McCulloch recalled:

"I assembled a list of about fifty questions and passed them on to a Hughes aide. About forty-eight hours later, the phone rang at 11 a.m., and the flat, nasal voice at the other end identified itself as that of Howard Hughes. That started weeks of tit-illation, intrigue, maneuvering, exhaustion and sheer damn foolishness. We were on a first-name basis after the second call, but his calls never seemed to have an end or a beginning. They were, in essence, monologues, in which he made the case for holding off the story until new financing for TWA could be arranged."

McCulloch noticed that his conversations with Hughes gravitated from day-time to nighttime and early morning, reflecting Hughes' night owl schedule and lack of appreciation for other people's sleeping habits. "One night, I vowed to accept no calls, and my wife agreed that she would handle Howard," McCulloch wrote. "We fell into bed exhausted and waited for the calls we knew would come. The first came at 11. 'Mr. Hughes,' my wife explained, 'Frank is exhausted. He went to bed early, and I think he should get a good night's rest, don't you?'"

Hughes responded, "Good heavens, yes, Mrs. McCulloch, and I'm sorry to have been so thoughtless. A pleasant good night. Rest well." But thirty minutes later, Hughes called again. He apologized, saying that he had been so busy with other things that he had forgotten the earlier call. His third call arrived at one a.m. McCulloch, still exhausted, answered the phone. Hughes assumed the journalist must be feeling rested after two hours of sleep. "Then he suggested that I should drive to the intersection of Olympic and Sepulveda boulevards, park at the southwest corner, blink my lights twice, and wait for a two-tone, 1954 Mercury sedan to come alongside."

McCulloch hopped in his car and headed for the intersection. The Mercury pulled up, and McCulloch got in the back seat. "We made our way by back roads to the unfinished western end of the Los Angeles International Airport. There the driver left me stranded in the middle of an unfinished runway. I became aware that I was actually standing in a half-moon of parked automobiles."

Journalist Frank McCulloch interviewed Hughes in the late 1950s. Courtesy of Candace S. Akers.

A few minutes later, Hughes walked up and greeted McCulloch, who stuck out his hand to shake. But Hughes awkwardly declined to shake hands, explaining both that he had been eating a hot dog and got mustard on his hand, and he was shaving and cut his hand.

"Hughes asked if I would like to take a ride. Of course. Right behind me, looming up in the dark was Boeing's prototype of the 707. Howard and I boarded and went to the pilot's compartment, where he indicated I should take the engineer's seat, behind the co-pilot's seat."

Hughes and McCulloch soon were joined by a co-pilot and the actress Jean Peters, who had married Hughes the year before in Tonopah, Nevada. "The semi-circle of automobiles turned on their lights, illuminating part of the lumpy runway," McCulloch wrote. "Howard—dressed in nondescript gray slacks, white shirts and loafers but no socks—kicked on the engines. Away we went—to, I am certain, the utter astonishment, if not horror, of the unapprised men in the airport control tower."

They flew for four hours, down the Baja coast, up through Arizona, over Las Vegas. McCulloch made small talk with Peters, while Hughes talked about the merits of the 707. "At his invitation, I took the co-pilot's seat, and he calmly told me that I now had control of the airplane. That was somewhere over the Arizona desert at 30,000 feet; I had never so much as piloted a Piper Cub."

As they returned to LAX, the copilot "all but had a spasm" as he observed Hughes' approach to the landing and Hughes assured him he had everything under control. "We hit awfully hard—again without having so much as acknowledged the existence of the tower—bounced about five times, and rolled to a screeching, dusty halt just short of the last fence at the southwest edge of the airport." Hughes and his bride jumped into a waiting car and disappeared.

Only later did McCulloch realize the purpose of the "midnight ride" in the Boeing prototype. "What Howard was trying to show me, though he never articulated it, was that the 707 was a helluva airplane, and if he could just get the money he needed to buy enough of them, he could bail out TWA."

Not long after the flight, McCulloch and Hughes spoke again by phone, with Hughes continuing to urge McCulloch to delay the story. McCulloch decided to pay a visit to *Time*'s publisher, Henry Luce, who was living in Phoenix. "Very cagily—since by this time I was certain that Howard knew every detail about my every move—I booked to Phoenix not on TWA but on United. When I got there, I rented not a Hertz or an Avis but a local firm's car. I drove to the Luce home not by established routes but by enormous circles. Then I drove to the back of the circular driveway and hid my rented Ford behind a large lilac bush."

Luce and other editors at his home quickly concluded that the story should be published, and suggested that McCulloch's fears about Hughes tracking his movements were absurd. "I left the house and made my way to the lilac bush and my rented, locked Ford," McCulloch recalled. "As I slipped the key in the door, I noticed with a start that there was something white slipped beneath the rim of the horn. It was a business card, printed with the name of the TWA manager in Phoenix. On the other side was a message: "Mr. McCulloch—please call Mr. Hughes immediately.""

Hughes made contact with McCulloch a few times after their face-to-face meeting in 1958. When the McCullochs' son was born at St. John's Hospital in Santa Monica, California, Hughes sent a giant bouquet of tropical plants to the hospital. Candy Akers, one of McCulloch's daughters, described the bouquet as a "forest. They had to get a dolly to bring it upstairs."

Akers said the display "sat in our entryway for a long time, until all the plants died. It was designed to be a planter and then turned upside down to become a white wicker bench. Mom and Dad used it at the foot of their bed as a bench."

In 1966—in the months before Hughes moved to Boston, then Las Vegas—McCulloch returned to New York after a stint covering the Vietnam War. He got a call asking him to come to Los Angeles to talk to Hughes. McCulloch traveled to L.A., checked into a hotel and met a Hughes aide to let him know he had arrived.

"But the next morning a headline caught my eye: the Buddhist riots were flaring again in Saigon and Danang. I didn't even call the aide back. Within two hours, I was on the next flight to Asia. I do wonder, though, what it was that Howard wanted to talk about."

McCulloch had another telephone conversation with Hughes in the midst of the controversy over Clifford Irving's purported Hughes autobiography. Irving's book was going to be serialized in *Life* magazine. Hughes called McCulloch and said the book was a fake. McCulloch personally stopped the presses in Chicago. His bosses were upset, at least at first.

"I did it on my own," McCulloch said in an interview with *Silver & Blue*, the University of Nevada, Reno's alumni magazine, in 1992. "It didn't sit too well with my superiors. But it would have been a lot worse if the edition had continued to run."

McCulloch said Hughes called him a few other times over the years. He called him at the *Time-Life* bureau in Saigon to talk about the Vietnam War, and he called him in Washington, D.C., urging him to give President Nixon a break.

McCulloch had one final Hughes encounter. Sitting at his desk at the *Sacramento Bee*, he received a call from Bill Gay, one of Hughes' top executives. Gay said "the man" wanted to talk to him.

"Of course. Put him on," McCulloch said. The phone was quiet for several minutes, and then Gay came back on. "Frank, my apologies," Gay said. "I don't think that will be possible today."

The next morning, when McCulloch entered his office, there was a printout of a wire service story on his desk reporting that Hughes had died. "The thought hit me like a hard blow," McCulloch said. "In his dying moments he wanted to talk to me."

In addition to his many years with *Time* and *Life* magazines, McCulloch was a top editor at the *Los Angeles Times*, *Sacramento Bee* and *San Francisco Examiner*, retiring in 1991. He was named a Distinguished Nevadan by the university Board of Regents on May 18, 2018, just four days after he died at age ninety-eight.

Ann Miller

Ann Miller, the actress, singer and dancer best known for her roles in *Easter Parade* and *Kiss Me Kate* and her Broadway run in *Sugar Babies*, had only one date with Howard Hughes but it was a memorable one. In her memoir, *Miller's High Life*, she explains that the date wasn't really a date in the traditional sense. Hughes was in a relationship with the actress Linda Darnell, Miller's good friend. Darnell, she said, seemed intent on marrying Hughes, even though she was married to someone else—though separated—at the time.

Hughes called Miller at two a.m. "You've got to help me," he said. "I've got a problem with Linda. I have to talk to you." They agreed to meet the following night at nine.

"So the next night I got all dressed up in a pretty cocktail dress and waited. Nine o'clock came. Then ten, then eleven, and still no Howard Hughes. Finally, about a quarter of twelve the doorbell rang and there stood Howard."

Miller was not impressed with what she saw. "He was wearing a dirty old coat with grease spots all over it and patches on the elbows, a beat-up shirt, wrinkled trousers, and old tennis shoes. He walked into the hallway and I said, 'Is that what you're going to wear to dinner?'" When Miller said she would not go out with him looking that way, Hughes ran out to the car to retrieve another shirt and pants.

"Howard disappeared into my powder room and came out looking very neat, with a clean shirt and a marvelous pair of trousers. But he still had on that awful jacket and the tennis shoes."

Leaving the house, they got into what Miller called "the most beat-up battered old Chevrolet I've ever seen." They drove to Perino's, one of the nicest restaurants in town.

As soon as they sat down, Hughes got up and walked into the kitchen. He reappeared with a big bowl of salad. "I mixed it myself," he said. "I never let anyone else touch food that I eat." Hughes asked the waiter to bring a toaster to the table and a loaf of bread, after which he made his own toast.

The food preparations concluded, Hughes told Miller he wanted her help to let Darnell down easy. "I think all the world of her but I don't want to get married," he said. Hughes also told her that Darnell's husband was demanding a lot of money from Hughes to agree to a divorce. Miller promised she would talk to Darnell.

The next stop for Hughes and Miller was his projection room at Goldwyn Studios to see the latest footage for his next film. But on the way, the car ran out of gas. "I saw a filling station about four blocks back there," Hughes said. "You wait in the car and I'll walk and get a can of gasoline."

Hughes returned, poured the gas in the tank, got behind the wheel and turned the key. The car wouldn't start. "Come on, we have to push," he said.

"Would you believe Miss Twinkle-Toes and Mr. Billionaire out there in the middle of the night pushing a beat-up, rust-buckety rattletrap of a car to make it start? Well, that's what we did."

They continued to the Goldwyn Studios, where Hughes impressed her with the special seats in the projection room. "The instant I sat down a big flap came out from under the seat, tilted me back and raised my legs up so that I was sitting there like a queen in a huge overstuffed chair."

The movie was played extremely loud, because he was hard of hearing. "He turned the sound up so loud he nearly blew me out of the projection room, chaise longue and all," Miller recalled.

Hughes took her home, and the next day Miller went to see Darnell. "I assured her that Howard was in love with her but wasn't ready for marriage just yet. And I thought it best to tell her about her husband—that he was demanding a money settlement from Howard before he would free her."

Darnell was distraught by what Miller told her, especially about her husband. Darnell later talked with Hughes about it and expressed how sorry she was about her husband's actions. Darnell died in 1965 at age forty-one from burns she suffered in a house fire. Miller died in 2008 at age eighty.

Shelley Winters

As a young actress, Shelley Winters met Howard Hughes at a New Year's Eve party at the Hollywood home of film producer Sam Spiegel. According to her autobiography, she was sitting by herself when a "tall, very skinny man" approached her. She did not recognize the billionaire aviator and film producer. "He introduced himself, but there was so much noise all I heard was 'Hugh something.'"

When Hughes, or "Hugh," went to find Winters something to eat, she noticed "he had on white tennis shoes, and I thought, Jesus, the poor guy must have borrowed someone's tuxedo, because it did look rather old and shiny. It occurred to me that he was a set decorator (they are always tall and lanky so they can reach up into the storage bins) and had crashed the party."

Hughes returned, accompanied by a butler carrying a tray with two plates of food. Winters, famished, "started eating everything in sight." She remembered that the party was strangely quiet, with "all eyes riveted, I thought, on me. I was so embarrassed I almost stopped eating. I finished the food on my plate, then, at Hugh's insistence, started on his."

Having eaten so much, her dress was suddenly so tight it was difficult to breathe. She asked Hughes to unzip the back of her dress. "He was doing pretty well with the zipper until the fringe of the shawl got caught in it." When Winters' friend approached, she suggested Winters adjust her dress in the restroom. But Hughes was intent on finishing the task right there. "I'm enjoying this," he said. "I've had many mechanical problems to deal with, but this is one of the most fascinating."

Later during the party, Winters was in the powder room with Ava Gardner, who had a long-running and tempestuous relationship with Hughes. "As I sat down at the dressing table and began fixing my hair, Ava said, 'I'm glad you took Howard Hughes off my hands, Shelley. He really keeps his women in isolation.'"

"I did *what*?" Winters asked.

"The only problem is," Gardner continued, "he gave me a new car for Christmas, and something went wrong with it. So I took it out to Hughes

Actress Shelley Winters saw some of Hughes' eccentricities firsthand. Courtesy of *Las Vegas Review-Journal* Archive.

Aircraft at his suggestion to have it fixed. When I went to pick it up, I drove it about two miles and the engine fell out. He had it wired, the son of a bitch. I thought he would be furious when I forced him to bring me tonight and then I ditched him to get even. But he obviously thinks you're so cute that I don't think he's noticed."

Winters did not grasp what Gardner was telling her. "That nice set decorator and I just had dinner together because I was a wallflower and he was alone, too. The poor guy doesn't even own a pair of shoes. He's wearing his tennis sneakers, for God's sake."

"He's no set decorator," Gardner said. "He's a millionaire many times over. Everyone at the party is talking about what a fancy he's taken to you."

When Winters returned to the party, she asked Hughes a few questions, including why he wears tennis shoes. "My feet hurt when I wear shoes," he said. "When you're as tall as I am, it's very hard on your feet."

Hughes offered to take Winters home. She expected to see a limousine pull up, but "instead we walked right past the car valets and halfway up the block until we came to a scratched-up little green Ford, circa 1938."

Hughes and Winters met the following evening for dinner and a movie. They dined in a Japanese restaurant and then "drove to some small movie house in Santa Monica with a marquee that read 'Closed for the Duration,' but we went in anyway. Hughes waved his arm to a man's head sticking out of the projection booth, and a film I'd never seen before called *Hell's Angels* started. Howard Hughes was listed as the director, and only a part of it was in sound. Jean Harlow was the star, and she was fantastic."

"You're the closest thing to her I've ever seen," Hughes told her. He said if he were to remake *Hell's Angels*, he would set it during World War II and Winters would play Harlow's role.

A few years later, Winters received an offer from the Flamingo Hotel in Las Vegas to star in a nightclub act. The resort would pay her $30,000 per week for four weeks. After a two-week practice run in San Diego, Winters was ready to debut in Las Vegas.

"Opening night, as I pranced near the edge of the stage, I slipped and fell three feet—into Howard Hughes' lap! He was sitting at a ringside table. He caught me, wiped me off and stood me back up on the stage."

Hughes, who was living in a Flamingo suite at the time, saw Winters backstage after the show. "I thanked him for the loan of his lap."

Before her second show, Winters received a phone call in her dressing room. "It was a vicious obscene caller. I slammed the phone down and stood there in terror." The Flamingo's operator tracked the call to another room in the hotel. Flamingo security, with Winters in tow, went directly to the room. "The guard asked me to stand aside, drew his gun, then pounded loudly on the door. The door opened, and what looked to me like a naked, hairy and drunken gangster started to swear at the guard. I was hiding around the corner. The guard put away the gun and politely asked the man to 'cool it' because some of the other guests were complaining and the owner of the hotel would get upset if the entertainers got so insulted they refused to go on. That's the strongest language this 'policeman' dared use to this creep. The guy mumbled something about 'fun' and slammed the door in our faces. The guard took me back to my room rather sheepishly. I stared at him with disbelief and could think of nothing to say."

The security guard's reserved handling of the frightening call—one imagines the "gangster" was connected at a high level—left Winters ready to leave town. But as she started her next show, she saw Hughes again in the audience. He sent her a note to join him afterward at his table. Winters tearfully told him about the phone call and the security guard. Hughes assured her she would be safe.

"Shelley, we are old friends," he said. "You can trust me. Nothing, and I mean nothing, will happen to your child or your mother or you while you are playing here at the Flamingo. I will personally guarantee it."

After the show, Winters ran up to her suite, where she saw a man "who looked like a caricature of an FBI man, complete with gun in holster under his arm, sitting in a chair in front of the room, another one standing up. She asked them what they were doing there. "Miss Winters, Mr. Hughes wants us to stay with your mother and baby and you for as long as you are in Las Vegas."

And they did. "Whether we went out to the pool or I took the baby for a walk in the stroller or my mother gambled in the casino . . . or went to the restaurants or shops, there were always two large men following [us]."

A year later, Hughes, as head of RKO, offered Winters $50,000 to co-star in *The Treasure of Pancho Villa*. Winters said she would do it if she were paid $1,000 per month for four years rather than a lump sum of $50,000. Her rationale was that she wanted a steady income while pursuing a return to the theater in New York. Hughes asked why she would want $48,000 instead of $50,000. He instead paid her $1,000 per month for *five* years.

Winters died in 2008. She was eighty-five.

Greg Bautzer

Greg Bautzer was one of Hollywood's most powerful lawyers from the 1950s through the 1980s. Howard Hughes was the catalyst for his success.

"Having Hughes as a client paid off in more ways than earning high fees from the billionaire," explained B. James Gladstone, author of *The Man Who Seduced Hollywood*. "It made other important businessmen want Bautzer to be their lawyer. If he was good enough for Hughes, he was good enough for them."

Hughes and Bautzer were involved in all sorts of legal skirmishes and developed a close relationship. One of the side effects of this relationship was Hughes' desire to get in touch with Bautzer no matter where he was or what he was doing. "The billionaire called Bautzer at restaurants. He called him at home. He called at all hours of the night," Gladstone wrote.

Bautzer had a second telephone installed in his office just for calls from Hughes. Further, Bautzer's secretary, Lea Sullivan, had a second phone installed in her home so that Hughes could reach her if he couldn't find Bautzer.

But Hughes usually could find Bautzer. In 1955, Bautzer took a vacation to Italy, in part to get a break from Hughes. On a whim, he took a room at an inn in a small village. He had told no one he was there. "He had been in his room only a few minutes when the phone rang," Gladstone wrote. "It was Hughes." The billionaire had dispatched detectives to keep tabs on Bautzer's movements.

On a business trip, Bautzer and Sullivan discovered that Oklahoma City was a dry town. A cab driver took them to a private club outside the city. Not long after sitting down, a waiter brought a telephone to their table. "Are you Bautzer?" the waiter asked. "There's a phone call for you." It was Hughes.

Despite these exasperating episodes, Bautzer was devoted to Hughes. In the early 1960s, he proclaimed, "There are only three things I'm really sentimental about. First, there's my son. Second, there's money. And third, there's Howard Hughes. In that order of priority. I just love that goddamned guy."

Bautzer died in 1987 at age seventy-six.

Elizabeth Taylor

Did Howard Hughes try to buy Elizabeth Taylor from her mother? That is the story told by Hughes biographer Charles Higham, and repeated by countless media sources ever since.

Hughes first saw Taylor in 1949 in the lobby of the Beverly Hills Hotel. He invited the teenage movie star and her parents for a weekend excursion. They agreed, but Taylor was not interested in Hughes, whom she considered to be too old for her.

A few years later, Hughes, through attorney Greg Bautzer, tried again. He asked Bautzer to ask Taylor's mother, Sara, if she would agree to an arranged marriage in exchange for $1 million.

Bautzer reluctantly went to see Sara. "I have a very unusual proposal to make," Bautzer said. "Howard Hughes wants to marry your daughter. . . . There's an inducement attached. He's prepared to pay a million dollars for her."

"Tax free?" Sara replied. She and Bautzer had a good laugh. The bold proposal was rejected out of hand.

In his memoir, Noah Dietrich tells a different story. After Taylor's first marriage, to Nicky Hilton, ended, Hughes sent associate Pat DiCicco to talk with her. Hughes invited Taylor to his house in Palm Springs, California. When they met there, Hughes offered to make her a bigger star at his RKO studio than she was at MGM. She had other plans.

"She told him that she was going to London to see [British actor] Michael Wilding, whom she intended to marry," Dietrich wrote. "Howard was distraught. Elizabeth was adamant. No amount of sweet-talk could dissuade her. As a last desperate measure, he sent DiCicco on the plane with her to London. Pat argued all the way, but the young lady had her mind set on marrying Michael Wilding. And she did."

Kitty Kelley, in her 1981 biography of Taylor, quotes the actress as saying she refused to marry Hughes because "he was such an out-and-out bore, I wouldn't have married him for all his money."

While Hughes was unsuccessful in wedding Taylor, others had better luck. She was married eight times to seven men. She died in 2011 at age seventy-nine.

Mitzi Gaynor

The singer, dancer, and actress Mitzi Gaynor dated Howard Hughes for several months when she was eighteen years old. That would have been around 1950. Seventy years later, Gaynor discussed Hughes with correspondent Mo Rocca on *CBS Sunday Morning*.

As Gaynor and Rocca leafed through a large scrapbook, Gaynor pointed to a picture of Hughes. "That's the hot number," Gaynor said. "That's Mr. Howard Hughes."

Rocca asked, "What was your connection, do you think? Was it emotional? Was it—"

Singer, dancer, and actress Mitzi Gaynor dated Hughes for several months around 1950. Courtesy of *Las Vegas Review-Journal* Archive.

"I think he wanted to get into my pants," Gaynor replied.

Asked if she loved Hughes, Gaynor said, "I thought I did. He asked me to marry him. Then I found out he'd asked 47 other women at the same time."

While still dating Hughes, Gaynor met the Hollywood producer and agent Jack Bean, who eventually became her husband of fifty-two years. She broke up with Hughes, but he wanted to leave her with something. "He said, 'Okay, I want you to buy some dirt.' I said, 'Some dirt?' He said, 'Yes, in Las Vegas—$25 an acre, which I sold maybe eight years ago for two million bucks.'"

In another 2019 interview, this one with *Closer Weekly* magazine, Gaynor's recollection of the Las Vegas land deal was a little different. "He had some property in Las Vegas and said, 'I want you to buy some dirt.' I said, 'I don't want to buy dirt, I want an apartment house.' He said, 'Well, you can do that later.' So, for $25 an acre, I bought five acres on the Las Vegas Strip. You know what that's worth? Well, I sold it for $6 million. So that's what I love about him!"

Whether Gaynor sold the property for $2 million or $6 million, she profited handsomely from the modest investment Hughes encouraged her to make. In the intervening years, Gaynor became well acquainted with Las Vegas. After her movie career stalled in the late '50s, she put together a highly successful Las Vegas stage show. She performed at the Flamingo Hotel for four years starting in 1961, then moved to the Riviera for six years. Her third stop on the Strip was the Tropicana.

In a 1972 interview for *Ladies Home Journal*, Gaynor recalled that Hughes was an excellent dancer—"the best dancer of them all, the rhumba, foxtrot, everything." She also said "often he used to fly me and my mother from one city to another just to take us to dinner."

Gaynor stopped performing in Las Vegas in the late '70s, instead touring theaters around the country. She did not return to the Las Vegas stage again until 2011, presumably about the time she cashed in on that long-ago real estate investment.

Part 6:

Hughes
in Pop Culture

The Fictional Hughes: Movies, Novels, and Beyond

Fictional portrayals of Howard Hughes seem to fall into two categories, in the same way that fictional portrayals of Elvis Presley do. There is the young, dashing Hughes, with only a hint of the bizarre behavior of his last twenty years, and there is the older, eccentric recluse.

The Amazing Howard Hughes

In 1977, a year after Howard Hughes' death, CBS produced a four-hour television miniseries about the billionaire starring a young Tommy Lee Jones.

Jones, a Texan who once worked for Hughes Tool Company, is easily the best thing about this workmanlike chronicle of Hughes' life. *TV Guide* reporter Dwight Whitney, describing Jones' performance, wrote that "the physical resemblance is frightening."

"Tommy chopped off his hair, went on a diet, read all the published books and articles on the subject, listened to the tapes, studied the newsreels, boned up on the studio research, cheerfully endured five-hour makeup sessions . . . and seldom dropped a line," Whitney wrote.

Jones, who went on to a highly successful movie career, is particularly good at portraying Hughes from his late teens through the early 1950s. Once Hughes becomes reclusive and his paranoia and obsessive-compulsive tendencies come to the fore, Jones is hampered by makeup work that at times makes him look more like a character from *Planet of the Apes*, or, as one critic described him, the Geico insurance cave man.

The movie is based on Noah Dietrich's memoir, so much of the story is told through the lens of Hughes' top administrator from the 1920s through the 1950s. The story covers most of the highlights and lowlights of Hughes' life, from his teenage years when his parents died through his final days in an Acapulco hotel room. Jean Harlow, Billie Dove, Katharine Hepburn, and Jane Russell are portrayed, as is the U.S. Senate hearing at which Hughes faced down critics of his *Hercules* airplane.

The film makes a point of emphasizing key philosophical aspects of Hughes' life. As a young man, Hughes tells Dietrich, "I'm going to be the best at whatever I do." Later, Hughes tells a screenwriter, "Everybody has a price." Even if Hughes never literally uttered these assertions, the record seems fairly clear that he believed them.

Although Jones does a fine job as the lead character, he was not the producers' first choice. As Whitney of *TV Guide* reported, the producer, Roger Gimbel, offered Warren Beatty $1 million to play Hughes. "When Beatty turned him down, he cast Tommy Lee Jones for $25,000, thereby effecting a saving of $975,000 going in." (As we shall see, Beatty finally produced a Hughes movie of his own almost thirty years later.)

The producers faced a number of threatened legal actions, including intimidating letters from Summa Corporation and concerns expressed by Hepburn, who ultimately declined to sue.

Dietrich, meanwhile, was thrilled by the movie. "I was terrifically impressed with the script and the casting," he told Whitney. "I met Tommy. I thought it really was Howard there for a while."

One challenge in evaluating this movie is that only a two-hour version of it is available today. CBS released a VHS version of the film that cuts it by almost half. As a result, it has a decidedly choppy feel, with story lines left unresolved and certain segments of Hughes' life barely explored. The two-hour version skips over the Las Vegas years once Hughes decides to buy the Desert Inn rather than move out. The 185-minute version is undoubtedly better—more cohesive and engrossing.

After watching this made-for-TV movie, one can see why Martin Scorsese decided to focus on just the first half of Hughes' life in *The Aviator*. There's simply too much to cover over Hughes' seventy years, and the story goes in all different directions. *The Amazing Howard Hughes* tries to cover it all, and the result is a surface-level hodgepodge that can't build up much momentum.

The Aviator

Certainly the most ambitious portrayal of Hughes is found in the 2004 Martin Scorsese film *The Aviator*. Leonardo DiCaprio does an impressive job of capturing the young Hughes—the hard-driving filmmaker, pilot, and actress-chaser. The movie received eleven Academy Award nominations and won five. It also received six Golden Globe nominations and won three, including Best Picture. While the movie focuses on roughly the first half of Hughes' life, it strongly suggests the gradual decline in his mental health.

It's a movie best appreciated by those who already know something about Hughes. It's hard to imagine someone understanding what's happening and why it's significant without knowing the basic facts of his life. Furthermore, the biopic ends abruptly, leaving some disappointed that it doesn't tackle key developments later in Hughes' life.

Las Vegas does not figure in the movie's plot at all. There is just one brief suggestion of his later years in Las Vegas. In the midst of a mental breakdown, during which he is naked and bearded and with long fingernails, he is shown watching a movie showing desert scenes. "I like the desert," he says mysteriously. "It's clean."

The movie documents some of the major events and accomplishments in Hughes' life, including the arduous filming of *Hell's Angels*, his romance with Katharine Hepburn, his near-fatal crash of the XF-11 spy plane and his dramatic U.S. Senate testimony over war profiteering accusations. The Hepburn subplot is particularly engrossing, largely because Cate Blanchett delivers such an endearing performance as the earthy actress.

But the overriding theme of Scorsese's movie is Hughes' mental decline. His germ phobia is ever present. At his favorite restaurant, he orders milk in a bottle with the cap still on it. There are several scenes in public bathrooms, including one in which he washes his hands until they bleed. When he starts to walk out, he stops when he sees the doorknob and realizes he doesn't want to touch it. He ends up waiting by the side of the door for someone to come in so he can walk out without having to touch the doorknob.

Paranoia also begins to set in during the 1940s as Hughes engages in high-stakes business and political battles. His volatile relationship with actress Ava Gardner (Kate Beckinsale) erupts when she discovers he has installed bugs in her house and phones.

The movie winds down with Hughes getting behind the controls of the flying boat, called *Hercules* by Hughes, the Spruce Goose by a doubting public. "All right, boys, let's fire it up," he says. As the plane gains speed across the water, the tension builds until *Hercules* triumphantly takes flight.

But the movie ends on a more poignant note, with Hughes beginning to break down again, repeating the phrase, "The way of the future." Escaping into a bathroom, Hughes tries to get a hold of himself while continuing to mutter those fateful words, which hold a double meaning: Hughes' unrelenting desire to pursue new frontiers contrasted with a foreshadowing of his later years dominated by drug addiction, mental illness, and seclusion.

Scorsese is one of the all-time great filmmakers, and *The Aviator* reflects his talents. People who don't know anything about Hughes might find the movie a little odd and slow-going, but for those familiar with Hughes' story, it is equals parts triumphant and heart-rendingly tragic.

The Carpetbaggers

Harold Robbins' 1961 best seller *The Carpetbaggers* features a main character, Jonas Cord Jr., who is clearly modeled on Hughes. The book embodies the phrase "roman à clef," defined by Webster's as a "novel in which real persons or actual events figure under disguise."

The Carpetbaggers was Robbins' breakthrough novel, the one that made him the best-selling author on the planet for many years. Few would suggest that Robbins was a literary lion, but he knew how to tell a compelling story. The advantage he had with *The Carpetbaggers* was borrowing liberally from the notable events of Hughes' life.

The book is pulp fiction through and through, but the cast of characters is undeniably interesting and the plot developments compelling. You find yourself eagerly inhabiting this rough-and-tumble world of aviation, movies, sex, and murder that Robbins creates, even if it is a mile wide and an inch deep. And it is eerily similar to the world one inhabits while researching the life and times of Howard Hughes.

Cord's basic story is Hughes', with just a few alterations. His mother dies when he is a child. His father makes his fortune in explosives (Hughes' father made his fortune inventing a mining drill bit). Cord's father dies suddenly, and he takes over the company at a young age. He buys out minority shareholders in his father's company, just as Hughes did.

There's much more:
- Cord loves to fly airplanes, makes record-breaking flights, starts an aircraft company, tests new aircraft himself, and buys an airline. He builds a "flying boat" during World War II and is involved in a near-fatal crash.
- Cord gets into the movie business, converts a silent movie into a talkie, invents a special bra to accentuate an actress' breasts on screen, and puts scores of promising young actresses under contract. He makes a big-budget war movie with elaborate dogfights called *Devils in the Sky* (Hughes' war picture was called *Hell's Angels*).

- Cord is a big-time womanizer, bedding young actresses particularly.
- Cord discovers a beautiful young woman with no acting experience and puts her in a sexy role that makes her a big star. He then hampers her career by refusing to allow her to accept the subsequent roles she's offered. (The scenario is reminiscent of Jane Russell's early career, although the actual character seems closer to Marilyn Monroe.)
- Cord abhors being in the public eye, and starts to shut out the world. Even his top executives can't get in touch with him.

This long, sprawling novel offers more than a rehash of the biography of Hughes. Robbins' characters also parallel the lives of some other famous people. For example, the character Rina Marlowe seems to be based on Jean Harlow, whose career was promoted by Hughes. The character Nevada Smith resembles the cowboy movie stars Tom Mix and Ken Maynard.

While Robbins was never a Pulitzer Prize nominee, parts of *The Carpetbaggers* do reflect a writer hard at work trying to get things right. Amid the frequent sex scenes and too-abrupt plot turns, his descriptions of the workings of the movie business, in particular, show an impressive store of firsthand knowledge. Robbins also does a credible job of getting inside the head of Cord/Hughes. "In my world, you made up your own rules," Cord says. "And everybody had to live by them whether they liked it or not."

Robbins had one annoying tick in *The Carpetbaggers* that really stands out reading it decades later: Seemingly everybody in the novel smokes like a chimney. In scene after scene, characters are lighting cigarettes, taking drags on cigarettes, and snubbing them out. They smoke anywhere and everywhere. Cord lights a cigarette in an elevator and a hospital. Even a pregnant doctor smokes. Obviously, the America of the 1920s, '30s, and '40s was unaware of the deadly effects of smoking, but it's worth noting that Hughes himself was not a smoker. Nor was he a heavy drinker, which marks one other difference between him and Cord.

The Carpetbaggers movie, released in 1964, stars George Peppard as Jonas Cord Jr., Carroll Baker as Rina Marlowe, and Alan Ladd miscast as the half-Indian Nevada Smith. It follows the basic plot of the book until the end, when the story goes in a couple of bizarre directions. Practically out of nowhere, we learn that Cord had a twin brother who was "incurably insane" and died when he was nine years old. This, along with his father's insistence on forgetting the twin ever existed, apparently is why Cord is such a mean-spirited jerk. Then Cord's wife, whom he abused and ignored emotionally for years, suddenly returns, and she and Cord reunite to raise their child. Happily ever after.

The movie, directed by Edward Dmytryk, was a blockbuster in 1964, due largely to the smut factor. Though a pale representation of the novel's blunt sexuality, *The Carpetbaggers* challenged Hollywood's Production Code, showing women in lingerie, aggressive love scenes, and dialogue featuring sexual innuendoes. By today's standards, the movie hardly deserves a PG-13 rating.

Peppard does a credible job of portraying the brash, ruthless Cord, but he doesn't remind one of Hughes the way DiCaprio does in *The Aviator*. Baker is a stunning platinum blonde, but she is not given the material needed to capture the complexities of the novel's Rina Marlowe. Her most memorable scene finds her in Paris, doing a striptease on a large chandelier that crashes to the ground.

The movie's campy nature is reflected in a ridiculous fight scene between Cord and Nevada Smith, in which they trade punches that obviously don't connect and flip over furniture for no apparent reason.

The eleventh-hour subplot about the crazy twin appears to have been incorporated because the sprawling novel lacked the big payoff one expects with a movie. But that's far from the biggest problem. When it came out, the *New York Times* trashed the movie, calling it "manufactured claptrap, superficial and two-dimensional."

Melvin and Howard

Melvin and Howard (1980) focuses on the older, bedraggled Hughes, played by Jason Robards. The film, directed by Jonathan Demme, received three Oscar nominations, winning two.

The Hughes of *Melvin and Howard* is the unkempt recluse of his later years. But this artfully done movie isn't really about him. It's about the charmingly ramshackle life of Melvin Dummar.

The film opens with a motorcyclist gleefully racing across a desert dry lake. Words appear on the screen: "Desert outside Tonopah, Nevada." But then the cyclist crashes while trying to leap a water reservoir.

Cut to a motorist driving down a remote highway at night, listening to the radio. He pulls off the highway onto a dirt road, stops, and gets out to urinate. Returning to his pickup truck and turning it around, he notices something in his headlights: a disheveled old man lying on the ground. Dummar (Paul Le Mat) carries the guy to his truck and helps him into the passenger seat.

Dummar heads back to the highway and gradually gets into a conversation with the old man, suggesting he needs medical care for his bloody ear.

"No doctors," the man gruffly responds. "I'm going to Vegas. . . . No stops, please."

Dummar mentions that he once applied to work at aircraft companies, including Hughes Aircraft, but had no luck.

"I'm Howard Hughes," the old man says.

Dummar doesn't believe him, but he's easygoing about it. "I believe anybody can call themselves whatever they want."

As they drive along, Dummar urges Hughes to sing along to a Christmas song he has written called "Santa's Souped-Up Sleigh." Hughes doesn't want to. Sing "or you walk," Dummar warns.

Hughes begrudgingly sings along. Then Dummar wants Hughes to sing a song he knows. Hesitatingly at first, Hughes sings "Bye Bye Blackbird." Eventually the two of them enjoy themselves singing the old standard.

Arriving in Las Vegas in the morning light, Hughes instructs Dummar to drop him off behind a Strip hotel. Hughes gets out, but then asks Dummar, "You got any money?" Dummar gives him the change in his pocket and drives off. Hughes starts walking toward the hotel and tosses the change aside.

The movie turns to Dummar's comically tumultuous life. He goes home to his pretty but ditzy wife, Linda (Mary Steenburgen), and their daughter, all living in a rattletrap trailer in Gabbs, Nevada. Times aren't good. Melvin's motorcycle is repossessed. Linda leaves him.

The real-life Melvin Dummar makes a cameo as a worker in a bus station.

Melvin goes after Linda, finding her working as a stripper in a Reno club. They get divorced.

Linda quits her job and moves to Anaheim, California, where she is pregnant. She calls Melvin to give him the news, and he says he wants to get married again. She agrees, and they have a $39 quickie wedding (presumably in Las Vegas).

The happy family moves to Glendale, California, where Melvin works as a milkman. Financial problems continue. Melvin convinces Linda to go on a popular game show. She wins a furniture set, a piano, and $10,000.

They buy a new house. But Melvin goes too far: He also buys a Cadillac and a boat. They can't afford it, and Linda leaves again. "Melvin, you're a loser!" she screams.

Melvin falls for a co-worker at the dairy. They move to Willard, Utah, to run a gas station. It's hard work, but they're getting by all right. They see on the news that Hughes has died. Dummar reminds his new wife of the story he told her about picking up Hughes in the desert.

A man in a dark suit comes into the gas station and asks for directions to Las Vegas. With Dummar distracted by another customer, the man leaves an envelope on Melvin's desk. Dummar notices it's something about a Hughes will. He drives to Salt Lake City, goes to the Mormon Church headquarters, and leaves the envelope on a secretary's desk.

A Hughes will has been discovered. One of the beneficiaries is Dummar, who stands to get $156 million. TV reporters descend on Willard, Utah.

At the courthouse in Las Vegas, Melvin is on the witness stand. Everybody is skeptical of his story. Why was the will left with him? He doesn't know. The judge asks Melvin if his story is true. Melvin replies, "It's the truth."

Back home, Melvin is subdued. "I'm not going to see that money," he says. But he isn't too bummed about it. He feels good that "Howard Hughes sang Melvin Dummar's song."

The movie ends with a flashback to Dummar and Hughes driving to Las Vegas. Hughes asks if he can drive. Hughes slides over, puts the truck in gear and pulls back onto the road. As Dummar dozes, Hughes sings "Bye Bye Blackbird."

The end.

Melvin and Howard roughly follows Dummar's tale, unlikely as it may be. The movie does not attempt to explain why Hughes was riding a motorcycle alone in the middle of the Nevada desert, though it suggests that he was thoroughly enjoying the freedom of racing around in the desolate area.

This is definitely a kinder, gentler Hughes, revealing the human being behind the public image. The same can be said of the Dummar character, suggesting that he was just a regular guy who by dumb luck got caught up in something far bigger than he ever imagined. True or not, it's a good story.

Tucker: The Man and His Dream

Another acclaimed film offering a brief appearance by Hughes is 1988's *Tucker: The Man and His Dream*, directed by Francis Ford Coppola.

In *Tucker*, Hughes, played admirably by Dean Stockwell, makes a cameo. He summons Preston Tucker, the would-be manufacturer of the "car of tomorrow," to the Southern California plant where he is working on his flying boat. Hughes shares a connection with Tucker: Besides both being inventors and independent entrepreneurs, they are being harassed by Senator Homer Ferguson of Michigan.

Hughes, eager to get back at Ferguson, tips off Tucker that he should contact a small helicopter company in Cincinnati that can provide steel at competitive prices and has an aluminum engine that might work well in the Tucker automobile.

In the perhaps one-minute scene, Hughes is portrayed as odd and mysterious, with his giant flying boat looming in the background.

I Was Howard Hughes

With his 2003 novel *I Was Howard Hughes*, Steven Carter takes an unusual approach to the Hughes story. The novel is structured in the form of a biography of Hughes, authored by a man named Alton Reece. Reece's "biography" is not the usual birth-to-death narrative. Rather, it is a compilation of interviews and diary entries focused on certain periods in Hughes' life.

At times, Carter's novel is very funny, such as the inclusion of a variation on an actual memo dictated by Hughes complaining to his aides about their lack of effort in finding his wife's missing cat. Carter clearly studied Hughes' writing style before crafting the memo:

"Now, it just seems to me that if Bill gave a goddamn in hell about my predicament down here he would have obtained from somewhere—I don't know where—from Los Angeles or someplace, he would have got some expert in the way of animals, cats in particular, and had him come down here and then put about eight or ten of Maheu's men at his disposal and they would have conducted an intelligent search based upon being instructed by somebody who knows the habits and ways of an animal of this kind. But, instead of that, so far as I have been able to make out, not one thing has been done."

Carter also has a young Hughes dreaming of building an empire in Nevada: "Nevada will be a mecca in two areas: aviation and tourism. Right now the possibility of the growth of either in this state seems remote because it is so barren; however, that is exactly why this plan should work. This is a pie that no one except me wants a piece of."

Hughes envisions building, testing, and servicing airplanes in Nevada, while the tourism would come from building golf courses: "I am thinking about the possibility of popularizing golf and making it the all-American game instead of just recreation for the upper tier. Land costs almost nothing here and so it would be the perfect place to build golf course after golf course if I can design a cost-effective irrigation system that would be practical on this barren land."

In Carter's novel, the young Hughes does not envision gambling as Nevada's economic future.

The real story within *I Was Howard Hughes* is that of Alton Reece, who, during the course of researching the biography, begins to take on some of the characteristics of his famous subject. But halfway through the novel, I found myself asking: What is the point? As a mix of fact and fiction about Hughes, it is confusing and frustrating. I spent much of the time wondering which anecdotes were true and which were invented. I can't imagine what readers with considerably less knowledge about Hughes are thinking as they wade in.

Fact and fiction, of course, are hard enough to sift through with much of the legitimate biographical material about Hughes. Carter's novel, clever though it is, doesn't really try to offer anything enlightening about Hughes. Its deceptive structure serves only to add to the static.

The Howard Hughes Affair

Howard Hughes was the focus of a 1979 novel by the prolific mystery writer Stuart Kaminsky. *The Howard Hughes Affair* was the fourth installment (of twenty-four altogether) in Kaminsky's light-hearted series about private eye Toby Peters.

The setting is Los Angeles, 1941. War is raging in Europe, and Americans are growing concerned that they soon will be joining the war, perhaps against Japan. Hughes hires Peters to find out which of the guests he invited to a dinner party snuck into his office and examined his secret plans for new military airplanes.

Peters embarks on a classic hardboiled detective odyssey, asking questions and gauging the truthfulness of the responses. He has skirmishes of various kinds, and several people end up dead. One of Hughes' dinner guests is mobster Bugsy Siegel, who assures Peters he hasn't done any of the killing. "In my business, we only kill each other," he says, echoing the title of a Siegel biography.

Kaminsky's depictions of Hughes are accurate enough, clearly based on having read a couple of books about the billionaire. Hughes is hard of hearing, and he wears ill-fitting suits. He obsessively flies his planes, looking for ways to improve them. He has an aversion to germs. At one point, Peters meets with Hughes on the set of the *The Outlaw*.

But unfortunately, Kaminsky does not really involve Hughes in the murder mystery. As a result, he misses one of Hughes' few charms, which was his love for the sort of intrigue that a private eye would naturally encounter. The real-life Hughes hired plenty of private investigators for various assignments and reveled in the stories they told him afterward. Kaminsky's Hughes is far too business-like and aloof.

Kaminsky has a lot more fun with another dinner guest, the actor Basil Rathbone, who accompanies Peters during parts of his investigation and offers clever Sherlock Holmesian insights.

The Shining

Horror writer Stephen King included a Hughesian character in his 1977 novel *The Shining*. The story's setting, the haunted Overlook Hotel in Colorado, was purchased in the 1940s by Horace Derwent, described as a California "millionaire inventor, pilot, film producer, and entrepreneur." Parts of Derwent's biography differ substantially from Hughes', but the parallels are clear, such as inventing a strapless bra to accentuate an actress' cleavage and living a reclusive lifestyle.

Everything Derwent touched "turned to gold"—except the Overlook Hotel. Derwent, "rumored to have substantial Las Vegas holdings," poured millions of dollars into renovating the hotel, but he lost money and eventually sold it. Derwent plays a role in the strange goings-on at the hotel that drive the Torrance family crazy, but since Derwent is essentially a ghost, he is not really fleshed out in the narrative.

Iron Man

An even more unusual portrayal of Hughes is found in the Marvel comic *Iron Man*. The weapons inventor Anthony Stark, who becomes the superhero Iron Man, seems to be patterned after Hughes in his prime:

"Anthony Stark . . . rich, handsome, known as a glamorous playboy, constantly in the company of beautiful, adoring women. . . . Anthony Stark is both a sophisticate and a scientist! A millionaire bachelor, as much at home in a laboratory as in high society!"

Set during the Cold War, the comic has Stark in the front lines of the battle against the "Communist Menace." His inventions are constantly helping the military, such as transistor-powered roller skates that "enable an entire infantry division to race down a highway at 60 miles an hour."

The similarities between Stark and Hughes essentially end with his rich playboy image and inventive efforts to defeat communism. The comic book series, penned by Stan Lee in the early '60s, does not attempt to extend the parallel any further.

Rules Don't Apply

Warren Beatty first expressed an interest in making a movie about Howard Hughes in the early 1970s. He finally made one in 2016 called *Rules Don't Apply*. The movie, co-written by award-winning *Melvin and Howard* screenwriter Bo Goldman, was highly anticipated. Unfortunately, it does not deliver on those expectations.

Beatty plays Hughes, and he wisely does not try very hard to impersonate his real-life subject. His character is more light-hearted and charming than Hughes was, which is not necessarily a bad thing in what amounts to a romantic comedy. A more fundamental challenge: He is playing Hughes in his fifties at a time when Beatty was seventy-nine years old.

The story begins in the late 1950s in Los Angeles. It focuses on a beautiful young woman named Marla (Lily Collins, the daughter of singer Phil Collins) whom Hughes puts under contract and sets up in an apartment along with her mother (Annette Bening, Beatty's real-life wife, whom he met on the set of *Bugsy*). The young actress, of course, wants to be a Hollywood star. But when she is ignored by Hughes, she takes an interest in one of his young drivers, Frank (Alden Ehrenreich), although such a liaison is, of course, strictly forbidden. When Hughes finally enters their lives, complications ensue.

The best part of *Rules Don't Apply* is the romance between Marla and Frank. When Hughes becomes part of the story, the narrative meanders into a muddled mess. It might have been more compelling to tell the story of the young lovers navigating the rules and eccentricities of the Hughes organization without ever introducing Howard himself.

To be fair, while it failed at the box office, some seasoned critics liked the movie. Stephen Holden of the *New York Times* called it "hugely entertaining." He particularly liked the film's "good-humored" tone. *Rolling Stone* magazine's Peter Travers said that Beatty's performance, "filled with comic bite and aching confusion, teases a much deeper portrait."

Rules Don't Apply most likely will be remembered for the breakout performance by Collins, who received a Golden Globe nomination for Best Actress.

Weird Tales: *Obscure Books about Hughes*

So, you haven't written a book about Howard Hughes? Well, why not? What are you waiting for? Everyone else has.

Hughes has been the subject of an incredible number of books, most of them published in the 1970s, before and after his death in 1976. But many others have been published over the past forty years, covering almost every aspect of Hughes' life and business. A handful of these books make up the respected canon of Hughes biography and form the foundation for any serious study of the man. Many more books teeter on the periphery of scholarship, offering some tangential piece of the Hughes puzzle that may or may not be true, but may be entertaining nonetheless. Most of them are out of print, available only in used bookstores or the dark corners of the internet. This chapter outlines some of these memoirs and tell-all tomes and shares the best and worst parts.

I Caught Flies for Howard Hughes
By Ron Kistler
Playboy Press, 1976

As Kistler explains on the first page of this insightful and entertaining memoir, he was one of several men employed round-the-clock to, among other things, keep flies from invading Hughes' bungalow at the Beverly Hills Hotel. He explains why this could be a formidable challenge:

"On hot sunny days flies made kamikaze dives to get into the darkness of Bungalow Four. It was dark, because my employer kept the lights off and the drapes closed. It was also warm, since he kept the air conditioners off, preferring to sit nude in a white leather chair—nude, that is, save for a pink hotel napkin, which he kept on his crotch."

Further complicating Kistler's flycatching were the restrictions under which he had to fulfill his duties: "I wasn't allowed to use a fly swatter, newspaper or magazine, sticky paper, or spray can when I went after a fly in Bungalow Four. It was hand-to-wing combat, and the Kleenex was there to ensure that the hand would never come into direct contact with the foe."

Kistler worked for Hughes for about three years, starting right after Hughes removed himself completely from the public eye in 1957. For thirteen months of his employment, Kistler says he was "with Hughes more than any other person on the face of the earth." Although Kistler ostensibly was a "bodyguard" for Hughes, in reality he was more of a babysitter.

Kistler's stint with Hughes started on the graveyard shift watching a parked airplane. The Convair 440, covered in dust and sitting on flat tires, obviously had not flown in years, but Hughes demanded that somebody keep an eye on it and let nobody touch it. The job was ridiculous—mostly sleeping and reading—but it paid two dollars per hour at a time when Kistler was unemployed.

Because Kistler was not a Mormon, he was told that his prospects for advancement within the Hughes company were not good. But after a couple of months of mindless airplane guard detail, the monotony was broken when Hughes visited the airfield. Kistler apparently had impressed Hughes with his frantic efforts to keep gawkers away, and soon he was reassigned to the "drivers' pool."

Because there were many more drivers than driving assignments, this job, too, required finding inventive ways to pass the time. A favorite activity was ping-pong: "I feel certain that a team from Hughes Productions could have held its own with the Red Chinese national team," Kistler quipped.

Most of the driving assignments were mundane, such as taking a Hughes company executive somewhere or picking up the mail. But escorting Hughes' stable of starlets various places could be more interesting. Besides taking the young women to dancing and singing lessons, the drivers often accompanied them to restaurants and shows. "We could not have dinner with the starlet alone," Kistler wrote. "It was compulsory that she have her parents or her agent along." In addition, Kistler says, the routine included a private investigator tailing the up-and-coming actress and her entourage.

After a year in the drivers' pool, Kistler was rewarded with a new assignment: bodyguard. He started by providing security for Hughes during exclusive movie screenings at Goldwyn Studios. Naturally, the screenings weren't the usual two-hour outings. Kistler says Hughes sometimes would watch movies for forty-eight to seventy-two hours straight, requiring employees to drive all over the city to pick up films from various sources.

Also, Hughes was not a typical movie watcher. Kistler wrote: "He'd watch some of the films from beginning to end. Others he would signal to be stopped after five, ten, forty, or eighty minutes. To this day I cannot figure out why he stopped some films when he did. On many occasions he would watch a movie for two hours and stop it five minutes from the end." Hughes also would have the projectionist rerun a portion of a film numerous times, often when he identified a female extra or cast member whom Hughes wanted to put under contract.

Just when Kistler had reached the breaking point with this dead-end job, he received a new assignment: round-the-clock handmaiden to Hughes. While the opportunity to be near Hughes kept Kistler on the job, it turned out to be even more monotonous than his previous work. Hughes occasionally expected his keepers to perform mundane tasks, but mostly they chatted with their colleagues, read magazines, and called their wives on the phone.

Things got more interesting when Hughes asked Kistler to take some dictation. Kistler found himself "in the middle of one of the greatest dramas in American corporate history": the battle for control of TWA. One marathon dictation session occurred while Hughes sat on the toilet, trying desperately to conquer his chronic constipation problem.

Hughes deteriorated physically before Kistler's eyes. Because of his weight loss, "his bones seemed to be trying to cut through his flesh; there was no cushion of fat to impede them," Kistler wrote. "His cheekbones were grotesquely out of proportion to the rest of his sunken face. The black circles under his eyes appeared to be the work of a makeup artist trying to recapture the look of Lon Chaney in *The Phantom of the Opera*." Kistler says he reported his concerns about Hughes' health to his bosses, who expressed alarm but took no decisive action—a stance that would continue for years as Hughes' health plummeted.

Kistler's primary task while on duty for Hughes at the Beverly Hills Hotel was film projectionist. "If he wanted movies screened, I screened them. If he didn't, I would sit in silence. Often I would be there for twelve hours straight, or longer, without an opportunity to take a drink of water or go to the toilet."

Hughes used Kleenex obsessively, Kistler wrote: "He used them to wipe his nose, to blow his nose, to dab his nose. To wipe his eyes. To clean out his ears. With the corners twisted, to clean under his fingernails and toenails. He used Kleenex to clean the amplifier of his hearing aid, as well as the earpiece.

He continually cleaned the telephone, his chair, the ottoman—he cleaned every damned thing he could reach from his chair."

And the used Kleenex? It was tossed over his shoulder onto the floor, forming a mountainous pile of tissues that Kistler was not allowed to dispose.

Kistler had a front-row seat during Hughes' most intimate business dealings. Besides hearing what Hughes had to say during phone conversations, he often could hear the person on the other end of the line. "I was privy to these calls because of Hughes' hearing problem," Kistler wrote. "He was forced to wear a hearing aid, so he did not hold the telephone in a normal manner. He reversed it, holding the earpiece to the amplifier of the hearing device and the mouthpiece in front of his mouth. I could hear both sides of the conversation from where I sat, and Hughes knew it. Whenever there was something he didn't want me to hear, he'd send me to my room. But most of the time I stayed, and more than once Hughes asked me, after he had completed the call, to recall for him something that had been said or how it had been put."

Despite the bizarre scene within the bungalow, Hughes sometimes was an enchanting presence on the telephone. During one such phone conversation, "Hughes was so completely charming that it was difficult to believe a naked, scraggly-haired millionaire hidden in a darkened bungalow could be uttering the words he uttered," Kistler wrote.

Kistler says he was perplexed by Hughes' relationship with his wife, actress Jean Peters, who stayed in a separate bungalow at the hotel. They would talk on the phone for hours, but did not see each other in person. Hughes also insisted on controlling her comings and goings. "She went from hobby to hobby—ceramics, needlepoint, welding sculpture out of metal—while Hughes wouldn't allow her to go out and do the things she wanted to do. She loved baseball, and the Dodgers had just come out to L.A., but Hughes wouldn't allow her to go to the Coliseum. If she wanted to go out shopping, she'd make it one time out of ten."

The long hours and monotony of the job eventually became too much for Kistler, who began to rebel against Hughes' bizarre orders. Finally, he quit, telling off Hughes and storming out of his bungalow. But looking back, Kistler wrote that for all the stresses and oddities of the job, he enjoyed being with Hughes. "On balance, he had never really treated me with anything less than respect. He gave me credit for my intelligence, humor, dedication to an impossible job, and loyalty. He had, under his own pressures . . . pushed me hard, but he'd had the good sense and decency to back off when he knew that he had gone too far. Yes, that was it: I found myself admitting that I liked Howard Hughes."

My Life and Opinions
By Howard Hughes, edited by Robert P. Eaton
Best Books Press, 1972

This has to be one of the strangest books ever published—about Hughes or anything else.

The premise is that the book's editor, Robert P. Eaton, met numerous times with Hughes in 1967 and 1970 while the billionaire was living at the Desert Inn in Las Vegas. Eaton says Hughes gave him stacks of handwritten notes on "legal-size yellow pages" documenting his life and opinions and asked Eaton to put together a book. The reason, Eaton says, is that Hughes wanted to set the record straight, to counter the distortions and misrepresentations in the media about him and his business dealings.

Eaton laments that Hughes' notes didn't turn out to be a bonanza of revelations. Instead, they are more of a rambling commentary on a range of personal experiences and political topics, from his first flight at age thirteen to the making of *Hell's Angels* to his Las Vegas investments. There's really nothing in the Hughes notes that couldn't have been imagined from studying biographies and news clippings.

Eaton immediately raises credibility questions when he describes visiting the Desert Inn to meet Hughes. Two claims in particular are highly suspect:

- Eaton says that when he entered the private elevator taking him to the ninth floor, he noticed a red circle painted on the floor. "I stepped into the circle and the doors closed. I waited. . . . The elevator didn't move, and I wondered about it until I remembered the dark glasses. Howard's germ phobia had progressed so far that visitors had to be sterilized before they were admitted to his presence. I put the glasses on. I sensed rather than saw the change in the light. Then I smelt the distinctive odor of an ultraviolet-ray unit and hoped that whoever was manipulating the damn thing would not overexpose me. . . . I was now hygienically sanctified."

No one who worked for Hughes at the Desert Inn corroborates this fantastical sterilization procedure.

- When Eaton meets Hughes at the DI, his description of the man includes a key inconsistency with other witness accounts. Eaton says: "His hair— what there was of it—was almost white. A few thin strands were brushed back across the top of his head, but they hardly covered his scalp. . . . He had grown a stringy beard to go with his mustache, and he reminded me very much of a tall Ho Chi Minh."

People who actually saw Hughes during his Desert Inn years say he often had long hair and a long beard. The Ho Chi Minh comparison isn't close.

In one section, Hughes describes taking a trip to Germany just before World War II. This was just after his highly publicized round-the-world flight in 1938. He says he met with military leader Hermann Goering and other Nazis, toured Germany's aviation facilities and watched Luftwaffe aerial demonstrations. Hughes says he was impressed with Germany's aviation program, and says he was shown supposedly top-secret drawings for jet-powered aircraft. "My impression was that they had shown me the drawings deliberately, knowing that I would pass the information on to the United States government," Hughes allegedly writes.

Hughes says that when he returned home, "I wrote my impressions and sent them to the War Department. After several weeks I received a polite note of thanks from an aide to General Henry Arnold, then head of the Army Air Corps, and that was all. Apparently the Lindbergh affair was on everybody's mind, and the acquisition of vital military intelligence was not as important as political considerations."

No biographies mention Hughes traveling to Germany after his round-the-world flight, nor do they report that he met with Nazi leaders.

Hughes' musings conclude with some not-very-introspective assessments of his life. "While I cannot lay claim to being a very good man, neither am I a very bad man," he writes. Also: "I have hurt some men, for which I have felt regret. I have helped others, for which I claim no credit."

The book widens the credibility gap by starting and ending with fictionalized chapters in which Eaton dramatizes Hughes being preserved through cryogenics and brought back to life in 2025. It's not clear why these sections were included, except, perhaps, to spice up what is otherwise a very dry text.

Eaton's entire premise is certainly fictional. He clearly did a lot of research on Hughes' personality and attitudes, and the prose allegedly written by Hughes seems consistent with the billionaire's life story and publicly expressed views. One has to wonder: If Eaton had wanted to make a big splash with a supposed Hughes memoir, why not give Hughes more interesting things to say? Clifford Irving certainly did that in his fake autobiography written around the same time. Yet the blandness of Hughes' recollections and political comments in Eaton's book leaves you thinking they just may be real. Or, that Eaton purposely made them bland to give them the air of authenticity.

It's possible that Eaton did, as he describes, meet Hughes back in 1957 at the Beverly Hills Hotel and got to know him a little at that time. But all reliable sources insist that during his four years at the Desert Inn, Hughes never met in person with anyone outside his small entourage of personal aides. In addition, Hughes' leading biographers give Eaton's book zero credibility. Neither

Eaton nor his book merits a mention in Donald L. Barlett and James B. Steele's respected *Empire: The Life, Legend, and Madness of Howard Hughes*, published in 1979. Nor does the book make an appearance in Richard Hack's comprehensive 2001 biography, *Hughes: The Private Diaries, Memos and Letters*. If anybody believed Eaton actually had obtained Hughes' memoirs, they would serve as primary source material and would be quoted liberally.

Before the book's release, excerpts appeared in *Ladies Home Journal*—but not before Hughes tried to stop it, as he did most books about him. Attorney Chester Davis filed suit to stop the magazine from printing the excerpts, but the judge refused to stop publication.

In 2014, Eaton briefly resurfaced in an article published in the *Palm Beach Post*. Reporter Barbara Marshall said that after the controversy over the Hughes book, Eaton moved to Europe. He returned to the States forty years later, looking for vindication.

It turns out Eaton was something of a Hollywood playboy in the 1950s, his movie star good looks and charm earning him entrée to the movie capital's elite circles. He rubbed shoulders with Frank Sinatra and played tennis with Gene Kelly. He also became friends with attorney Greg Bautzer, who often represented Hughes.

Eaton's celluloid career was paltry, but he married Lana Turner, with whom Hughes had an affair in the 1940s. Eaton and Turner tied the knot in 1965, but the marriage lasted less than four years. It fell apart in 1969 after Eaton's grand idea for Turner to make a comeback as the star of a television series called *The Survivors* was a ratings and financial disaster. His experiences in Hollywood and with Turner became the basis for a highly autobiographical novel he wrote, *The Body Brokers*, published in 1970.

According to Eaton, it was Bautzer who gave him a bag of yellow legal pads full of handwritten notes. He said Bautzer also gave him more than $100,000 to transform the notes into Hughes' life story. Eaton set to work, and a few months later returned the notes and the manuscript to Bautzer. They never spoke again.

According to Marshall's article, "more than a year later Eaton spotted *My Life and Opinions* by Howard Hughes, edited by Robert P. Eaton, in a New York bookstore window. Included was a foreword about his relationship with Hughes that he says was fictitious and written by someone else."

The book was widely proclaimed to be a fake, and nobody came to Eaton's defense. That's when he moved to Greece.

In 2014, then living in West Palm Beach, Eaton was promoting an unpublished memoir he had written called "Beverly Hills Racket" that he hoped would lead to a TV series about his life.

Howard Hughes, His Other Empire, and His Man
By Clint Baxter and Jim Haworth
Vantage Press, 1996

Jim Haworth was a longtime rancher who managed Howard Hughes' "secret empire" of rural Nevada acreage, including the Warm Springs Ranch, about fifty miles northeast of Las Vegas.

Haworth says Hughes was drawn to acquire his vast desert holdings while flying over them in the 1940s. They became "the answer to Howard Hughes' dream, his escape to untainted air, pure water, and land."

Hughes bought the Warm Springs Ranch in the Moapa Valley in 1968. Haworth had managed the ranch for the previous owner, New York millionaire Frank Taylor, and stayed on after Hughes took over, managing cattle and horses.

The authors suggest that Hughes bought the Warm Springs Ranch for the same reason he bought actress Vera Krupp's ranch in Red Rock Canyon, west of Las Vegas, that year: as a place to entice his estranged wife, Jean Peters, to live with him in peaceful seclusion.

Haworth helped Hughes expand his ranching empire across Clark and Lincoln counties.

The first half of the book primarily recounts Hughes' life, a scattershot chronology cobbled together from other biographies. This narrative is intercut with brief biographical interludes about Haworth's life, including his skill in raising and training horses. The book also detours into a history of Hughes' purchase of mining claims across Nevada.

It doesn't take long for the reader to realize that Haworth never spoke with Hughes or received any direct written communication from the billionaire, despite the title's claim that Haworth was "His Man." The authors contend that Hughes monitored ranch operations from the air, but reliable sources agree that Hughes never left his penthouse suite at the Desert Inn from 1966 to 1970.

It's also clear that Hughes' executives took only reluctant interest in the ranch. Haworth was flown to Los Angeles once a month to report to Hughes executives on ranch activities.

"Being part of a multimillion-dollar outfit, Jim thought he could relieve the strains on the ranch, but soon found that those in command had no intention of helping Mr. Hughes make the ranch a pleasure and success," the authors wrote.

Haworth makes some interesting assertions. For example, he contends that Hughes executives did a sorry job of managing the Krupp Ranch (now Spring Mountain Ranch State Park). "Through mismanagement by the property division, Hughes could not help but lose the majority of the Krupp cattle the first year," Haworth wrote. "They did not die. These good breeding animals were taken to slaughter by [Bill] Gay's men, probably for Hughes' hotel beef.

"Meanwhile, several hundred thousand dollars were wasted on the Krupp ranch, fixing it up as a playhouse for Hughes' high executives from Las Vegas and Los Angeles."

Haworth says the first thing Hughes executives did once they took over the Warm Springs Ranch was to "sell off the valuable Brahma cattle that Frank Taylor and Jim had developed. They didn't know a damn thing about ranching."

Haworth speculates that Hughes longed for the peace and tranquility of the ranch: "I am sure that if Mr. Hughes could have been turned loose by his Mormon aides and lived on Warm Springs Ranch before being drugged and destroyed, he would be alive today and a very happy man."

The book's second half consists largely of cowboy-on-the-range stories, campfire recipes, and Howarth's rough charcoal sketches of bucking broncos, angry bulls, and such.

After Hughes' death in 1976, the executor of his estate, cousin Will Lummis, put the Warm Springs Ranch up for sale, originally for $8 million. The ranch was eventually sold to the Mormon Church for $4.5 million in 1978, with the condition that Howarth continue to manage the operation, which he did for several years.

His Weird and Wanton Ways: The Secret Life of Howard Hughes
By Richard Mathison
William Morrow & Company Inc., 1977

Based largely on stories recounted by Hughes' longtime security chief, Jeff Chouinard, Mathison's book is well-written and entertaining, though a fairly minor contribution to the Hughes canon.

Mathison contends that during Chouinard's employment by Hughes from 1949 to 1968, the former private detective, who was better known by the name Mike Conrad, was closer to Hughes than anyone, including the executives who ran his companies and the women he courted. "Chouinard was his daily personal contact with the outside world of women, other employees, his houses, his planes," Mathison wrote. "For days on end during a crisis he'd call the detective every hour with orders and questions."

But Mathison says Chouinard's close contact with Hughes did not necessarily make him privy to Hughes' business maneuvers. "In the neurotic world of Howard Hughes there was only one insider," Mathison notes.

Part of Chouinard's job was to monitor the harem of young women

Hughes identified as potential movie starlets. "By official count he kept detailed case histories on 108 girls," Mathison wrote. Hughes gave detailed instructions to his potential starlets. "The girl must sleep in her bra every night, and she was never, never to turn her head more than fifteen degrees or it might put lines in her neck. The drivers were cautioned as usual never to cross railroad tracks and to slow down to two miles an hour at bumps to avoid injuring the girl's breast tissue."

Chouinard met Hughes in 1948 after soliciting RKO Pictures, which Hughes owned, to sponsor a round-the-world flight in a single-engine plane. Hughes, a world-famous pilot, was skeptical of Chouinard's plan, but offered him a job as an investigator. Chouinard took the job, hoping to eventually persuade Hughes to finance his flight.

Before long, Chouinard became Hughes' top private eye, focusing in the early years on various ploys to foil the "Red Menace" that Hughes believed was seeking to destroy America. Hughes had fired numerous employees of RKO Pictures who were suspected of being Communists. Working with Chouinard, Hughes plotted to expand the battle, though nothing much ever came of it.

Chouinard recalls the classic Hughes obsession with details, a trait that would later frustrate Bob Maheu as he tried to run the billionaire's Las Vegas empire: "The most minute item would suddenly focus his whole attention: on which corner a guard was to stand, northwest or southeast; how a car was to park at sunset. Days would be taken up in game plans about such nonsense. Everything would stop while the Hughes tunnel-vision took over."

Hughes loved to play amateur detective, and charged Chouinard with carrying out his often-ridiculous and petty plans. For example, Hughes became interested in a Las Vegas showgirl whose boyfriend was a police officer. Chouinard was told to follow the officer and report back to Hughes every hour. "Within a day Chouinard had discovered the cop was a family man and the showgirl wasn't aware of it," Mathison wrote. "Hughes delightedly gave her the news that her boyfriend was married and heard her break into tears on the phone. Once he'd destroyed the romance, he lost all interest in her and never called her again."

Chouinard was a central player in many of Hughes' bizarre plots involving women. One time, Hughes concocted a complex plan to celebrate New Year's at midnight at the Beverly Hills Hotel with three women, but none of them was to know about the others. "It was all intricately laid out, involving a dozen people who had to follow the timing of the choreography down to the second," Mathison wrote. "Jean Peters was to be in the dining room of the hotel, Susan Hayward was to be at a table in the Polo Lounge, and his Number 3, a would-be starlet . . . was to be in a bungalow at a candlelit table."

Of course, Hughes' farcical B-movie scheme involving a series of phone calls interrupting his meetings with the women went awry. First, a suspicious Hayward discovered Hughes with Peters and stormed out. Peters followed, while the third woman, Yvonne Shubert, never knew what happened. Naturally, Hughes blamed his employees. "For three days, he hurled accusations at different members of the staff for fouling up his elaborate scheme," Mathison wrote.

Hughes' relationship with Peters was far from over, however. He later married her in a secret ceremony in Tonopah, Nevada. (Mathison mistakenly reports that the wedding occurred in Hawthorne, Nevada.)

Chouinard quit working for Hughes after the billionaire moved to Las Vegas, effectively ending Mathison's tale, except for this biting final assessment of Hughes:

"Hughes was no genius. His wealth grew, thanks to employees and the value of the dollar, out of all proportion to his personal contribution. One can only guess—as with all famous and fascinating psychotics—what he might have done had he been well and sane. As it was he was the skunk at the lawn party of his own corporate world."

A final note on Jeff Chouinard: His youngest brother, Yvon, is the owner of the Patagonia outdoor gear empire.

Howard Hughes and His Mormon Family
By Jerry Bell
Granite Publishing, 2005

This book is an unabashed hagiography. Nary a negative word is offered about Hughes, whom the author says he came to "respect and love." In fact, Bell manages to justify many of Hughes' eccentricities and obvious effects of mental illness as products of his genius.

Bell wrote the book partly as a response to Ron Kistler's *I Caught Flies for Howard Hughes*, which he says made Hughes "look ridiculous." "While my respect for The Boss did not allow me to publish a book on him during his lifetime, I felt that eventually I should tell the public the positive side of working in Hughes' employ."

Bell grew up in Provo, Utah. After a stint in the US Army he became a hairdresser in Hollywood, where his clients included models and movie stars. But after developing an allergy to hair-coloring chemicals, Bell quit the trade and, in 1956, landed a job working for Hughes as a security guard.

The book is oddly organized, starting with a long chapter in which Bell outlines fourteen secrets to Hughes' success in business (number five: "Possess a 'millionaire mentality'").

Bell first was assigned to guard one of Hughes' old Convair airplanes. Then he was transferred to Hughes' Bel Air, California, home. In the process he briefly became a member of Hughes' infamous "Mormon Mafia," the men who attended to his personal needs in the later years of his life.

Bell elaborates on a familiar theme among the various Hughes employees who have written about their experiences: the company hierarchy.

"The difference between a driver and a staff member was a substantial one. The staff member was rather like a nobleman or a general in the royal army. All his wishes and needs were provided for him; a truly ambrosial life was his for the asking. He was provided with the most rare delicacies from the list of authorized restaurants. The staff member also attended the best of current plays and other theater performances, and escorted beautiful starlets (along with a driver) to bright spots after dark. Staff members could drive their cars if they chose, or they could use one of the drivers always available.

"On the other hand, a driver must always be available to serve either the royal army people or others designated by the King, or the King himself. He must spend hours waiting or guarding the royal possessions. He had many privileges, of course, but not as many as a member of the staff."

After Hughes married Jean Peters in 1957, Bell says they quietly moved into a home in Palm Springs, California, where Bell served as a guard during the couple's "six-month honeymoon." The newlyweds kept to themselves, with few visitors and little exposure to employees such as Bell.

Bell observes that a rich man such as Hughes should have a permanent residence, a large estate "filled with original paintings of the masters, with manuscripts of internationally renowned authors, with comfort and luxury and collections and music and objets d'art, and more importantly, surrounded by family and friends. But that was not Hughes' way. This particular king was castle-less and estate-less; he didn't have a permanent residence, he collected almost nothing, he didn't give dinner parties, or have as guests the significant people of the world."

Instead, Hughes restlessly moved from place to place, a highly involved process that kept his employees busy with an array of tasks, from scouting prospective residences that offered sufficient privacy to preparing the home for his unique occupancy. This process included taping the windows and doors "so no unfiltered air could get in; then it must be air-conditioned by equipment Hughes had personally designed, and all the plants and foliage around the house and inside the house were either destroyed or neglected."

During his stint guarding Hughes' house in Palm Springs, Bell got married, which proved to be a fortuitous move in more ways than one. First, his bosses told him to find a nice house in Palm Springs (he had been staying in a motel), and that the company would take care of the expenses. Bell ended up with a house that actually was nicer than the one in which Hughes and Peters were staying. Then he was asked where he was going for his honeymoon, and the company paid for the trip.

Bell describes a variety of Hughes employees he encountered over the years whom he calls "the Forgotten People." These were employees such as an airplane mechanic and a chef who had next to nothing to do, except to be on call if they were needed. Since they were rarely if ever needed, they collected twice-a-month paychecks for nothing. Bell explains why these people were allowed to linger on: "One of the rules in working for Hughes was to be silent unless spoken to, not to bring up a subject unless Hughes initiated it, not to explain anything unless asked. . . . The result was that people were kept on the payroll who hadn't contributed any work for many years."

Bell devotes a chapter to explaining why Hughes had so many Mormons on his staff, concluding that the "frugality and sacrifice" they practiced during their missionary service made them well-suited to the job. "This strict type of living would most certainly produce a much disciplined and devoted individual," he explains. "Many of the individuals closest to Hughes had had such an experience and understood the meaning of hard work, honesty, discipline, long hours, devotion, and even some deprivation."

While Hughes undoubtedly appreciated his Mormon staffers' discipline and clean living, the primary reason for the large number of Mormon employees was that they were hired by Hughes' top aides, Bill Gay and Kay Glenn, who were devout Mormons and had access to young recruits through their church connections.

Bell resigned from the monotony of the tasks assigned by Hughes, moved to Hawaii, and became a college professor there for twenty years. He later moved to Provo, Utah, where he performed missionary work.

Boxes: *The Secret Life of Howard Hughes, second edition*
By Douglas Wellman and Mark Musick
WriteLife Publishing, 2015

This book has a preposterous premise, but it has received so much attention over the years that it must be addressed here.

The story in a nutshell: Howard Hughes did not die in 1976. When he was living in the Desert Inn in Las Vegas in 1968, he concocted a scheme to escape his miserable billionaire's life. He installed an impersonator in the hotel's penthouse suit and assumed the identity of another man, one Verner Nicely of Ohio, allowing Hughes to live out his days as a regular person.

Nicely—known as "Nik"—met a woman named Eva McLelland in 1969 at a military base in Panama. They fell in love and married. They lived in various places until settling in rural Alabama.

Eva tells the authors that Nik was very secretive about his past. He was eccentric. He was hard of hearing. He was fanatical about cleanliness. He had blond hair but colored it from its natural black. He had burn scars all over his body. He always wrote on legal pads. And mysterious people were always watching them and talking with Nik.

In 1975, Nik revealed to Eva that he was in fact Howard Hughes. After six years of marriage, this answered a lot of questions for Eva. For one, "the constant presence of the aides made more sense."

After Hughes died in 1976, Nik became even stranger and more reclusive, according to Eva. "Nik preferred to stay on their property or spend his time alone, hiding in the woods, naked. For some reason, Nik felt compelled to shed his clothes and commune with nature at a very basic level."

As the years passed, Nik opened up more and more to Eva about his life, doing a respectable job of adhering to the biographical record. Nik died of cancer in 2001. Co-author Mark Musick met Eva about a year later, and, although skeptical at first, he took an interest in her story.

Musick and Wellman painstakingly dissect the chronology of the latter years of Hughes' life, looking for logical ways to surgically embed Nik's story into the known record. The big question of who replaced Hughes at the Desert Inn is answered with the conjecture that a body double hired to distract the press in the late 1950s—a fairly well documented fact—was retained for the monumental task.

The authors make a valiant effort, but in the end there are just too many factual and logistical hurdles to overcome. One problem is that pictures of Nik included in the book—none of them close up—don't look as much like Hughes as the authors contend. Another is that records of a medical exam in 2000 revealed Nik to be six feet tall, a full four inches shorter than Howard. Even though many of us lose height in old age, four inches would be extreme. These issues, however, are dwarfed by the audacious notion that Howard Hughes, one of the world's most famous people, could have lived another man's life in obscurity for more than thirty years without the ruse being leaked or discovered. Are we to believe that all these "aides" coming and going from Nik and Eva's house in rural Alabama have kept their lips sealed all this time? That all the people who would have known about the Hughes impersonator have resisted all temptations to reveal the story? That this story was suppressed throughout the contentious battle over the Hughes estate? Not to mention the idea that Hughes would have been satisfied with the strange and modest lifestyle—gardening, living in travel trailers—that Eva describes in the book.

No matter how sincere the authors were—I believe they saw themselves on a noble quest—this story is akin to the legend that Elvis Presley faked his death in 1977 and later was spotted waiting in line at a Burger King in Michigan.

Still, the authors have done an admirable job of promoting *Boxes*, and in the process have gained a fair stable of believers. This should not be surprising, considering the wild myths and conspiracy theories that otherwise sensible people are willing to believe. The true story of Hughes' life is so odd and intriguing, what's one more crazy twist in a life full of them?

31

Hughes on Display:
He's Everywhere and Nowhere in Las Vegas

It's difficult to avoid the name Howard Hughes in Las Vegas, largely because the community's largest master-planned community, Summerlin, is being built by the Howard Hughes Corporation. He's also the focus of several educational and museum displays.

In 1984, eight years after Hughes' death, Summa Corporation donated $2 million to UNLV's engineering school, which was named the Howard R. Hughes College of Engineering. A replica of Hughes' famed H-1 *Racer*, with which he set the flight speed record in 1935, hangs in the engineering building. The replica incorporates many details of the original plane, which is displayed in the Smithsonian's National Air and Space Museum in Washington, D.C. Photos and information about Hughes' aviation achievements also line the walls of the engineering building.

The Summerlin Library has a large permanent exhibit chronicling Hughes' life, focusing on his flying exploits, filmmaking, and Las Vegas years. The highlight is a collection of model airplanes hanging over the children's section. They are replicas of the aircraft Hughes flew and designed, from the H-1 *Racer* to the H-4 flying boat, or Spruce Goose.

Three local museums also have Hughes exhibits.

The Howard W. Cannon Aviation Museum at McCarran International Airport has several exhibits about Hughes, who owned an airport and an an airline in Las Vegas and was at the controls during a tragic 1943 crash at Lake Mead. Hughes is featured in displays above the baggage claim area as well as in the A gates. The prize artifact is located in the A gates: the flight suit Hughes wore during his record-breaking round-the-world flight in 1938. In a strange twist, Howard Cannon, for whom the aviation museum is named, helped arrange Hughes' Tonopah wedding to Jean Peters when he was an attorney in Las Vegas.

The Nevada State Museum, located within the Springs Preserve historical and environmental complex, has a Hughes exhibit featuring objects salvaged from the Green House, the home Hughes leased in the early 1950s when he lived in Las Vegas for about a year. After Hughes returned to Los Angeles in 1954, the house was sealed up and left untouched until Hughes' death in 1976. It was reopened during the search for a will, and a few of the relics found their way to the state museum.

The Mob Museum in downtown Las Vegas has an exhibit focusing on the role Hughes played in nudging the mob out of the Las Vegas casino business. Artifacts donated by Hughes' right-hand man, Bob Maheu, help to explain his role in Las Vegas as well as his participation in a CIA-Mafia plot to assassinate Fidel Castro.

For many years, the Tournament Players Club clubhouse in Summerlin featured an extensive display of artifacts and photos from Hughes' younger days as a promising two-handicap amateur golfer. A trophy Hughes won in 1927 at the Bel Air Country Club highlighted a collection of artifacts that included his golf bag and clubs. Hughes won his first amateur tournament when he was seventeen and strove to become the world's best golfer. He played almost every day, even during the filming of his war epic *Hell's Angels*. But Hughes abruptly gave up playing competitively in 1932—at age twenty-six—when he realized his dream of being the best wasn't going to happen. He became the world's fastest pilot instead. The TPC no longer displays the Hughes memorabilia.

While the golf exhibit is gone, the Howard Hughes Corporation found another way to honor its namesake. The company purchased the local minor league baseball team, the Las Vegas 51s, in 2013 and then built a $150 million stadium for the team in Summerlin. Starting with the 2019 season, the 51s became the Aviators, in honor of Hughes' achievements in aviation.

There are no shrines to Hughes on the Las Vegas Strip. All six casinos he owned have been torn down. Wynn Las Vegas has replaced the Desert Inn. The Venetian is where the Sands once stood. The Mirage has eclipsed the Castaways. The Silver Slipper gave way to a parking lot for the adjacent Frontier, which was demolished in 2007. The Landmark site served as a parking lot for the Las Vegas Convention Center. Today the property is part of a $935 million convention center expansion.

Pilgrimage: *Visiting the Flying Boat*

Howard Hughes died when I was ten years old. I lived in rural Wisconsin at the time, and I don't remember noting the news event. I probably was too busy playing baseball or watching *Happy Days* to acknowledge that some old businessman had died.

But after I started my newspaper career in Las Vegas in 1988, I soon became aware that Hughes had played an important role in the city's history. His name was closely associated with the area's biggest new residential community, Summerlin, built by his heirs. In addition, local journalists and historians often mentioned Hughes as the man who helped drive organized crime out of the casino industry. In those days, every Las Vegan absorbed the fact that the eccentric billionaire had lived in the Desert Inn penthouse in the 1960s.

I was intrigued by Hughes. But Las Vegas history is loaded with interesting characters, and I didn't consider him worthy of greater attention than any of the others. That began to change about 2002, when I started working on my first book, *Sun, Sin & Suburbia: The History of Modern Las Vegas*. I decided to devote a chapter to Hughes. The more research I did about the man, the more I wanted to learn about his life and the persistent legends and mysteries swirling around his name.

When the Martin Scorsese film *The Aviator* came out in 2004, I noted that the story ended in 1947. Hughes lived for twenty-nine years beyond the end of the movie, and he spent key parts of that period in Las Vegas. I saw an opportunity. Why not put my growing desire to learn more about Hughes to productive use?

Thus, the idea for this book was born. It was time to push beneath the surface of the Hughes story and dig for the truth—or at least some deeper understanding of this enigmatic figure. I studied all the books about Hughes, mined the newspaper morgue, conducted in-depth interviews with several people who knew him, and talked to others who had informed opinions about him. I became something of an authority on Hughes.

But it was a bookish, academic authority at best. My bank of knowledge lacked a tangible link to the man. I knew plenty of facts about him, his accomplishments and failures, but I did not really understand him better than anyone else.

I had a brainstorm: I would travel to Oregon to see Hughes' most famous creation, the flying boat. This, I thought, would provide the tangible connection I needed to give readers a brilliant final assessment of Hughes.

The pilgrimage

It's a job to get to the Evergreen Aviation & Space Museum. After I flew into Portland, Oregon, I picked up a brochure for the museum and there was a map on the back suggesting the drive to McMinnville—about forty miles—would be a piece of cake. But it turns out the highway, 99 West, is not really a highway at all. It's a glorified commercial street slogging through the suburban landscape, traffic signals at regular intervals halting heavy commuter traffic.

Finally, 99 West escapes metro Portland and enters Willamette Valley wine country, dominated by untold shades of green foliage spreading across rolling hills. One passes dozens of vineyards, with modest signs offering wine tastings. More than two hundred wineries operate in this region, which is highly regarded for its pinot noir grapes.

There's no mistaking the Evergreen Aviation & Space Museum as you approach McMinnville. The massive structure immediately suggests that something very large is kept inside. Of course, I know exactly what this huge thing is: Howard Hughes' flying boat. *Hercules*. The H-4.

The Spruce Goose

Howard Hughes hated that one of the great achievements of his life was best known by this derogatory nickname. The name wasn't even accurate. The flying boat was indeed made out of wood, but mostly birch, not spruce. Still, the name Spruce Goose stuck, so much so that even reverent museum officials have embraced it. For many years, the museum's eatery was called the Spruce Goose Café. You can purchase Spruce Goose Amber Ale. Rows of grapevines adjacent to the museum constitute the Spruce Goose Vineyard.

Hughes' flying boat is on display in the Evergreen Aviation & Space Museum outside Portland, Oregon. Author's collection.

The flying boat must be seen in person to be believed. The airplane occupies the entire width, breadth, and height of the museum. It dwarfs everything in its vicinity. The wingspan is 319 feet, 11 inches—longer than a football field. It is 218 feet, 8 inches in length and 79 feet, 4 inches in height. It weighs 300,000 pounds and is powered by eight 3,000-horsepower engines.

Despite the size of the museum building, it is impossible to get far enough away to see the entire aircraft at once. You look at the front of it, the side, the back, part of one wing. The idea of one man at the controls dictating the speed and direction of something this big is hard to imagine.

Visitors are encouraged to climb a flight of stairs to look inside the flying boat, but the experience is limited. Looking to the back through a glass partition, you see the cargo space, capable of carrying 750 soldiers. Looking through glass toward the front, you see the spiral staircase leading to the flight deck. Unfortunately, the average visitor cannot proceed farther.

The flying boat isn't pretty. It is painted primer gray, with no flourishes of any kind. It lacks the sleek lines of a fighter jet. It doesn't have the geometric complexity of the early biplanes. It is hulking and plain, but these aesthetic deficits do not diminish the engineering awe it inspires, or the significance of its place in aviation history.

Flying boat's origins

The flying boat was conceived in response to the German U-boat crisis during the early stages of World War II. German submarines—or U-boats—were a destructive menace to Allied shipping in the Atlantic. Shipbuilder Henry J. Kaiser thought a "flying boat" would nullify the submarine threat. He turned to Hughes, the famed aviator, to help him build the unprecedented aircraft.

Kaiser estimated a prototype flying boat could be built in ten months. Hughes drew up preliminary sketches, and the Defense Plant Corporation approved an $18 million contract in November 1942. The contract called for the construction of three prototypes. Hughes would design and build them and Kaiser would handle their mass production. The contract, not a high priority to military leaders, precluded the partners from using metal, a precious resource during the war. Hughes decided to build it out of wood, using a Duramold glue that made the wood as light and strong as aluminum.

Ten months passed and Hughes was still working on the designs and specifications. Then he started building a giant hangar in Culver City, California, in which to build the plane.

As the flying boat project inched along, the U-boat crisis diminished. The Allies developed new tactics and technologies, such as radar and sonar, to counteract the U-boats. In addition, the British cracked Germany's Enigma code and could track the U-boats' movements. Discouraged by the lack of progress and seeing the unlikelihood that he would secure a contract to mass produce flying boats, Kaiser dropped out in 1944.

The government tried to cancel the contract, but Hughes lobbied federal officials to sign a new contract with him to build a single prototype. He reportedly received behind-the-scenes support from President Franklin Roosevelt. Originally called the HK-1 (for Hughes-Kaiser), the plane was renamed the H-4, representing the fourth aircraft project spearheaded by Hughes. Hughes called it *Hercules*.

When the war ended in 1945, Hughes was still working on the flying boat. Republican U.S. Senators Homer Ferguson of Michigan and Owen Brewster of Maine were critical of Hughes' spending of taxpayer money on what they called a boondoggle—a "flying lumberyard." Hughes was called to Washington to testify before a committee investigating the contract. He was grilled for four days, but his powerful testimony overwhelmed his critics. "I put the sweat of

Hughes piloted the flying boat when it took flight in 1947. Courtesy of Howard Hughes Public
Relations Photo Collection, Special Collections and Archives, University Libraries, University of
Nevada, Las Vegas.

my life into this thing," Hughes said. "I have my reputation rolled up in it, and
I have stated that if it was a failure I probably will leave this country and never
come back, and I mean it." In addition to the "sweat of my life," Hughes spent
$7 million of his own money on the plane.

The senators backed off, but Hughes felt compelled to prove his detrac-
tors wrong. He returned to California, determined to ready *Hercules* for flight.
Because the plane was so large, it was impossible for a human being to move the
controls manually, so Hughes and his engineers devised a power control system
that was the forerunner of power steering in modern automobiles.

On November 2, 1947, Hughes drew huge crowds and dozens of reporters
to Long Beach Harbor to witness several high-speed taxi runs of the flying boat.
After several forays on the water, Hughes decided to up the ante. He would see
if the thing would fly.

"This was the greatest challenge of his twenty-year career as a pilot," wrote
George J. Marrett in *Howard Hughes: Aviator*. "Either he would go down in history as the pilot who flew the world's largest aircraft or be remembered as the
pilot who caused the biggest aviation catastrophe."

Without telling the thirty people on board what he was planning, Hughes accelerated past ninety miles per hour and the plane lifted seventy feet off the water. It was airborne for about one minute and twenty seconds—more than long enough to prove to Senators Brewster and Ferguson that the flying boat was no boondoggle. Hughes landed it smoothly back on the water.

After the flight

After its maiden voyage in 1947, the flying boat left the public eye for thirty-three years. Hughes kept staff on site to maintain the plane and keep people away from it—at a cost of more than $1 million per year. For years, he insisted he would resume work on the project. But it never moved.

A crisis ensued in the late '50s when the U.S. government's General Services Administration, which owned the flying boat, wanted to dispose of it. From the perspective of government bureaucrats, it was merely gathering dust and taking up space—a lot of space.

After other appeals failed to persuade the GSA to save the flying boat, Hughes called Bob Maheu, who would later serve as his chief executive in Nevada. "I'm at the Bel Air Hotel on a Friday and I get this urgent phone call," Maheu said. "Hughes is on the phone. He says, 'Monday is the last day I can preserve my project.' He says forget everything else you are doing and get involved with this project."

Maheu first contacted Len De Lissio, the GSA's director of security and a fellow former FBI agent. Maheu convinced De Lissio to vouch for his integrity with Max Medley, the GSA controller. "I called Medley, and he was pissed," Maheu recalled. "He said things like, 'No one's going to push me around.' Apparently whoever had been handling it for Howard at the Washington level had exercised muscle on him."

Medley agreed to see Maheu in his office at nine a.m. Monday, and Maheu got on a cross-country flight. "I walk in, and Medley is still pissed. He tells me he's never been pushed around this much. I said let's just talk. Medley had checked me out over the weekend with two of his best friends, who just coincidentally happened to be two of my dear friends. We spent all day working on this, and I finally made an arrangement to buy the flying boat for $50,000. When I reported back to Hughes, he was in ecstasy. But the next day, my phone rang and Hughes said, 'We can't do it that way. My attorneys say it has to stay in the name of the government.'" Apparently if Hughes bought the airplane, his tax burden to maintain it would be severe.

Maheu managed to work out a new deal for Hughes to lease the flying boat from the government for $9,600 per month, thereby avoiding the tax implications.

The lease deal protected the flying boat for more than twenty years. But when the lease on the Long Beach hangar expired in 1980, the plane's fate again hung in the balance. A leading proposal would have broken up the aircraft and divvied the pieces among nine Smithsonian museums, none of which was large enough to accommodate the whole thing. Instead, the Aero Club of Southern California obtained the plane and leased it to the Wrather Corporation, which built a $4 million domed exhibit hall. Alongside the Queen Mary ocean liner, it served as a tourist attraction in Long Beach from 1983 until 1990.

Then the Walt Disney Corporation acquired Wrather and announced plans to use the hangar space for a sea park it never built. At long last, the flying boat would have to move. The Aero Club considered several proposals, including one from a Las Vegas group led by Bob McCaffery to move it to the Strip. The winning proposal came from aviation executive Del Smith and his son, Michael King Smith, who vowed to make the flying boat the centerpiece of their planned Evergreen Aviation & Space Museum in McMinnville, Oregon.

The Smiths disassembled the flying boat, and the pieces were placed on barges to travel nine hundred miles up the Pacific Coast and along the Willamette River. It arrived in McMinnville in 1993. The airplane was reassembled, and the museum opened in 2001.

Place in history

The flying boat arguably was the crowning achievement of Hughes' life. He built faster airplanes, made hundreds of millions of dollars, dated the world's most beautiful women, produced popular movies, and played an important role in the growth of Las Vegas. But as noteworthy as those things are, they do not hold the singular fascination of the flying boat. Between 1943 and 1947, Hughes was, as always, a furious multi-tasker, but he dedicated the most time and effort to the construction of the H-4. During this period, Hughes survived two serious plane crashes and a nervous breakdown, yet he worked harder on this project than on any other in his life. That's saying something about a man who routinely ignored life's necessities—eating, sleeping, etc.—in pursuit of a goal. Testifying before the Senate committee investigating the flying boat contract, Hughes said:

"If I made a mistake on this airplane it was not through neglect. It was through supervising each portion of it in too much detail. In other words, as I look back on it, if I could do the job over, I would have delegated more of the work to other people, which might possibly have resulted in a faster job. But I am by nature a perfectionist, and I seem to have trouble allowing anything to go through in a half-perfect condition. So if I made any mistake it was in working too hard and in doing too much of it with my own two hands."

It flew only once, but the flying boat's legacy is secure. It was an important step forward for aviation, although not necessarily a major engineering advance. The other major aircraft contractors were capable of doing the same thing. But they didn't. Hughes did. He eschewed financial reward to pursue a worthy goal. Just as he had done when he shattered air speed records, he pushed the industry forward through sheer force of will. And he was proud of it. As the authors of *Empire* explained: "All through the 1950s, before he slipped into seclusion, the highest honor he could bestow on another was a personal tour of the flying boat, to let a visitor pad around inside its wooden belly, gawking at its enormous size."

The flying boat's most obvious offspring was the C-5 Galaxy cargo plane, used during the Cold War and Vietnam and still in operation today. It benefited greatly from technology that Hughes did not have at his disposal. But Hughes' flying boat still holds the title of the largest airplane ever built. It is larger than the Airbus A380 (2005), the Boeing 747 (1969), and the Antonov 225 (1988).

Today, the flying boat is generally viewed with awe and respect, but that's a fairly recent phenomenon. In its day, it more often was described as a famous flop, or a farcical product of Hughes' giant ego. Maheu, for one, considers it a major contribution to aviation. "The real guys in the aviation industry told me it accelerated the type of frames that could fly," he said. "It was not a failure."

Visitors to the Evergreen Aviation & Space Museum can't help but agree.

The final word

My pilgrimage to the flying boat did not yield an epiphany. I admired the airplane's size, and the skill, commitment, and hard work required to see it to completion. But while the flying boat was a tangible link to Hughes, it didn't open any new paths to greater understanding.

In the meantime, however, I came to realize something about Hughes that was more important than the airplanes he built or the money he made. I learned that Hughes was a man to whom other men were fiercely loyal. He possessed an undefinable charisma that drew thousands of people into his orbit, not for money or glory, but for the chance to work for him, to help him achieve his goals.

First, consider the "inside aides" who catered to Hughes' every personal want and need. They came from all walks of life and somehow fell into bizarre menial jobs taking care of an eccentric, hermetic billionaire. Most were well paid, but they worked hard for their paychecks. Hughes would make completely unreasonable demands, and they would comply. They were separated from their families for long periods. They worked holidays. They submitted to these and other hardships out of loyalty to Hughes.

The "outside aides" performed all sorts of tasks, from watching Hughes' airplanes parked around the country to driving his contracted starlets to acting lessons. These individuals may have come into direct contact with Hughes only a few times, if at all, but many of them became longtime employees who would do anything for the boss.

As for the executives and lawyers employed by Hughes, many of them could have made more money and had easier lives working for others. But they relished the opportunity to help Hughes fulfill his business plans, to debate the next legal maneuver with him. Hughes was strange, but he was smart and bold, too, and his lieutenants enjoyed working for a man who was not deterred by any obstacle.

The Hughes Circle—the small group of individuals who knew the man—is shrinking fast. Old age is taking its toll. But those few who spoke with me for this book revealed a boundless devotion to Hughes. He always will be a big part of their personal story, and they are proud of it. Many have dedicated part of their golden years to debunking myths about Hughes and setting the record straight. They don't deny Hughes' faults and oddities, but they don't want them to be the main things people remember about him.

And, for these folks, there is always time to talk about Hughes—to reminisce about specific events, to compare notes, to discuss what was achieved and what went wrong. One evening, I stopped by Paul Winn's house to drop off a photograph I borrowed for use in this book. He invited me in, and before long we were going over a random series of Hughes topics. Somehow, we got on the subject of Hughes' golf game. Hughes was a good golfer, and as a young man wanted to be the best. He eventually gave up that quest in favor of making movies and flying airplanes. But contrary to one leading legend, Hughes did not give up the game entirely in the early 1930s. He played later that decade with Katharine Hepburn, and reportedly was on the links in Las Vegas in the early '50s. Winn questioned that latter assertion, but didn't know for sure. He did know where to turn for confirmation, though: former Hughes aide Kay Glenn, now living in Salt Lake City. Glenn did not generally talk to reporters, but Winn quickly punched his number into the phone and Glenn answered. Glenn said he did not think Hughes played golf in Las Vegas in the early '50s.

So there it was. A few minutes later, Glenn called Winn to talk about some movies starring John Travolta. Glenn apparently had heard that Travolta wanted to play Hughes in a movie. These kinds of conversations are common among the Hughes Circle.

One might conclude that these old guys need to move on, that living in the past is not healthy. But Hughes played such a large role in their lives that even if they wanted to move on, they could not do so. He is an indelible part of their stories.

And now he's part of mine. After thirteen years of research and writing, I am haunted by Howard Hughes. My wife enjoys watching old movies on TV. At least half the time, the lead actress dated Hughes. I can't help but mention this. In conversation with friends and colleagues, I find myself telling Hughes stories and drawing parallels with current events. I try not to be annoying.

But all things considered, I'm glad to have ventured this deeply into the Hughes story. His life features all sorts of valuable lessons in what to do and what not to do—in business, in politics, in life. He remains an enigma to me. But my experience affirms an old cliché: The journey is the reward.

Acknowledgments

Stephens Press published the first edition of this book in 2008. Carolyn Hayes Uber, the first and only publisher of Stephens Press, backed the book from the outset and did everything in her power to make it a success. From the beginning, she planned to eventually publish a paperback edition. Tragically, Carolyn died of cancer in 2014, and Stephens Press was dissolved soon thereafter. I know she would be incredibly pleased that the University of Nevada Press is keeping this book alive, and allowing me to substantially expand the story.

University of Nevada Press staffers past and present have been wonderful to work with as this new edition evolved. Thank you to former director Joanne O'Hare for agreeing to publish a new edition, and to current director Clark Whitehorn, former editorial, design, and production manager Alrica Goldstein, and copy editor Paul Szydelko for their skill and patience in guiding the book into its final form.

University of Nevada, Las Vegas history professor Michael Green has been a supporter and editor for both editions of this book. Even though we are the same age, I consider Mike my mentor in the history field.

My former bosses at the *Las Vegas Review-Journal*, Sherman Frederick, Allan Fleming, and Mike Ferguson, showed consistent support for this book, cutting me slack when I needed some. Many colleagues in the Las Vegas news media provided inspiration, insights, and support.

My current boss, Mob Museum President and CEO Jonathan Ullman, has given me the opportunity to work as a historian and the means to improve my knowledge and craft in this field. This second edition is a better book as a result. Thanks also to my Mob Museum colleagues, including Ashley Miller, Mark Achenbach, and the Content team for their support and assistance.

My heartfelt thanks to those individuals, some now deceased, who gave so generously of their time to enhance my understanding of Howard Hughes and Las Vegas: Bob Maheu, Gordon Margulis, Ralph Denton, Bob Stoldal, Arelo Sederberg, Peg Crockett, Melvin Dummar, Dean Elson, Mark Smith, Don Digilio, Dan Newburn, Ron Brooks, Burton Cohen, Bill Friedman, Peter Maheu, Bernie Sindler, Gus Russo, G. David Schwartz, Wally Boundy, Bob Perchetti, Linda Gray, Bob McCaffery, Candy Akers, Gene Lassers, Harry Reid, Robert List, Richard Bryan, Frank Lewis, John Livermore, Su Kim Chung, Mark Hall-Patton, and Stuart Stein.

A special thanks to Paul Winn, who has dedicated many hours of his life to helping me separate fact from fiction in the chronicles of Hughes' life.

I must thank the many journalists, historians, and memoirists who have written about Hughes over the years. Without their research and their contributions to the public record—and this cannot be overstated—this book could not exist.

A nod to *Desert Companion*, Nevada Public Radio's monthly magazine, which published, in slightly different form, a couple of segments of this book.

Thank you to my wife, Tammy, and my daughters, Erin and Sara, for their endless patience and support. Considering the long nights and weekends that went into this book, I know they sacrificed as much as I did.

Thanks also to Jon and Sally Schumacher, Barbara Sowards, and John and Eulah Wallis.

Bibliography

Barlett, Donald L., and James B. Steele. *Howard Hughes: His Life and Madness*. New York: W.W. Norton, 1979. (Originally published under the title *Empire: The Life, Legend, and Madness of Howard Hughes*.)

Brown, Peter Harry, and Pat H. Broeske. *Howard Hughes: The Untold Story*. New York: Dutton, 1996.

Ceplair, Larry. *The Marxist and the Movies: A Biography of Paul Jarrico*. Lexington, Kentucky: University Press of Kentucky, 2007.

Chandler, Charlotte. *The Real Kate: A Personal Biography of Katharine Hepburn*. London: JR Books, 2011.

Davenport, Elaine, Paul Eddy, and Hurwitz. *The Hughes Papers*. New York: Ballantine Books, 1976.

Dean, Josh. *The Taking of K-129: How the CIA Used Howard Hughes to Steal a Russian Sub in the Most Daring Covert Operation in History*. New York: Dutton, 2018.

Denton, Ralph L., and Michael S. Green. *A Liberal Conscience: Ralph Denton, Nevadan*. Reno: University of Nevada Oral History Program, 2001.

Denton, Sally, and Roger Morris. *The Money and the Power: The Making of Las Vegas and Its Hold on America, 1947-2000*. New York: Alfred A. Knopf, 2001.

Dietrich, Noah, and Bob Thomas. *Howard: The Amazing Mr. Hughes*. Greenwich, Connecticut: Fawcett Gold Medal, 1972.

Drew, William M. *At the Center of the Frame: Leading Ladies of the Twenties and Thirties*. Lanham, Maryland: Vestal Press, 1999.

Drosnin, Michael. *Citizen Hughes*. New York: Holt Rinehart and Winston, 1985.

Evans, Peter and Ava Gardner. *Ava Gardner: The Secret Conversations*. New York: Simon & Schuster, 2013.

Fay, Stephen, Lewis Chester, and Magnus Linklater. *Hoax: The Inside Story of the Howard Hughes-Clifford Irving Affair*. New York: Viking, 1972.

Finstad, Suzanne. *Heir Not Apparent*. Austin, Texas: Texas Monthly Press, 1984.

Gardner, Ava. *Ava: My Story*. New York: Bantam Books, 1990.

Garrison, Omar. *Howard Hughes in Las Vegas*. New York: Lyle Stuart, 1970.

Gerber, Albert B. *Bashful Billionaire: The Story of Howard Hughes*. New York: Lyle Stuart, 1967.

Gladstone, B. James. *The Man Who Seduced Hollywood: The Life and Loves of Greg Bautzer, Tinseltown's Most Powerful Lawyer*. Chicago: Chicago Review Press, 2013.

Gragg, Larry D. *Benjamin "Bugsy" Siegel: The Gangster, the Flamingo, and the Making of Modern Las Vegas*. Santa Barbara, California: Praeger, 2015.

Hack, Richard. *Hughes: The Private Diaries, Memos and Letters*. Beverly Hills, California: New Millennium Press, 2001.

Hepburn, Katharine. *Me: Stories of My Life*. New York: Alfred A. Knopf, 1991.

Higham, Charles. *Howard Hughes: The Secret Life*. New York: St. Martin's Griffin, 1993.

Higham, Charles. *Kate: The Life of Katharine Hepburn*. New York: W.W. Norton, 1975.

Hopkins, A.D., and K.J. Evans, eds. *The First 100: Portraits of the Men and Women Who Shaped Las Vegas*. Las Vegas: Huntington Press, 1999.

Hyland, L.A. "Pat." *Call Me Pat: The Autobiography of the Man Howard Hughes Chose to Lead Hughes Aircraft*. Virginia Beach, Virginia: The Donning Company, 1993.

Irving, Clifford. *The Hoax*. E-reads, 1999.

Keats, John. *Howard Hughes*. New York: Random House, 1966.

Kemm, James O. *Rupert Hughes: A Hollywood Legend*. Beverly Hills, California: Pomegranate Press, 1997.

Kistler, Ron. *I Caught Flies for Howard Hughes*. Chicago: Playboy Press, 1976.

Lasky, Betty. *RKO: The Biggest Little Major of Them All*. Upper Saddle River, New Jersey: Prentice-Hall, 1984.

Laxalt, Paul. *Nevada's Paul Laxalt: A Memoir*. Reno: Jack Bacon & Company, 2000.

Laxalt, Robert. *Nevada: A History*. New York: W.W. Norton & Company, 1977.

Laytner, Ron. *Up Against Hughes: The Maheu Story*. New York: Manor Books, 1972.

Madden, Nelson. *The Real Howard Hughes Story*. New York: Manor Books, 1976.

Magnesen, Gary. *The Investigation: A Former FBI Agent Uncovers the Truth Behind Howard Hughes, Melvin Dummar, and the Most Contested Will in American History*. Fort Lee, New Jersey: Barricade Books, 2005.

Magnesen, Gary. *Stolen Justice: The True Story Behind the Howard Hughes Will*. Las Vegas: Houdini Publishing, 2015.

Maguglin, Robert. *Howard Hughes: His Achievements & Legacy*. Sequoia Communications, 1984.

Maheu, Robert, and Richard Hack. *Next to Hughes*. New York: HarperCollins, 1992.

Mann, William J. *Kate: The Woman Who Was Hepburn*. New York: Henry Holt and Company, 2006.

Marrett, George J. *Howard Hughes: Aviator*. Annapolis, Maryland: Naval Institute Press, 2004.

McBride, Joseph. *Hawks on Hawks*. Berkeley, California: University of California Press, 1982.

Miller, Ann, and Norma Lee Browning. *Miller's High Life*. Garden City, New York: Doubleday, 1972.

Moore, Terry. *The Beauty and the Billionaire*. New York: Pocket Books, 1984.

Moore, Terry, and Jerry Rivers. *The Passions of Howard Hughes*. Los Angeles: General Publishing Group, 1996.

Odessky, Dick. *Fly on the Wall: Recollections of Las Vegas' Good Old, Bad Old Days*. Las Vegas: Huntington Press, 1999.

Parsons, Louella. *Tell It to Louella*. New York: Lancer Books, 1961.

Pearl, Ralph. *Las Vegas Is My Beat*. Secaucus, New Jersey: Lyle Stuart Inc., 1973.

Phelan, James. *Howard Hughes: The Hidden Years*. New York: Random House, 1976.

Phelan, James, and Chester Lewis. *The Money: The Battle for Howard Hughes's Billions*. London: Orion Business Books, 1997.

Phelan, James. *Scandals, Scamps, and Scoundrels: The Casebook of an Investigative Reporter*. New York: Random House, 1982.

Rappleye, Charles and Ed Becker. *All American Mafioso: The Johnny Rosselli Story*. New York: Doubleday, 1991.

Real, Jack G., and Bill Yenne. *The Asylum of Howard Hughes*. Xlibris, 2003.

Reid, Harry with Mark Warren. *The Good Fight: Hard Lessons from Searchlight to Washington*. New York: G.P. Putnam's Sons, 2008.

Rempel, William C. *The Gambler: How Penniless Dropout Kirk Kerkorian Became the Greatest Deal Maker in Capitalist History*. New York: Dey St., 2018.

Rhoden, Harold. *High Stakes: The Gamble for the Howard Hughes Will*. New York: Crown, 1980.

Richardson, D. Kenneth. *Hughes After Howard: The Story of Hughes Aircraft Company*. Santa Barbara, California: Sea Hill Press, 2011.

Russell, Jane. *Jane Russell: My Path and My Detours*. New York: Franklin Watts, 1985.

Russo, Gus. *Supermob: How Sidney Korshak and His Criminal Associates Became America's Hidden Power Brokers*. New York: Bloomsbury, 2006.

Sederberg, Arelo C. *Hughesworld: The Strange Life and Death of an American Legend*. Bloomington, Indiana: iUniverse Inc., 2013.

Serling, Robert. *Howard Hughes' Airline: An Informal History of TWA*. New York: St. Martin's, 1983.

Sheehan, Jack, ed. *The Players: The Men Who Made Las Vegas*. Reno: University of Nevada Press, 1997.

Sheehan, Jack. *Quiet Kingmaker of Las Vegas: E. Parry Thomas*. Las Vegas: Stephens Press, 2009.

Schumacher, Geoff. *Sun, Sin & Suburbia: The History of Modern Las Vegas*. Reno: University of Nevada Press, 2015.

Smith, John L. *No Limit: The Rise and Fall of Bob Stupak and Las Vegas' Stratosphere Tower*. Las Vegas: Huntington Press, 1997.

Smith, John L. *Sharks in the Desert: The Founding Fathers and Current Kings of Las Vegas*. Fort Lee, New Jersey: Barricade Books, 2005.

Snyder, Jimmy. *Jimmy the Greek*. Chicago: Playboy Press, 1975.

Thomas, Tony. *Howard Hughes in Hollywood*. Secaucus, New Jersey: Citadel Press, 1985.

Wilkerson, W.R. III. *Hollywood Godfather: The Life and Crimes of Billy Wilkerson*. Chicago: Chicago Review Press, 2018.

Winters, Shelley. *Shelley: Also Known as Shirley*. New York: William Morrow and Company, 1980.

Index

Page numbers in *italics* refer to photographs.

About the Author

Geoff Schumacher is the senior director of content for the Mob Museum in Las Vegas, responsible for its exhibits, artifacts and public programs. He earned his bachelor's degree in journalism from the University of Nevada, Reno, and his master's degree in history from Arizona State University. He had a twenty-five-year career in newspaper journalism, with positions of increasing responsibility at the *Las Vegas Sun, Las Vegas CityLife, Las Vegas Mercury, Las Vegas Review-Journal* and *Ames* (Iowa) *Tribune.* He is the author of *Sun, Sin & Suburbia: The History of Modern Las Vegas* (University of Nevada Press) and served as editor of *Nevada: 150 Years in the Silver State,* the official book commemorating the state's sesquicentennial. He is associate editor of the *Nevada Historical Society Quarterly* and has edited, co-edited or contributed to seven editions of the annual Las Vegas Writes anthology for Nevada Humanities. Schumacher is married and has two grown children.